T0386682

Mothers
of the
Mind

Mothers of the Mind

The Remarkable
Women Who Shaped
Virginia Woolf,
Agatha Christie
and Sylvia Plath

Rachel Trethewey

For my Mum,
with Love.

Quotes from Virginia Woolf used by permission of The Society of Authors as the Literary Representative of the Estate of Virginia Woolf. The Society of Authors, 24 Bedford Row, London WC1R 4EH.

Quotes from *The Hound of Death and Other Stories* ('Wireless' and 'The Last Séance'), *Unfinished Portrait*, *Appointment with Death*, *Towards Zero*, *Death Comes as the End*, *Come, Tell Me How You Live*, *Ordeal by Innocence* and *An Autobiography*. Reprinted by permission of HarperCollins Publishers Ltd © 1933, 1934, 1938, 1944, 1945, 1946, 1958, 1977 Agatha Christie.

Quotes from 'Ocean 1212-W' in *Johnny Panic and the Bible of Dreams*, *The Bell Jar by Sylvia Plath*, *The Journals of Sylvia Plath 1950-62*, 'Medusa' in *Collected Poems by Sylvia Plath*, *Letters Home*. © Sylvia Plath. Used by permission of Faber and Faber Ltd.

Quotes from *Letters Home by Sylvia Plath*. © 1975 by Aurelia Schober Plath. Used by permission of Faber & Faber Ltd and HarperCollins Publishers.

Quote from *The Journals of Sylvia Plath*. © Sylvia Plath. Used by permission of Penguin Random House.

Quotes from Archive Material MS88993/1/1 from The British Library PER 3, *Letters of Ted Hughes*. © Ted Hughes. Used by permission of Faber and Faber Ltd.

First published 2023

The History Press
97 St George's Place, Cheltenham,
Gloucestershire, GL50 3QB
www.thehistorypress.co.uk

© Rachel Trethewey, 2023

The right of Rachel Trethewey to be identified as the Author of this work has been asserted in accordance with the Copyright, Designs and Patents Act 1988.

British Library Cataloguing in Publication Data.
A catalogue record for this book is available from the British Library.

ISBN 978 1 80399 189 4

Typesetting and origination by The History Press
Printed and bound in Great Britain by TJ Books Limited, Padstow, Cornwall.

MIX
Paper from
responsible sources
FSC® C013056

Trees for Life

Contents

Introduction

We think back through our mothers if we are women.[1]

When I first read this quotation from Virginia Woolf, as I was viewing an exhibition at the Tate of St Ives, its truth resonated with me. Seeing Virginia's statement alongside a bewitching photograph of her mother, Julia Stephen, I was even more intrigued. As this mesmerising woman's soulful eyes stared out at me from across the century's divide, I wanted to find out who she was. She looked like Virginia, but there was also something elusive about her. I wanted to discover what she was really like and explore her relationship with her daughter.

As I thought about Virginia and Julia, I began to wonder whether the quotation was equally true for other female writers. I soon learnt that the Bloomsbury author was certainly not the only one who was moulded by her maternal heritage; Agatha Christie and Sylvia Plath were also inextricably entwined with their mothers, Clara Miller and Aurelia Plath. Their attitudes to life, literature and feminism were shaped by these formidable women. Virginia argued that not enough had been written about women's relationships with each other and she was right;[2] too often in the past, these authors have been defined by their relationships with their lovers rather than their formative affinity with their mothers. And yet, the maternal bond laid the foundation on which they built the rest of their lives, for good or ill.

There have been many previous biographies of Virginia, Agatha and Sylvia, but here for the first time Julia, Clara and Aurelia are put centre stage. They are the leading ladies, their daughters the supporting actresses and rather than just receiving a passing mention, their remarkable life stories are told in full. They deserve to be better known, as they were as passionate, complex, and at times contradictory, as their more famous daughters.

All three mothers were aspiring writers themselves, and by reading what they wrote, rather than just what was written about them, we hear their voices rather than just seeing them through the distorting lenses of other people's eyes. Their voices need to be heard because they were always whispering in their daughters' ears. Exploring their stories, we gain a new insight into the authors and why they developed in the way they did. The importance of these mothers should never be underestimated; Virginia admitted that for much of her life her mother obsessed her; even for three decades after her death, Julia haunted her every step. One Christie biographer portrays Clara as the love of Agatha's life,[3] while her daughter Rosalind described her grandmother as a dangerous woman because Agatha never thought she was wrong. A leading Plath scholar claims Sylvia and Aurelia were a team who worked together to achieve literary success.[4] However, Sylvia's psychiatrist encouraged the poet to believe that the mother–daughter relationship was at the root of her mental health problems and gave her permission to hate Aurelia.

Looking at the three writers through their mothers provides a new perspective on their lives and work. As a feminist icon, Virginia Woolf's ideas about women's roles can be seen as a rebellion against her anti-feminist mother. While Julia Stephen publicly campaigned against women having the vote, Virginia reacted by fighting for their rights in both the private and public sphere. For Virginia, the personal was political; her mother represented the ideal of Victorian womanhood, the self-sacrificing 'angel in the house' whom she had to 'kill' if she was to survive.

The most controversial moment in Agatha Christie's life is her disappearance in 1926. Usually the break-up of her marriage is seen as the main reason for her breakdown, but was it just the catalyst while the underlying reason was the death of her beloved mother? The answer to this question depends on who was most important to her mental well-being – her husband or her mother? As Agatha's grandson Mathew Prichard notes about the relationship between his grandmother and Clara, 'The closeness with which they lived their lives is self-evident and much closer than the relationship I think most people have with their mothers.'[5]

Sylvia Plath biographies often focus on her passionate relationship with her husband, Ted Hughes, but her relationship with her mother was equally tempestuous. Aurelia Plath thought she had a close and loving bond with her daughter, but it was only after Sylvia's death that she discovered what she really thought about her. It was devastating to find that the version of their relationship in Sylvia's novel, poems and journals was so different from her affectionate letters home. In *Mothers of the Mind* Aurelia finally answers back and we learn what she really thought about the way her daughter treated her.

All six women were women who loved too much. They experienced what Agatha Christie described as 'a dangerous intensity of affection', meaning their love for their lovers and each other had the potential to destroy them. The bond between each of the mothers and daughters was uncanny, involving what Aurelia Plath called 'psychic osmosis', which allowed them to imagine themselves into each other's minds. Being so close to another person could be claustrophobic and made it hard to establish a separate identity. In fact, the hyper-sensitivity, intensity, and imagination the daughters inherited from their mothers made them the outstanding writers they became. It gave their work an innate understanding of human relationships and an integrity which made each of the authors so successful in their different genres.[6] Their sensitivity made them vulnerable, however, and each of the writers needed a great deal of mothering. When their parents were not there to provide protection, their lovers, friends and family stepped in to fill that role.

The mothers' influence on their daughters' writing was crucial. They were the first to recognise their child's genius and then they did everything they could to help them fulfil that potential. The mothers were their daughters' first teachers, readers and critics. For all three authors, their earliest experiments in writing were to please their mothers. Later, Clara and Aurelia encouraged their daughters to make the transition from amateur to professional writers.[7] Once the daughters became famous authors, their mothers inspired some of their most compelling characters. As the people they knew best, all three writers wrote about them in both autobiographical and fictional forms. In her novel *To the Lighthouse*, Virginia recaptured the spirit of her mother in Mrs Ramsay. In Agatha's fictionalised version of her early life, *Unfinished Portrait*, the character of Miriam is modelled on Clara. Less flatteringly, Sylvia's unsympathetic portrayal of Mrs Greenwood in her novel *The Bell Jar* is based on Aurelia. In these works, the writers literally imagined themselves into their mothers' minds, but as Aurelia later angrily explained, her daughter could only write what she *thought* her mother *thought* – her true feelings were very different. By finding out who the mothers really were, on their own terms, we discover how closely their daughters' portrayals of them matched the reality.

Observing their family dynamics also helped to form their attitudes to feminism. In the Stephen, Miller and Plath households, lip service was paid to the dominance of men, but in each of the families a matriarchy, made up of generations of strong women, was really in charge. Both Virginia and Sylvia were critical of the sexist status quo which they believed turned their mothers into self-sacrificing martyrs. In contrast to the other authors, Agatha felt no desire to challenge her mother's conventional role. Although she became one of the bestselling authors of all time, she was never a feminist.

The three authors wrote about their mothers and motherhood frequently in their novels, poetry, memoirs, letters and journals. Agatha Christie is best known for her detective stories, but she also wrote six novels under the pseudonym Mary Westmacott, which are very different from her usual genre. In these complex psychological studies, she explored family relationships in all their complicated forms. The Westmacott novels are windows into Agatha's inner life, and they are examined for the insight they provide into Agatha's attitude to the mother–daughter bond. Sylvia Plath's most famous poems are about her father; who can forget the brutal portrayal of the Nazi in 'Daddy'? However, this book is more interested in her poems about her mother; the pushy mother in 'The Disquieting Muses' and the life-smothering jellyfish in 'Medusa' are equally unforgettable and show how toxic her relationship with Aurelia had become.

The daughters provide only half the material, and they were not the only ones to leave fascinating written sources. Julia wrote children's stories, essays and a book on nursing; Clara penned poems and short stories; Aurelia wrote poems, an academic thesis, and the introduction to her daughter's *Letters Home*. Reading their mothers' writing helps us to understand where the daughters' talent came from. What was just a seed in one generation grew to fruition in the next.

This book is for admirers of Woolf, Christie and Plath, but it is also for anyone interested in mothers and daughters. Through three very different relationships, written about in separate but interrelating sections, we explore the maternal bond in all its diversity. We see both the positive effects of unconditional love and the negative repercussions of possessiveness. We discover how dangerous it can be to live vicariously through another person and explore how far a parent should interfere in their child's life. These stories raise profound questions about how well we can ever know another person, even those we love best. Tracing each daughter's journey through the painful rite of passage of separating from her mother and establishing her own identity, it ultimately shows that the emotional umbilical cord which ties us so tightly to our mothers is never completely severed, even by death.

Part One

Julia and Virginia

1

The Dutiful Daughter

One thing everyone always agreed on about Julia Jackson was that she was exceptionally beautiful. Her appearance was classical and austere, reminiscent of a marble Greek statue in its perfection. Her flawless features also conformed to the Pre-Raphaelite aesthetic ideal of her era, making her allure both timeless and fashionable. Descended from a long line of beauties, Julia's good looks were treated as her birth right and remarked upon wherever she went.

Born in India on 7 February 1846, like the other mothers in this book, Julia was an outsider, but for her it was a positive rather than a negative, adding an air of mystery to her many attractions. Part of the Anglo-Indian governing class, her mother's family, the Pattles, were high-profile members of society in Calcutta and London, yet in both places they never quite belonged. In India they exuded French chic; when they returned to England, they brought the aromatic atmosphere of the sub-continent with them.

The family inspired many myths; there was no room for dull characters, everyone had to be larger than life, either a romantic hero or an outrageous villain. Although the reality was sometimes more prosaic, the romanticised versions reveal the colourful self-image the family cultivated.[1] As she grew up, Julia identified with her French aristocratic ancestors; Virginia believed that her mother's 'wit and her bearing and her temper' came from them.[2]

The most dashing figure in their ancestry was the Chevalier de L'Etang. Born at Versailles in 1757, Antoine Ambroise Pierre de L'Etang's life was defined by his love for Marie Antoinette. According to family folklore, which may be more fantasy than fact, he was made her page when she first arrived in France from Austria. Spending time with the lonely young girl, he grew devoted to his royal mistress.[3] After becoming an officer in Louis XVI's Bodyguards, he was about to be created a marquis when rumours reached the king that Ambroise was the queen's lover. In a fit of jealousy, Louis banished his rival to India. The chevalier's departure from France saved his life because he was absent during the French Revolution. In India, he married Therese de L'Etang, who was part Bengali; the original family beauty, her lustrous hair and dark eyes passed down the generations.[4] Although Ambroise created a fulfilling new life for himself in India, he never forgot his tragic queen. When he died, he was buried with the miniature of Marie Antoinette, resting on his heart.[5]

Less evocative but equally memorable was the story of Ambroise's daughter Adeline and her husband, James Pattle, who became a judge in the Calcutta Court of Appeal. Recent research suggests he was a respectable public servant whose reputation was damaged by being unfairly confused with his notorious brother, but his family preferred the more dramatic version.[6] His descendant Quentin Bell described him as 'a quite extravagantly wicked man', who was known as 'the greatest liar in India'.[7]

James and Adeline had seven daughters including Julia's mother, Maria. Educated in France, the Pattle sisters were high-spirited and unconventional, creating a stir wherever they went. Tall and graceful, Maria was quieter and more intellectual than her vivacious siblings. Known as 'a blue-stocking', in 1837 Maria married John Jackson, a well-respected physician.[8] The couple started a family, but Maria took their two daughters, Adeline and Mary, to England for the sake of their health.

In 1845, Maria had just returned to India when a double tragedy struck. In September, her father, James, died having apparently drunk himself to death. According to one story, his corpse was preserved in a barrel of rum and sent back to England aboard a ship. During a storm, his body burst out of its container. The sight of her malevolent husband supposedly coming back to life so terrified his widow that she died of shock shortly afterwards and was buried at sea. An alternative version of the story had James's remains being transported aboard a ship which then caught fire. When his body was consumed in the flames, the sailors said, 'That Pattle had been such a scamp that the devil wouldn't let him go out of India!' Whatever the true story, the basic facts were tragic enough: both James and Adeline died within a few months of each other. Their devastated daughters recorded the tragedy on a memorial, stating that 52-year-old Adeline was 'a victim to affliction and suffering produced by the calamity of her husband's death'.[9] The story was so memorably macabre it circulated in society for generations. Decades later, Virginia heard gossips say, 'Oh the old Pattles! They're always bursting out of their casks.'[10]

Julia was born a few months after this traumatic incident. Her first years were spent in Calcutta, living in a luxurious mansion, staffed by many servants.[11] When Julia was 2 years old, Maria returned to England with her youngest daughter. Reunited with her two daughters Adeline and Mary, for several years Maria and her children lived with her sister and brother-in-law, Sara and Thoby Prinsep. Known for her 'impulsive warmth' and 'restless energy', Aunt Sara had inherited her vivacity from her French mother.[12] Her husband, Thoby, was a calming influence among the excitable women in the family. A former director of the East India company and a Persian scholar, he became like a father to Julia.

When Julia was 5, Maria and her daughters moved to their own house in Hampstead. With her father still in India, Julia grew up in a matriarchy, where the women, not the men, mattered. In his frequent letters home, John Jackson comes across as an affectionate father, who missed his wife and daughters dreadfully. He sent them carefully thought out presents and wanted to be kept informed of all their news. He longed to be with them again, but his work continued to keep them apart.[13]

In 1855, Dr Jackson finally rejoined the family, and they moved to a larger house in Hendon. After the anticipation, it was an anti-climax and he made little impression on the female-dominated household. As Leslie Stephen, his future son-in-law, wrote, he became a 'bit of an outsider' and 'somehow he did not seem to count – as fathers generally count in their family'.[14] Although Maria respected her husband, she could not 'ardently love' him because he did not fit the Pattles' romantic self-image. A passionate woman, who admired heroism, Mrs Jackson found little to inspire her in this affectionate, dutiful man.

As mother and daughters were exceptionally close, his exclusion from the charmed circle became particularly obvious to observers. Even Julia, who felt such a powerful love for the rest of her family, could only muster a lukewarm affection for him. This was partly because father and daughter had been separated for much of Julia's childhood, but, according to

Leslie, it was also because Dr Jackson was a 'comparatively uninteresting character'.[15] Admittedly, he was ill-at-ease in the intellectual and artistic circles his wife and daughters favoured, but he was a highly respected doctor.[16] The denigration of this worthy medic passed down the generations, as his granddaughter Virginia described him as 'a common place prosaic old man; boring people with his stories of a famous poison case in Calcutta; excluded from this poetical fairyland'.[17]

Maria created the 'fairyland' she craved elsewhere. She found a kindred spirit in the poet Coventry Patmore, who became a lifelong friend. His sentimental image of self-sacrificing femininity in his poem 'The Angel in the House' became the Victorian touchstone for what women were expected to be. Ironically, although Maria had rarely put her husband or anyone else first, she readily accepted these values, in theory if not in practice, and passed them on to her daughters who grew up to become models of saintly womanhood. Her inscribed copy of the poem from the poet passed down the generations from Julia to Virginia.[18] The Bloomsbury author was to spend much of her life trying to escape from this limiting legacy.

Like many girls of her class and generation, Julia received only a limited education from a governess, which left her with 'an instinctive, not a trained mind'.[19] Valued for her beauty not her brains, she acquired the accomplishments expected of a Victorian wife; she spoke French with an excellent accent and played the piano well. Always a romantic, she read widely and developed a passion for De Quincey's *Confessions of an English Opium Eater* and Sir Walter Scott's novels. As her later writing shows, she was highly literate and logical, but her own experience left her with a negative attitude to formal education for girls which was to have repercussions for her daughters.

From an early age, Julia's striking good looks set her apart. Her mother did not want her to be spoilt by becoming too self-conscious about her appearance. Mrs Jackson had an irrational belief that every man who met her daughter, even fleetingly in a railway carriage, fell in love with her.[20] When Julia went out, her older sister Mary was sent with her to distract her from noticing that people could not resist looking at her. Many sisters might have become jealous of such an attractive sibling, but Mary never resented her younger sister. Her protective instincts ran deep; even when Julia had become a mother herself, she still called her by her family nickname, 'my darling Babe'.[21] Perhaps there was no competition between the

Jackson girls because there was a substantial age gap between Julia and her two older siblings. By the time Julia was grown up, her sisters were already married. In 1856, Adeline wed the Oxford History Professor Henry Halford Vaughan and six years later Mary married Herbert Fisher, tutor and private secretary to the Prince of Wales. Throughout their lives, Maria and her three daughters constantly exchanged gossipy, intimate letters sharing the minutiae of their lives. They trusted each other completely and knew this mutual understanding would never fail them.

Mrs Jackson was 'passionately devoted' to all her daughters, but Julia was 'the cherished jewel of her mother's home'.[22] In a reversal of roles, as Maria became increasingly disabled from rheumatism, Julia cared for her. She nursed her mother when she was unable to get out of bed and accompanied her to spas on her quest for cures. At an early age, Julia learnt to put someone else's needs before her own. Soothing her mother on her sickbed, she first discovered her lifetime's vocation for nursing. This nurturing side of Julia was to become as fundamental to her image as her beauty. For the rest of her life, Maria totally depended on her self-sacrificing youngest daughter. She wrote to her sometimes three times a day and often sent an additional telegram to her 'dear heart, her lamb'.[23] Leslie Stephen wrote that there grew up between them 'a specially tender relation; a love such as exceeded the ordinary love of mother and daughter and which became of the utmost importance to both of them'.[24] A photograph of them together captures the dynamic: seated above her daughter with one hand resting on her cheek, Mrs Jackson looks gaunt and miserable while Julia leans into her mother, gazing up at her and looking concerned.

2

The Muse

Through her well-connected aunts, Julia was introduced to an exciting cultural world. Maria's sisters were at the heart of Victorian society, counting the leading artists, writers and politicians of the age as personal friends. However, although they mixed with the elite, they never quite fitted in because they did not want to; confident in themselves, they had no desire to conform. Wearing cashmere shawls, chunky jewellery and silver bracelets and serving curry to their guests, the Pattles relished being different.[1] While other women straitjacketed themselves in corsets and crinolines, they floated into a room in sweeping robes. Talking in Hindustani to each other or speaking English with French accents, they were a self-contained clan with their own set of values, which was humorously referred to as 'Pattledom'.[2]

Their bewitching niece became the much-admired darling of their circle. Since being a child, Julia had spent a great deal of time with her Aunt Sara and Uncle Thoby at Little Holland House in Kensington. Years later, when Julia showed her children where it had been, it brought back the happiest memories; she 'clapped her hands and cried, "That was where it was!" as if a fairyland had disappeared.'[3]

The Prinseps' Sunday afternoon salons were legendary. Like the other writers in this book, Virginia imagined herself into her mother's mind and wrote about her youthful experiences as if she was there. Virginia described Little Holland House as 'a summer afternoon world'. At the centre of the melee was Julia, a cool, calm 'vision', standing silently with a dish of strawberries and cream.[4] In *To the Lighthouse*, through Mrs Ramsay, the fictionalised version of her mother, Virginia imagines the impression

Julia made on the young men she met. 'Astonishingly beautiful', she was absorbed in her own thoughts with her eyes downcast, looking 'so still […] so young […] peaceful'.[5]

At Little Holland House, Julia was introduced to the Pre-Raphaelite artists. When Edward Burne-Jones became seriously ill, motherly Aunt Sara took him into her home and nursed him. Soon his fellow artist and sculptor G.F. Watts also moved in, setting up his studio on their upper floor. Nicknamed by the Pattles 'Signor', the sisters and their daughters provided him with the perfect models. Carrying a sketch book with him, he never missed an opportunity to draw them.[6] When Julia was a child, Watts drew a head of her in chalk; he later did two more paintings of her, but she disliked one of them so much she refused to ever see it when it was exhibited. Shortly afterwards, the sculptor Pietro Marochetti used her as the model for Princess Elizabeth, the 14-year-old daughter of Charles I, who died at Carisbrooke Castle on the Isle of Wight. A teenage Julia posing as a dead princess set in stone her image as a tragic heroine.

Julia's calm, often wistful, appearance personified the Pre-Raphaelite idea of beauty which was the height of fashion in her youth. As she embodied their other-worldly fantasies, these artists clamoured to capture her elusive essence. For a modern woman, there is something unsettling about their desire to portray her as a vulnerable victim. When Edward Burne-Jones painted her as the Princess Sabra being led to the dragon, she was once again turned into an icon of serene sacrifice – one who can only be saved by a chivalrous man.

Mrs Jackson began to have misgivings, worrying that Julia's simplicity might be ruined by this homage to her beauty. When the sculptor Thomas Woolner asked if he could make a bust of her, his request was refused. The Pre-Raphaelite artists' admiration for Julia was not purely professional; apparently, both William Holman Hunt and Thomas Woolner wanted to marry her. One of the leading religious painters of his day, Hunt met Julia through Little Holland House circles. In June 1864, he spent an enjoyable summer afternoon with Julia and her family at their Hendon home. It seems that it was at around this time that he proposed to her.[7]

Evidently, Hunt fell intensely in love with Julia; he was so devastated by her rejection that, even after a year, he could not bear to visit her home. When Mrs Jackson invited him to a party, he politely declined – writing that although he appreciated 'the gentleness and kindness' they all showed him during 'the trying ordeal', he could not risk coming. He explained, 'I must not put myself in danger of suffering unnecessary bitterness now I feel at peace at last and I must be a wise man and take care to avoid sacrificing a state of mind which it took me so long to re-establish.'[8] Despite his rejection, Hunt remained lifelong friends with Julia. He was attracted by her character as much as her looks and asked her to be godmother to his child. Like so many of her admirers, he regarded her with 'reverence', as if she were a saint instead of a real woman.[9]

Although the paintings of Julia were memorable, the series of photographs by Julia's aunt, Mrs Cameron, came closest to capturing her essence. Impulsive and enthusiastic, Julia Margaret Cameron was the most talented of the Pattle sisters. When her daughter gave her a camera, she became obsessed by the new medium. Rejecting realism in favour of a more emotionally expressive approach, her innovative work revolutionised portrait photography. Taking the world's first close-ups, she created intimacy and psychological intensity by suppressing detail and using soft focus and dramatic lighting.[10]

In 1860, Mrs Cameron moved to a house called 'Dimbola' at Freshwater, on the Isle of Wight. Like all the Pattle sisters, Mrs Cameron had a penchant for collecting and hero-worshipping great men, leading one visitor to exclaim, 'Everybody is either a genius, or a poet, or a painter or peculiar in some way. Is there *nobody* commonplace?'[11] Her neighbour, the poet laureate, Alfred, Lord Tennyson became a close friend and often visited with his illustrious guests.

Although Mrs Cameron photographed the most famous men of the era, Julia was her muse. There was a special bond between the two women because Julia had been named after her aunt who was also her godmother. Mrs Cameron's photographs of her niece look surprisingly modern. Unlike most of her portraits of women, she depicted Julia as herself, rather than in costume as a religious or literary character. Usually, this approach was reserved for her male sitters, which suggests she recognised that Julia's powerful personality made her any man's equal.[12] The haunting picture of Julia, hair streaming down her back, face half in shade, her eyes staring uncompromisingly at the camera as though she can see into a person's soul, is unforgettable. When Mrs Cameron's work was exhibited in London, the *Evening Standard* singled out for praise the 'forcible likenesses' of Julia over the portraits of Darwin, Longfellow, Tennyson and Carlyle.[13]

Mrs Cameron played a major role in creating Julia's image as a great beauty. Without those mesmerising photographs, her good looks would have been ephemeral; her aunt made sure she would never be forgotten. Inevitably, with all this attention Julia could not avoid realising she was beautiful, but, according to Leslie Stephen, she did not have a shred of vanity. He wrote, 'Nobody could have been more absolutely unspoilt and untouched by the slightest weakness of self-complacency.'[14] However, Virginia believed there was a penalty for her mother's beauty: 'it came too readily, came too completely. It stilled life – froze it.'[15] It made her seem aloof and untouchable. No doubt thinking of Julia, years later when writing her novel *Jacob's Room*, Virginia described beauty as 'important; it is an inheritance; one cannot ignore it. But it is a barrier, it is in fact rather a bore.'[16]

3

The Perfect Match

Looking at the images of Julia, even in her youth there is a sadness that underlies the beauty; she seemed very alone as though no one could reach her. Growing up in the world of Tennyson and the Pre-Raphaelite Brotherhood, her dreams were imbued with Arthurian legends where demure damsels patiently waited for courageous knights to awaken them from their somnolent state. For Julia, a young barrister called Herbert Duckworth was that gallant figure; he awoke in her the grand passion she had dreamt of.

Their love story conformed to her romantic vision. Herbert and Julia met in Venice in 1862. When Mary and Herbert Fisher were on honeymoon he was suddenly taken ill. The Jacksons rushed out to support Mary and, while there, Fisher introduced Julia to his university friend Herbert Duckworth. After their first encounter, they met again at Lake Lucerne and although they had only talked briefly, Julia was soon 'head over heels in love with him'.[1]

Fourteen years her senior, Herbert was her perfect physical match; he was as handsome as she was beautiful. Tall and well-built, with broad shoulders and a generous, open face, he had high cheekbones, and a radiant smile which lit up a room. He epitomised the Victorian cult of the gentlemanly amateur, one who played the game for the sake of taking part rather than winning. He had been a good sportsman at Eton and Trinity College, Cambridge, without being excessively competitive. Similarly, he passed his examinations at university creditably without aiming for distinction. Much admired by his contemporaries, he measured up to their masculine ideal by being 'the perfect type of the public-school man'.[2]

The son of a wealthy Somerset family, his ambitions were limited to practising as a barrister for a few years and then retiring to become a magistrate and country squire. His easy-going temperament was just what Julia needed; he diluted her intensity, chasing away her melancholy moods. Most importantly, unlike other suitors, it seems he treated her as a flesh and blood woman rather than a plaster saint on a pedestal. By doing so, he grounded her in this world rather than the next. She responded to him with a depth of passion and devotion which no other man had been able to unleash.

In February 1867, Julia and Herbert got engaged. Photographs of the couple taken at this time exude happiness. In a fashionable dress with ruffled sleeves and a miniscule nipped-in waist, Julia leans back with a serene but knowing look as though she was suppressing a smile. In his companion portrait, there is a glint in Herbert's eyes; it looks as though he is about to say something amusing to his fiancée or burst out laughing. Dapper, with a boater on his lap and a large bow tie around his neck, he looks very pleased with himself. Certainly, many of the men in their circle considered him to be a particularly fortunate man, while some women thought Herbert 'not <u>hero</u> enough for Miss Jackson'.[3]

Julia's mother and sisters realised it was a rare love match. Mary Fisher described Herbert as 'a beam of light [...] like no one I have ever met'. This charismatic young man fitted perfectly into the Pattle mythology, visualising him as a Greek hero, the Great Achilles.[4] As a serious young woman, Julia thought very carefully about what she was doing. When she made her vows, she gave herself unconditionally, body and soul. Believing their two lives had become one, she experienced 'entire unity with him'.[5]

After the wedding in May, Julia and Herbert went on honeymoon abroad before setting up home in the Duckworths' London town house in Bryanston Square. As Julia could not bear to be separated from her husband, unlike many young wives of barristers she joined him travelling around the Northern circuit. Living in lodgings, she entertained his admiring colleagues to tea and attended court to watch Herbert perform. However, her appearance proved to be rather a distraction. One barrister explained, 'I spent the whole morning in court looking at a beautiful face.'[6] Once Herbert was married, he became even less concerned about his career. In one letter he admitted that he was penitent for caring so little for his profession, but he was quite content with having such a wife.

For Julia and Herbert, they were each other's world, they needed nothing else to complete their happiness. Yet, Julia's perfect contentment came with a fear of losing it. If ever Herbert was late, she panicked that something had happened to him. When Julia was on a picnic with some friends, Herbert was delayed because he missed the train. She could not relax until he had arrived, pacing up and down the road near the railway station looking out for him in 'a state of painful anxiety' which seemed to her friends to be unreasonable. Her sister Mary recalled that she always got in such a state when she was apart from her husband. She told Mary, 'I could not live if I had to be separated from him as much as you have to be separated from Herbert Fisher.'[7]

In March 1868, Julia and Herbert had their first child, George Herbert. Even with a baby, Julia still insisted on travelling with her husband on circuit. Herbert's university friend and fellow barrister, Vernon Lushington, told his wife, Jane (who stayed at home with their small children), that Mrs Duckworth had 'gallantly followed her husband' first to Manchester and then Liverpool.[8] In May 1869, the Duckworths had a daughter, Stella. Julia described this period in her life as a time of complete fulfilment. For four years she experienced 'a full measure of the greatest happiness that can fall to the lot of a woman'.[9]

Later, Virginia wondered if her mother's relationship with her first husband could really have been so perfect. She suspected that Julia romanticised it. Was Herbert really such a paragon? Virginia complained, 'Youth and death shed a halo through which it is difficult to see a real face.'[10] In her view, Herbert was so obviously Julia's inferior in all ways that it was unlikely he could have permanently satisfied her 'noble and genuine passions'. She wondered whether her mother just cloaked 'his deficiencies in her own super abundance', and made her marriage fit the narrative she had created. So far, Julia's life had run smoothly. As Virginia wrote, she had 'passed like a princess in a pageant from her supremely beautiful youth to marriage and motherhood without awakenment'.[11]

Julia soon experienced a rude awakening from which she would never completely recover. In May 1870, Herbert's father wrote to Dr Jackson saying that he was concerned about his son's health. He worried that a London life might be unsuitable for him. Mr Duckworth was considering increasing his allowance so that Herbert could give up work and live in the country. In September 1870, the Duckworths went to stay with

Julia's sister Adeline and her husband, Henry Vaughan, at Upton Castle in Pembrokeshire. Heavily pregnant, Julia was in the garden with Herbert when he stretched to pick a fig from a tree for her. As he reached up, he felt an acute pain; an undiagnosed abscess had burst. He deteriorated rapidly and within twenty-four hours he was dead aged only 37. Although this was the story passed down to Julia's children, like so many of the family legends it may not be totally accurate. A contemporary newspaper article stated that Herbert sustained an internal rupture while carrying one of his children upstairs.[12] Usually so scrupulously truthful, Julia preferred the more romantic version. Adding to the legend surrounding this tragic love story, after Herbert was laid to rest at his childhood home, Stella recalled that her distraught mother lay inconsolable upon his grave.[13]

Left a widow at the age of 24, Julia's faith in fairy tales ended the day Herbert died. She never felt so happy again; from then on there was always a shadow and she saw life in stark terms as something to be endured rather than enjoyed. As well as the tragic human loss, she suffered from disillusionment. Stripped of her dreams, according to Virginia, she looked at the world with clear eyes, and became 'more scornful than was just of its tragedy and stupidity'.[14] Julia lost her religious faith, leaving her without the solace of believing she would be reunited with Herbert in an afterlife. Naturally, she turned to her mother in this crisis. After the bleak funeral, Julia and her children stayed with the Jacksons. As Mrs Jackson was so close to Julia, she felt it acutely, writing to a friend, 'Our domestic happiness has been much troubled by our poor child's irreparable loss. To us it was that of a son, so much did we love him.'[15]

Six weeks after Herbert's death Julia gave birth prematurely to another son, Gerald. Having three children under the age of 4 just made her loss more poignant. Two-year-old George, who was the image of his father, kept asking, 'Where's Georgie's Papa?'[16] Photographs of Julia taken by Mrs Cameron at this time suggest Julia suffered from postnatal depression as well as grief. She appears unable to bond with her children. As she sits listless in a chair, looking into the distance, they cling on to her as though they are afraid of losing her too. Her arms lie languidly by her sides as if she does not even have the will to hold her baby. Always ethereal, she is spectral in these photographs, so thin that her bones show through her skin, and she looks in danger of literally fading away. Mrs Cameron recalled her niece's large blue eyes filling with tears as she told her, 'Oh aunt Julia, only pray God that I may die soon, that is what I most want.'[17] She told a friend that she was 'as unhappy as it is possible for a human being to be'.[18]

When Julia looked back on this time, she realised that she had suppressed her grief and tried to just carry on with life for the sake of her children, but this behaviour had been detrimental to her mental health. She later told Leslie that it 'all seemed a shipwreck'. Her existence had become 'a dream, a futile procession of images which seem to have in them no real life or meaning: the only real world is the world of intense gnawing pain which may be gradually dulled, but which refuses to admit any of the brighter realities from outside'.[19]

Her attempt to keep soldiering on after Herbert's death was to be echoed in Aurelia Plath's reaction to her husband's death decades later. With three small children depending on her, Julia had no choice but to try to be cheerful by keeping busy and thinking as little as possible. But repressing her grief was damaging, she explained:

> I got deadened. I had all along felt that if it had been possible for me to be myself, it would have been better for me individually; and that I could have got more real life out of the wreck if I had broken down more. But there was Baby to be thought of and everyone around me urging me to keep up, and I could never be alone which sometimes was such torture. So that by degrees I felt that though I was more cheerful and content than most people, I was more changed.[20]

A year after Herbert's death, Julia moved into a house in London. Friends and family expected her to resume her old life as she was a very eligible young woman and her widowhood just added to her mystique. Her old admirers, including her flamboyant cousin, the artist Val Prinsep, were ready to comfort her. As Julia's friend Jane Lushington wrote to her husband, 'Mark my words – and don't think me an unfeeling wicked monster – she will be Mrs Val Prinsep before she is thirty!'[21] Even those closest to her underestimated the depth of her grief, however.

Julia had never been frivolous, but after Herbert's death she became positively austere. She admitted that life in a convent appealed to her and, with her hair drawn back from her face and wearing severe clothes, she began to look like a nun. Her only real solace was helping others and during these years she found her vocation in caring for the poor and sick. She became 'a kind of sister of mercy', and her friends and family sent for her whenever there was illness or death. Yet even this relief came at considerable cost to herself because seeing such suffering reinforced her melancholy view of life. She admitted that she saw the world 'clothed in drab' and 'shrouded in a crape-veil'. She felt most at home with the suffering and once she had rescued one person, she was looking for the next. As Leslie said, it seemed that she had 'accepted sorrow as her life-long partner'.[22]

Although Virginia understood that the sudden shock had made Julia react as she did, like Sylvia Plath decades later, she was critical of her mother's behaviour. Virginia wrote, 'She reversed those natural instincts which were so strong in her of happiness and joy in a generous and abundant life, and pressed the bitterest fruit to her lips.' Whereas before she had imagined herself as a romantic heroine, she now saw herself as a tragic one, someone who had looked into the abyss and was enlightened. According to Virginia, Julia believed she was free from all illusion and 'possessed of the true secret of life at last'. It was a bleak realisation, however, for she saw 'that sorrow is our lot, and at best we can but face it bravely'. [23]

4

A Meeting of Minds

On a cold winter's evening in November 1875, Julia visited her friend Minny Stephen, who was heavily pregnant. The two women had known each other since those carefree days at Little Holland House. During some of the darkest times in Julia's widowhood, Minny's warm-hearted elder sister, Anny, had encouraged her to take an interest in life. As Anny lived with the Stephens, Julia often visited her old friends. When Julia dropped in on that chilly night, she found Minny and her husband Leslie sitting harmoniously together 'in perfect happiness and security'. Not wishing to intrude and thinking 'the presence of a desolate widow incongruous', she did not stay long and hurried home to 'her own solitary hearth'.[1]

A few hours later, Minny went to bed in some discomfort. During the night she had a convulsion and never regained consciousness; by the middle of the following day she was dead. Her death had been as sudden and unexpected as Herbert's. Like Julia five years before, Leslie Stephen was in complete shock, left reeling as in a matter of hours his secure world collapsed. Although their partnership was not as perfect as Julia and Herbert's relationship, Leslie and Minny had enjoyed eight years of happy marriage. She had been the first woman to stir him out of his donnish ways.

The Stephen family were middle-class liberal intellectuals who had been at the forefront of reform for generations. Part of the Clapham Sect, they had campaigned against slavery. Leslie's father, James Stephen, was one of the most influential colonial administrators of the nineteenth century. The Stephens' circle formed an 'aristocracy of intellect', who felt secure in a sense of superiority based on moral and mental attributes, not wealth or birth.[2] After being educated at Eton and Cambridge, Leslie became a tutor at his old university college. He looked set for an impressive academic career until a crisis of faith transformed his plans. To qualify for his position, he had to take religious orders, but he began to have doubts about the truth of the Bible. Unable to hide his scepticism, he resigned as a tutor at Trinity Hall.

In 1864, he moved to London and became a writer on several newspapers. Mixing in literary circles, he got to know Lord Tennyson, Robert Browning, George Eliot and Anthony Trollope. Through mutual friends he was introduced to Thackeray's daughters Anny and Minny. A great admirer of their father's novel *Vanity Fair*, it was hardly surprising that the bookish bachelor fell in love with one of his favourite author's daughters. Minny was attractive and full of fun with a playful sense of humour. She was not an intellectual, but her childlike simplicity and straightforwardness appealed to Leslie.[3] When they sat next to each other at a dinner party in Hampstead, the attraction was obvious. A fellow guest, the novelist Mrs Gaskell, said afterwards that she foresaw they would marry.[4]

At the same time as Leslie was falling in love with Minny, he met Julia for the first time at a picnic. She was dressed in white with blue flowers in her hat and Leslie thought she was the most beautiful girl he had ever seen, like 'the Sistine Madonna'.[5] He did not speak to her, but he would never forget that vision. A few months later, Leslie became engaged to Minny; they married in June 1867, shortly after the Duckworths' wedding. Occasionally, the two newly married couples' paths crossed at dinner parties. When Julia was placed next to Leslie, she felt rather intimidated. He was known for being fiercely intellectual and opposed to anything fanciful, which he described as 'humbug', 'sham' or 'sentimental'.[6] Lacking confidence in her intellectual abilities, Julia feared he would be bored by her. In fact, he always admired and respected her, but at this time he was too wrapped up in his own life to give her much thought. He became known for the anti-conservatism of his writing. He attacked religion for encouraging intolerance and hypocrisy, and supported parliamentary and university reform as well as Irish independence and Church disestablishment.[7]

In 1870, the Stephens' daughter, Laura, was born prematurely. Weighing less than three pounds at birth, she was a delicate baby. Although she was slow to teethe and speak, her mother did not realise there was anything seriously wrong.[8] Minny devoted herself to being a full-time wife and mother. When she became pregnant again, five years later, the future looked promising, but all that changed in a matter of hours.

After Minny's death, Leslie turned to the women in his circle to console him. The day after the tragedy, Julia came to support her old friend Anny. When she saw Leslie, she kissed him tenderly and asked him whether he had kept many letters because they were the greatest comfort. Her manner was too restrained for Anny's taste; she would have preferred a greater out-pouring of emotion, but that was not Julia's way. She was used to helping the bereaved and knew the best support was practical not hysterical. A few days later, when Anny and Leslie went to Brighton, Julia took a lodging nearby to support them. Shortly after they returned to London, Leslie and his sister-in-law moved into a house next door to Julia's home at Hyde Park Gate.[9]

Growing up with a devoted mother and doting sister, Leslie was used to women pampering him. When Minny died, he automatically expected her sister Anny to step into her shoes. However, Anny had other plans, and, to Leslie's horror, she promptly fell in love with her much younger cousin, Richmond Ritchie. Seventeen years her junior, Richmond was a student while she was a mature woman of nearly 40. When Leslie walked into the drawing room and found the unconventional couple kissing, he was so appalled he gave Anny an ultimatum: she should make up her mind one way or another. His approach backfired and Anny got engaged that afternoon. She left her demanding brother-in-law to begin a new life with her youthful lover. Always a romantic, Julia encouraged the love affair and acted as peacemaker between Leslie and Anny, telling him he 'ought to be glad of anything that increases happiness'.[10]

Once Anny was married, Julia stepped in to fill the gap. She became a sympathetic listener who gave good advice. Leslie was becoming increasingly worried about his daughter, Laura, who was displaying signs of emotional and behavioural difficulties. Julia and Leslie met frequently, and he began to depend on her judgement. The bond between them was based in their mutual grief; each felt there was someone who really understood. Julia was truthful with Leslie about her feelings for Herbert, and although his feelings for Minny were not so intense, his grief was fresher. What started as mutual consolation gradually developed into something more.

Leslie had always been attracted by Julia's beauty, but now he became aware of her remarkable character too. Although initially Julia was not physically attracted to Leslie, she admired his intelligence and integrity. He suited the woman she had become. Their daughter Virginia believed that after Herbert's death Julia began to exercise her mind more and now sought to satisfy her intellect.[11] She admired Leslie's essays before she fell in love with him. His writing about his agnosticism put into words her own sceptical attitude to Christianity. She was not looking for love; no one could replace the perfect Herbert, but the meeting of minds she experienced with Leslie made her feel less alone.

After a year, Leslie realised that he wanted to be more than just good friends with Julia. One day, walking past Knightsbridge Barracks, he suddenly had 'a flash of revelation', and said to himself, 'I am in love with Julia.'[12] As he faced his true feelings, he began to experience a sense of 'joy and revival'.[13] When she came to a dinner party, after all the other guests had left he gave her a note telling her that he loved her in the way a man loves the woman he would marry. He thought there was no hope of him being her lover, but he was desperate to remain her friend. Promising to do whatever she wanted and to never speak to her of love again if that was her wish, he hoped they could find a mutual understanding. After reading the note, Julia came to Leslie's study and told him that although marriage was out of the question, they could be close friends.[14]

During the next year, they continued to see each other often, and when apart they wrote to each other daily. Julia invited Leslie to her aunt Julia Margaret Cameron's house at Freshwater. Mrs Cameron was relieved to discover that he was not just a dry academic but had a poetic side too. Appealing to the Pattle romantic streak, he stood in the hall at 'Dimbola' reciting Swinburne's *Hymn to Proserpine* and from the *Rubaiyat of Omar Khayyam*.[15] Afterwards, she wrote to her sister, Mrs Jackson, that she realised he was 'not made of iron or stone as these Gods of pure intellect so often are'.[16]

Mrs Cameron believed that Leslie was Julia's fate. She wrote to her niece that she believed his intellect 'would unlock the closely barred doors of your heart' and that love would flow from 'that reverence which intellect and wisdom always inspire'. She did have some qualms as she detected a shadow around Leslie, and she believed this shadow waited for Julia. Observing Leslie's 'mournful manner', as he sat very close to her niece 'tall, wrapt in gloom, companionless, silent', she knew his neediness would appeal to Julia's nurturing nature.[17]

When Julia first introduced Leslie to her mother as her friend, Mrs Jackson was not impressed. He was rude about her hero, Coventry Patmore, telling her that he 'despised' the poet because he was 'effeminate' with 'a cowardly view of the world'. Afterwards, Leslie had to apologise, blaming a fit of 'temporary insanity'.[18] Hardly surprisingly, at first Julia wanted to keep the importance of her relationship with Leslie secret from her mother. Knowing how possessive and protective Mrs Jackson was, Julia realised that she would interfere. Leslie urged Julia to tell her the truth. When Julia eventually confided, Mrs Jackson told her frankly that she did not believe their unconventional relationship could last. She thought her daughter should either give Leslie up or marry him. As always, Julia was very influenced by her mother and began to have concerns.

Throughout this time, Julia was honest with Leslie about her feelings. Her letters were loving but she still would not marry him. She continued to consider death would be the greatest blessing.[19] She felt the situation was unfair for him because it made him restless, and it stopped him from finding a fulfilling relationship elsewhere.[20] Leslie told her he would take her on whatever terms she wished, because he knew that he would love her for as long as he lived. Although they were not married, he believed they had become 'one in spirit'.[21]

Reassuring her that whatever she decided he was there for her, he wrote, 'Dearest, whether you marry me or not I will love you with all my heart, I will make it my whole purpose to give you [...] such happiness as I can.'[22] Assuring her that they were so emotionally in tune that he understood her without her needing to say anything, he signed off, 'Goodbye, my own – for you are my own, are you not?'[23]

Finding love again seemed miraculous to them both. Julia felt 'peaceful and sheltered' with Leslie, but she was too afraid of loving and losing again to commit completely. There were moments when she was still overwhelmed by depression and believed she had little to offer him. She wrote:

> Knowing what I am, it is no temptation to me to marry you from the thought that I should make your life happier or brighter – I don't think I should [...] All this sounds cold and horrid – but you know I do love you with my whole heart – only it seems such a poor dead heart. I cannot tell you that it can never revive, for I could not have thought it possible that I should have felt for anyone what I feel for you.[24]

Recognising this as a step forward, Leslie replied that this was enough for him. But Mrs Jackson was right; this unsettling state could not last forever. As Leslie needed someone to manage his household, he decided to employ a German housekeeper. Julia realised that this might set the seal on the terms of their relationship. During a Christmas visit to her mother, she agonised about what to do. When she told Leslie that she feared having another woman in the house would come between them, he once again assured her that 'you have got me so fast that you can do with me whatever you like'.[25] Leslie's patience and understanding paid off. On Julia's return to London, he spent the evening with her. Sitting in her armchair by the fire, she finally told him, 'I will be your wife and will do my best to be a good wife to you.'[26] Leslie was ecstatic, telling her that it was a 'marvellous thing' and that she was 'making sunshine and peace for me'. He recognised that they would have to face sorrows as well as joy together but told her, 'If I can see your face as I have seen it sometimes lately, I shall think that I have been one of the happiest of men.'[27]

Once her decision was made, Julia's doubts vanished, and she wondered why she hesitated for so long. In a letter to a friend, she wrote, 'I had thought that no such brightness could ever have come to me, but it has.'[28] Mrs Jackson was anxious about her daughter's decision, but her sister, Mrs Cameron, reassured her that it was the best thing for Julia's happiness. She hoped her joy would now be as deep as her grief. She admitted that Leslie had a 'rather incomprehensible exterior', but she believed his shadow had now become Julia's light.[29]

The couple were married at Kensington church on 26 March 1878. Her first and second husbands could not have been more different. With his long beard and wiry, eccentric appearance, Leslie could never replace the romantic hero who had first captured Julia's heart. Her new husband was thirteen years older than her and incredibly self-centred. Unlike easygoing Herbert, he combined vanity and self-doubt and demanded constant reassurance. While Herbert lacked ambition, Leslie was driven by a desire to be recognised as a literary genius.

The fact Julia could be attracted to such different men reflected her complexities. Virginia wrote, 'Her character was sharpened by the mixture of simplicity and scepticism. She was sociable yet severe; very amusing; but very serious; extremely practical but with a depth in her.'[30] Like Mrs Durrant in Virginia's novel *Jacob's Room*, she was 'equally poised between gloom and laughter'.[31] An actress friend of Julia's described her as 'the most beautiful Madonna and at the same time the most complete woman of the world [...] She would suddenly say something so unexpected, from that Madonna face, one thought it vicious.'[32] Few people could totally understand her contradictions; her first husband connected with the woman of the world, while her second saw only the Madonna.

Knowing she did not want to be just valued for her appearance, Leslie told her, 'I always wonder that anybody can tell a woman that she is beautiful it seems to me to be insulting; and I shall not tell you what I think of your looks.'[33] Instead, he focused on her noble character, explaining that he would always feel for her 'reverence as well as love. [...] You see I have not got my Saints and you must not be angry if I put you in the place where my Saints ought to be.'[34] But, by turning her into a plaster saint, Leslie had just replaced one female stereotype with another. He failed to understand the real her, just as much as the men who could not see beyond her beauty.

In many ways, Leslie, more than Herbert, fitted the image of what people expected Julia's husband to be. As another intellectual, he formed a cerebral triumvirate with his brothers-in-law, Mary's and Adeline's husbands Herbert Fisher and Henry Vaughan. Julia's family were relieved that she had found love again. Mrs Cameron wrote to her niece that she believed Leslie was the perfect man for her. He was kind and would take care of her, but he was also the right person to balance her strong independent will.[35] Most of their friends believed they were well matched too; the writer George Meredith wrote to Julia's daughter many years later that Leslie was 'the one man in my knowledge worthy of being mated with your mother. I could not say more of any man's nobility.'[36] Henry James had his doubts, however. He was surprised that someone as charming as Julia had 'consented to become matrimonially the receptacle of Leslie Stephen's ineffable and impossible taciturnity and dreariness'.[37] Even Leslie's biographer recognised that Julia was more remarkable than her husband.[38]

For Leslie, his second wife was 'the romance of my life'.[39] For Julia, it was more complicated. She had given herself to Herbert unconditionally and it was not easy to do that again. Leslie complained that Julia would not say 'I love you' to him. She would write it in letters, and he felt loved, but he would have liked her to say it.[40] For her part, Julia would have liked Leslie to be more physically demonstrative to her.[41] While Herbert had been her physical match, Leslie was her spiritual one. In her second marriage, Julia had found a man who felt as intensely as she did. It did not make their relationship easy, but it did make it real; in their complex way they were soulmates. Virginia believed her mother's second marriage was 'the true though late fulfilment of all that she could be; and, but that it was rather late, rather crowded, and rather anxious, no match was more truly equal, or more ceaselessly valiant'.[42]

5

The Absent Mother

During the Stephens' honeymoon at Eastnor Castle,[1] when Leslie playfully pushed his new wife down a slope, 7-year-old Gerald rushed to defend his mother, attacking his new stepfather.[2] Witnessing Julia's inconsolable grief during her widowhood, her three children were protective of her. After five years alone together, they were afraid that this new man might come between them. While they were courting, Julia voiced her concerns about introducing a stepfather into their lives. Leslie reassured her that her children 'attract me for their own sakes and not for yours', and that he would do for them whatever he would do for his own daughter.[3] However, merging the two families was never going to be easy.

At first, Leslie was uncomfortable with his stepchildren. It was the only subject he did not feel able to speak freely to his wife about. Not feeling like a real father to them, he tactfully kept his distance when their mother needed to discipline them.[4] He knew that intervening could be counter-productive. Julia's eldest son, George, could do no wrong in her eyes. Their admiration was mutual; she doted on him and in return he adored her.[5] Her second son, Gerald, was delicate, so Julia worried constantly about his health. Leslie felt more empathy with Stella. Noticing that his wife was often stern with her little girl he mentioned this to her. Julia explained that she did not love her boys better, it was just that Stella seemed a part of herself.[6]

Leslie's relationship with his daughter, Laura, was equally ambivalent. Valuing intellect, he found it hard to accept she had learning difficulties. When Leslie tried to teach her to read, he lost his temper because he believed she was just being wilful. Yet, before his second marriage, other than Julia, she was the centre of his world. He took her on holidays to the Lake District and planned outings that she thoroughly enjoyed. During their courtship, he frequently wrote to Julia about Laura, admitting that he felt helpless and out of his depth when dealing with her, but his love for her ran deep. He wrote, 'When she (Laura) is good, she is a little witch. She claims me altogether and I could not wish her altered.'[7] However, Laura's position in his life gradually changed after he remarried.

Over the next five years, Leslie and Julia added four more children to the complicated mix. In May 1879, Vanessa was born, then a year later Julian Thoby. Leslie was concerned that childbearing was damaging Julia's health. His letters suggest that he was willing to practise sexual abstinence, but she laughed at the idea, so was soon pregnant again.[8] On 25 January 1882, Adeline Virginia was born; a year later, their last child, Adrian, completed the family. Having so many children so close together in her thirties sapped Julia's strength. The experience also did little to dispel her gloomy outlook. When Edward Burne-Jones painted her in the early stage of pregnancy as the Virgin Mary in his picture of the Annunciation, her pallid skin tone and dead eyes make Julia look like a ghost rather than a blooming mother-to-be. As she looked at one of her babies, she told Leslie she thought her little boy could never be so happy again. Virginia's birth was also tinged with sadness. Born a year after the death of her sister Adeline, Julia named her new baby after her sibling, although (to dilute the painful associations), she added the name 'Virginia', and the little girl became known as 'Ginny', 'Ginnium' or 'Ginia'.[9]

In the *Mausoleum Book*, Leslie portrayed all the children as one big happy family, but this image was far from the reality and beneath the surface there were serious underlying tensions. Virginia described the Duckworths as 'the others', not brothers and sisters.[10] She felt even less affinity with Leslie's daughter, Laura, merely describing her as 'Thackeray's granddaughter'.[11]

No longer getting as much attention from her father and thrown together with other children in a noisy, extended family, Laura found it hard to cope. She was tongue-tied and stammered when she joined the rest of the family for dinner. Laura's frustration led to behavioural problems; she sometimes spat out her food or threw a tantrum.[12] On one occasion, she threw the scissors into the fire. The gap between her bright half-siblings and the little girl with learning difficulties became a chasm; Virginia described her as 'a vacant-eyed girl whose idiocy was becoming daily more obvious'.[13] Poignantly, Laura was aware that she was being compared unfavourably with the others. Leslie wrote to Julia, 'She seems to be a little more ashamed of herself than she used to be; and it makes me pity her, poor little thing!'[14]

They employed a governess for her, but Laura's emotional and behavioural problems deteriorated.[15] Julia's friend Jane Lushington described it as unusual for Laura to have a lesson without screams or punishment. Every morning the little girl would wake up and say that she had not slept a wink and that it was 'wicked to make her get up – and then she screams – this *every* day.'[16] Tellingly, Laura's behaviour was better when Julia was away. Perhaps her stepmother made her nervous or she sensed this woman was a rival for her father's love. Certainly, Julia had little patience with her stepdaughter; she believed Laura was naughty and perverse and she was stricter with her than Leslie had been.[17] Even Julia's usually uncritical friend Jane had qualms about her treatment. Mrs Lushington wrote to her husband:

> I confess I think her manner stern – but I am sure she's kind at heart and takes <u>endless</u> trouble about her – but I sigh for a real mother for the poor little strange demon – she must feel how beautiful and attractive Stella is and if you can <u>believe</u> it they are nearly the same age.[18]

It seems that the tensions between mother and stepdaughter became so acute that Leslie feared Laura might be violent to Julia. Eventually, she was sent to an asylum, Earlswood, in Redhill. They occasionally visited her, but she never permanently returned home.[19] Part of Leslie felt guilty, but he reassured himself, 'I do not doubt that we have done the best we could.'[20]

Biographer Hermione Lee examines to what degree Leslie and Julia should be criticised for their handling of Laura. She puts it into the context of the treatment of children with learning difficulties in the Victorian era, concluding that they were not guilty of 'a sadistic patriarchal conspiracy, but an unimaginative and disciplinarian response'.[21] This is true, but before his second marriage Leslie was more imaginative and flexible and his daughter had responded better to this approach. There is no doubt Leslie loved Laura, but once he had Julia and his younger children, she no longer mattered as much to him. Julia came first and when Laura added to the strain on his already exhausted wife, he made a choice.

Julia's treatment of her stepdaughter was one of the few times she fell from grace in the eyes of observers. However, her relationship with her own daughters was also far from perfect. With Stella, she replicated the inseparable bond she had with Mrs Jackson, but it took a darker form. Mother and daughter's inability to recognise each other as separate individuals made it hard for Stella to forge her own identity. Virginia wrote, 'They were sun and moon to each other; my mother the positive and definite; Stella the reflecting satellite.'[22] Modest and self-critical, the younger woman lived in her mother's shadow, always comparing herself unfavourably to her. Stella believed that she was not as intelligent or attractive as Julia. That was not how other people saw her. Although she was less classically beautiful, there was a softness and sweetness about her which was more approachable.[23]

Julia did little to boost her daughter's confidence. She saw Stella as an extension of herself, but 'a slower and less efficient part [and] she did not scruple to treat her with the severity with which she would have treated her own failings'.[24] Reflecting this attitude, Julia nicknamed Stella 'Old Cow'. Admittedly, teasing pet names were an integral part of the Stephen family's sense of humour; Virginia was known as 'the Goat', Adrian as 'the Dwarf', but it can have done little to bolster Stella's already shaky self-esteem.

Julia exploited Stella's uncritical devotion. While she pursued her good works outside the home, her eldest daughter was expected to take on many of the household responsibilities. She did it uncomplainingly because she adored her mother. To an observer, it appears that Stella not Julia was the real saint in the family.

Most of our knowledge about their relationship comes from Virginia, who was not the most objective observer because the close relationship that Stella and Julia enjoyed was denied her. Virginia believed there was something 'almost excessive' and not quite 'wholesome' about her half-sister's feelings for their mother. Like Julia's separation anxiety about Herbert, Stella could not bear to be apart from her mother. Shortly before one trip, she burst into tears saying, 'What can it matter where we are, so long as we are together.'[25] There was too little distance between them for the two women to see each other clearly. What Julia felt passed almost immediately through Stella's mind, leaving 'no need for the brain to ponder and criticise what the soul knew'.[26]

The relationship between them is captured in a photograph reminiscent of the earlier one of Julia looking up at Mrs Jackson, but now Julia has become the gaunt older woman while Stella is the adoring acolyte. In this generation, mother and daughter appear even more inseparable as Stella is standing so close to her mother there is absolutely no space between them. The few surviving letters between Julia and Stella paint a slightly different picture from the one Virginia gives us. There is a warmth and solicitousness in Julia's correspondence which challenges her youngest daughter's assessment of their bond.[27]

Compared with their half-sister, Virginia and Vanessa had a distant relationship with their mother. There were moments of intimacy, but they were rare. Virginia's first memory was sitting on Julia's lap on a train or bus with her cheek pressed against her. She vividly recalled her mother's dress with its red and purple flowers on a black background, and the scratchiness of her beads against her skin.[28] A photograph of mother and toddler shows Julia cuddling her little girl, her eyes downcast, smiling serenely as Virginia stares confidently at the photographer. This was one of Leslie's favourite photographs of his wife; he wrote that its 'tenderness' made his 'heart tremble'.[29] Another cherished memory for Virginia was her mother coming to the nursery at night with a candle to see if the children were asleep. A nervous child, Virginia sometimes lay awake, afraid of the dark and longing for her mother to come. When she finally arrived, Julia told her daughter to think of all the lovely things she could think of, such as rainbows and bells.[30] A similar scene appears in Virginia's novel *Jacob's Room* when Mrs Flanders tells her young son to imagine fairies and a mother bird feeding a baby bird in its nest when he cannot sleep.[31]

Julia was too busy to be a hands-on mother. Stella and Vanessa mothered their little sister more than she did. Stella took Virginia for walks, while Vanessa, although she was only a few years older, used to massage her with scent after her bath and put her to bed.[32] The image Virginia creates of Julia is far from maternal. In *To the Lighthouse* she repeatedly describes Mrs Ramsay, the fictionalised version of her mother, as severe. In her memoirs, Virginia recalled her being 'offhand' and 'sharp'. She disapproved of affectation, telling her as they arrived at a friend's house, 'If you put your head on one side like that, you shan't come to the party.'[33]

Looking back on her childhood, Virginia could never remember being alone with her mother for more than a few minutes without someone interrupting.[34] Even as a baby, her time with her mother was strictly limited; she was weaned at 10 weeks old, an unusually early separation.[35] The only time Virginia had her mother's undivided attention was if she was ill or in some crisis. Even when Julia taught her lessons, she shared her with Vanessa. Rather than being a bonding experience, these sessions were stressful because Julia had a 'quick temper' and was 'impatient of stupidity'. Virginia believed it would have been better if she had employed a governess, but Julia was too 'impetuous, and also a little imperious; so conscious of her own burning will', to do that. She thought she could do everything more effectively than anyone else.[36]

Although her sons had a public-school and university education, like many parents of her generation, Julia did not believe her daughters should have the same. It was decided that Vanessa and Virginia would be educated at home. There were Swiss and French governesses, but most of the teaching was done by Julia and Leslie. Virginia resented it and in later life one of the main elements of her feminism was that girls should have the same educational opportunities as boys. Interestingly, Leslie was more supportive of female education than Julia. Indeed, his ideas, at least in theory, were so progressive they sound like forerunners of his daughter's arguments. In an era when mental health specialists advised against the education of women because it might damage their physical and mental health and make them incapable of 'performing their functions as women', he was ahead of his time.[37]

During their courtship, Julia and Leslie discussed the issue in depth. He believed that women ought to be well educated, learning the basics in Greek, Latin and arithmetic and then, if they showed aptitude for a subject, they should be taught by the best teachers. He wanted them to develop skills which could be used to earn their own living rather than merely for amusement. He did not intend his daughters to be taught just the accomplishments that would turn them into respectable young ladies. He wrote to Julia, 'I hate to see so many women's lives wasted simply because they have not been trained well enough to have an independent interest in any studies or to be able to work effectively at any profession.'[38]

Reading Leslie's views, Julia was offended and took this as an attack on her own limited education. More conservative than him, she wanted her daughters educated to have many interests in life rather than a career. Realising he had upset her, Leslie backtracked and reassured her that he did not want her to be a scholar.[39] He was telling her the truth because although in theory he wanted women to be better educated, in practice he often found erudite women irritating.[40] It bolstered his self-esteem to feel superior; however, Julia's attitude to girls' education was to have repercussions for her daughters. She taught them Latin, history and French, while Leslie gave them lessons in mathematics. Determined they should become accomplished young ladies, she also made sure they learnt the piano, singing, 'graceful deportment', riding and dancing.

Although Virginia later resented this arrangement, as her father was a retired don and his extensive library was available to her, she was better educated than many of her contemporaries. Her extensive knowledge of English literature was encouraged by him. When she tapped at his study door asking for another book he was delighted saying, 'Gracious child how you gobble.'[41] After Julia's death, Leslie's belief that his daughters should be able to develop their talents was followed. Virginia took courses in German, History, Latin and Greek at King's College Ladies' Department in Kensington.[42]

Although Julia was not an ideal teacher, she encouraged Virginia's love of literature. The little girl inherited her literary talent from her mother as well as her father. Julia was a skilful storyteller whose children's stories demonstrate her fertile imagination and literary ability. Combining a vivid turn of phrase, colourful caricatures and witty dialogue, they are delightful but also didactic with a strong moral message: cruelty to animals or humans is unacceptable. Sadistic children experience nightmarish adventures which terrify them into behaving properly. Revealing the sense of humour her daughter inherited, Julia's stories are full of in-jokes.[43] With her menagerie of magical talking animals, including 'pert' Miss Piggling, a bear with gout, and 'bashful' elephants, many of the stories read like precursors of Beatrix Potter. Confirming her literary ambitions, Julia unsuccessfully tried to have them published by Routledge.[44]

Julia did not shy away from the harsh realities of life in her stories or her conversations with Virginia. In the one surviving letter she wrote to her daughter, she recounted a conversation she overheard between two old ladies about a younger woman who accidentally killed her first child by waltzing it around the room until the baby could not breathe.[45] This seems a strange story to tell a sensitive 6-year-old, but there was black humour in the way Julia told it. Perhaps, she also felt it was better to expose her daughter to the darker side of life early rather than let her discover it later.

The children were soon making up their own stories, producing the *Hyde Park Gate News*, a chronicle of family life. Starting as a group effort, Virginia increasingly took the lead role; from the age of 9, for the next four years she produced a weekly edition. Her editorial selection was aimed at pleasing her mother, with accounts of her matchmaking, coping with burst pipes, and nursing included.[46] In it we hear Julia's voice mimicked by her daughter, as Virginia echoes her mother's views and sayings on everything from health to women's suffrage.[47] As well as articles, it contained Virginia's first surviving story 'The Midnight Ride'.[48] Inspired by *Punch* magazine, the overall tone of the *Hyde Park Gate News* was satirical rather than sentimental.[49]

Julia was her daughter's first critic, and Virginia craved her approval. After leaving a copy of the paper beside her plate at breakfast, she watched anxiously as her mother read her newspaper. Years later, she remembered her excitement if Julia liked something she had written. Making her laugh was the greatest accolade; Julia had a distinctive laugh which ended with three diminishing ahs 'Ah-ah-ah'.[50] This welcome sound made Virginia 'blush furiously' with pride.[51] Recognising her daughter's literary talent, Julia observed to Leslie, 'Rather clever, I think.'[52] She was so proud of Virginia's exceptional imagination that she sent one of her stories to a friend.[53] She also shared the *Hyde Park Gate News* with her mother, Mrs Jackson, who admired Virginia's graphic accounts of family visits.[54]

Rationed time alone together, Virginia craved intimacy with her mother. She relished the 'snatched moments' when before dinner she chose the jewellery Julia would wear, then walked arm in arm downstairs to the dining room with her.[55] These glimmers of a closer relationship left Virginia wanting more, but it never materialised. There was none of that conspiratorial chatter and sharing of confidences that the other mothers and daughters in this book enjoyed; Julia kept her secrets to herself. When Virginia asked how Leslie proposed, instead of replying, her mother just gave her little laugh.[56]

Like Sylvia Plath, Virginia felt more of a rapport with her father than her mother. Although she would later portray Leslie as a domestic tyrant, during her childhood he comes across as a loving parent who was more involved in his children's lives than most Victorian fathers. Father and daughter had a special bond. When Virginia asked Vanessa which parent she preferred, while her sister immediately replied she liked their mother, Virginia chose their father.[57] Her feelings were reciprocated; Leslie thought his youngest daughter was like him, but she had more life in her than he had at her age.[58]

When Julia was away, Leslie often wrote to her about 'the little rogue'. Virginia would tell him a story every night or make a speech in front of the whole family about a crow and a book, which was such 'a long rigmarole' that her siblings got bored and coughed her down.[59] Then she nestled up close to him on the sofa and gazing up at him through her shock of hair, her eyes flashing and looking mischievous, she would say, 'Don't go Papa.'[60] In the nursery, Virginia would regale her siblings with stories about the Dilke family next door. Intellectually curious, to Leslie's delight his precocious daughter discussed history with him.

Although Leslie recognised how bright Virginia was, he did not have the same career aspirations for her as he did for his sons. Hoping Thoby might one day become Lord Chancellor, he told Julia that he did not want him to be an author. He explained 'that is for ladies and Ginia will do well at that'.[61] Leslie could not decide what type of writer Virginia should be, but he hoped she might take up history so that he could give her some hints.[62] Reading these letters, it is easy to understand where Virginia got her inspiration for Shakespeare's sister, the talented daughter in *A Room of One's Own* who did not have the same opportunities as her brother.

Julia had less complicated relationships with her sons than her daughters. Virginia believed her mother's favourite child was her brother Adrian. In the *Hyde Park Gate News*, Virginia observes Julia's tenderness towards her youngest child. When he was ill, she described her 'fond mother' feeding him medicine from a spoon like a bird feeding its young titbits.[63] In *To the Lighthouse*, Mrs Ramsay has a special affinity with her youngest son, James. Leslie also recognised that Adrian was particularly close to Julia. She hated sending all her sons away to boarding school, but it was even more painful when her youngest went.[64] She kept a photograph of him by her bed and called him her 'joy'.[65]

Another favourite was George. Tall and good looking but not very bright, he was very like his father. His exuberant displays of emotion cut through Julia's reserve. Virginia recalled coming into the drawing room to find George on his knees with his arms extended, addressing his mother 'in tones of fervent adoration'. He had only been away for a short time, but on his return he 'lavished caresses, endearments, enquiries, embraces' on her as if he had been away in the Australian Bush for forty years.[66] An admirer of Julia's also noticed the intense relationship between mother and son, writing, 'He adores you in a way that delights me and – makes me half jealous too!'[67]

Julia's relationship with her sons also made Virginia envious. In the *Hyde Park Gate News*, she frequently recorded her mother tearfully welcoming her sons home from boarding school or university. She was more concerned with their well-being than any academic success. Quoting one of her mother's sayings, Virginia noted that Julia would rather see her children 'roll in health than roll in wealth'.[68] Even though her daughters turned out to be more talented than her sons, she instilled in them that men were superior to women. One friend, the novelist George Meredith, criticised her conventional attitudes, telling her that he would like to see Thoby 'before his father has taught him that he must act the superior, and you have schooled the little maids to accept the fact supposed: for it is largely (I expect you dissent) a matter of training'.[69]

Leslie portrayed his wife as a perfect mother, but the reality was different. Unable to get the balance right between being either too close or too distant from her daughters, she was a better mother to her sons. However, her greatest deficiency as a mother was failing to be aware of what was really happening in her home. When Virginia was aged about 6, her half-brother, Gerald, who was twelve years older than her, sexually abused her. Virginia recalled being caught looking at herself in the glass in the hall and feeling ashamed or afraid of her own body. There was a shelf outside the dining room and Gerald lifted her on to it and began exploring her body. She remembered resenting and disliking it, but she instinctively felt it was too shaming to mention. Afterwards, she would dream that she was looking in the mirror when the face of a horrible creature would suddenly appear over her shoulder and frighten her. The abuse she suffered at her half-brother's hands was to affect the rest of Virginia's life.[70] Shortly before her death decades later, she confessed to a friend, 'I still shiver with shame at the memory.'[71] Her mother had failed her in the most fundamental way; she had not been there to protect her youngest daughter from her own son.[72]

6

The Hostess

While something far darker lurked behind the flawless façade, to the outside world the Stephens seemed the perfect family. Acolytes gathered around them both in London and at their holiday home in Cornwall. They seemed to offer a combination of stability and stimulation which attracted a diverse range of people, from literary lions to lonely souls. Julia was the central figure around whom all her family and friends revolved. She created an ambience which totally absorbed people while they were in her orbit.

Virginia described the power of her mother's personality, which overwhelmed all objectivity in the people she met. As her daughter, Virginia felt that she lived 'so completely in her atmosphere that one never got far enough away from her to see her as a person'.[1] Both Leslie and Virginia tried to analyse exactly how Julia exerted such a hold over people, but like a butterfly which becomes lifeless once pinned down, that indefinable quality remained elusive. She was enigmatic – that was part of her power – even those closest to her never completely penetrated that mystique. There were many facets to her character, and no one saw all of them; the charming hostess was very different from the severe mother.

When Leslie moved into Julia's house in Hyde Park Gate, they created the ultimate Victorian home. From its raspberry red and black drawing room with its plush velvet furniture, to the marble busts and ornaments cluttering every surface, it epitomised its era.[2] For modern tastes it sounds oppressive, but at the time it was the height of fashion. As the family grew, so did their tall town house. To save on architect's fees, Julia sketched what she wanted, then an extra storey would be built on top of the house, or a dining room added at the bottom.[3] With eight children and seven servants, there was no privacy; only Leslie had the luxury of a room of his own, and when family life became too much he retreated to his study.

Leslie and Julia's home reflected their relationship. No attempt was made to hide their memories of their lost loves; Herbert's barrister's wig was kept in the nursery wardrobe, while a cast of Minny's hands was displayed in the drawing room cabinet. Keeping these physical reminders of the dead suited the morbid sensibilities of the Victorian era. The Stephens were following Queen Victoria's example of keeping even the smallest relic of Prince Albert until her dying day.

In a stable relationship again, both husband and wife thrived. Leslie became an increasingly influential man of letters. He wrote about ethics and literary history, but his greatest commitment was to biography. In 1885, he became the first editor of *The Dictionary of National Biography*. He counted the writers Thomas Hardy, George Meredith and Henry James as friends. Younger men hung on his every word and flattered his ego, while with his children he had 'a godlike, yet childlike standing'.[4]

In her second marriage, Julia came to life again.[5] Her friend Jane Lushington noted she was 'looking, if possible, more beautiful than ever'.[6] She attracted many admirers, and Leslie's friend James Russell Lowell, the American ambassador and poet, became particularly devoted to her. When she addressed him in her letters as 'Excellency', he replied by writing to her as 'Dear Super-Excellency'. Enjoying paying her convoluted compliments, he described how when he saw a girl with 'hair just your ripening-corn-in-the-wind colours' he 'thanked her inwardly for recalling you'.[7] Couched in terms of courtly love, he wrote poems to her, and in return she sent him photographs of herself and her family. What started as a playful flirtation grew into something deeper as her friendship comforted him during his wife's final illness and she confided in him about Leslie's depressions. In the later letters, he told her that he loved her 'with all my heart'.[8]

Although he was twenty-seven years her senior, Lowell was just the sort of man to appeal to her. A charismatic diplomat and romantic poet, he had used his poetry to express anti-slavery views. Like Leslie, he was an academic and writer, who combined being a professor of languages at Harvard and editor of *The Atlantic Monthly*. When he was appointed to the Court of St James, Queen Victoria commented that she had never seen an ambassador who 'created so much interest and won so much regard'.

A ladies' man, he occasionally piqued Julia's jealousy by mentioning his aristocratic lady friends.

James and Julia's flirtation made them feel young and attractive again. Now in her early forties, Julia's looks were fading, but her admirer always treated her as the beautiful girl she had been. When she complained that she was looking older and had to wear glasses, he reassured her that 'not even smallpox could do anything more than bring you nearer the level of your competitors'.[9] Calling her 'My Pallas Athene', he told her, 'Age can never disfigure a face like yours.'[10]

Important as their relationship was to them both, it was kept strictly within platonic bounds. He described his affection for her as 'sweetly-sacred'.[11] Treating her as a saint, he wrote, 'I keep a candle burning always before your image in the shrine of my soul.'[12] Half-joking, he told her that she bore the burdens of others with such forgetfulness of herself that 'you are beginning to look top-heavy with the heap of halos you win and wear'.[13] Implying that he was too elderly for a physical relationship, the ambassador emphasised how 'enormously old' he was.[14] Respecting his friendship with her husband, his letters always ended with love to Leslie and the children.

As Julia was so fond of Lowell, she made him Virginia's godfather. 'Vinnie', as he nicknamed her, was always singled out for special mention. When Julia sent him a picture of her daughter for Christmas, he said that while reading he looked up from his book now and then 'to distract myself with a bit of flirtation with a pair of eyes that are running over with it in happy expectation of worthier objects than a dreary old greybeard like me'.[15] A few years later he wrote to Julia, 'Don't let Vinnie be too like you or I shall be falling in love with her by mistake.'[16] At the end of another letter he wrote that he felt so 'like kissing somebody, that I must beg you to give me that felicity by proxy on the lips of my goddaughter'.[17]

Such remarks written by an elderly man about a little girl could be seen as sexualising a child and would be unacceptable in our own era. Like Mrs Cameron's photographs of scantily clad children, they make a modern observer feel decidedly uneasy. However, the Victorians had different standards. It seems that Lowell was treating Virginia as an extension of her mother and using her as a surrogate to pay yet more compliments to Julia. He wrote that Virginia had 'the good taste to look (so far as she, or anybody can) like you'.[18] Ironically, in Victorian culture it was more acceptable for him to make flirtatious comments about a prepubescent girl than her married mother. This was an era when relationships between children and adult men were assumed to be innocent; the friendship between the bachelor Charles Dodgson (Lewis Carroll) and Alice Liddell, the little girl who inspired his *Alice's Adventures in Wonderland*, took place in overlapping intellectual circles to the Stephens as Mrs Cameron photographed Alice.[19]

The correspondence between Julia and Lowell suggests that they were both aware that Virginia was special. Proud of her daughter's precocious skill with language, Julia told him amusing anecdotes about his god-daughter and repeated the words she coined. He wrote 'her "annydogs" coursing unmuzzled the paths of history are a joy forever, and her "botanical husband" is the same vintage as "mobbled Queen"'.[20] He described one of Virginia's letters to him as being 'delightful' as a Japanese drawing.[21] He recognised that, 'She seems to have that knack of saying things which makes life endurable. I hope she will keep it.'[22]

Although Lowell was Julia's most serious admirer, he was one among many. According to Leslie, Henry James 'always loved her' too. None of her devotees were a threat to her husband, however; she inspired courtly not carnal love. They knew Leslie's devotion left no vacuum, as Henry James observed to a mutual friend, 'Good God, how that man adores her!'[23] In return, Julia gave her husband the confidence which made him increasingly attractive to the opposite sex. One female friend said, 'He did by instinct all the little things that women like.'[24] Basking in the company of beautiful women, Julia teased him about 'flirting with pretty ladies', but she knew none of them could rival her in his eyes.[25] He told her, 'Nobody in the whole world has a more devoted or loving or <u>beautiful</u> wife and he must be a perfect donkey if he was not aware of it.'[26]

Neither Leslie nor Julia cared for 'society', but they enjoyed gathering like-minded people together.[27] The Stephens considered it bad taste to care too much about appearances; they preferred their home and clothes to be shabby rather than flashy and their dinner parties were stimulating but certainly not smart. The children sometimes helped to wait at the table and fought over who would have the honour of taking an illustrious guest's plate. After the meal, everyone retired to the drawing room to chat by the fire or sing around the piano.[28] Virginia wrote, 'The patriarchal society of the Victorian age was in full swing in our drawing room.' Women were expected to be passive and decorative, admiring and applauding as their men showed off their intellectual prowess.[29]

Unlike her daughter in later life, Julia played by society's rules. At her Sunday tea parties, presiding over the oval tea table with her shell-like pink china, Julia was the perfect hostess. Her manners were impeccable; there were never awkward silences as her mastery of small talk was 'a concoction, a confection'.[30] She gave everyone just enough of her time to make them feel special. The bevy of beauties, who treated her as a second mother, could rely on her for advice. Lonely old bachelors were supplied with copious cups of tea, spiced buns and sympathy.[31] In contrast to his charming wife, Leslie could be rude. He could not tolerate bores and made his feelings known, groaning and muttering very audibly under his breath.[32] He admitted that spending time with dull people made him 'restless as a hyena'.[33] When he had had enough, he escaped to his study, leaving them to bore Julia.

The chosen few from the Stephens' London circle were invited to join them on their holidays in Cornwall. In 1882, the family leased Talland House in St Ives; they loved it so much that every year the family spent their summer there. Those holidays took on a golden light in Leslie and Virginia's memories. Aged 6 months when she was first taken there, Virginia described 'feeling the purest ecstasy I can conceive', as she lay in bed in the nursery listening to the waves break on the shore.[34] Leslie shared her passion for the place, describing it as 'a pocket-paradise'.[35] The three or four summer months spent at Talland House were the happiest time for all the family.

From the moment they set off on the long train journey the fun began. Like Virginia, Julia was a keen people watcher who could humorously caricature people in a few sentences. While waiting at the station, she kept her children laughing till the train set off.[36] Once in St Ives, the family immediately felt at home. The spacious Victorian house had 2 or 3 acres of terraced gardens which ran down to the sea. Divided into a dozen little plots, it seemed full of romance to the children. There were nooks and crannies surrounded by escallonia hedges where couples could meet for assignations. A sheltered spot behind the grape-house, where Julia enjoyed sitting in the sun, became known as love corner. In the early evening she sat on the porch, knitting and watching her children play cricket. Later, she would stroll in the garden picking flowers. Always in the background were the sounds and smell of the sea. As one guest, Margaret Lushington, told her sister, 'The blue bay from every window that I see as I write is more improbably beautiful than anything I ever saw.'[37] Inside, the décor was decidedly dilapidated, the faded wallpaper peeled and the threadbare furniture had seen better days, but it just added to the relaxed atmosphere. The children walked sand into the house, while Leslie marched in with muddy boots from his tramps along the coast, but it did not matter – they were on holiday.

During the Stephens' time at St Ives, the little fishing town was unspoilt. Few visitors wandered through the narrow streets lined with granite cottages, although the arrival of a branch railway line in the 1870s had made it easier for travellers from all over the country to reach the picturesque town and it was gradually growing in popularity. From the 1880s, artists were attracted by the exceptional quality of the light. One summer, Whistler, with his assistant, Walter Sickert, painted beach scenes.[38]

We get the clearest image of holidays at Talland House from Virginia's novel *To the Lighthouse*. Although the fictional account is set in the Hebrides, it captures the essence of the family's Cornish idyll. Mr and Mrs Ramsay, the fictionalised versions of Julia and Leslie, are in many ways indistinguishable from the real people. However, like Sylvia Plath's and Agatha Christie's writing about their past, it should be read as Virginia's imaginative perspective on what she observed rather than a verbatim account.

Inevitably, Julia invited more guests than the nine-bedroom house could accommodate, so once every camp bed was occupied and it was crammed to the attics, extra guests lodged in the town. Julia threw together an eclectic assortment of famous writers, earnest young academics, and pretty girls. Virginia complained that she was 'a little indiscriminate in her choice of friends', but if the children laughed at the more eccentric characters, Julia reprimanded them. She expected everyone to be treated with respect.[39] The consequences of mixing such a diverse range of people could be unpredictable, but it just added to the excitement of the holiday.

During the day, everyone would do their own thing. Some went on outings to local beauty spots, others spent the day on the beach, while the more artistic guests painted or photographed the ever-changing scene. The children had lessons with Julia in the morning and walks with Leslie in the afternoon, but for the rest of the day they were free to do their own thing. Virginia and Vanessa were tomboys who loved climbing trees or going out sailing with a fisherman in a lugger. In the evening, they played cricket with their brothers and soon Virginia became known as a demon bowler.[40] Once it got dark, they would go moth hunting. Armed with butterfly nets and lamps, they caught the bugs in jars laced with rum provided by Julia.

At the end of every busy day, guests had dinner together. Sometimes fifteen people would crowd into the candlelit dining room for a meal consisting of the freshest local produce. Lobster from the local fishermen and Cornish clotted cream from a nearby dairy were bought in; grapes, strawberries and peaches were eaten straight from the garden. While Leslie sat at the head of the table, Julia held court at the other end. The intellectual atmosphere could be intimidating; one young guest, Margaret Lushington, wrote to her sister, 'Why people don't die of fright and terror when first they come here I don't know. No one speaks one word, and everyone looks savage.'[41] It was Julia's role to meld the diverse range of guests into a cohesive whole. She conducted them as though they were her orchestra. One moment she would be drawing out a shy guest, the next defusing a potential explosion from her irascible husband.

Julia managed to be both charming and surprisingly direct. She had strong opinions and expressed them with conviction. If a subject interested her, she became animated using her hands to make her point. Speaking quickly, she had a lively turn of phrase and a good sense of humour; her distinctive laugh often punctuated the conversation.[42] If a guest was in favour, she completely focused her attention on them and made them feel they were the only person in the room. If they had annoyed her, she could be 'cool, amused and even faintly malicious'.[43]

It was during these holidays that Virginia first discovered how absorbing writing could be. Sitting on the green plush sofa in the drawing room while the adults dined, she scribbled a story in the style of the American novelist Nathaniel Hawthorne.[44] When dinner was over, Julia went up to the attic to say goodnight to the children. Sometimes she would tell them a story set in St Ives. Copying her mother's example, Virginia made up equally enthralling tales which she recounted to Julia and her godfather Mr Lowell. Every night, Virginia added the latest instalment to her serial about Beccage and Hoodwinks, evil spirits who lived on the rubbish heap in the garden and disappeared through a hole in the escallonia hedge.[45]

Julia was in her element on holiday. Virginia remembered her coming out on to her bedroom balcony in a white dressing gown, to gaze serenely at the sea.[46] While her friends and family played on the beach she would write letters, contentedly listening to them having fun. Mr Lowell recalled her pitching her tent upon the sands and watching her 'pretty little Merman and maids paddling in the surf'.[47] Occasionally, she would brave the sea herself; her nephew remembered her bobbing about in the water in a large black hat.[48]

Julia was a dedicated matchmaker and eligible bachelors were thrown together with attractive young women. Daughters of old friends were excited to be invited. The highly charged atmosphere is captured in letters written by Margaret Lushington to her sister. She enthusiastically analysed each potential suitor and was ready for a holiday romance.[49] Although Julia was kind to the girls, she was more attentive to the young men. Virginia believed this was partly for sexist reasons; Julia's alter-ego Mrs Ramsay was drawn to the opposite sex because of 'their chivalry and valour, for the fact that they negotiated treaties, ruled India, controlled finance'. But it was also because she found their 'trustful, childlike, reverential' relationship with her appealing.[50] For a woman who had been so admired by men in her youth, it would have been hard to become invisible to them in middle age. In her new role, she continued to have sexual power. She became their trusted confidante and made them feel better about themselves. In return, they offered her 'a kind of chivalrous devotion' and many of them fell a little in love with this compassionate older woman.[51]

She decided who should marry whom and then worked on her project till her mission was accomplished. Young couples were sent off on walks together, then seeds were subtly sown in impressionable minds; one girl was told about the stellar career awaiting her suitor, while Margaret Lushington learned it would break George's heart if she left before he arrived.[52] Julia was more successful with some matches than others. In 1890, one of her favourite protegees, Kitty Lushington, got engaged to the political editor, Leo Maxse, in the aptly named 'love corner' at Talland House.[53] Another success was the match between the historian Frederic Maitland and Julia's niece Florence Fisher. Julia did far more than just introduce the couple; she actively intervened when things went wrong. Although Florence and Frederic seemed to be getting on well, the relationship stalled when he failed to propose. Rather than accepting defeat, Julia tackled Frederic about what the problem was. When he explained that he had thoughts of suicide and feared he might go insane, she told him she did not believe it and suggested he should consult the best expert in London. Given a clean bill of health by the doctor, Frederic's qualms vanished, and he was soon happily married to Julia's favourite niece.[54]

Unfortunately, Julia was less successful with her own daughter. When Stella came out in society, many young men fell in love with her. As they crowded into the Stephens' drawing room it 'excited many instincts long dormant in her mother'.[55] Perhaps remembering her own youthful romance, Julia could not resist getting involved in her daughter's love life. She was 'intensely amused' by all the intrigue,[56] yet her involvement at times backfired. Julia particularly favoured an eligible young lawyer called Jack Hills. Like Herbert Duckworth, he was a thoroughly decent 'English country gentleman type'[57]. He courted Stella for several years, pursuing her with the tenacity of a 'wire-haired terrier'.[58] It seems, however, he got on better with the mother than the daughter. When Jack proposed, for once Stella did not give in to her mother's wishes and she refused. No matter how eligible the suitor, Stella was not ready to leave Julia.

Like Sylvia Plath in *The Bell Jar*, Virginia in *To the Lighthouse* sometimes attributed the worst motives to her mother; she suggested Julia's match-making came from a wish to dominate, to interfere and make people do what she wanted.[59] Perhaps there was an element of truth in Virginia's view, as the Lushington sisters also sometimes found her intrusive. Margaret wrote to Susan, 'How trying of Mrs Stephen to come to your room.'[60] A more generous interpretation came from Leslie; he believed that Julia liked to make other people happy and knowing the joy she had experienced when she first fell in love, she wanted those around her to share that ecstasy.[61]

Virginia's criticism was ideological as well as personal; she was critical of her mother's behaviour for feminist reasons. Virginia saw Julia's matchmaking as another example of her mother's conventional attitude to female roles. In the novel, Mrs Ramsay thinks the only way a woman could be truly happy was if she married and had children. She could not understand women with different desires from her own. It seems she would never have been able to accept that her daughters might want a different life 'in Paris perhaps; a wilder life; not always taking care of some man or other'.[62] Many years later, Virginia was to challenge her mother's conservative views with her feminist ideas. Her lifestyle was to be a rebellion against Julia's world view.

The Angel Outside the House

As a Victorian woman, Julia was expected to model herself on 'the angel in the house', the creation of Coventry Patmore, her mother's friend. Confined to the domestic sphere, a woman's role was to be a good wife and mother, running the house and nurturing numerous children. Both Leslie and Julia accepted this idea of separate spheres for men and women. She was the unchallenged mistress of the household and a force to be reckoned with in her caring roles both at home and in the community, while her husband's domain was the public sphere – the world of literature and academia.

As so often with the Stephens, however, the situation was not quite what it seemed. Although on the surface Julia was the model of Victorian femininity, there was far more to her than that. She stretched her separate sphere to its limits, and she was outside their home more than Leslie. While he remained cocooned within his study absorbed in his own thoughts, she escaped from this esoteric atmosphere to make a real difference in the wider world. She never openly rebelled, but Julia lived her life on her own terms. Although she was part of a patriarchal society, she had grown up in a matriarchy where women got their own way. Personal experience made her view of the world matriarchal; she saw herself as a mother to not just her children but also her servants and the wider community.[1]

Considering that he was lucky to have her, Leslie rarely prevented her from doing what she wanted. Unlike her husband, she did not crave fame, nor did she publicise or politicise her actions. Instead, she quietly worked to achieve her humanitarian aims. Since being a child, Julia's vocation was nursing. During her widowhood, she found solace in that role; therefore, when she remarried, she was not going to give it up. If anyone in her family was ill, they called for her. During her engagement to Leslie, Uncle Thoby became seriously ill. As his wife was unable to cope, Julia left Leslie in charge of the children and immediately rushed over to the Isle of Wight to support her aunt and uncle.[2] She soon took charge of the 'paralysed household', but her no-nonsense approach was not to everyone's taste. Thoby's granddaughter wrote, 'Her manner was reserved and authoritative, so that she rather frightened us.'[3]

Beneath the calm exterior, Julia was a very sensitive woman who was deeply upset by her uncle's suffering. She could only express her true feelings in her letters to Leslie. Providing her with the reassurance she needed, he told her that he longed to put his arms around her and comfort her. He wrote, 'I love you more tenderly [...] when I see you tormented by these heavy blows.' Yet, as always with Leslie, his thoughts soon returned to himself. He admitted to being rather jealous of Uncle Thoby getting Julia's attention. Morbid as ever, he pondered what he would want if he was dying.[4]

Leslie often had to share his wife because Julia's family relied on her in every crisis. When her eldest sister, Adeline Vaughan, was dying from heart disease, Julia left her own family to nurse her. Watching her sister die slowly and painfully was harrowing enough but being at Upton Castle again must have brought back memories of her first husband's tragic death. According to Leslie, the letters he received from her at this time were the saddest she ever wrote.[5] Suggesting that her depressive streak ran deeper than his, he wrote to her:

> What grieves me in your pessimism is that I know the cause of it. You think the world unhappy because you are melancholy: and I would give all that I have and ever shall have in the world to make you cheerful.[6]

With Adeline dead, Julia's close relationship with her surviving sister, Mary Fisher, became even more important to them both. They wrote to each other frequently, confiding their concerns. One of Mary's sons was often ill, and she described the minutiae of his illness and treatment to Julia, knowing no one was better equipped to offer sound advice. As Virginia later noted, to dip into this generation's letters 'is to be immersed in the joys and sorrow of enormous families, to share their whooping coughs and colds and misadventures, day by day, indeed hour by hour'.[7]

As Julia's mother grew older, her dependence on her daughter also increased. Describing herself as 'feeling like a restless old Panther', Mrs Jackson constantly fussed about her family's health. As well as displaying a colourful turn of phrase, she also showed an overactive imagination worthy of a novelist.[8] In one letter, she feared that the candles would set fire to the fourposter's drapes or the children would catch cold or be stung to death by bees.[9] In another, she tried to persuade Leslie not to go to Switzerland in case he was killed by an avalanche.[10] This was the norm in her letters; in her anxious mind anything from eating an indigestible sausage to swimming in the sea might prove fatal. However, her greatest concern was always for Julia; like Leslie, she considered her youngest daughter was perfect but delicate. She impressed on Stella that her first duty was to look after her mother. While they were on holiday in St Ives, she wrote to her to keep an eye on Julia to make sure she did not get sunburnt if it was hot or rheumatism if it was damp. She added, 'Kiss her sweet face for me. I am counting the days until I shall see it.'[11] In letters to Leslie, she always called Julia our 'darling of darlings', and they often conspired together to try to save her from her self-sacrificing streak.[12] Yet they were the ones who demanded most from her.

After Dr Jackson died in 1887, his wife's health deteriorated. Julia took the children with her and stayed with Mrs Jackson in Brighton. Her absence irritated Leslie and he resorted to emotional blackmail to try to make his wife come home. Complaining that she was sacrificing herself and being bullied by her mother, he told her that if she was away much longer he would 'plunge into dissipation – only I don't know what it would be – not evening parties, nor dinners nor theatres – perhaps the public house. It looks the pleasantest.'[13] No doubt, the incongruous idea of Leslie sitting in a pub nursing a tankard of beer hastened Julia's return.

Torn between two arch-manipulators who competed for her attention, Julia tried to juggle everyone's needs. Unable to cope on her own, Mrs Jackson divided her time between her two surviving daughters. As her mother was bedridden and very demanding, Julia did her best to make her as comfortable as possible. She kept her entertained by fully involving her in family life. Mrs Jackson remained fiercely protective of her daughter to the end. When the artist William Rothenstein drew an unflattering sketch of Julia, looking gaunt and elderly, her mother roused herself from her bed and staggered downstairs to give him a piece of her mind.[14]

When Mrs Jackson died in April 1892, it was a great blow to Julia; afterwards she went to stay at her cousin's house for six or eight weeks to recover.[15] Mother and daughter had relied completely on each other. Just about concealing his jealousy, Leslie wrote:

> I have never seen nor can I imagine the relation between mother and daughter more beautiful and perfect. Our 'darling of darlings' loved her mother so well that it might seem as if they had been alone together in the world.[16]

Although Julia was an experienced nurse, she never became immune to suffering. She remained an empathetic person who was affected by what she witnessed. She was particularly upset by the mental health problems of Leslie's nephew, James Kenneth Stephen, known as Jem, a tall, broad-shouldered young man of whom she was very fond. A brilliant student at Eton and Cambridge, he became a tutor to the Duke of Clarence, who was the eldest son of the Prince of Wales. Unfortunately, after a blow to his head, Jem began to suffer from manic-depressive episodes which some-times took violent sexual forms.[17] On one occasion, he rushed upstairs to the nursery in Hyde Park Gate brandishing a sword, which he plunged into the bread. Another time, in a state of euphoria, he seized Virginia and carried her off to his house, insisting that he was a painter of genius and wanted the little girl to pose for him.[18]

Julia's peaceful presence usually calmed him down, so when Jem's parents suggested she should turn him away, Julia replied that she could not shut her door upon him.[19] When he became obsessed with Stella, Julia found herself in a dilemma. She wanted to help her nephew, but her first duty was to protect her daughter. When Jem arrived at Hyde Park Gate, wild-eyed, looking like 'a tormented bull', determined to find the object of his desire, Stella had to be sent to stay with the Lushingtons in Surrey for her safety.[20] At this time, Julia wrote affectionate letters to her 'Beloved Female', from 'Your loving Old Ma'. She told Stella, 'I do want you to get rid of all this nightmare time and enjoy yourself darling.'[21]

Treating mother and daughter as extensions of each other, Jem told Leslie that if he could speak to Julia alone, he might not want to see Stella. It was an emotional meeting. Julia asked Jem not to write her unkind let-ters because she had kept her word to him and had tried to be kind. He promised that he would never visit the house again until she invited him. Before leaving, he kissed her again and again. Julia told Stella, 'It was such a great relief to me to have this talk – but of course I feel that he will probably unsay it all as he did smell so much of drink.'[22]

Even Julia could not save Jem. After his landlady at Cambridge found him standing at his bedroom window naked, singing and throwing all his belongings out of the window, he was sent to an asylum. He refused food and within three months starved to death.[23] Julia never forgot Jem; she regularly visited his grave and told her husband it was one of the losses to which she found it hardest to become reconciled.[24]

Julia's caring role extended far beyond her family. Her interest in other people was genuine and she was never off duty. Leslie confessed that he rather grudged 'this incessant round of kindly services', but he could not stop her. He knew that these acts of kindness were 'a kind of religious practice' for her.[25] Julia was aware that her children also resented her frequent absences. In her children's story *Cat's Meat*, Maggie and Bob miss their philanthropic mother, Lady Middleton, so much that they go missing in a bid to get her attention.[26] However, Julia was never willing to give up her vocation to appease her family.

Travelling around London on an omnibus, she would chat to the conductor or other passengers and find out about their lives to see if she could help.[27] Virginia described her as having 'great clearness of insight, sound judgment, humour, and a power of grasping very quickly the real nature of someone's circumstances'.[28] Reading Leslie's account of her good works there is the danger of imagining Julia as blandly worthy, but Virginia corrects this impression, explaining, 'All her gifts had something swift, decisive, witty even, in their nature; so that there could be no question of dullness or drudgery in her daily work, however lugubrious it seemed of itself.'[29]

When Julia was on holiday in Cornwall, she would surreptitiously slip out to help the needy. A very upright figure, dressed in her shabby grey cloak, a basket in one hand, a parasol in the other, she walked briskly from one appointment to another, never wasting a moment. Her help was practical and well thought out. When Julia realised there was a lack of healthcare provision in St Ives, she raised money to set up a nurse for the town. Rather than an interfering lady bountiful, she became a respected member of the local community. One local woman said:

When she heard my poor lad was ill she came at once to see what she could do. She stayed with me and helped me to nurse him herself and got a trained nurse for him; and when she saw him lying dead, she cried over me and kissed me and comforted me.[30]

As a child, Virginia remembered watching her mother wearily wander up the path at Talland House after one of her mercy missions. Virginia stopped playing to talk to her, but wrapped up in her own thoughts, her mother turned away and lowered her eyes. 'From that indescribably sad gesture I knew that Philips, the man who had been crushed on the line and whom she had been visiting, was dead.' A vicarious shadow was cast over Virginia, making her think about death.[31] Sometimes, when Julia returned late from helping others, Virginia would wait up for her because she was terrified something had happened to her mother.[32]

In *To the Lighthouse*, there is a note of criticism in Virginia's view of Julia's philanthropy. She describes Mrs Ramsay thoughtfully providing old magazines for the lighthouse keeper's little boy who has a tubercular hip, but there is the sense that she sees other people's problems through middle-class eyes. Encouraging her children to empathise with the lighthouse keeper's family, she suggests they would miss having letters and newspapers and no one to see.[33] As with her attitude to what women needed to be happy, she could only see the situation from her own perspective. She tried to use her imagination, but Virginia was aware of its limitations.

In fact, like her daughter, Julia did have a strong imaginative streak and natural literary talent, but she believed it should be used for practical rather than artistic purposes. Using her extensive experience, she wrote a book on nursing called *Notes from Sick Rooms*. The title sounds deadly dull, but thanks to her skilful turn of phrase and her compassion, as one reviewer commented it is 'very delightful reading'.[34] Another critic wrote, 'It would almost be worthwhile to be ill if you could count upon being nursed with the sympathetic tenderness which pervades the little work of Mrs Leslie Stephen.'[35]

The book emphasises how much Julia enjoyed her work. Describing nursing as 'an art', she wrote, 'A nurse's life is certainly not a dull one and the more skilful the nurse the less dull she will be.' It seems that she found her professional life easier than her personal one, as she explained, 'The ordinary relations between the sick and the well are far easier and pleasanter than between the well and the well.' It made her feel fulfilled because 'to give relief, even if it be only temporary [...] is perhaps a greater pleasure than can be found in the performance of any other duty'.[36]

On most issues, Julia had strong opinions and once she had made up her mind she would not be moved. As mistress of a large household, she wrote an essay on the duties of employers to their domestic staff. Showing respect for her employees, she gave status to domestic work, writing that 'to serve is no bad office' or 'degradation'. Believing in the interdependence between people, she championed a strong bond between servants and their employers and claimed former employees were often seen as old friends.[37] Her children's stories also reinforce this message, teaching her sons and daughters that it is wrong to mistreat servants. Leslie and Virginia provide different images of Julia as an employer. Leslie portrayed her as the perfect mistress, whose servants rarely left. A Swiss maid called Suzette, who was employed by her while she was married to Herbert, stayed with her for two decades until she developed cancer. A children's nurse named Leyden remained with her equally long.[38] Virginia was more sceptical about her mother's benevolence, criticising the servants' sleeping quarters at Hyde Park Gate as 'a little pinched and bare' and their basement as 'a dark insanitary place'. She recalled that when one maid burst out 'It's like hell', Julia 'assumed the frozen dignity of the Victorian matron' and was not sympathetic.[39]

Once again, Virginia suggests that Julia was more charitable outside than within her own home. She felt passionately about providing healthcare and good nutrition for the poor. Sometimes this led to controversy and confrontation. In 1879, she argued with the medical officer and guardians of the Fulham workhouse about their decision to no longer give their elderly and sick paupers half a pint of beer each day. She believed it helped to make them more comfortable and alleviated some of their suffering. The argument escalated when she wrote an eloquent letter to the *Pall Mall Gazette*. Articles appeared in national and local newspapers debating whether she was right, or was she just an illogical do-gooder ruled by her heart instead of her head?[40] Undeterred, she stood by her principles and refused to back down.

Although she was an amateur, Julia was very professional in her work. In her novel, Virginia describes Mrs Ramsay taking a notebook and pen with her, which she used to carefully list details about the circumstances of the people she visited. She would have liked to become an investigator of social problems.[41] This was hardly surprising as the Stephens were friends with the great social investigator of the Victorian era, Charles Booth, and his family.

In another era, when more careers were open to women, it seems likely Julia would have become a doctor, nurse or social worker. Surprisingly for such a strong-minded woman, she was not a feminist. She did not believe women should have the vote and actively campaigned against it. In 1889, she joined 100 well-known women in signing a letter opposing the extension of the parliamentary franchise to women. Among her co-signatories were a diverse range of aristocrats and the wives of politicians and famous men. Representing all shades of political opinion, they were united in the view that if women became directly involved in politics, rather than just exerting their influence, it would 'blunt the special moral qualities of women, and so lessen the national reserves of moral force'. While they desired 'the fullest possible development of the powers, energies and education of women', they believed their roles differed from those of men. They concluded, 'The pursuit of a mere outward equality with men is for women not only vain, but demoralising. It leads to a total misconception of woman's true dignity and special mission.'[42]

Julia's friend George Meredith was shocked by her old-fashioned views. When she told him that it was enough for her that Leslie 'should vote, should think', he criticised her 'irrational obstructiveness'. Describing her 'beautiful posture of the Britannic wife' as outdated, he warned her 'the world is moving on' and it would pass her by.[43] However, Julia was certain of her special mission and proud of her role in society. She explained that although women's work was different from men's, it was not 'lower or less important'. She claimed equality with the opposite sex in moral courage.[44] No doubt, it helped that Leslie also recognised her contribution. In an essay on 'Forgotten Benefactors', written after her death, he claimed she was morally his superior. He explained that although women's 'domestic influence' was 'confined within narrower limits', it could 'really mould the character of a little circle and determine the whole life of one little section of the next generation'.[45] This assessment was certainly true of Julia; she was such a strong character that she exerted a great influence on everyone she came across.

At times, the demands from so many directions exhausted her, but she needed people to need her. Once again denigrating her mother's motives, in *To the Lighthouse* Virginia portrays Mrs Ramsay pondering whether her desire to help was vanity and for her own self-satisfaction. Lily Briscoe also wonders if Mrs Ramsay's predisposition to pity people sprang from some need of her own, rather than theirs.[46] Perhaps there is a degree of truth in Virginia's analysis of Julia's motivation, but she was viewing it from her own rather than her mother's perspective.

For Julia, caring for those less fortunate than herself became her 'practical religion'.[47] There were deep-rooted personal and cultural reasons that made her dedicate her life to this cause with no desire for public recognition or reward. Nineteenth-century literature glorified self-sacrificing characters, who toiled in obscurity, doing good for no ulterior motive. Wordsworth extolled those 'little, nameless, unremembered, acts of kindness and of love', as the 'best portion of a good man's life'.[48] The onus on women to live in this way was even greater. Mrs Gaskell's novel *Ruth* tells the story of the 'fallen woman' who finds redemption by literally giving up her life to nurse others. Most memorably, George Eliot's *Middlemarch* ends with the celebration of Dorothea's selfless contribution to society. Like Eliot, Julia differed from many of her contemporaries because she was not driven to do good deeds by Christianity. She explained her humanitarian motivation in her essay on agnostic women:

We are not thinking that we shall gain a glorious immortality, that we shall be crowned as saints because we have helped our fellow creatures, but they are our work. We are bound to these sufferers by the tie of sisterhood and while life lasts we will help, soothe, and if we can, love them.[49]

Part of a different generation, although Virginia was interested in the unsung heroines of history, she rejected many of the Victorian values her mother was steeped in. It was not just theoretical for Julia; when she was widowed, she discovered that identifying with those who were suffering was the only way to deal with her deep depressive streak which never totally went away. As she wrote in *Agnostic Women*, without work 'night will overtake us while it is yet day, the night of deepest death, of sloth, of hardness of heart, of wasted opportunity'.[50] Keeping active and focusing on others helped her to cope with her anxiety and prevented her imagination from running wild. In the *Mausoleum Book*, Leslie described his wife's 'rather anxious temperament'.[51] In *To the Lighthouse*, Mrs Ramsay has a tendency to catastrophise. She worries about her children walking on the cliff edges. When they go sailing, she tries to rationalise her fears telling herself that 'holocaust on such a scale was not probable. They could not all be drowned.' But her coping techniques did not completely work because once again 'she felt alone in the presence of her old antagonist life'.[52] By an act of will, Julia managed to keep her fears under control, but only just, and the repression of her feelings was exhausting.

8

The Martyr

Prematurely aged, white hair pulled back from her skull-like face, Julia looks severe in the photographs of her in middle age. Glancing in the mirror, she was aware that she had lost her good looks. When Leslie denied it, she accused him of being 'silly', but it seems she secretly appreciated his reassurance. Her husband meant what he said; although he realised that she had lost her bloom and that she often looked very stern, the 'dignity and nobility' of her character shone through. He wrote, 'She always seemed to me to be beautiful, all through, beautiful in soul as in body.'[1]

Rather than revealing who Julia really was, Virginia saw her mother's vestiges of beauty as like a mask which 'she lived behind, and could do nothing to disturb'.[2] Her daughter wanted to find out what lay beneath. Watching her mother during their lessons together, she noticed that when Julia was not talking, she looked very sad.[3] In *To the Lighthouse*, she writes about Mrs Ramsay, 'Never did anybody look so sad.'[4] These lasting images of Julia beg the question, was she so deeply unhappy? And did the suffering she had witnessed crush the life out of her, or was the problem within her? Did she, like her daughter Virginia, suffer from depression? In the years that followed her death, Leslie and Virginia were to ask themselves these questions as they tried to understand the woman they loved.

As Julia reached her late forties, she was completely worn out. She gave so much of herself to others that it left her with few reserves. As well as nursing her family and friends and her community work, Leslie's egotistical emotional demands added to her exhaustion. Her marriage was complicated; he was difficult to live with, but in many ways, he was the right man for her. Still aspiring to be a genius, he exaggerated his sense of inadequacy and fished for compliments, which gratified him but drained her. Protecting him as though he was a child, she filtered out any bad reviews before he could read them and accompanied him when he lectured. During his speeches, she gave him 'bright glances' to assure him he was doing well, then afterwards she told him he had never spoken better.[5] Yet even Julia's soothing support could not always stop him from feeling a failure.

When Leslie felt bad about himself, his frustrations were taken out on his wife and children. He had a violent temper which he could not control. We get an idea of what his outbursts were like from Virginia's portrayal of his alter ego, Mr Ramsay, who would slam the bedroom door, get up from the table in a fury, or throw a plate through the window.[6] When Leslie became angry, his reason disappeared. Virginia wrote about the 'horror and the terror' of his violent rage, describing his actions as having 'something blind, animal, savage in them'.[7] He believed these outbursts were a sign of his genius which exempted him from the normal rules of behaviour, but they were hard for his family to bear.[8] Although he experienced remorse and usually apologised to Julia afterwards, he had no intention of changing and it did not make up for his tantrums. His outbursts upset her, and it took her some time to forgive him.

In *To the Lighthouse*, Lily Briscoe criticises the way Mrs Ramsay handled Mr Ramsay. Lily thinks she was 'weak with her husband. She let him make those scenes.'[9] This seems to have been Virginia's view; she complained that Julia was too willing to sacrifice her daughters to him. It would have been better for the family if she had made him less dependent on her. Instead, she made 'a fetish of his health'.[10] Even Leslie realised his wife should have stood up to him more, writing to her:

> You are only too ready to make yourself a slave to me and give way to my whims. [...] I wish you would take your own part a little more and make me have my turn of giving in.[11]

He also told her that she should not encourage him to be so selfish.[12] Perhaps Julia was just too exhausted to do anything else or, in her relationship with him, as in all her relationships, she needed to be the giver and carer.

Leslie's crisis of confidence culminated in a breakdown when he doubted the value of his work. He had wanted to make his mark as a philosopher but instead he was known as a critic and biographer. A perfectionist and workaholic, as well as editing *The Dictionary of National Biography*, he took on other literary projects. It all became too much for him and by 1887 he was describing his office as 'my place of torture'. [13] The following year he collapsed from overworking. Julia found him in a state of unconsciousness and as he came around, he saw her staring anxiously into his face.[14] On another occasion, he collapsed on the floor of the Athenaeum library.

Friends were worried about the whole family. Vernon Lushington wrote to his daughter Kitty, 'Leslie seems to be in a strange condition, which I can't quite understand, still less measure; but evidently he gives cause for anxiety.'[15] Staying with the family during this crisis, Kitty described how sensitive he was. She dared not mention reading one of his essays in case it upset him. She wrote to her father, 'I love him, but he does live in such a shell.'[16]

During these stressful years, Julia managed every aspect of her husband's life. She liaised with his publishers to find a compromise which would prevent him from feeling a failure.[17] Physically and emotionally, it took a toll on her health. Tossing and turning, Leslie disturbed her most nights. Awaking in a fit of 'the horrors', he panicked that he would not get back to sleep again. As though he was a baby, Julia calmed him down and lulled him to sleep. When Julia confided in her admirer, James Russell Lowell, he became concerned about the effect of Leslie's illness on her. He wrote, 'I know what a brave woman you are, and this makes me all the more sorry.'[18]

Eventually, in 1891, Leslie faced the inevitable and resigned as editor of the dictionary.[19] Unlike her first husband, Herbert, whose sunny temperament chased away any clouds, Leslie's gloomy moods reinforced Julia's depressive tendencies. In fact, although he often moaned, she was the one with the more pessimistic view of life. He believed happiness was possible, while she saw it as always 'tinged with sadness'.[20] It seems that throughout her life, Julia had to fight depression. It could be attributed to the trauma of Herbert's death, but there are hints that it was always part of her temperament. It seems that her experiences just reinforced an underlying depressive streak. As Leslie explained, she was not always unhappy; there were moments of great joy, but Julia's overall view of life was bleak.

In *To the Lighthouse*, Virginia imagines Mrs Ramsay's thoughts. Lacking a religious faith, they are nihilistic, 'There is no reason, order, justice; but suffering, death, the poor. [...] No happiness lasted; she knew that.'[21] Such existential anguish was not unique; since Darwinism challenged religious orthodoxy, there had been an intellectual crisis of confidence in Victorian society. Mrs Ramsay's attitude is reminiscent of Matthew Arnold's poem *Dover Beach* in which the world 'Hath really neither joy, nor love, nor light, / Nor certitude, nor peace, nor help for pain'.[22] With the certainty of faith taken away, Arnold turns to his love for consolation. To a degree, Julia and Leslie did the same. Although their relationship was complex and they were both by 'no means easy-going people', Virginia believed they had 'found in the other the highest and most perfect harmony which their natures could respond to'.[23] A photograph of them peacefully reading together at Talland House, with Virginia in the background, captures the harmonious side of their relationship. In *To the Lighthouse*, she wrote about 'the glow, the rhapsody, the self-surrender', on Mrs Ramsay's face when she had given her husband the sympathy he demanded.[24] Observing them as a child, Virginia was aware of the 'pure and unutterable delight' they took in each other. It did not mean they were always happy, but like irregular pieces of a jigsaw they slotted together. Within the limitations of their temperaments, they were able to be their best selves. In each other's eyes they were the people they aspired to be; Julia was the nurturing saint, Leslie the demanding genius. Most importantly, they always loved each other. As Leslie wrote, 'I loved her with my whole heart, and I loved her without qualification. She knew it – as well as I know it.'[25]

In the early months of 1895, their relationship was particularly strained. There were frequent petty disagreements. Less patient than usual, Julia complained about Leslie sitting up too late. He accused her of attacking him 'illogically' when he indulged in one of his rants about his inadequacy.[26] Julia did not seem herself, probably she was not feeling well, but she would not give in to illness. In January she rushed around as much as usual, travelling to Somerset for a Duckworth wedding then later that week organising her orphaned niece Millicent Vaughan's wedding and hosting the reception at Hyde Park Gate.

When she caught influenza in March she did not have the strength to fight it. Friends and family noticed a change in her mood; Margaret Lushington wrote to her father after seeing her, 'I thought her very ill and sadly irritable.'[27] When Henry James visited, he found her looking 'so intensely beautiful on her sofa [...] that one felt it to be a sort of blessing in disguise'.[28] Any blessing was short-lived, however. Overdoing it as usual, although she was not supposed to move from the sofa, Virginia observed, 'She hops about writing letters and generally superintending the house as if she had never been ill in her life.' She went for a carriage drive in the park and was desperate to visit her youngest son, Adrian, at boarding school, but she was just not well enough.[29] Her daughter wrote that 'her respites were fewer; she sank, like an exhausted swimmer, deeper and deeper in the water.'[30] She developed rheumatic fever, which weakened her heart.[31]

By April, Leslie was aware of 'a painful sensation of tragedy in the background' and told his wife that he was 'still rather haunted by your looks – you were so tired and weak'.[32] Stella was also worried about her mother, but Julia minimised her health problems and insisted that her eldest daughter continue with a planned trip abroad. During the holiday, Stella became increasingly concerned by the shaky handwriting in her mother's letters. She wrote to Vanessa to try to find out what was happening, but Julia would not let Stella know the truth and she claimed that her illness was only slight. Mother and daughter were too close for this deception to work, and Stella rushed home like 'some tormented dumb animal'. Over the next ten days Julia became increasingly ill.[33]

On the morning of 5 May, George was sitting by his mother's bed, when he realised she was deteriorating. He called Leslie who immediately knew she was dying.[34] Virginia recalled being brought in to see her mother alive for the last time. After kissing her, as her youngest daughter crept out of the room, Julia whispered, 'Hold yourself straight, my little goat.'[35] It was a characteristic comment from the dying woman, who, even in her final hours, expected her daughters to behave in a certain way.

In later years, Virginia often tried to recreate what happened on that fateful day. Her versions differ a little, but the essential story remains the same. After Julia died, she recalled leaning out of the nursery window at about six in the morning and seeing the doctor walking away from their house with his head bent. Watching the pigeons settling, she had a feeling of 'calm, sadness, finality'. It was as if 'everything had come to an end'. When George took Virginia to say goodbye, Leslie staggered out of the bedroom and cried out something indecipherable. Wrapped up in warm towels and given brandy in warm milk, Virginia was led into the candlelit room. She went up to the bed to kiss her dead mother, whose body was still warm. Reacting to all the pent-up emotion, when Virginia noticed that one of the nurses was sobbing, 'a desire to laugh' came over her. She recalled, 'I felt nothing whatever.' [36] For years afterwards, Virginia worried that she had not felt enough as the shock numbed her emotions.[37] In her novel *Mrs Dalloway*, Septimus Warren Smith's inability to feel, after the death of a loved one, lies at the root of his insanity.

The following day, Stella took Virginia in to kiss Julia's body for the last time. She described her mother's face as looking 'immeasurably distant, hollow and stern. When I kissed her, it was like kissing cold iron.' The young girl pulled back in shock. She then watched as Stella stroked their mother's face and undid a button on her nightdress, to make it the way she had liked it. As usual, Stella thought about others rather than herself and she noticed that Virginia was afraid. When she came up to the nursery, she apologised to her younger sister and the girls cried together. Virginia told Stella, 'When I see mother, I see a man sitting with her.' It was then Stella's turn to be frightened, but she reassured her sister, saying, 'It's nice that she shouldn't be alone.'[38] Later, Virginia could not be sure whether she had really seen a man or whether she had just said it to draw attention to herself.[39]

The trauma of losing a parent would be disturbing for any child, but the Victorian obsession with making a 13-year-old girl confront her mother's corpse and kiss it must have added to Virginia's distress. She was a sensitive girl and her worst fears had been realised. The enormity of the situation only gradually sank in. Virginia wrote that her mother's death was 'the greatest disaster that could happen'.[40] Nothing would ever be the same again for the whole family.

Immediately after Julia's death, it was as if her husband and children were trapped in a mausoleum with her. The atmosphere at Hyde Park Gate was suffocating. Virginia described the days before the funeral as 'so melodramatic, histrionic and unreal that any hallucination was possible'. The house, which had before been bustling with Julia's energy, became a dead place. Everything was black and dull as, shrouded in mourning, people crept in and out talking in hushed tones. The cloying smell of funereal flowers filled the rooms. All Julia's children sat around Leslie's chair in the drawing room, sobbing.

Julia's funeral at Kensal Green cemetery was grim. Considered too young, the Stephen siblings did not go, so a distraught Leslie attended with his Duckworth stepchildren. Susan Lushington wrote to her father, 'Yesterday was too terrible, Stella like marble holding and supporting Mr Stephen [...] what will they do?'[41] That was the question on everyone's lips.

9

The Family Falls Apart

Julia's absence now became as powerful a catalyst as her presence had been, influencing every aspect of her husband and children's lives. Virginia later wrote, 'The effect of death upon those that live is always strange, and often terrible in the havoc it makes.'[1] Julia had been a magnetic force and without her to pull them together, they fell apart. All their relationships shifted and became out of kilter. In *To the Lighthouse*, Virginia wrote that without Mrs Ramsay, 'it was a house full of unrelated passions', which descended into 'chaos'.[2]

Leslie's grief was so all-consuming, it felt as if his children had lost their father as well. His groans created an atmosphere of gloom which passed the normal limits of sorrow and obscured the genuine tragedy.[3] Virginia felt her father's reaction was self-indulgent and unhealthy. In her novel, she describes Mr Ramsay's melodramatic grief as 'horrible' and 'indecent'.[4]

Shortly after Julia's death, Leslie began writing the *Mausoleum Book* to keep the memory of Julia alive. Surprisingly, despite the maudlin title, it is very readable, and does not avoid dealing with the difficult parts of their relationship. He agonised about whether he had been a good husband. However, he did not apply the same objectivity in his portrait of his wife, depicting her as an infallible icon. Six months after Julia's death, in a lecture on 'Forgotten Benefactors', he once again turned her into '"the perfect woman", who is also the fitting vehicle for the angel light'.[5] By shaping reality to fit his fantasy, it was as if he killed her again for her children. It blocked out the real woman – imperfect but deeply loved by them. Virginia wrote that it did 'unpardonable mischief by substituting for the shape of a true and most vivid mother, nothing better than an unlovable phantom'.[6]

Although Leslie claimed that his first duty was to his children, he was too self-centred to give them what they needed. Wrapped up in his own grief, he was unable to help them make sense of what had happened. At meals he would say that he wished to die.[7] This was the last thing his children wanted to hear; they needed their surviving parent to remain strong for them. Rather than being able to grieve for their mother, they had to repress their emotions and care for their father. The lack of reality in the world Leslie created was detrimental, particularly for Virginia, whose mental health was seriously affected.

At first, she experienced waves of heightened perception, writing that it was as though something was 'unveiled [...] as if something was becoming visible without any effort'. One spring evening, lying in the grass in Kensington Gardens with Vanessa, she read a poem and felt she understood it in a whole new way. 'I had a feeling of transparency in words when they cease to be words and become so intensified that one seems to experience them; to foretell them as if they developed what one is already feeling.'[8] The fine line in Virginia's life between madness and genius first appeared after the trauma of her mother's death. This heightened feeling for words was to make Virginia the innovative writer she became, but it took her close to the edge of sanity.

Not sure how to grieve, she became increasingly apprehensive. Observing Stella's silent mourning and her father's melodramatic misery, neither provided a perfect model. Even the pain she felt was welcome in a world in which nothing seemed real.[9] Interestingly, her description of her feelings is similar to Julia's after Herbert's death. Mother and daughter reacted in the same way to tragedy, experiencing a lack of reality and the pressure to repress their grief for the sake of others.

Shortly after her mother's death, Virginia had her first 'breakdown'.[10] It manifested itself in physical as well as emotional symptoms. She suffered from a racing pulse and feelings of anger, terror and excitement.[11] Her doctor advised that she should do fewer lessons and be careful not to excite herself, but no real counselling was given.[12] This pattern of mental health problems recurred throughout Virginia's life. Her doctors described her illness as 'neurasthenia', but she would possibly now be diagnosed as having bipolar disorder. She suffered from manic episodes and refused to eat.[13] Hermione Lee describes Virginia as 'a sane woman who had an illness'. She argues that we cannot be sure what caused her mental illness, but it seems to have been attributable to genetic, environmental and biological factors. Her breakdowns were usually, but not always, triggered by major events in her life. Periodically, she suffered from severe episodes of mental illness and on several occasions tried to kill herself.[14] There were phases of intense happiness and few people were more excited by life than her.[15] Sadly, after each breakdown she lived with the fear of it happening again.

During this traumatic period, Stella tried to fill the chasm left by Julia. She became like a second mother to Virginia, ran the household and looked after her stepfather. Spending hours with Leslie, she listened to him wallow in self-pity. Caring for everyone else, she concealed her own suffering in case it upset them, but her half-sisters occasionally found her in tears, sitting at her desk with a photograph of Julia in front of her.[16] Friends knew 'the heroic struggle' Stella was making to survive and the toll it took on her health.[17] She became increasingly pale, as though she too was about to fade away.

As a dutiful Victorian daughter, the only escape was marriage, so when her faithful suitor, Jack Hills, proposed again in August 1896, she accepted. Perhaps part of the reason was she knew Julia would have approved. When Stella broke the news to her half-sisters, Virginia asked, 'Did mother know?' and she replied, 'Yes.'[18] During her engagement, Stella grew in confidence and, out of Julia's shadow, she finally established her own identity. At last, she had someone who put her first. Even Leslie noticed the change, writing that 'she showed her true self more clearly and brightly'.[19] As usual, however, he could not help looking at the situation from his own selfish perspective. He was jealous and complained about his stepdaughter leaving him. At first, he expected the young couple to live with him at 22 Hyde Park Gate, but eventually, a compromise was reached, and they agreed to move into a house in the same street. Virginia also had mixed emotions about Stella leaving home and she resented other people taking her sister's attention away from her.

On 10 April 1897, at Kensington church, Jack and Stella were married. It was one of the many occasions when Julia's absence was agonising. Leslie admitted his wife would have been delighted, writing, 'It has seemed to me as if I felt a presence all day and I know that she would have rejoiced. Alas! How much happier we should all have been.'[20] The following day, he went with their children to take the wedding flowers to her grave.[21]

Just as Stella was about to finally live her own life, tragedy struck again. Shortly after she returned from honeymoon, she became ill. Peritonitis was diagnosed but she was not operated on for three months. When Stella became unwell, Virginia stayed with her. Even when she was seriously ill, Stella sat up late with her sister, soothing her nerves. The day before Stella's operation, George took Virginia home; the half-sisters were never to see each other again.[22] Surgeons removed an internal abscess too late; Stella died on 19 July 1897 aged 28. Adding to the poignancy of the story, she was pregnant.[23]

Decades later, Vanessa told her son that Stella died because she could not live without Julia.[24] For her siblings, her death was like a cruel repeat of their mother's death such a short time before. The funeral was held at the same cemetery with the same people. As Stella was placed in the grave next to her mother, there was a thunderstorm with flashes of lightning, pouring rain and hailstones. Her old friend Kitty Maxse wrote, 'It all seems so impossible [...] I almost expected to see Stella in her black cape.'[25]

The loss reopened barely healed wounds for the family. As they grew older, Virginia and Vanessa saw Stella's story as epitomising 'all the old abuses' of the family system.[26] The two sisters rebelled against their father and the society which sanctioned his behaviour. Virginia explained:

We made him the type of all that we hated in our lives; he was the tyrant of inconceivable selfishness, who had replaced the beauty and merriment of the dead with ugliness and gloom. We were bitter, harsh, and to a great extent, unjust; but even now it seems to me that there was some truth in our complaint.[27]

Biographer Lyndall Gordon argues that they turned their father into a scapegoat.[28] Virginia's husband, Leonard Woolf, also thought they were unfair to him and exaggerated his faults due to a 'complicated variety of the Oedipus complex'.[29] It seems that like Sylvia Plath, Virginia was looking for someone to blame for the tragedies that had marred her early life. Her attitude to her father was ambivalent, alternating between love and hate; she admired him but also resented how he behaved. She believed that she was more like Leslie than Julia and that made her more critical of him.[30]

Scholars debate whether Virginia's criticism was justified. His marriage was more equal than many Victorian partnerships, but his treatment of Stella was different. Leslie exploited his stepdaughter more than her mother, partly because a wife had more status than an unmarried daughter but also because Julia was a stronger character. The older woman was determined to do her own thing within the confines of Victorian society. She made the system work for her and would not have seen herself as a victim, but her acquiescence did nothing to protect more vulnerable women. Virginia blamed the system but also Julia for letting Leslie behave so badly and thus creating the situation her daughters inherited. Her analysis suggested that the problem lay in the Victorian matriarchy as well as the patriarchy. Women like her grandmother, mother and aunts allowed men to treat them as 'part slave, part angel'. Virginia recalled her aunt Mary Fisher whispering to her about her father, 'He is one of those men who cannot live without us. And it is very nice for us that it should be so.'[31] But the experience had turned out to be far from 'nice' for his daughters.

10

An Abuse of Trust

After Julia's death, Virginia had a recurring dream in which her mother lifted a wreath of white flowers on to her head and then walked with her distinctive quickness away from her across the fields. Following the loss of Stella, Virginia dreamt of her sister joining their mother in this ethereal procession, leaving her behind.[1] The shock of Stella's unexpected death exacerbated Virginia's feelings of instability. She found it worse than losing her mother, thinking, 'But this is impossible; things aren't, can't be, like this.' Like Julia, after her first husband Herbert's death, for a time Virginia lost her faith in life itself. She felt 'violently cheated of some promise' and that she had been 'a fool to hope for things'.[2]

In later life, she put her mental health problems down to the 'emotions and complications' of her family life.[3] Her suffering was made worse by the behaviour of the men in her family. Virginia and Vanessa were left exposed; as their friend Kitty Maxse wrote to her sister, 'They are so utterly stranded.'[4] Rather than a place of sanctuary, the threat to them came from inside their home; the people they should have been able to rely on abused their trust.

Their father was the first to exploit his position. Aged just 18, Vanessa was expected to run the household and dedicate herself to his care. As Virginia angrily observed, their father was 'quite prepared to take Vanessa for his next victim'.[5] But, unlike Julia and Stella, she refused to give in to Leslie's intolerable demands and temper tantrums. She had seen what had happened to the women who submitted and had no intention of becoming another martyr. When her father was unreasonable, she just ignored him.

Resentful of her father's behaviour, Virginia wholeheartedly supported her sister. The already close bond between them grew even stronger as they stood together in sisterly solidarity.[6] Both girls had inherited different shades of their mother's beauty; as their cousin noted, they were 'so beautiful even the dogs in the road turned round to look again'.[7] Unfortunately, their good looks made them more vulnerable to the younger men in their family as they related to them in an inappropriately sexual way.

Without Julia to care for him, Leslie's physical as well as his mental health deteriorated. A few years after his wife's death he was diagnosed with terminal cancer. With their father abdicating his position, George Duckworth became, for all practical purposes, the head of the family. Their eldest half-brother had been the girls' childhood hero and they looked to him for stability in an insecure world. Virginia explained that he became 'father and mother, sister and brother in one' to them.[8] Family and friends praised his selfless behaviour but, rather than protecting his half-sisters, George preyed on them.

It started innocently enough as, bonded by their mutual grief, the half-siblings grew closer. George claimed that Julia would have wanted him to look after his sisters and they were all he had left of his adored mother. When he asked them to go to grand parties they agreed, but it soon became clear that his feelings were far from fraternal. He first overstepped brotherly boundaries with Vanessa. After showering her with expensive gifts, he hugged and kissed her then begged her to go to more society events with him. When she refused, he turned to Virginia. Although she felt uneasy, she thought it was what Julia would have wanted, so she gave in. She wrote, 'Over that turbulent whirlpool the ghosts of mother and Stella presided. How could we do battle with all of them.'[9]

Virginia's intuition that there was something unhealthy about George's interest was right. One evening, when Virginia had gone to bed, the door opened, and George came in. 'Don't be frightened', he whispered to her. 'And don't turn on the light, oh beloved. Beloved.'[10] He then flung himself on the bed kissing and fondling her. Apparently, Vanessa later told the family doctor about what happened but when questioned George claimed that he was just trying to comfort Virginia because she was upset about Leslie's illness.[11]

George concealed his true motive from himself and everyone else. Virginia wrote, 'Under the name of unselfishness he allowed himself to

commit acts which a cleverer man would have called tyrannical; and, profoundly believing in the purity of his love, he behaved little better than a
brute.'[12] We cannot be sure about the extent of George's sexual abuse, but
the effect on Virginia was long lasting. She only dared to confront it decades later.[13] She told her friend Ottoline Morrell, 'He sent me mad.'[14] As
Hermione Lee argues, we cannot know whether the sexual abuse both her
half-brothers subjected her to at different stages in her life was the cause
of her mental instability, but Virginia certainly believed it had been very
damaging. She blamed George for her volatility, inability to feel properly
and her sexual inhibition.[15]

Virginia and Vanessa needed to escape from this unhealthy atmosphere,
to live lives that were true to themselves, but for a time they were trapped.
They were only released when their father died from cancer in February
1904. Never recovering from losing Julia, Leslie died in the marital bedroom with a picture of her hanging in front of him.[16] A few months after
his death, Virginia had a serious breakdown and attempted suicide. She
spent several months in a mental health institution. While Virginia was ill,
Vanessa sold 22 Hyde Park Gate, the once happy home which had become
a prison for them.[17]

11

The Rebellion

Like Agatha Christie and Sylvia Plath after their breakdowns, Virginia realised that she had to start a new, very different life if she was to survive. Free at last from their toxic family, Virginia and Vanessa left Kensington for Bloomsbury. It was a symbolic move, representing a shift from their parents' Victorian values into the modern world. Their experimental life-style challenged the sexual and social mores of the society they had grown up in. Virginia wrote they made up their minds that 'everything was going to be new; everything was going to be different. Everything was on trial.'[1]

In their Gordon Square town house, even their choice of décor was a rebellion against Julia. Instead of her oppressive red and black colour scheme, they created a light, airy atmosphere with pastel shades and naturalistic chintzes. When family friends came to visit their new home, they realised that the change in style went far deeper than the wallpaper. One critical visitor made it clear that Julia would have disapproved of this for her daughters, but that was what her daughters wanted. Virginia wrote, 'There was something in the atmosphere; something hostile to the old traditions of the family.'[2] However, Virginia could never completely leave her mother behind and in the hall Mrs Cameron's haunting photographs of Julia kept a watchful eye on her children's antics.[3]

She would not have liked what she saw. The Bloomsbury set, which grew up around the Stephen siblings, brought out into the open topics that Julia had shoved under her heavily patterned carpets. During their Thursday evenings with Thoby's Cambridge friends, nothing was off limits. Julia's polite small talk was replaced with philosophical discussions in which the young women were encouraged to have opinions instead of just looking pretty and listening to the men debate. As Vanessa's son Quentin Bell explained, the Bloomsbury group was feminist as women were on a completely equal footing with men. They challenged the idea that men should be the source of power and authority.[4] Unlike at their mother's parties, Virginia and Vanessa were able to reveal their true thoughts, instead of concealing their intelligence beneath a submissive feminine façade.

Virginia was relieved that the young men in their circle did not notice what women looked like. Rather than the handsome specimens of Victorian muscular masculinity Julia admired, her daughters felt safer with these 'dingy' intellectuals who were totally 'lacking in physical splendour'. They could not have been more different from Herbert Duckworth, but perhaps more importantly, they bore no resemblance to his son George, whose overt masculinity threatened Virginia. Her nephew Quentin Bell believed that her aversion to male lust was not just due to her half-brothers. He thought that Virginia had some deeper inhibition. Vita Sackville-West made a similar assessment; she wrote that Virginia disliked men's possessiveness and love of domination, in fact she disliked 'the quality of masculinity'.[5]

Although Virginia was afraid of sex in practice, she relished breaking taboos by talking about it. While Julia spent hours discussing 'love and marriage' but shied away from discussing sex, her daughters revelled in hearing about the intimate details of their friends' love lives. Virginia wrote, 'We discussed copulation with the same excitement and openness that we had discussed the nature of good.'[6] It seems that Virginia was relieved that many of the men were homosexuals because it meant there was no question of them wanting to marry her. All the pressure was removed as her mother's matchmaking became yet another relic of a bygone age.

Virginia's attitude to marriage challenged her mother's views. Unlike Julia, who believed women could only be happy if they were married with children, Virginia wanted to live a different life. She saw marriage as 'a very low-down affair'. When Vanessa warned her that they would both eventually have to settle down, she felt 'a horrible necessity impending over us; a fate would descend and snatch us apart just as we had achieved freedom and happiness'.[7]

Her premonition was right. In November 1906, Thoby died of typhoid fever aged only 26. Shortly after Thoby's death, Vanessa married one of her brother's friends, the art critic Clive Bell. Although the sisters remained incredibly close, Virginia had to establish a separate life for herself. She took a house in Brunswick Square and invited some of her male friends to share it. Unmarried men and women living together was shocking in Edwardian society and family friends knew how Julia would have reacted. Virginia wrote, 'My mother's ghost was invoked once more [...] to deplore [it].'[8]

When Vanessa had her first child, Julian, in 1908, Virginia wrote a memoir for her nephew about their family life. Her *Reminiscences* was her answer to Leslie's *Mausoleum Book*, and in it she portrays her mother in a more critical way. Vanessa was deeply moved by Virginia's memoir. She saw it as a poignant recreation and wondered how they survived so much tragedy.[9] Virginia was not satisfied with her work, complaining, 'You will not find in what I say [...] any semblance of a woman whom you can love.'[10]

Attempting to recapture her mother influenced Virginia's attitude to biography. Aware of its limitations, she believed that the layers of anecdotes and descriptions surrounding a person could obscure their essence. She was also frustrated by the inadequacy of language. She had tried to recreate her mother's voice but was thwarted, writing, 'What would one not give to recapture a single phrase even! Or the tone of the clear round voice.'[11] This frustration with the genre became a theme she returned to periodically. She realised that in biographies the characters were always much smaller than life sized. The biographer arranged the subject in patterns of which they were ignorant and read into what they said meanings which they never intended.[12] She believed that a narrative which traced a life chronologically from birth to death was just a convenience. It was more enlightening to approach it imaginatively, focusing on key moments and hidden actions, as in the lives of most people there were a few essential 'moments of being' from which everything else proceeds.[13]

Revisiting her childhood and memories of her mother was to continue for the rest of Virginia's life. It was as if by understanding Julia she would find the key to making sense of who she was and why she felt as she did. Innovatory as she was, Virginia could never completely escape her mother's expectations. She explained, 'what she said has never ceased.'[14] At times, she struggled with not fulfilling Julia's stereotype of femininity. She was undermined by an inner voice, which sounded remarkably like her mother whispering that she was not a real woman.

When Virginia was 29, she became severely depressed and suffered another breakdown. She compared her own unmarried, childless state with her sister's life. Perhaps seeing herself through Julia's eyes, she described herself as a failure, 'insane too, and no writer'.[15] Later she recreated these self-critical thoughts in *To the Lighthouse*, when Lily Briscoe is wracked with self-doubt as she is unable to offer Mr Ramsay the self-sacrificing support he needs. She blames herself, thinking that she must be 'not a woman, but a peevish, ill-tempered, dried-up old maid'.[16] This constant tension between being true to herself and the expectations of her dead mother was finely balanced. Reflecting Virginia's experience, Lily Briscoe thinks Mrs Ramsay has faded from her life, taking her old-fashioned views with her, but then she appears again as forceful as ever 'mockingly' saying, 'Marry, marry!'[17]

The societal pressure and emotional need to marry became increasingly intense for Virginia. In 1912, aged 30, she stopped resisting and married Leonard Woolf, a friend of her brother. She wanted a 'modern' partnership and she questioned whether her parents' model of a monogamous marriage was the highest form of married life.[18] The Woolfs' marriage was unconventional, but it worked because they genuinely loved each other. Virginia was not interested in sex with Leonard, but they were affectionate to each other.

For a woman who often compared herself unfavourably with her mother, Virginia must have been delighted that Leonard preferred her appearance to Julia's classic good looks. When he saw the Cameron photographs of his mother-in-law, he described her beauty as 'rather insipid'; it was 'too feminine, and not sufficiently female' and even 'slightly irritating'. He was glad that Virginia and Vanessa inherited the more masculine Stephen good looks, rather than 'the saintly dying duck loveliness' of their mother.[19]

Going against Julia's expectations of a woman's role, the couple did not have children. Although Virginia wanted them, doctors advised against it because of her instability.[20] Blaming herself, she sometimes regretted not forcing Leonard to take the risk.[21] She believed that if she had shown more 'self-control' it might have happened.[22] Envious of Vanessa having three children, she thought about whether motherhood would have suited her. Her feelings fluctuated; at times her childlessness made her feel a failure.[23] At others, she believed motherhood would have compromised her writing and that she would not have liked 'the physicalness' of having children of her own.[24]

Rather than being a mother, Virginia needed mothering. In her first novel, *The Voyage Out*, written during these years, the heroine Rachel Vinrace misses a mother who could teach her the facts of life and instruct her 'in feminine graces'.[25] She looks for someone to replace her dead mother, both in her friendships with older women and her romantic relationships. Part of her lover Terence Hewet's attraction is he has 'something of a woman in him',[26] and he seems to offer Rachel the intimacy she has missed out on.[27] The novel is dedicated to Leonard, and his appeal was similar. He became her main protector as, like Julia with Leslie, he looked after the 'shell-less little creature'.[28] Nurturing her genius, Leonard calmed her down and reassured her about her work. He became essential to her stability, but the security Leonard supplied was not always enough.

In 1913, Virginia made a suicide attempt and for the following two years, on and off, she experienced severe mental health problems. One morning in early 1915, she seemed calm and perfectly sane, having breakfast in bed with Leonard. Suddenly she became violently excited and distressed; she thought her mother was in the room and she began talking to her. Virginia then rambled incoherently for several days. Eventually, she was taken to a nursing home where she gradually improved.[29]

Leonard believed these episodes could be controlled by making sure that she had a regular routine. He believed her breakdowns were related to her creative genius and that they were most likely to happen if she became stressed about finishing a book.[30] Carefully cared for by her husband, Virginia enjoyed a fulfilling life for prolonged periods. In her diary she wrote that few people were more interested by life and happy.[31]

Supportive as Leonard was, there remained a void that needed filling. In her bond with Vanessa and her closest women friends, she continued looking for the female nurturing relationship and unconditional love which she had never fully experienced with her mother. Her sister was her first and most important mother replacement. Emphasising Vanessa's maternal instinct and similarities to Julia, Virginia referred to herself as her sister's 'first born'.[32] Accepting this mothering role, Vanessa wrote to Virginia when she had a breakdown, 'My own baby [...] You must be well cossetted for a year.'[33] Even at the age of 23, on a rough Channel crossing, Virginia had sat in her sister's lap.[34]

Virginia was attracted to mature women who offered comfort and guidance. Mixed with a maternal appeal, there was often an erotic element. Her first romantic friendship was with Violet Dickinson, a family friend who was seventeen years older. Supporting her through Leslie's death, Violet listened to her worries and petted her. Virginia nicknamed Violet 'Kangaroo' with 'a pouch for a small kangaroo to creep to'.[35] Another important friendship was with her cousin's wife, Madge Vaughan. Addressing her in letters as 'Mama' and calling herself 'your infant', Virginia wrote that she wanted to be treated like 'a nice child'.[36] Repeating this idea, she told her friend Katherine Arnold-Forster, 'I think all good mothers ought to consider me half their child, which is what I really like best.'[37]

Virginia's most intense relationship with another woman was with Vita Sackville-West. The two authors first met at a dinner party in 1922 and were soon fascinated by each other. Their descendants are cautious about using the word 'affair' to describe their relationship as according to Vita they only went to bed together twice.[38] Sexual attraction was only part of their complicated bond – a large part of it was about Virginia's continuing search for a mother figure. Although Vita was younger than Virginia, the older writer was attracted by the idea that her lover was a mother. She wrote in her diary that Vita's 'maturity and full-breastedness' as well as 'her motherhood' appealed to her because Vita was 'in short (what I have never been) a real woman'. She gave her the 'maternal protection which, for some reason, is what I have always most wished from everyone'.[39]

Like her father with her mother, Virginia craved Vita's sympathy.[40] When she was ill, Virginia believed that 'everything would be warm and happy' if Vita came.[41] Her childlike vulnerability inspired tenderness in Sackville-West, who had never known anyone so sensitive.[42] Even once the physical side of their relationship waned, Vita continued to feel protective.[43] She told Virginia that she would look after her like a nanny with a new baby.[44] However, no woman could fill the chasm left by Julia for long and Virginia's quest continued. When she got involved with the older composer Ethel Smyth, she explained she had, 'that maternal quality which of all others I need and adore'.[45]

12

Haunting Virginia

Virginia was haunted by her mother for decades. Ironically, Julia's ghost was with her more than the flesh and blood woman ever had been. After her death, she lived on in her daughter's imagination, becoming a constant presence in her life and work. Virginia wrote:

> Now and again on more occasions than I can number, in bed at night or in the street, or as I come into the room, there she is, beautiful, emphatic, with her familiar phrase and her laugh; closer to me than any of the living are.[1]

Virginia admitted that until she was in her forties:

> the presence of my mother obsessed me. I could hear her voice, see her, imagine what she would do or say as I went about my day's doings. She was one of the invisible presences who after all play so important a part in every life.[2]

According to Virginia, this was not purely by chance. In her draft of *To the Lighthouse*, Mrs Ramsay believed that she gained immortality by being psychically intertwined with her children. It pleased the mother 'to think how all their lives long in their memories she would be woven [...] so that her own death would matter rather less'.[3]

Virginia's ongoing relationship with Julia was never static. There were phases when she drew closer to her mother and others when she rejected everything she stood for. Although part of Virginia wanted to be totally different from Julia, there was another side which desired to be just like her. Thirty years after her mother's death, Virginia was still dressing up in her clothes. Shortly after a person dies there is a poignancy in seeing an item of their clothing and it is difficult to get rid of this last tangible link – but to be wearing a dead person's clothes decades later suggests a deep psychological need. Was Virginia trying to become her mother? Did she do it to know what it felt like to be her? Whatever her reasons it was not a one-off aberration, but something Virginia experimented with for several years.

In January 1923, she wore one of her mother's old dresses to Vanessa's fancy-dress party. Three years later, she was photographed for *Vogue* in Julia's lace trimmed dress. The expression on her face is reminiscent of Julia; her eyes are slightly downcast, and a half-smile plays on her lips, but Virginia looks inauthentic. There is something bizarre about her angular body trussed up in an ultra-feminine, wasp-waisted dress. There is a knowing look in her eyes as if she realises how incongruous it is for a modernist author to be playacting at being a Victorian lady.

We get an insight into her motivation in her short story 'The New Dress', written in 1924. The heroine, Mabel, has a new outfit made inspired from her mother's Paris fashion books because she thought 'how much prettier, more dignified, and more womanly they were then'.[4] Mimicking this overt femininity failed, however; when Mabel wore the new dress to a party she was mocked by the other guests and felt inferior. The dated dress symbolised Virginia's conflicted attitude towards femininity and her difficulty establishing a separate identity from her mother.

Observers noted the inconsistency between the image Virginia projected and her inner self. In *The Book of Beauty*, Cecil Beaton wrote, 'Her old-fashioned dowdiness are but a conscious and literary game of pretence, for she is alertly contemporary, even a little ahead of her time.'[5] His description of her could have been applied to Mrs Cameron's photos of Julia half a century earlier. Virginia looked like 'a terrified ghost', who had 'all the chaste and sombre beauty' of a nun. Describing Virginia in terms used about her mother, he added, 'When one sees her so sensitively nervous and with the poignant beauty of the lady in the faded photograph [...] one realises that a face can be a reverend and sacred thing.'[6]

It was not only Beaton's description which was reminiscent of Julia. When Hugh Walpole in his novel *Hans Frost* caricatured Virginia in the character Jane Rose, it sounded like her mother. He wrote:

Jane Rose looked like the wife of a Pre-Raphaelite painter, her dark hair brushed back in waves from her forehead, her grey dress cut in simple fashion, her thin pale face quiet and remote [...] There was something terrifying in her gentle remoteness.[7]

Responding to Hugh, Virginia repeated the feelings she expressed in her short story, 'I feel rather like the wife of a Pre-Raphaelite painter who has blundered in among Rubens and Matisse and Cocktails and Champagne and sits in a simple grey dress looking very odd and causing some alarm to her hostess.'[8]

During this phase, Virginia also imitated her mother in her writing. In 1926, her essay 'On Being Ill' was published in *The New Criterion*. Drawing on her history of migraines, pneumonia and mental health problems, it questioned why illness was not written about more frequently and complained about the poverty of language to express it.[9] In her novel *The Voyage Out* she wrote brilliantly about the experience of being ill; her descriptions of the mental and physical torment are visceral. Although written from the perspective of a patient rather than a nurse, 'On Being Ill' has much in common with Julia's book *Notes from Sick Rooms*. Written with a similar compassion and subtle humour, the similarities between the two books were not accidental. When her first biographer, Winifred Holtby, noticed a resemblance, Virginia was delighted.[10] Suggesting her pride in Julia's book, Leonard and Virginia reprinted it at their Hogarth Press.[11] Reading mother and daughter's writing on sickness together is poignant; a reader cannot help thinking how much Virginia needed her mother to nurse her through her illnesses.

The culmination of Virginia's imitation of Julia came when she wrote *To the Lighthouse*. Like Agatha in *Unfinished Portrait* and Sylvia in *The Bell Jar*, Virginia blended her memories with imagined experiences. In the novel she sought 'psychic osmosis' with her mother by writing much of it from Julia's perspective. In some of the stream of consciousness passages, which imagined what Mrs Ramsay was thinking, she tried to get into her mother's mind. She wanted to know 'her thoughts, her imaginations, her desires'.[12]

Writing *To the Lighthouse* turned out to be a dangerous but exhilarating experiment. The joy of bringing her mother back to life was followed by the sorrow of losing her again.[13] One day while walking around Tavistock Square, Virginia started making up the book in her head; it then came in an 'involuntary rush'.[14] She began writing the novel at her home Monk's House on 6 August 1925. Writing very quickly, it flowed fluently because the ideas behind it had been germinating for decades. She sensed that facing her complicated feelings towards her mother would unlock her latent gifts as a writer.[15]

Delving into her deepest emotions made her ill and she had to stop writing for several months. She started again in January 1926, but it continued to affect her and in July she had 'a whole nervous breakdown in miniature'. Once she finished her first draft in September she suffered from intense depression and feelings of unreality. She later confessed in her diary that after writing the novel she was nearer to suicide than she had been since 1913.[16] Symbolically, *To the Lighthouse* was published in May 1927 on the anniversary of her mother's death.[17]

Once her novel was finished, she was pleased with the result. She realised it was 'easily the best of my books' and Leonard agreed, calling it a 'masterpiece'.[18] Vanessa believed Virginia had completely captured their mother, writing:

> You have given a portrait of mother which is more like her to me than anything I could ever have conceived possible. It is almost painful to have her so raised from the dead. You have made one feel the extraordinary beauty of her character, which must be the most difficult thing in the world to do. It was like meeting her again, with oneself grown up and on equal terms.[19]

Virginia was delighted, writing:

> I'm in a terrible state of pleasure that you should think Mrs Ramsay so like mother. At the same time, it is a psychological mystery why she should be: how a child could know about her; except that she has always haunted me.[20]

Like the *Mausoleum Book*, *To the Lighthouse* is as much about the author as the subject. Although the novel is autobiographical, the character of Mrs Ramsay is a fusion of people. Virginia admitted she was inspired by Vanessa as well as Julia.[21] Vita Sackville-West thought that Virginia was very like her heroine.[22] Virginia replied, 'I don't know if I'm like Mrs Ramsay: as my mother died when I was thirteen probably it is a child's view of her: but I have some sentimental delight in thinking that you like her.'[23]

What Aurelia Plath later emphasised about her daughter Sylvia's fictional portrayal of her was also true for Woolf's novel; it could only be what *she* thought her mother thought. Virginia was such a different woman from Julia that the thoughts she attributes to her are perhaps no more accurate than Leslie's interpretations of his wife's motivation. However, the book has an emotional truth and gives us an unparalleled insight into Virginia's feelings for her mother. She wanted to call *To the Lighthouse* an elegy rather than a novel.[24] In this work more than in any of her other writing, Virginia expressed her yearning for Julia. The feeling of emptiness is most explicitly expressed through Lily Briscoe, as she looks at the vacant step where Mrs Ramsay used to sit. She thought:

> To want and not to have, sent all up her body a hardness, a hollowness, a strain. And then to want and not to have – to want and want – how that wrung the heart, and wrung it again and again! Oh Mrs Ramsay! She called out silently, to that essence [...] that abstract one made of her. [25]

Writing *To the Lighthouse* proved cathartic for Virginia. Afterwards, she claimed that her mother no longer haunted her, explaining, 'I ceased to be obsessed by my mother. I no longer hear her voice; I do not see her.'[26] Writing about Julia had been a cross between psychoanalysis and an exorcism. Virginia believed that by expressing long-suppressed feelings she laid them to rest. Her mother's presence lost much of its potency, but there was a sadness in this diminution, as well as a degree of relief, because it erased many of her memories of Julia, leaving her 'rubbed out and featureless'.[27]

Virginia's relationship with Julia was never fully resolved. Even once she had confronted her mother in her fiction, the shade of the dead woman still came and went. In her novel *The Waves*, published in 1931, she wrote about the dead still leaping out at her on street corners and in dreams.[28] She described the voices in her head as 'those half-articulate ghosts who keep up their hauntings by day and night; who turn over in their sleep, who utter their confused cries, who put out their phantom fingers and clutch at me as I try to escape'.[29] Six years later, in *The Years*, she once again fictionalised the harm caused by the patriarchal family and returned to the trauma of losing her mother in her portrayal of Rose Pargiter's illness and death-bed scene.[30]

13

Killing the Angel

Julia influenced Virginia's feminism as much as her fiction. Writing *To the Lighthouse* was a turning point and afterwards she had a less internalised, more public debate with her mother's old-fashioned ideas.[1] Her attitude to women's roles reflected her ambivalence towards her mother; sometimes she seemed to reject everything Julia stood for, at others she wanted to preserve aspects of her mother's legacy. Her ideas evolved over many decades and there were different phases in her feminist journey.

Before the First World War, she had supported the Votes for Women campaign, but her involvement was limited.[2] In her forties, Virginia brought the feminist theories she had been formulating for decades out into the open. In 1928, she gave two lectures at Cambridge arguing for a space for women writers within a literary tradition which was dominated by men. Calling for better education for women, she claimed that they were unable to achieve their potential due to lack of opportunity not talent.

Drawing on these lectures, in September 1929 Virginia published *A Room of One's Own*. This important feminist tract examined the obstacles in the way of women fulfilling their potential. She argued that a woman required money and a room of her own if she was to write fiction.[3] Evidently, the dynamics in her family influenced Virginia's ideas. Emphasising the importance of female education, she complained that her lack of a university training made it harder to marshal her research into a coherent argument. Perhaps recalling the contrast between her brothers' opportunities and her own, she imagined Shakespeare had 'an extraordinarily gifted' sister called Judith, whose ambitions were thwarted because of her sex.[4] In her view, this inability to use their talents drove many clever girls mad.

Pandering to the male sense of superiority by acting as though women were inferior also came in for attack. No doubt recalling how Julia constantly bolstered Leslie's fragile ego, Virginia wrote that for centuries women had served 'as looking glasses possessing the magic and delicious power of reflecting the figure of man at twice its natural size'. If men were told the truth about the quality of their work 'the figure in the looking glass shrinks'.[5] However, rather than bolstering the male ego, women should fulfil their own ambitions. Instead of letting other people impose a narrative on their lives, they should write their own autobiographies. In the past biography had been too much focused on great men; it was time 'obscure' lives were recorded, as this could be a potent weapon in the battle for women's freedom.[6]

In 1931, Virginia developed her feminist ideas further in a speech about 'Professions for Women'. Knowing her family history, it reads as intensely personal as well as political. In the paper, she described her battle against 'the phantom' in her life which she called 'The Angel in the House'. This spectral figure can be read as both her mother and the sexist values of Victorian society which she embodied. Although Virginia did not mention her mother by name, there can be little doubt who was in her thoughts as she described the 'angel'. Intensely sympathetic and charming, this mythical figure was utterly unselfish and self-sacrificing. There was a woman like this in every Victorian household, and in the previous generations, who failed to rebel.

Although the angel's idealised existence was fictitious, she cast a long shadow. When Virginia first wrote reviews of novels by men, 'The shadow of her wings fell upon the page; I heard the rustling of her skirts in the room.' This phantom whispered in her ear, making her censor her writing to flatter and deceive rather than tell the truth. Virginia realised she had to silence this voice. She wrote:

> I turned upon her and caught her by the throat. I did my best to kill her [...] Had I not killed her she would have killed me. She would have plucked the heart out of my writing [...] She died hard [...] She was always creeping back when I thought I had despatched her.[7]

This violent matricidal image illustrates what a long and painful battle Virginia fought to silence that undermining inner voice and how essential it was for her to establish her own identity. Decades later, Sylvia Plath was to fight a similar battle and describe it in equally brutal terms.

Once Virginia had killed the angel she could be herself, but first she had to discover who that self was. She had to fight against the sheltered upbringing Victorian girls experienced. Ignorance about sexual matters and the habitual silencing of feelings were pernicious. Virginia argued that a female author needed to develop her unconscious imagination and tell the truth about female passion and bodily experiences, but the attitudes of men continued to impede her. Nor was male censorship the only limiting factor – she still had 'ghosts' to fight within herself.[8] Sylvia Plath was to continue Virginia's battle; she wrote about these visceral female experiences with an even greater freedom than her predecessor.

In 1938, the personal once again became political in Virginia's book-length essay *Three Guineas*, which formulated a feminist response to war.[9] It gives an insight into her evolving attitude towards her mother. Although Julia is not mentioned by name, Virginia took on points made in the anti-suffrage letter signed by her. She demolished the argument that women did not need political power because they wielded indirect influence over men. The idea that a wise woman used her feminine wiles to make a man think he was in charge, while doing what she wanted, was anathema to Virginia. Relying on female charm and male chivalry might have worked for a few exceptional individuals, but not most women. She wrote:

> If such is the real nature of our influence [...] it is either beyond our reach, for many of us are plain, poor and old; or beneath our contempt, for many of us would prefer to call ourselves prostitutes.[10]

Virginia also challenged her mother's views set out in her essay on agnostic women. Julia doubted that women would ever surmount the obstacles preventing them entering the professions. She did not want them to because of the effect it might have on men. She wrote, 'Will their chivalry have no reward? We can see no hope for them when this millennium for women arrives.'[11] While as usual her mother put men first, Virginia's emphasis was on women's needs. Woolf wrote that thankfully, now a woman could enter the professions and earn her own living, she no longer had to use 'the charm element' to procure money from her father or husband.[12]

While rejecting many of her mother's values, Virginia did not discard them all. Instead, she wanted to combine the best elements of the past in her blueprint for the future. Although equal educational opportunities for men and women were central to her ideas, she did not want education to be judged purely by its power to gain employment and earn money. Recognising there was some merit in her mother's and grandmother's informal education, she wrote that even though they were not educated they were civilised women.[13] Nor did she want women to just fit into a professional life created by men. Instead, she wanted them to still have time for the leisured cultural activities women like Julia had excelled at because this created fully rounded human beings

Nor did she expect every woman to enter the traditional professions. Showing respect for the nurturing role women like her mother played, she wanted a change in society's attitude to their importance. She argued that bringing up a large family, running a house and nursing the sick should be treated as a profession.[14] Reflecting the importance of these unsung heroines, she wanted a living wage paid by the state to mothers. This salary would give a married woman freedom to have a mind of her own.[15]

In the final part of *Three Guineas*, as Virginia examined the causes of war, she drew parallels between the domestic tyranny of Victorian fathers and the oppressive regimes of the fascist dictators. Insisting that war and tyranny had their roots in the power dynamics of the home, she wrote, 'It is our duty to catch Hitler in his home haunts.' The enemy was not just a threat in a faraway place; he was at the heart of the family structure.[16] To illustrate her point, she claimed that the fathers of Elizabeth Barrett Browning and Charlotte Brontë demonstrated an 'infantile fixation' in their attempts to control their daughters and prevent them becoming independent.[17] Her argument suggests she had not forgiven Leslie for the way he treated his daughters.

Virginia returned to the parallels between domestic and political tyranny in 'Thoughts on Peace in an Air Raid'. Arguing that women of ability were held down because of 'a subconscious Hitlerism in the hearts of men', she criticised the masculine desire for aggression and need to dominate and enslave; she admitted that women were partly to blame, however, as they tried to enslave men through sexual attraction. She explained, 'If we could free ourselves from slavery, we should free men from tyranny. Hitlers are bred by slaves.'[18] Virginia's theory about the similarities between fascism and patriarchal society reads like a forerunner of Sylvia Plath's ideas in her poem 'Daddy' which portrays the dominating father as the jack-booted Nazi. For both writers the public and private worlds were inseparably connected.

As war loomed on the horizon, Virginia's mind was once again invaded by 'invisible presences'. Reading Freud made her look at her childhood from a new perspective.[19] Reconsidering her relationship with her father, she discovered 'this violently disturbing conflict of love and hate is a common feeling and is called ambivalence'.[20] She became convinced that she needed to confront him in her writing to dispel the authority he still held over her.

Retreating into a lost world, she wrote her autobiographical essay 'A Sketch of the Past'.[21] She tried to capture her parents as people who were separate from her. But just as Julia seemed to be within her grasp she slipped away again, leaving Virginia wondering why she found it so difficult to describe her feelings for her mother and the woman herself. She could easily portray other characters, but she could never see Julia 'completely undisturbed by later impressions'.[22]

Dwelling on the past was always a double-edged sword for Virginia and rather than helping her escape it added to her problems. In the last months of her life, as the threat of a German invasion terrified her, she could not stop thinking about her parents and her childhood. Rereading Leslie's memoir and his love letters to her mother she simplified their relationship, writing:

How beautiful they were, those old people – I mean father and mother – how simple, how clear, how untroubled. [...] How gay even their life reads to me: no mud: no whirlpools. [...] Nothing turbulent; nothing involved; no introspection.[23]

She soothed herself to sleep with thoughts of St Ives and tried to recapture the security she felt sitting on Julia's lap as a child.[24] Inevitably, dwelling on the past brought back memories of her half-brothers' sexual abuse and her resentment towards her father, which triggered feelings of worthlessness. Leonard recognised the risk she was taking and after she had spent the afternoon arranging Leslie's old books, he begged her to put her father away.[25] It was equally dangerous to conjure up the ghost of her mother;

its hazardous potential was captured through Lily Briscoe's thoughts in *To the Lighthouse*:

> It had seemed so safe, thinking of her, Ghost air, nothingness, a thing you could play with easily and safely at any time of day or night, she had been that, and then suddenly she put her hand out and wrung the heart thus [...] If they shouted loud enough Mrs Ramsay would return [...] the tears ran down her face. 'Mrs Ramsay!' Lily cried, 'Mrs Ramsay!' but nothing happened. The pain increased. That anguish could reduce one to such a pitch of imbecility.[26]

Invoking those spectres in the dark days of the war added to Virginia's instability. In the final weeks of her life, she was terrified about having another breakdown.[27] The suddenness and intensity of this attack reminded Leonard of the episode in 1915 when over breakfast she imagined her mother was in the room. He thought her deteriorating mental health was triggered by finishing her book.[28] She became stressed about her writing and unable to sleep or eat. In her final letter to Vanessa she told her that she was certain she was going mad again and she was always hearing voices.[29]

On 28 March 1941, Virginia left a letter to Leonard thanking him for giving her 'complete happiness', then she walked across the water meadow to the River Ouse, filled her pocket with stones, and drowned herself. In the past she had imagined the ghostly figures of Julia and Stella, floral wreaths in their hair, walking away from her across a field. Finally, she followed them.

Part Two

Clara and Agatha

14

The Poor Relation

Superficially, Agatha Christie's mother, Clara Boehmer, could not have been more different from Julia Jackson. Unlike Virginia's mother, she had no pretensions about being a beauty. Considering herself 'dumpy' and rather plain, her attractions were not as obvious, but Clara's soulful hazel eyes showed she experienced intense emotions. Beneath her unassuming image there was a woman of strong passions, deep emotional intelligence, and intense intuition.

By observing her mother, Agatha discovered that the most fascinating characters are not always the ones who immediately attract attention. It is no coincidence that while Virginia wrote about Clarissa Dalloway and Mrs Ramsay, women who were at the centre of society, Agatha's most famous female character is Jane Marple, an unpretentious provincial lady, who observes from the sidelines but understands more than anyone else exactly what is going on. For Agatha, her mother was her greatest heroine and, unlike Virginia's relationship with Julia, or Sylvia's with Aurelia, there was little ambivalence in their bond. They adored each other and that unconditional love was the bedrock on which Agatha built her life.

Clara was not as fortunate as her daughter to grow up feeling secure in her mother's love. Her childhood deprived her of a sense of belonging. It left her determined that her children should never know the unhappiness she had experienced. Her mother, Polly West, was born in Chichester, Sussex. She was the daughter of Thomas West, a painter, plumber and glazier, and his wife, Mary Ann Kelsey. According to Agatha's Mary Westmacott novel, *Unfinished Portrait*, which like Virginia's *To the Lighthouse* fictionalises her family life, Thomas and Mary Ann's marriage was a love match which produced ten children. When Mary Ann died of consumption aged only 39, her husband was heartbroken and died just six months later.[1]

Orphaned at the age of 10, Polly and her siblings went to live with their mother's brother and his wife on their farm at Prinsted, Sussex.[2] As Polly grew up, intense sibling rivalry developed between her and her eldest sister Margaret. For the rest of their lives, they argued about who was the more attractive; apparently Polly had the prettier face, but Margaret the better figure.[3] Believing that delicate health was a sign of femininity, they even competed about who was the most physically frail.[4]

Growing up in an era when few careers were open to women and attracting an eligible man was the easiest way to move up in the world, both girls competed to see who could make the best match. As Agatha wrote in *Unfinished Portrait*, they 'had been brought up in the days when men were considered to be the hub of the universe. Women merely existed to minister to those magnificent beings.'[5]

When Polly was 16, she fell in love with an army officer, Captain Frederic Boehmer. Born in Martinique during the Napoleonic wars, Frederic's German father served in the British Army in the West Indies. Aged 19, Frederic also joined the army. Starting as a private, he served in Ireland, the Mediterranean, Jamaica and Canada and rose through his own merit to become an officer in the Argyllshire Highlanders Regiment. He married and had four children, but by the time his regiment returned to England in 1847, his first wife and all his children had died.[6]

An urbane widower, Frederic was twenty-one years older than Polly, but his experience just made him more attractive to the innocent country girl. With his neat moustache and elegant physique, Frederic was known as the handsomest man in the regiment.[7] Polly's family thought she was too young to wed, but as Frederic was about to be posted abroad, she went against their wishes and the couple married on 11 February 1851 at St John the Baptist church in Westbourne, Sussex.[8]

Over the next decade, Polly and Frederic had five children; one died in infancy, but the rest survived. While Frederic's regiment was garrisoned in Dublin in February, 1854, Clarissa (known as Clara) was born. As an army family, Clara and her brothers, Frederick, Harry and Ernest, travelled with their parents to Malta and Greece. Back in England, in 1859 Frederic became a director of The Great Central Mining Company of Devon. The plan was to mine the minerals in Ilsington near Newton Abbot, which was close to areas already known for yielding large quantities of copper and tin. Unfortunately, the mine did not live up to expectations and a year later the business was wound up, leaving Captain Boehmer and the miners with nothing to show for their hard work.[9]

In September 1860, Frederic retired from the army and the family moved to St Helier, Jersey. His retirement was brief as he died in April 1863 aged 49. According to family mythology, he was killed when he was thrown from his horse. Like the story about Herbert Duckworth's death, the reality seems to have been less romantic; the local parish register recorded he died from bronchitis.[10] Left a widow at the age of 27, Polly was devastated, saying that she wanted to be buried with her beloved husband in the cemetery in St Helier. Although she was young and attractive, she never married again. After Frederic's death, Polly had just enough money to live on but not sufficient to provide her children with the opportunities she desired. A skilled needlewoman, Polly supplemented her income by taking in sewing, but even working an eight-hour day she could not afford to send her sons to boarding school.

In the snakes and ladders of their sibling rivalry, as Polly went down, Margaret was on the up. In April 1863, just a fortnight before her sister lost her husband, she married a much older wealthy American business-man, Nathaniel Frary Miller. Mr Miller was a widower with a son called Frederick. A self-made man, he worked his way up from being an office boy to a partner in the firm of H.B. Claflin, a dry goods business based in Manhattan, New York. As his business had a branch in Manchester, he visited Britain frequently and on one of these trips he met Margaret.

The Millers lived an affluent life at Timperley Villa, Timperley in Cheshire, but the one thing they lacked was children. Ever pragmatic, Margaret thought of a way to help her sister and herself: she offered to adopt one of Polly's children. It was decided that 9-year-old Clara should come to live with her aunt and uncle. To a modern reader it sounds a strange bargain between two sisters, but it was not unusual at the time. A similar deal was done by Jane Austen's family; her brother Edward was also adopted by wealthy childless relatives. They made him heir to their fortune, and, in return, he took their name, becoming Edward Austen Knight. However, even though this type of practical arrangement was accepted at the time, the repercussions could be profound. Agatha believed that her mother never completely got over being given away. She was told that it was to provide her with a more comfortable lifestyle and a better education, but it still felt like a rejection.[11]

The deal allowed Polly to send her eldest son to Wellington College, the prestigious boarding school in Berkshire. Mrs Boehmer's decision, Agatha believed, made Clara feel that her mother loved her brothers more than her.[12] It was so deeply instilled that boys were worth more than girls that when, aged 17, she was asked, in the family pastime of 'Confessions', who she would like to be if not herself, she replied 'A schoolboy'.[13] Clara's separation from her mother and siblings left a lasting scar. Agatha wrote, 'I think the resentment she felt, the deep hurt at being unwanted, coloured her attitude to life. It made her distrustful of herself, and suspicious of people's affection.'[14]

As so often in their relationship, Agatha was protective of Clara and empathised so much that she may have felt the experience more acutely than her mother did herself.[15] In her *Autobiography*, Agatha wrote that nothing could replace for Clara a 'carefree life' in 'her own home'. This emphasis on the importance of home is at least as much about the daughter's feelings as her mother's. Agatha adored her childhood home, and it was essential to her security even when she was an adult. In her memoir, Agatha added that when she heard anxious parents wondering if a child should be brought up by someone who could give them more material benefits, she always wanted to say, '"Don't let the child go." Her home, her own people, love – the security of belonging – what does the best education in the world mean against that?'[16]

Clara's experience influenced Agatha's fiction. Like Virginia in *To the Lighthouse* and Sylvia in *The Bell Jar*, Agatha imagined what her mother felt. In an unpublished short story about 'Witch Hasel' the character is based on Clara. At first, she lived with her parents and brothers in small, cramped rooms with few material comforts, but where she felt 'secure, accepted'; it was 'certainly not glamorous but warm, warm with the warmth and intimacy of close knowledge'. When her father suddenly dies, her mother agrees to her being adopted by her Aunt Mildred and Uncle Edward. Hasel is angry about the decision, thinking, 'She wasn't an orphan. She had a mother, she had brothers. Why should she be adopted by strange people?'

Although the little girl enjoyed a luxurious lifestyle in her aunt and uncle's large 'smug' white house, she is unhappy. Separated from her close family, a cold tide of hatred flows through her, and she wishes her aunt and uncle were dead. She resents them for 'their unwanted, painstaking kindness and their humiliating neglect of her as a real person'. Feeling like a refugee who was in exile, she could never feel at home because 'none of it was hers, it didn't belong to her – she didn't belong to it. She had lost everything that she belonged to.'[17]

This desire to be understood and to belong are recurring themes in Agatha's work. Adoptions are rarely successful in her novels.[18] In *Ordeal by Innocence*, desperate to become a mother, wealthy heiress Rachel Argyle adopts five children, but rather than loving her they resent her. Through the character of her adopted son Micky, who was 'sold' by his biological mother to the Argyles for £100, we get an insight into what Agatha imagined Clara felt. He never looked on his adoptive mother as his real parent and bore a 'deep, almost pathological grudge' against her.[19] Micky knew that he ought to be grateful for his privileged upbringing, but that obligation just made it worse. He had not wanted to be taken away from his own home and would have preferred to stay with his own family, where he belonged.[20]

Mrs Argyle was rich enough to buy many things; she gave her adopted family love, care and security but she could not buy their love. The message is clear; it is wrong to treat a child like a commodity which can be bartered. A similar attitude appears in Agatha's early short story 'Wireless', as a wealthy childless aunt tries to buy her niece's affections but fails. Mrs Harter intended to make Miriam her heiress but when her niece does not pander to her whims she is returned to her mother as if she had been 'goods on approval'. Mrs Harter then makes a 'new acquisition', her nephew Charles.[21] The fact the niece was called Miriam, the name Agatha uses for the character modelled on Clara in *Unfinished Portrait*, suggests that she was thinking of her mother as she wrote it.

Although in later life Clara always treated her mother and aunt kindly, Agatha believed the resentment remained.[22] Clara wanted for nothing materially in her new home and her aunt was kind to her, but the little girl cried herself to sleep every night and became withdrawn. She found solace in reading her favourite book from her Jersey home, *The King of the Golden River*. She modelled herself on the determined little boy in the story, who conquered his unhappiness by being considerate and sensible.[23] Clara was so obedient her aunt assumed she was naturally quiet. But when her niece lost weight and grew pale, Mrs Miller called a doctor who diagnosed homesickness. After confessing her feelings, Clara became more settled.

One of the great advantages of Clara's life with the Millers was that she received a better education than many girls of her generation. She attended a local private school where she became an avid reader, with an eclectic taste in literature which ranged from the poetry of Tennyson to the novels of Louisa May Alcott. Her favourite character was the feisty heroine Jo in Alcott's *Little Women*.[24]

Clara was intelligent, and in a different era, when more careers were open to women, she might have become a doctor. When her brother Ernest studied medicine, she begged him to share his knowledge with her. Agatha believed that her mother was more suited to becoming a medic than he was. Instead, Clara had to content herself with being an amateur doctor.[25] For the rest of her life she would read the medical journal *The Lancet*.[26] She passed on her love of medicine to her daughter. When Agatha worked as a nurse and pharmacist in the First World War, she was fulfilling an ambition which had been denied her mother.

As she grew older, Clara's relationship with her aunt remained complicated. In 1877, she wrote a poem to Margaret Miller, which expresses the sentiments of a dutiful daughter but suggests that she respected rather than deeply loved her. Like Julia Stephen, Mrs Miller is portrayed as a selfless model of Victorian womanhood; there is 'no truer woman, nobler friend'. Continuing with platitudes about her kindness, the poem ends with an appeal to God to 'keep her long on earth / To dwell among our loving hearts / Who feel her priceless worth'.[27] These trite lines do not tally with Agatha's recollection of her mother's feelings towards the woman who brought her up. Margaret Miller *should* be loved but, like Rachel Argyle in *Ordeal by Innocence*, is she really? In Clara's poem, Margaret Miller comes across like the smug do-gooders in Agatha's novels, who give people what they think they should have, rather than what they really need.

According to Agatha, when Clara was a young woman Mrs Miller did not treat her exactly as she would her own daughter. Clara was denied a debutante season. While Margaret always bought herself couture clothes from Paris, she dressed Clara in drab dresses more suitable for a little girl than a young woman.[28] Clara loved clothes and in later life dressed in the latest fashions. When zips were first invented, she had a corset made which zipped up the front. However, it was practically a surgical operation to get out of it and, due to her Victorian modesty, she feared being permanently trapped as 'a kind of modern Woman in the Iron Corset'.[29] Her desire to look her best ran deep, in her Confessions, when 17-year-old Clara was asked what her present state of mind was, she wrote 'wishing for a long dress'.

Reading between the lines of the Confessions album tells us more about Clara's true emotions than her carefully contrived poem. Asked to note her chief characteristic, she wrote 'a great love for children'. Reinforcing her desire to have a large family after missing out on growing up with her brothers, she recorded that her idea of misery would be 'never to see or be with children'.[30] Clara was a determined young woman, who knew just what she wanted from life and was going to do her best to get it. Like one of the heroines in her favourite romantic novels, by sheer willpower she would change her circumstances. In her Confessions, she recorded that her favourite motto was 'Upward and Onward', adding, 'Where there's a will there's a way.'[31]

15

The Wonderful Hero

Unlike Julia, few people would have cast Clara as a romantic heroine, but she was equally capable of a grand passion. As a teenager, she wrote poems about romantic love with an almost religious fervour; it was sacred to her and an intimation of heaven on earth. Believing in soulmates, she imagined a relationship where her 'inmost spirit' could connect with her lover.[1] She was looking for a 'wonderful hero' to worship and when she met her aunt's stepson, Frederick Alvah Miller, she thought she had found him.[2]

Easy-going Frederick was an unlikely candidate to inspire such intensity but, echoing the partnership of Herbert Duckworth and Julia Jackson, the combination of the passionate young woman and the placid young man worked. The couple first met when Frederick was visiting his father and step-mother in England. Born in Manhattan, after his mother died Fred divided his time between his American grandparents and his father in England. Educated in Switzerland, he seemed intriguingly cosmopolitan to the quiet little girl who was eight years his junior. Well connected in New York society, he lived like a Henry James or Edith Wharton character. After languid days spent reading newspapers and writing letters at the Union Club, in the evenings he went out to dinner or dancing with friends. Trips to the theatre and concerts provided opportunities to flirt with society beauties.

Although he appeared a debonair man of the world, what appealed most to Clara about Fred was his kindness. She stayed quietly in the background, but he noticed her. When he remarked to Margaret what lovely eyes her niece had, for the first time Clara thought that perhaps she was not so plain after all.[3] When the warm-hearted young man left, Clara could not stop thinking about him. Her self-esteem was too low for her to hope that he would fall in love with her, but she daydreamed that after a 'brilliant but unhappy' society marriage, his first wife would die, and he would come back to his shy cousin, who had been pining away for him.[4]

Although at first Fred thought of Clara as an affectionate little girl, there was a genuine rapport between them. Gradually, he began to see her in a different light and when she was 17, he sent her a volume of Southey's poems bound in blue and gold, inscribed 'To Clara, a token of love.'[5] In return, Clara embroidered a pocketbook for her 'Cousin Fred'. On the cover are daisies and a heart with two arrows through it, with the message, 'See me as a seal upon thine heart. My love is strong as death.'[6] Fred was so touched by her gift that he kept it for the rest of his life.

Clara was very different from the society belles he knew in New York, but it seems the depth and complexity of her character attracted him. Perhaps, as they had both lost parents in childhood and lacked a permanent home, they were drawn to each other. Together they discovered a sense of belonging which had previously eluded them. Reading their separate answers to the Confessions, it is evident that they offered each other what they needed. Fred wrote that his idea of happiness was 'to be perfectly loved', and noted that his favourite qualities in a woman were 'amiability to reason, with a good temper'. In her Confessions, Clara rated a woman's 'fidelity' as most important and wrote that her idea of happiness was 'always doing the right thing'.[7]

When he first proposed, Clara refused, thinking she was not attractive enough and that she might disappoint him. But when he asked again, she could not resist. During their engagement she gave him a maroon and gold album of poems she had composed during their courtship. Although they are very Victorian, sentimentally linking love and death, they demonstrate that she took her writing seriously because they are carefully crafted. They tell us much about her feelings for her future husband. In *The Ideal*, she admitted that all her life she had dreamt with 'passionate longing' of an 'ideal noble and sweet' hero, and now she had found him.[8] In *Violets*, when Fred picked her favourite flowers and gave them to her, she no longer felt alone, instead she was:

Understood at last
Breathing joyful trust and peace
Blotting out the past.[9]

In another poem, *Two Loves Two Lives*, she recalled how when Fred first gently stooped and kissed her face, he awoke powerful emotions in her. She recognised that it was an attraction of emotional opposites; while he returned to America 'lightly careless', she was left feeling desolate and discontented. She loved him with 'the passionate love once only given on earth', and, if she could not be with him, she wanted to die. Fortunately, on his return Fred was won over by 'the little faithful heart' which 'trusts to him its life its soul'.

Clara was frightened by the intensity of her feelings for him, and the poem ends with a plea to God to:

Take back this unreasoning love ere it doth fade and die
It is a love which nought on earth should claim or call its own.[10]

When Fred was away, Clara was determined he should never forget her. In another poem she repeated the phrase 'Forget me not', and reminded him that although 'others love and others smile / They will not love or smile for long'. He should remember that true love lies with her because, 'I would gladly <u>die</u> for thee.'[11]

Reading Clara's poems, a reader cannot help thinking her single-minded love might have been claustrophobic. It seems Clara was aware of this and in one poem she mentioned 'the burden of my song'.[12] A recurring theme in Agatha's Westmacott novels is that loving another person too much could place a burden on the beloved. However, as Fred had never been the most important person in anyone's life before, it seems Clara's undying devotion gave him the security he wanted. She promised him he would never feel alone again, writing in 'A Love Song':

Fast in my arms will I hold you
Sheltered till death shall come
Never again to unfold you
Love who with love I have won.[13]

In April 1878, Clara and Fred's marriage took place at St Peter's, Bayswater. A pastel miniature captured Clara's moment of triumph. She looks delicate and feminine in her Elizabethan-style, white lace dress, with its stand-away collar and sprigs of orange blossom on the sleeves and bodice matching the wreath which holds her gauzy veil in place. Her steady hazel eyes look on the world with a new-found confidence. The delight the whole family felt at this match is clear from the celebration afterwards. No expense was spared on the wedding breakfast which was held at the Palace Gardens Terrace in Kensington. Reflecting the family's enjoyment of good food there were copious courses, including two soups, followed by hot and cold meats, salmon, lobster and foie gras, then a choice of six puddings and two ice creams.

Family was important to Fred and Clara but being together was what really mattered. They spent an idyllic honeymoon in Switzerland. Once again, Clara turned to poetry to express her love for her husband; in her verse she prayed for God to send her 'an angel friend' to protect 'my darling'. Suggesting that she could not believe her good fortune to have married him, she prayed:

Make me worthy, though so lowly
All his love of life to share
Give a heart where he may never
Sound the end or depth of love.

For Clara, like Julia during her first marriage, finding her 'kindred spirit' was clouded by insecurity and both young wives were afraid their happiness could not last. Fear of death stalks Clara's poem as she asked God to take 'all love's vague forebodings' and leave only 'peace and rest'.[14] To remember this precious moment in her life, she pressed a sprig of edelweiss, a gentian, a violet and some clover they picked together during their Alpine idyll. Almost disintegrating, it remains folded in her poem to this day.[15]

The Millers' marriage was as much a love match as Julia's marriage to Herbert Duckworth had been and the dynamic between the two couples was very similar. While Clara was intense, Fred was laid back. In the family game of Confessions, he noted his greatest dislike was getting up in the morning, and his favourite occupation was 'doing nothing'. Agatha believed that the happiness of her parents' marriage and their family life was largely due to Fred. She described him as 'a very agreeable man'.[16] He was not particularly clever, but he was happy in his own skin. When he was asked in Confessions if he was not himself who he would want to be, he replied 'nobody'. He described his present state of mind as 'Extremely comfortable, thank you'.[17]

Like Julia with her first husband, Fred's simple, straightforward personality was just what Clara needed to shake her out of her introspection. In her autobiography, Agatha described her mother as 'an enigmatic and arresting personality – more forceful than my father – startlingly original in her ideas, shy and miserably diffident about herself, and at bottom, I think with a natural melancholy'.[18] Like the other authors in this book, there was a history of mental health illness in Clara's family. New research by Lucy Worsley reveals that her eldest brother Frederick shot himself.[19] A first cousin and second cousin drowned themselves and Clara's great uncle died in an asylum for the insane.[20]

Clara never took her happiness for granted. Although her husband was devoted to her, she was always afraid he might leave her for a more attractive woman. In *Unfinished Portrait*, the mother tells her daughter that she was always on her guard against even the hint of a flirtation. She once saw a buxom maid put her hand over her husband's; the brazen servant was promptly sacked.[21] Clara was taking no risks, and decades later she advised her daughter to be equally wary.

Looking back at her parents' marriage, Agatha believed that although it was a strong partnership, Clara could be a challenge to live with. In her novel, she described the mother as having some 'devil' in her, meaning she had the 'guts' to stand up to her husband and he did not 'always have an easy life with her. She adored him, but she tried him too.' Agatha believed men liked that sort of stimulus and, because she had less of 'the little devil' in her, she had a less successful first marriage.[22]

Assessing her many years later, Agatha believed her mother was an exceptional person who had a touch of brilliance in her complex character.[23] She was like a butterfly who flitted from one idea to another, rarely coming to rest. Impulsive and with a quick mind, she was easily bored and constantly sought new experiences to stimulate her. Agatha wrote, 'thoughts dart [through her brain] with the swiftness of swallows in flight. [...] She is usually thinking about three things at once.'[24]

In *Unfinished Portrait*, Agatha describes her mother's alter ego, Miriam, as having a 'very vivid personality', which was enchanting. Like Virginia's view of Julia, Agatha seems to have thought her mother was more special than she was. She wrote, 'She had, I fancy, a charm that Celia (Miriam's daughter) did not inherit.'[25] Agatha inherited a great deal from Clara, however; she passed on gifts which would help to make her daughter the brilliant writer she became. Clara felt things incredibly intensely and had heightened perception. As Agatha explained, her mother's ideas:

> were always slightly at variance with reality. She saw the universe as more brightly coloured than it was, people as better or worse than they were. [...] Her creative imagination was so strong that it could never see things as drab or ordinary.'[26]

Seeing beneath the surface, her children believed that she was psychic. Her sixth sense combined with acute emotional intelligence meant she often intuitively knew what people were thinking and what was going to happen.

Agatha's second husband, Max Mallowan, had no doubt about Clara's legacy. He believed his wife inherited her mother's 'inner sensitivity together with an intuitive understanding of situations hidden from more normal mortals'.[27] As she channelled this imaginative gift into her writing, Agatha created the ingenious plots which were to make her so famous.

16

The Homemaker

Ashfield, the home Fred and Clara created in Torquay, Devon was to be for Agatha the equivalent of Talland House in St Ives for Virginia. The rambling white Victorian villa with its large garden provided the little girl with 'the lovely, safe, yet exciting world of childhood'. It gave her a place of sanctuary which she would return to, first physically, then in her imagination, for the rest of her life.[1] Even when she had her own home, it would remain the house of her dreams.[2] It is no coincidence that a large white house set on a hill appears frequently in Agatha's fiction. In her autobiography, she described what Ashfield meant to her, 'It has been my background, my shelter, the place where I truly belong. I have never suffered from the absence of roots.'[3] Like Talland House for Virginia, the house became inextricably bound up with Agatha's relationship with her mother. Ashfield was Clara's house, where she created a haven for her family.

The Millers first visited Torquay when they returned from their honeymoon. Developing rapidly after the Napoleonic wars, the town had become a fashionable seaside resort. Reminiscent of Italy or the French Riviera, with its balmy climate and Italianate villas, it had a continental atmosphere – although it always had a rather risqué reputation. After his visit, Charles Dickens wrote that it was 'a place I consider to be an imposter, a delusion and a snare'. Another critical visitor observed, 'It is a place of ease, luxury, riches, convenience and prettiness.'[4] This sybaritic atmosphere perfectly suited Fred and he immediately fell in love with the place. The couple moved into rented accommodation and in January 1879, their first child, Margaret (known as Madge), was born.

When Madge was 8 months old the Millers travelled to America to visit Fred's grandparents. They expected to make their permanent home there. During their visit, in June 1880, their second child, Louis Montant (known as Monty), was born in Morristown, New Jersey.[5] However, when the family returned to England in September 1880 their plans changed overnight. Fred was unexpectedly called back to New York for business, so Clara and her Aunt Margaret, who was now widowed, went to look for a house to rent in Torquay. The two women visited Ashfield, a seven-bedroomed property set in 2 acres, with a distant view of the sea.[6]

Sensitive to atmospheres, Clara immediately felt it was a peaceful place. The Quaker lady who owned the house told her that it made her happy to think of the Millers moving in.[7] Seeing this as a blessing, according to Agatha, impetuous as ever, Clara bought the house immediately, using her inheritance from her uncle, without even consulting her husband.[8] Fred was surprised by her snap decision, but good-naturedly accepted her wishes. Research by biographer Lucy Worsley reveals Agatha's account is not strictly accurate. A married woman could not buy a house in her own right because she was legally a feme covert; the law treated husband and wife as one person and that person was the husband. Clara's legacy was tied up in a trust, so she could not access it without trustees agreeing. Nor could she own Ashfield outright as it was a leasehold not a freehold property.[9] Still, Agatha's story has an emotional truth and emphasises that she always saw Ashfield as very much her mother's house.

It became the home Clara had always craved, making her feel that she finally belonged. By the time their youngest child, Agatha Mary Clarissa, was born on 15 September 1890, her roots went deep. When the Millers' youngest daughter was christened at the parish church, Clara named her baby after herself and her grandmother. According to Agatha, her first name was chosen at the last minute on the way to the christening.[10] Her godparents included the president of the local hospital, an Honourable and a future viscount.[11]

Growing up at Ashfield, Agatha had everything she needed to thrive. As Clara was 36 when her youngest daughter was born, she saw her as an unexpected blessing. Unlike Julia who weaned Virginia as soon as possible, Mrs Miller was determined to make the most of every moment with her baby and did not employ a nurse to look after her for two months.[12] As Agatha's brother and sister were so much older, Agatha became a self-contained child who lived in her imagination. The garden was her special domain and, like Virginia's descriptions of Talland House, decades later Agatha could still remember every detail. There was the walled kitchen garden where she ate apples and raspberries, then the long stretch of lawn surrounded by trees, a tennis or croquet lawn and the magical woods which wrapped around Ashfield.

Max Mallowan described Agatha as living in 'a permanent condition of fantasy'.[13] The little girl created a dreamland peopled with imaginary friends and, making up elaborate stories about them, their world became more fascinating to her than the real one.[14] It was perfect training for the future author as later her characters would also come alive in her imagination. Her childhood prepared her for 'a life of boundless invention'.[15]

These were halcyon days for the whole family. More sociable than his wife, Fred immersed himself in every aspect of Torquay's vibrant social life. He went to his club every morning, to the cricket club on summer afternoons, then in the evenings he appeared in amateur dramatics, sang in a choir, or played cards. Fred had a wide circle of friends; everyone from cabmen to local tradesmen loved him. In contrast, Clara was selective about her circle, but her friends were more unconventional and her relationships more intense.[16]

While Fred was busy socialising, Clara spent her days running the house and looking after the family. On Saturday afternoons, she sometimes had tea with the Reverend Petty, the vicar of their parish church. His daughter Gwen remembered Mrs Miller as 'an imposing woman: a woman with presence. She had a natural elegance with an innate flair for stylish clothes.' Dressed in a long black coat of flowing marocain and a wide-brimmed picture hat, holding a silver-topped ebony cane, she would arrive while the Reverend Petty was busy in his study writing his sermon. He was always pleased to see her because she was so 'lively and charming'. Over wafer-thin bread and butter and madeira cake, their conversation ranged from world events and the latest books to parish gossip. Gwen Petty recalled, 'Mrs Miller loved people and whereas they began on a purely socially agreeable note they often ended in confidence.'[17]

The Millers regularly entertained at Ashfield. During Torquay Regatta, they held a house party for the sailing event. They went to tea parties at the Yacht Club and took a party to the Regatta ball, which culminated with a spectacular firework display.[18] Throughout the year the Millers gave dinner parties. The food was superb with at least five courses on offer, including locally caught fish, the finest meat and lashings of Devon clotted cream. The Millers' parties were relaxed occasions because Fred was funny and always made people laugh. Although Clara lacked any sense of humour, she was good company too. As Agatha noted, 'The women, like my mother, had good minds. They read and studied and were exceedingly interesting to talk to.'[19]

Unlike the Stephens, the Millers were not intellectuals, but nor were they completely cut off from literary circles. The author Eden Phillpotts was a neighbour, and the two families became friends. Eden's daughter Adelaide attended the same ballet classes as Agatha.[20] Each summer, Eden invited his local friends to join literary celebrities at a large party in his garden.[21] Perhaps because Fred was one of the leading Americans in the bay, the authors Henry James and Rudyard Kipling also visited Ashfield. While Henry James's visit seems to have been successful, apparently Clara did not get on well with Kipling's American wife, Carrie, as afterwards, Mrs Miller wondered why Rudyard had married her.[22] Dressed in a white muslin dress with a wide sash, Agatha was introduced to these men of letters at her parents' tea parties.[23]

The quiet little girl learnt a great deal by discreetly observing people. Her cast of characters was limited, but they provided her with miscellaneous material that she would later use in her novels.[24] The Millers' band of loyal staff were like an extended family. Clara's attitude to her employees was similar to Julia's. She taught her children to treat them with great respect, telling them that they should recognise they were 'experts'. Servants were to be spoken to politely and never interrupted during their time off.[25] The Millers recognised hierarchies and believed that these boundaries made people feel secure. Agatha wrote that the servants 'knew their place' but rather than being subservient they took pride in their professionalism.[26]

Members of the Miller household knew they were valued. Clara had a natural authority which made people do what she wanted, but her thoughtfulness meant that her employees remained working for her for years. According to Agatha, their cook Jane ruled the kitchen like a queen.[27] When she had produced a particularly sumptuous dinner, Fred came down to the kitchen to congratulate her.[28]

After her parents, Agatha's elderly nanny 'Nursie' was the most important person in her early life. Deeply religious, nanny instilled her own strict religious values in her protégée. As a Sabbatarian, Nursie opposed any leisure activities on Sundays. When her parents played croquet or sang songs around the piano, Agatha feared they might go to hell for breaking Nursie's rules. As usual, Clara discovered what was worrying her daughter and allayed her fears.

Unlike Virginia, Agatha was brought up in a household where faith was important. Clara's relationship with God was as intense as her relationship with the people she loved. According to Agatha, her 'naturally mystic turn of mind' meant no form of organised religion satisfied her for long.[29] Finding it difficult to discover her spiritual home, Clara's quest took her in some unorthodox directions. Most of her spiritual experimentation took place before Agatha was born. At one stage, Roman Catholicism appealed, then Unitarianism, a belief system which rejected the Trinity and the belief that Christ was the son of God. Her attraction to Unitarianism occurred when Monty was born – resulting in him not being christened.

Later, Clara was attracted to Theosophy, a religious movement which claimed to embrace 'essential truth'. It taught that there was a brotherhood of 'Masters' or 'Mahatmas', who had great wisdom and supernatural powers. They held the key to understanding miracles, the afterlife, and psychic phenomena. To modern ears, many of the Theosophists' theories sound bizarre, but it became fashionable in the late Victorian era.[30] When the Millers lived in Torquay, controversial topics concerning morality, spirituality and the occult were regularly discussed at the town's Theosophist meeting house.[31]

Shortly before Agatha was born, Clara abandoned Theosophy, briefly turning to Zoroastrianism.[32] Based on the teachings of the Iranian-speaking prophet Zoroaster, it taught that the purpose of life is to bring happiness into the world and that good thoughts, words and deeds contributed to the cosmic battle against evil. However, the attraction of this esoteric faith did not last long either and Clara returned to the 'safe haven' of the Church of England in time for Agatha to be christened in their parish church. As her daughter was growing up, Clara only went to church occasionally, but her faith remained an essential part of her life. A picture of St Francis hung by her bed, and she read *The Imitation of Christ* every day.[33]

Fred never tried to stop his wife's religious experimentation. He always provided a stable base for Clara to return to after one of her spiritual flights of fancy. His own faith was conventional and unquestioning; he liked to attend a weekly service at their Church of England parish church. As soon as she was old enough, Agatha relished going with him. As father and daughter sang hymns and confessed their faith together, she grew to love the ritual.

Absorbing different attitudes to religion from the adults in her life, Agatha eventually found her own spiritual path. One boyfriend tried to interest her in Theosophy, but she thought many of its ideas were nonsense.[34] Throughout her life, like Clara, she was a seeker after truth, and intellectually curious.[35] In later life, James Jeans's book, *The Mysterious Universe*, made her think about the meaning of time and the nature of God in a new way.[36] Yet she always came back to her strong conventional faith. Her God was one of loving kindness; her favourite psalm was 'The Lord's My Shepherd'. At the end of her life, when she paid for a new stained-glass window in her local church, she asked for Christ to be portrayed as the good shepherd rather than suffering on the cross. Her extensive knowledge of the Bible learnt in childhood remained with her and is evident in the many biblical phrases she used in her novels. Her faith was very private; her friend, historian A.L. Rowse, only realised what a deeply religious woman she was after reading her poetry and her book of Christmas fables, *Star Over Bethlehem*.[37] This book showed her thinking about what her faith really meant. As a mother and daughter, she imagined what it was like for the Virgin Mary to see her son crucified.[38] Like Clara, she always kept *The Imitation of Christ* by her bedside. It provided solace when times were hard, but also instilled the essential virtues of tolerance, humility and acceptance that guided her life.[39]

17

The Devoted Mother

Although Virginia's mother, Julia, was portrayed as the angel in the house, Clara conformed more to this model of Victorian femininity. Unlike Julia, all her energies were devoted to looking after her husband and three children and creating a happy home. Rather than feeling caged by domesticity, she felt protected. She was content within her bounded sphere; the outside world had less appeal because her inner rather than her outer life was most important to her.

While much of Julia's energy was devoted to charitable causes and caring for her extended circle, Clara's focus was on her immediate family. Perhaps because she had lacked those close relationships in her childhood, she never took them for granted. Nurturing her husband and children with infinite care, she handled them as if they were as fragile as the fine porcelain figures she collected. Fiercely loyal, she was protective and possessive of the people she loved.

Never having experienced a close mother and daughter relationship with her own mother or aunt, she was determined to create it with her two daughters. Unlike Julia, who favoured her boys, Clara was much closer to Madge and Agatha than to her only son. For her, Monty was 'the difficult one'. Agatha thought that this was because mother and son were too alike, both wanting their own way.[1] In contrast, Clara's relationships with Madge and Agatha were harmonious. The girls were not particularly like her or each other, but she was compatible with them. Due to their temperaments and secure upbringing, Madge was more outgoing and Agatha more self-confident than Clara had ever been. Photographs of Agatha as a child show a poised little girl who knew she was adored. She was an exceptionally attractive, photogenic child and the sheer number of pictures of her – in a sailor suit, posing with friends and with pets – illustrate how much her parents doted on her.

Both Fred and Clara were determined that their daughter should never experience the insecurity they had suffered. Whenever they were separated from Agatha, they wrote to her carefully setting out when they would return and making sure that she knew she was loved. During one absence, Clara wrote, 'Darling little girlie, Mother is longing to kiss and love her sweet pet again.'[2] Unlike many Victorian fathers, Fred was never afraid of expressing his emotions and his letters were even more effusive than Clara's. He reminded his little girl, 'You must not forget your dear old Daddie who loves you ever and <u>ever</u> and <u>ever</u> so much.'[3]

Cocooned in love from both parents, Agatha flourished, but her relationship with Clara was the most important. Her mother was not overly sentimental or demonstrative, but when she called her daughter 'Precious lamb, pigeony pumpkin [...] with a laugh in her voice and a sharp, short hug' Agatha had no doubt that she was deeply loved.[4] Unlike Julia, who was often absent for Virginia, Clara was always there when her daughter needed her. Whatever the problem, her mother was the person who could always make her feel better. In her autobiography Agatha described the security Clara's presence provided, 'There was something magnetic and healing in her touch. In illness there was no one like her. She could give you her own strength and vitality.'[5]

Most importantly, Agatha knew Clara completely understood her; no words needed to be exchanged between them because there was a natural rapport. In later life, Agatha recalled an incident when as a child she went on a walk with her father and sister. Her day was ruined when their guide pinned a live butterfly to her hat. Neither Madge nor Fred knew why she was so distressed, but as soon as Clara saw her youngest daughter, she understood. Agatha described 'the wonderful relief it is when somebody knows what's in your mind and tells it to you so that you are at last released from that long bondage of silence, that seems so inescapable'.[6] While Clara was alive Agatha never felt alone; their intimacy was intense and in *Unfinished Portrait*, Agatha described how the mother would smile at her daughter and squeeze her hand, 'as though <u>they two had a secret shared</u>'.[7]

While Virginia could rarely remember being alone with Julia, Agatha spent endless hours with Clara. Her mother gave her the priceless gift of her time and never seemed rushed. As Fred was such a sociable man and out of the house a great deal, she formed a particularly close unit with her children.[8] Looking back over her long life, Agatha explained the times she had been happiest were in the quiet moments of everyday life.[9] Able to see things from a child's perspective, Clara genuinely enjoyed playing games with her little girl. Perhaps it was a way of experiencing the carefree childhood she missed. They rarely played the same game twice and Clara made everything fun. The middle-aged woman literally got down to Agatha's level, making an elaborate play house with her and then crawling in and out on all fours.[10]

Like Julia, Clara was a gifted storyteller and Agatha inherited this talent from her mother. Max Mallowan described Clara as a woman of 'exceptional imagination which acted on her [Agatha] as a catalyst'.[11] She invented absorbing bedtime stories which engrossed her daughter. Clara's love of novelty meant that she never remembered them so even Agatha's favourite tales could never be repeated. Like the other mothers in this book, Clara had literary ambitions of her own. She wrote poetry and short stories under the pseudonym 'Callis Miller'. However, her storytelling ability did not translate on to the page and her work was not published.

For most of her childhood, Agatha, like Virginia, was educated at home by her parents. While Monty, as the only son, was sent to Harrow, Clara's attitude to girls' education was never static and she experimented with different models for her two daughters. Madge was sent to a pioneering school in Brighton, which later became Roedean. Agatha later recalled that her parents' decision not to educate Madge at home was unusual; it was seen as extraordinary in their circle.[12] Madge was so bright she could have gone to Girton College, Cambridge. Instead, the Millers sent their eldest daughter to a finishing school in Paris because they did not want her to ruin her marriage prospects by becoming 'a blue-stocking'.[13]

In contrast to her sister's education, Clara decided that Agatha should have a free-range childhood and not learn to read until she was 8 years old. Instead, the precociously bright Agatha taught herself to read before she was 5 and from then on was a voracious reader. In her final novel, *Postern of Fate*, Tuppence Beresford's recollection of learning to read seems to have been based on Agatha's experience. Tuppence explained that after she had been read a story she found the book on the shelf and read it. When travelling on the train, she would read the posters in the fields advertising items like Carter's Little Liver Pills. However, the downside to this informal method was she did not learn to spell properly. The excitement of entering an imaginary world was still palpable in Agatha's novel written nearly eight decades later. She enjoyed fairy tales, stories about animals, and one about an Eton schoolboy. Her favourites were children's classics, including Robert Louis Stevenson's *Treasure Island* and Mrs Molesworth's *The Cuckoo Clock*, *The Tapestry Room* and *Four Winds Farm*. These prized possessions were handed down the generations from her grandmothers and mother.[14]

Like the Stephens, the Millers did not employ a full-time governess; instead, Fred taught Agatha mathematics while Clara instructed her in history. In contrast to Julia, whose impatience made her lessons stressful, Clara's approach was playful and entertaining. Agatha believed that her mother would have made a first-class teacher because anything she told you immediately became 'exciting and significant'.[15] Clara was passionate about history and by editing out the boring bits and focusing on the most colourful characters, she brought the subject alive for her daughter. The romance rather than the facts appealed to them both and, as a child, Agatha identified with historical heroines, relating to them as real people.

Rather than relying on textbooks, Clara's history came from novels. In *Postern of Fate*, Tuppence mentions Charlotte Yonge's *Unknown to History*, which told the story of Mary, Queen of Scots' time in captivity.[16] The themes of adoption, hidden identities and romance fired the little girl's imagination. She pretended to be Mary, Queen of Scots throwing herself on the mercy of Queen Elizabeth.[17] As a teenager, Agatha's history lessons inspired her to write poems about 'Elizabeth of England', 'Isolt of Brittany' and pagan priestesses.[18]

Unlike Virginia, Agatha did not resent her parents educating her at home. Her friends enjoyed a similar upbringing, and it would have been seen as odd to send her to school.[19] She was glad to escape having a governess because her mother was more fun.[20] Claiming her childhood was not unusually solitary, she socialised with friends at dancing lessons, Swedish exercise classes and art school. She also had piano and singing lessons to provide her with the accomplishments expected of an Edwardian young lady. However, although she mixed with other children, *Unfinished Portrait* suggests she was so painfully shy that these encounters were often an ordeal; she preferred her own company. Max Mallowan thought that his wife's idiosyncratic education was part of the reason she became such a successful writer. He believed that if she had been forced into conventional learning at school it would have hampered her 'natural elan' and crushed her 'wonderful natural imagination'.[21]

Clara wanted her daughter to do well, but any success was for Agatha's own satisfaction, not a prerequisite for her affection. Unlike Sylvia Plath, Agatha never felt her mother's love was conditional upon achievement. In later life, Agatha praised Victorian parents who, unlike modern ones, did not put pressure on their children to fulfil their hopes. Instead, they were realistic about their talents. Looking objectively at their offspring, they did not expect more from them than they could achieve.[22]

Evidently, Clara judged her daughters to be exceptionally talented. Rather than behaving like Julia, who treated her eldest daughter Stella as an acolyte, Clara was happy for her daughters to be in the limelight, while she was the support act. She believed they could achieve whatever they desired. Her judgement proved to be right as both Miller girls turned out to be gifted. Madge was first to take centre stage. Attractive rather than good looking, she was great fun. Fred particularly enjoyed her company as she had the sense of humour his wife lacked.[23]

Madge was labelled 'the clever one' and Agatha felt dull in comparison. As a child she considered she was the 'slow one', but in later life she realised this was only compared to her mother and sister's quicksilver wit.[24] Agatha described Madge as one of those people who can do almost anything they put their mind to.[25] Madge was a brilliant storyteller, and, encouraged by Clara, she was the first to become a published writer. A series of her humorous short stories appeared in *Vanity Fair* magazine. Growing up in an environment where she observed both her mother and sister writing, Agatha soon took up her pen. From the age of 7, she staged her own plays. Her first recorded story was a melodrama about 'the bloody Lady Agatha' who was bad, and 'the noble Lady Madge', who was good. However, her elder sister refused to take part unless the epithets were switched around.[26] When Agatha was 11, her first published poem, about a new tram service, appeared in the local Ealing newspaper.[27]

The women in the Miller family were much more talented than the men. Reflecting the family dynamics, in many of Agatha's novels and plays the female characters are stronger than the males. In *Death Comes as the End*, set in Ancient Egypt, the matriarch, Esa, explains that women learn to play on the weakness of men. A younger woman, Kait, questions what males are for other than to breed children, because females provide the strength of the race.[28] Similarly, in her play *The Hollow* the women are in charge, running circles around the inept men.[29] Like the other authors in this book, Agatha grew up in a matriarchy where her great aunt and grandmother played a prominent part. Known as 'Auntie-Grannie', Margaret Miller dominated the scene, while her sister Polly or 'Granny B' was kept in her place as the poor relation.

Agatha's memories of staying with Margaret at Ealing evoke an atmosphere of a lost Victorian world, similar to Virginia's descriptions of Hyde Park Gate. Agatha recalled the heavy mahogany furniture, the lace and red damask curtains, and the clutter of ornaments and furniture in rooms which were dark and gloomy.[30] Margaret was a powerful character who was to influence Agatha's world view. She was the undisputed matriarch of the family and as Fred wrote to his little girl, 'You know Grannie is just like the Queen.'[31] Her wishes were always obeyed and both parents encouraged Agatha to show her due respect. When her daughter stayed with Mrs Miller, Clara wrote, 'You must be good to her and love her very much.'[32]

Mrs Miller was at the centre of a network of elderly friends, old retainers and staff. Agatha remembered her grannies chattering away unselfconsciously about intimate details of their extended circle's lives.[33] Listening to them, she learnt by osmosis how to write realistic dialogue. Years later she was to tell Lord Snowdon that her books came from an oral tradition; while out walking she spoke aloud the dialogue of her characters so that they grew up naturally around her.[34] The female conversations Agatha overheard as a child were to feed into her novels. She found it 'fun' writing dialogue; it was important to 'write pretty fast, keep in the mood and keep the talk flowing naturally'.[35] Reflecting her grandmothers' conversations, her dialogue was witty and fast moving, dealing with the whole spectrum of human experience, from the trivial to the profound with equal authenticity.

Margaret was an important figure in her granddaughter's life, but she was no substitute for her mother. In December 1895, Agatha stayed with Margaret for several months while Fred and Clara took Madge to America. During the visit, 5-year-old Agatha reacted in much the same way her mother had as a child. She wrote a fictionalised version of her experience in *Unfinished Portrait*. Although Auntie-Grannie was very kind to her, Agatha missed her mother terribly and could not wait to go home. Repeating Clara's experience decades before, Celia (the Agatha character) was so homesick she cried, but Grannie did not know how to comfort her. The little girl just wanted her mother as without her it was an 'empty, lonely world'.[36]

18

Nightmares

Although Agatha had a golden childhood, there were shadows as well as sunshine. She was a dreamy child, whose imaginative world was as vivid to her as the real one. Dreams fascinated her and in later life she was intrigued by the role of the subconscious, but as a child she reacted in a visceral way. In her poem 'The Road of Dreams', she described the joy of dreams as unrivalled, but the fear experienced in nightmares was equally intense.[1]

Her nightmares suggest she was aware of an underlying threat to her idyllic world. Just as in her novels, where the cosiness and stability are only transient, the little girl discovered that death was always lurking in the background. It could come from nowhere, out of a blue sky. Even Ashfield was not the safe sanctuary it superficially seemed.

In January 1893, when Agatha was a toddler, Ashfield's gardener William Callicott died by suicide. Fred found him in an outhouse. The whole Miller family was traumatised by the tragedy. Agatha was too young to remember the actual event, but it entered family folklore as a fictionalised version appears in *Unfinished Portrait*.

As a sensitive child, Agatha absorbed emotional undercurrents, and these tensions came out in her subconscious. She had a recurrent nightmare about the 'Gun Man', who was a malign spirit with penetrating blue eyes and a stump instead of his arm. He would appear unexpectedly at events and could possess the people she loved. One night, she dreamed his cruel blue eyes were staring out of her mother's face.[2] Agatha woke up screaming. This frightening dream suggests that from an early age she realised that people were not always what they seemed. In later life, Agatha could never trace where this nightmare came from; she claimed that it resembled nothing she had seen or overheard. Biographer Janet Morgan thinks the dream suggests Agatha may have doubted whether those who were supposed to love her really did.[3] This is possible, but as she was so surrounded by love in her childhood, it is more probable that Agatha absorbed Clara's childhood insecurity. They were so close that her mother's emotions permeated her daughter's subconscious. Similarly, Sylvia Plath was to later appropriate Aurelia's negative childhood experiences as if they were her own.

In her novel *Ordeal by Innocence*, Agatha's description of the feeling of insecurity experienced by the character of Hester after her adopted mother, Rachel Argyle, is murdered has echoes of the 'Gun Man' nightmare. Hester felt afraid of everybody. She was not sure whether her father was what he seemed or if she could trust anybody or know what they were really like.[4] Hester's family relationships were far more like Clara's than Agatha's.

This sense of the unknowability of another person, even those closest to you, was reinforced by a game Madge used to play with her. They called it 'The Elder Sister', and, using her considerable acting ability, Madge played a mad character who lived in a cave, but looked exactly like her except for a sinister voice. The performance was so convincing it terrified Agatha, making her question what was real or unreal. In her autobiography, Agatha confessed she got a frisson from being frightened. She wondered if this was because part of her rebelled against a life which was in every other way so safe. Did people need a degree of danger to challenge them?[5]

A more threatening shadow for the family was Fred's dwindling fortune. Like Herbert Duckworth, Fred had little ambition and minimal interest in his business affairs. He just assumed his substantial income would continue pouring in, but by the time Agatha was about 5 years old there were problems. The trustees of his father's trust had mishandled his financial affairs. The situation was so dire that one of the trustees eventually shot himself.[6] When Fred discovered much of his fortune had been lost, he was devastated.[7] To economise, the family let out Ashfield and travelled abroad, where the cost of living was lower. Loyally, Clara did not criticise her husband, instead she just made the most of the situation. Staying in hotels in France and then the Channel Islands, the family treated it as an adventure and enjoyed the novelty.

Affected by his financial worries, Fred's health deteriorated. Doctors were not sure what was wrong with him; one diagnosed kidney disease, another heart problems. When Agatha overheard her mother and sister discussing her father's illness, she felt a 'shadow' was cast over her happy childhood. She did not totally understand what was going on, but it was like 'one of those atmospheric disturbances which are to the psychic world as an approaching thunderstorm is to the physical one'. [8] Both parents did their best to make life as normal as possible for their daughter. How they handled this worrying situation was the final affirmation of their love. They fought against the illness as a team, each trying to stay strong for the other's sake, while secretly realising they were fighting a losing battle.

Fred continued with his normal routine for as long as possible. An undemanding patient, he was as affable in his illness as he had been during the rest of his life. Putting aside any melodramatic tendencies, when faced with a real crisis Clara hid her anxieties and devotedly nursed her husband. As Fred suffered a series of 'heart attacks' often late at night, she sat up with him when he was breathless and reassured him that he would be all right. In the Christie Archive there is a piece of paper on which Fred recorded the dates and severity of each of his 'heart attacks'. The frequency increased throughout the year. [9] All his doctor could recommend was fresh air, moderate exercise and dietary supplements.

Continuing to believe 'where there's a will there's a way', Clara desperately searched for alternative treatments. [10] She refused to give up hope. We get an insight into her attitude in *Unfinished Portrait*, as the mother was always talking of what they would do when Daddy was better. [11] However, even Clara's strong will could not pull her husband through. As Fred's illness escalated, so did his money worries. Once again overhearing snippets of conversation, Agatha's active imagination ran away with her, and she thought the family would be ruined. Rather than hide what was happening from her daughter, thus turning it into a frightening secret, Clara wisely decided to explain the situation honestly to Agatha. As usual, her mother allayed her fears, reassuring her that the situation was not as bad as she imagined, and the family would just have to economise. [12]

At this time of enormous pressure on the family, Clara was the person who had to be strong and keep calm for the sake of everyone else; she was the lynchpin who held the family together. Fred was worried all the strain was making her ill too. While they were separated, he wrote to her, 'I never dare ask about your own health for I fear you are but poorly and you would never tell me if you felt ever so badly. I shall not feel happy until I have you home again.' [13]

While he consulted a leading heart specialist, Fred stayed with Margaret in Ealing. The doctor told him the problem was with the nerves of the heart. Knowing how worried Clara was, Fred tried to reassure her. He wrote:

> I am now, please God, done with doctors and hope I may get better soon. Love to my dear ones. [...] I hope this letter will make you feel happier and I think you will see, as it's true, that I certainly am.[14]

While her father was away, Agatha sent him a letter saying how much she loved and missed him.[15] Reflecting how much it meant to him, Fred kept it safely in his wallet.

Returning to London in November to look for a job, Frederick developed pneumonia. Separated from Clara, he wrote a final letter expressing his feelings for her. He explained:

> You have made all the difference in my life. No man ever had a wife like you. Every year I have been married to you I love you more. I thank you for your affection and love and sympathy. God bless you my dearest, we shall soon be together again.[16]

Distraught at the news, his wife and daughters rushed to be with him. Clara stayed with him day and night. Nurses cared for him, but they could not save him. On 26 November 1901, Fred died aged 55 when Agatha was just 11 years old. Like Virginia and Sylvia who lost a parent at a similar age, she would vividly recall what happened for the rest of her life. She wrote about it in both her autobiography and her novel *Unfinished Portrait*; the descriptions are very similar and give a detailed picture of this traumatic time. Agatha was standing on the landing when her mother burst out of Fred's bedroom with her hands held over her eyes. She rushed to the next-door room and shut the door behind her without even noticing her little girl. In *Unfinished Portrait*, the mother is described as 'like a leaf driven before the wind', her arms 'were thrown up to heaven, she was moaning'. She had never seen her mother distraught before.[17] For Agatha it must have been reminiscent of her worst nightmare; the gunman's eyes staring out of the familiar face.

It was left to the nurse to tell Agatha that her father had died.[18] Never imagining such a terrible thing could happen, it came as a complete shock. She went out into the garden to try to take it all in and began to cry.[19] In similar terms to Virginia and Sylvia, Agatha later wrote about the disorienting experience of losing a parent. The familiar suddenly became unfamiliar. Like Virginia, she found the all-consuming Victorian approach to mourning oppressive and frightening. Margaret's house took on a 'somewhat ghoulish character', as it filled with whispering relatives dressed in black.[20] In the novel, the little girl did not like all the blinds down; it changed the atmosphere of the house.[21]

Agatha was considered too young to go to the funeral, which she thought was unfair. Instead, she stayed at home with Margaret, roaming around the house in a distressed state.[22] What was particularly destabilising for a child was that the bereavement not only deprived her of her father, it also altered her mother. Clara was no longer the indestructible figure she always seemed. In her novel, Agatha describes the widowed mother as looking unfamiliar and fragile in her mourning outfit.[23]

In the order of service for the funeral, Clara kept two cuttings which expressed her yearning for her husband. The first, entitled 'In Absence', describes how she longs for his physical presence but her feelings for him have not changed, 'I love thee, dream thee, love thee and adore.' Beneath this verse she clipped another quotation, which is equally poignant. 'I cannot reach thee with these arms [...] But closely in my soul do I embrace thee and hold thee.'[24]

Like Julia and Leslie when they lost their partners, Clara followed the morbid Victorian tradition of saving relics left by her loved one. She preserved some beech leaves from the Ealing cemetery and kept a few of his pale brown hairs. Unlike the Stephens, the Millers did not make a cult of mourning or prolong it more than necessary. After the funeral they tried to make life carry on as usual.[25] There is no doubt that Clara was as devastated as first Julia and then Leslie Stephen had been by the loss of their soulmates, but she handled the situation differently. At first, she shut herself away in her bedroom and did not eat anything.[26] However, unlike both the Stephens, Clara's love for her daughter was at least as powerful as her bond with her husband, and that was the saving grace for her. It made her control her own feelings and think about Agatha's needs more than her own. Knowing the depth of their mother–daughter relationship, the family realised Agatha was the one person who could provide Clara with a reason to carry on. The bewildered 11-year-old was told that she must be 'mamma's little comforter'. She should go to her mother's bedroom and tell her that Fred was now happy in heaven. It was a heavy burden to place on a little girl but, obedient as ever, she did as she was told.

In *Unfinished Portrait*, Agatha described the experience. As the little girl went into the dark room, she saw her mother lying on her side, with her brown hair streaked with grey fanning out around her. Her eyes looked strange, as if they were staring at 'something beyond'. Her mother then smiled at her, but it was not a genuine smile and it seemed as if she was not there.[27] When Agatha tentatively said to her mother, 'Mummy, father is at peace now. He is happy. You wouldn't want him back, would you?', Clara vehemently replied, 'Yes I would, I would do anything in the world to have him back – anything, anything at all. I'd force him to come back, if I could. I want him, I want him back <u>here</u>, now.'[28]

With her mother seeming so out of control, Agatha felt afraid. Noticing the effect on her daughter, Clara immediately changed her tone and resumed the role of a reassuring parent. Explaining that she was not well, she promised it would be all right. After her mother kissed her, Agatha felt more secure.[29] Once she had gone, the nurse told the widow that she must now live for her children. She replied 'in a strange docile voice', 'Yes, I've got to live for my children. You needn't tell me that. I know it.'[30]

This is one of the pivotal moments in Agatha's life, which perhaps partly explains why she recovered from the premature death of her parent with fewer long-term repercussions than Virginia or Sylvia. Unlike Aurelia Plath, who when she lost her husband repressed her emotions and hid her suffering from her children, Clara did not conceal from Agatha how devastated she was. Although it was painful to witness her mother's grief, in the long run it was probably better for her mental health because a child senses when an adult is hiding the truth. Clara's reaction reflected the closeness of their relationship; if she had put on a façade, Agatha might have felt that she had in effect lost both parents. It would have been as terrifying as her recurring nightmare of the gunman. In *Unfinished Portrait*, the daughter felt unhappy until she realised that she still understood what her mother was feeling.[31] Their indestructible bond meant that neither Clara nor Agatha felt so isolated.

Unlike both Julia and Leslie Stephen, there was no hint of self-indulgence in Clara's grief. After a period of mourning, she forced herself to get on with her new life. Perhaps because she had enjoyed such a good relationship with her husband and felt no guilt, she was able to move forward and put her daughters first. After a holiday in France with Madge, she returned to Ashfield with Agatha. Without her husband Clara would never be as content again, but she still had a compelling reason to live.

19

The Widow

After Fred's death, Agatha and Clara's relationship entered a new, more intense phase. When Madge got married on 11 September 1902, mother and daughter were left alone together. It was not easy for Clara to let her eldest daughter go so soon after losing her husband, and after the wedding she went to bed, totally exhausted.[1] However, she knew that it was the right thing for Madge. Her bridegroom was James Watts, an Oxford graduate, the son of Clara's best friend. He came from a wealthy family, who owned a large gothic mansion, Abney Hall, in Cheadle, Cheshire. Both Clara and Agatha were delighted with the match; James was an unassuming man who was kind to his mother- and sister-in-law. They enjoyed spending Christmases at Abney Hall and it was to provide Agatha with inspiration for her country house mysteries.

For Agatha, losing a parent ended her childhood and marked the end of normal family life. Inevitably, this abrupt alteration temporarily shattered her security. Although Agatha had always been more dependent on her mother, she had been brought up to believe that the man of the family gave the home stability.[2] Physically affected by her bereavement, Clara developed heart problems and for the first time Agatha experienced anxiety. Waking up in the night in a panic fearing her mother might also die, she would creep along the corridor and listen outside her bedroom door to make sure that she was still breathing. She moved into Clara's dressing room, so that she could be with her if she suddenly became ill. In her autobiography, Agatha admitted that she was 'always overburdened with imagination'; this could be a curse in her private life, making her worry, but it was a great gift in her career.[3]

During her teenage years, like Clara at the same age, Agatha enjoyed writing poetry. Her mother's influence was evident in her early verse. Clara's Dresden figures of the Italian *commedia dell'arte* inspired a series of poems about the Harlequin.[4] Her mother's history lessons also provided Agatha with colourful characters to write about. Even her love poetry was reminiscent of Clara's teenage verse as they were both romantically death obsessed,[5] though Agatha already showed a literary ability which surpassed her mother's. Some of her poems won prizes and were accepted by *The Poetry Review*; she later published them in a collection entitled *The Road of Dreams*.[6]

Agatha's poetry allowed her to express powerful emotions. One of her early poems, *Down in the Wood*, gives an insight into her fears. Reading like her descriptions of her intense reaction to the gunman in her dreams, it has a nightmarish quality as, 'Fear – naked Fear passes out of the wood!'[7]

Growing up fast, Agatha began to feel responsible for Clara. But, unlike Virginia or Sylvia, she did not blame her surviving parent and she willingly put her mother first. Alone together at Ashfield, mother and daughter became each other's world. They lived together harmoniously, sharing many cultural interests. As they both enjoyed the theatre, Clara organised outings to the latest plays. Agatha remembered the spellbinding performance by Sir Henry Irving in Tennyson's *Becket* at Exeter for the rest of her life.

Unlike Aurelia Plath, who expected Sylvia to study the text before seeing a production, Clara and Agatha associated plays purely with pleasure. The Miller family all loved the theatre and regularly went to performances. As Agatha grew older, she enjoyed taking part in local amateur dramatics; it was by chance rather than design, however, that these early experiences sowed seeds that would turn Agatha into one of the most successful women playwrights of all time. Rather than approaching Shakespeare as a scholar, she built a relationship with the bard as an audience member.[8] She believed that Shakespeare could be ruined by making children study it at school. Instead, if they saw it performed even young children responded enthusiastically to it.[9] Virginia Woolf shared Agatha's view about the importance of an instinctive rather than purely intellectualised reaction.[10] Throughout her life, Agatha related to Shakespeare as a real person and was fascinated by his characters.

Mother and daughter also spent companionable evenings reading the classics to each other. Unlike with Aurelia and Sylvia, this was not treated as an academic exercise. Bouncing ideas around, they started with Sir Walter Scott and moved on to Dickens then Thackeray. Neither woman was afraid to admit that they found some of Thackeray's novels difficult. Clara had no time for Sir Walter Scott's superfluous descriptions and if there were boring bits, she deftly edited them out. Nor was she interested in morbid sentimentality, cutting out 'the sob stuff in Dickens, particularly the bits about Little Nell'.[11] Clara's taste influenced her daughter's later literary style, as Agatha's plots were tight – without excess descriptions or mawkish sentimentality. She enjoyed writing plays because she could go straight to the plot rather than having to describe scenes.[12]

Mother and daughter got on so well because they were compatible but not too similar; Agatha believed that she was more like Fred than Clara. When she was 13, her answers in Confessions are reminiscent of his replies. Her chief characteristic was 'living in the present', her idea of happiness was 'to make the best of everything', and she gave the same answer as him when asked 'If not yourself, who would you be?' 'Nobody.' It seems that her father's death did not permanently upset her equilibrium and she was looking forward to the future with 'Expectation'.[13] In *Unfinished Portrait*, Agatha described the daughter as inheriting her 'placidity, her even temper, her sweetness', from her father.[14] Her paternal legacy tempered the sensitivity and imagination she inherited from Clara. With her husband gone, Mrs Miller found in Agatha the stable companion she needed. There were occasional tensions, but both women were considerate and willing to compromise.

Unfortunately, Fred's financial problems meant economising. Clara considered selling Ashfield and moving to something smaller, but her children were horrified at the idea. Agatha could not bear the thought of losing her home so shortly after the loss of her father. Influenced by her daughter, Clara changed her mind.[15] Instead, Mrs Miller sold some antique furniture and cut back on entertaining. Lavish dinner parties were replaced with simple suppers and the number of servants was cut.

In poor health, Clara rarely went out and was usually in bed early, so after supper Agatha was left to her own devices. In the evenings she played the piano and sang for several hours until her mother complained it was disturbing her sleep.[16] Alone for much of the time, Agatha turned again to her imaginary friends, creating elaborate plots about their lives.[17] Although she was too loyal to criticise the change in their circumstances, her autobiography suggests that life at Ashfield could be rather dull for an exuberant teenager. She longed for Madge's visits in the summer, when the house was once again filled with her sister's vivacity.[18]

Clara was too self-aware to allow Agatha's happiness to be sacrificed for long. Perhaps she was concerned that they were becoming too dependent on each other.[19] Widening her social circles, Agatha was sent to a girls' school in Torquay; her mother encouraged her to go to parties, roller-skate on the pier, play croquet and tennis with her friends, and take part in amateur dramatics. Wanting her daughter to have opportunities she missed, Clara decided that Agatha should go to finishing school in Paris. At a tea party in London, Mrs Miller met Mrs Hamilton-Johnston, who was sending her daughter Dorothy to France. It was agreed that the two girls would go together to Miss Dryden's finishing school near the Arc de Triomphe. Clara travelled with Agatha across the Channel and then left her there. For the first week the teenager suffered from dreadful homesickness because she had been inseparable from her mother. She could not eat and cried every time she thought of Clara. However, once she had seen her again and told her about her homesickness, Agatha felt better and made the most of her Parisian life.

Being apart made Agatha look at Clara more objectively. Seeing her as a separate person rather than just her parent, she loved her even more. In *Unfinished Portrait*, the daughter expressed Agatha's feelings, 'Her mother – oh, there was no one like her mother in the whole world.'[20] Fellow pupil Dorothy Hamilton-Johnston recalled Agatha's 'complete attachment to her mother'.[21] Fortunately, there was no more homesickness and Dorothy remembered Agatha as 'always vivacious, the life and soul of the party and ready for the next adventure'.[22] The time Agatha spent at finishing school introduced her to a wider world.[23] Vying within her were two opposing strands of her personality; part of her craved the security of home, but the other part wanted to be free. As she wrote in her poem 'Heritage', she was excited by the prospect of 'Halcyon days to be'.[24]

20

The Confidante

The most important characteristic Agatha inherited from Clara was 'a dangerous intensity of affection'.[1] This capacity to feel an overpowering love for another person was something all six women in this book shared. It was at the heart of who they were and it made their feelings for the people they loved incredibly intense and potentially dangerous. It was to shape all the mothers' lives and the daughters' writing, giving their literary works a power and authenticity which could never be achieved by less passionate authors.

Like Clara as a teenager, Agatha's romantic nature had been fired by the books she read. The novel which really captured her imagination was *The Prisoner of Zenda* by Anthony Hope. The daring hero, Rudolf Rassendyll, who fell in love with Princess Flavia, filled her dreams. Agatha's expectations were not just based in fantasy; she had observed her parents' relationship and she wanted to experience an equally enduring partnership. Clara's attitude to her daughter's love life had a degree of ambivalence. She wished Agatha to have a happy marriage, but part of her did not want her daughter's love for her husband to take her away from her. However, once again it seems that her self-awareness asserted itself and she realised this possessive attitude was unfair. In *Unfinished Portrait*, the mother admitted to her daughter that 'it's very hard [...] for mothers not to be selfish'.[2]

As Agatha grew into an attractive young woman, her mother wanted her to experience all the things that she had missed. Even though she could hardly afford it, Clara was determined Agatha should have pretty clothes and some sort of debutante season. Her attitude was very similar to Hannah, the mother of two daughters in Agatha's play *The Lie*. Hannah confesses, 'I live again in my children [...] There's nothing I wouldn't do for them, steal, borrow or beg for their sake. If only I could see them both happily married.'[3]

Despite coming from a long line of strong women, Agatha was no feminist. Unlike Virginia, she felt no need to rebel against her mother and her attitude to female roles was conventional and conservative. In her autobiography, Agatha claimed that she was never ambitious; she most desired to get married to a man she loved. Observing her mother's and grandmothers' lives, she understood the importance of marrying a respectable, financially secure man. Once married, she looked forward to being cherished, but she had no intention of becoming a subservient trophy wife. The young women in her circle planned to put their husbands' needs first, but they intended to get their own way in the things which mattered to them.[4]

In an era when eugenic ideas were fashionable, finding the right husband was not just for personal happiness, it was also seen as part of a woman's patriotic duty. Christie scholar Julius Green believes that Agatha was influenced by George Bernard Shaw's philosophy. In *Man and Superman* Shaw promoted the idea that the development of the species was driven by a woman's success in finding the right partner biologically rather than financially or socially. He described this quest as 'The Life Force'. [5]

It may have been Agatha's duty to find her soulmate, but she also found it great fun. Unlike Virginia, as a young woman Agatha was intoxicated by the idea of romance. She loved the frisson flirtations brought to her life and the sexual chemistry involved. She saw the dynamic between men and women as thrilling, not threatening.[6] In her autobiography she described with relish anticipating what would happen and whom she would marry. It was the big question in life, and all other concerns dimmed in comparison.[7] There was 'no worry about what you should be or do [...] You were waiting for The Man and when the man came, he would change your entire life!' She recognised that it was in the hands of Fate and a gamble, but that made it even more exciting.[8]

When Agatha was old enough to 'come out' in society, Clara could not afford to give her daughter a London season. She was determined Agatha should have the next best thing, however, so they went to Egypt. In 1910, Clara had been seriously ill with a condition which doctors had been unable to satisfactorily diagnose; they suggested she might be suffering from gallstones, paratyphoid or appendicitis.[9] Going to Egypt was an adventure which could provide Agatha with a stimulating social life and Clara with the warm weather to recuperate.[10] Auntie-Grannie disapproved and grumbled that it was an unnecessary extravagance, but Clara was not to be deterred.[11] Margaret had prevented her from making the most of her own youth; she would not allow the same mistake to be repeated with her daughter.

For a sheltered young girl from Torquay, Cairo seemed very glamorous. There was a heady exoticism in the atmosphere as convalescent invalids, matchmaking mothers and their eager daughters mingled with military men in the Egyptian heat. There was no shortage of eligible suitors in uniform to partner Agatha. Staying in the Gezirah Palace Hotel for three months, life became one long round of polo matches, picnics and parties. Agatha was at that ephemeral age where every experience is fresh; her first evening dresses, carefully chosen with Clara, confections of pastel chiffons and embroidered satin, would remain etched on her memory. Capturing 'the close conspiracy' which exists between mothers and daughters, Agatha described in *Unfinished Portrait* how, despite make-up being considered taboo, each evening before they went out the mothers used to dab some rouge on their daughters' cheeks to make sure they looked their most attractive.[12] Living vicariously through her daughter, the older woman felt it more intensely than the younger one if another girl outshone her.[13] This was rarely a problem for Agatha. Going to five dances each week, she was transformed from a shy teenager into a confident young woman who was well aware of her feminine power.[14]

After their three-month adventure in Egypt, Clara and Agatha returned to Devon reinvigorated. The Cairo sojourn turned out to be just as Clara had intended; Agatha had enjoyed some light-hearted romances which prepared her for finding the real thing once she came home. Acting as her chaperone, Clara had carefully steered her daughter's love life in the right direction. It was only on the boat back to England that she informed Agatha that one of her suitors had told her that he wanted to marry her. Clara had successfully deterred him by saying her daughter was not in love with him. For once Agatha was annoyed with her mother; she had not wanted to marry the captain, but she would have liked to make the decision for herself. As usual in their relationship, they listened to each other and compromised. Clara remembered what it was like to be Agatha's age and understood that naturally she would like to deal with her own proposals.[15] As they were honest with each other, no lasting damage was done to their relationship.

Back in Devon, Agatha's successful social life continued. With her Scandinavian good looks of long red-gold hair, flawless complexion and soulful, heavy-lidded eyes, she was attractive to men and received many proposals. Clara admitted that no man seemed good enough for her beloved daughter, but she liked some of Agatha's suitors more than others.[16] Aware of her daughter's 'peculiar vulnerability' and knowing her own health was fragile and money was in short supply, she wanted to see her daughter married to a kind man like her late husband.[17] He needed to be someone who would take care of Agatha when Clara was dead.[18] Reflecting the pervasive double standard of the era, Mrs Miller had no problem with the idea of her innocent daughter marrying an experienced older man who had sowed 'his wild oats'.[19]

Influenced by her mother, there were two men whom her mother liked that Agatha seriously considered marrying. One was the son of family friends, another a naval officer. However, although they were eminently suitable and marriage to them would have meant her relationship with her mother remaining largely unchanged, there was something missing – she was not passionately in love, and she would have been marrying to please her mother rather than herself. She wanted to make Clara happy but, aware of her own emotional needs, she realised that would not ultimately be enough.[20] Mrs Miller understood that Agatha could not marry until she was in a relationship which satisfied that deep yearning. In *Unfinished Portrait*, the mother warns her daughter, 'You're a romantic, and a Fairy Prince – that sort of thing doesn't happen. So few women marry the man they are romantically in love with.'[21]

Agatha's romances were always a family affair with not just Clara but the whole matriarchy vetting potential suitors and giving advice. When Margaret Miller could no longer live by herself in Ealing she moved in with Clara and Agatha in Torquay. A highlight of her grandmother's increasingly restricted life was joining Agatha and her friends in the schoolroom after supper. Wanting to share their fun and know what was going on, it was the one time she stayed up late. Agatha admitted that part of her wished her grandmother would not come but in retrospect she was glad that she never discouraged her.[22]

Auntie-Grannie had no qualms about intervening in her granddaughter's love life. Although at times it could be unhelpful, her intentions were to help her make the best possible match. Still in thrall to the Victorian idea of 'interesting illness',[23] she used to tell Agatha's boyfriends how delicate her granddaughter's health was in the belief that it would make her even more attractive to them. An indignant Agatha would insist she was perfectly healthy.[24]

In her play *The Lie*, both the mother and grandmother are deeply involved in the younger generation's love lives, intervening as they feel necessary. When she could do little else, Margaret used to sit in her chair knitting;[25] this image evidently inspired the grandmother in *The Lie*. The old lady says to her granddaughter, 'We old folk, who sit and knit so quietly see more than you think.'[26] In her autobiography, written near the end of her own life, Agatha writes with great empathy about her grandmother.[27] Although she was more thoughtful than most young people, looking back Agatha chastised herself for being self-centred and not sympathetic enough about her grandmother's suffering.[28] This understanding of the elderly was to inform Agatha's literature; she portrays old women with an accuracy which came from close observation.

Every day, Agatha read the newspapers to Auntie-Grannie, lingering on the more melodramatic stories which appealed to Margaret. Perhaps reading these lurid accounts helped to fire her imagination with future plots. Like her grandmother, she was fascinated by why some people deviated from normal behaviour. Margaret Miller had a strong moral compass which she passed on to her granddaughter. Agatha's detective novels are modern morality tales about the struggle of good and evil. There was no room for relativism in Agatha's world; she was a defender of moral absolutes, right and wrong.[29]

Auntie-Grannie inspired some of Agatha's most memorable characters. Although Agatha denied it was an exact portrait, there are shades of Margaret Miller in Miss Marple. Both shared 'powers of prophecy', expected the worst and were usually proved right.[30] Agatha explained that although Margaret had led the most sheltered of Victorian lives, she 'always appeared to be intimately acquainted with the depths of depravity. One could be made to feel incredibly naïve and credulous by her reproachful remark, "But did you believe what they said to you? I never do!"'[31] It was not just her most famous female heroine who drew on Auntie-Grannie. A recurring theme in Agatha's fiction is that elderly ladies should never be underestimated; they are often the cleverest characters, who observe every detail and come to the right conclusions.

A sense of duty had been instilled in Agatha by Clara. Although Margaret had not always been generous in her youth, Clara forgave her and treated her with kindness. Observing her mother, Agatha saw how a daughter should behave; it was not about sentimental words but sympathetic actions. This period bonded the three generations of women even more tightly because instead of just thinking of themselves, they thought of each other.

Sex was one of the few things Clara was not totally open with her daughter about. Like most Edwardian mothers, Clara did not explain to Agatha the facts of life. When Madge was pregnant, Agatha imagined the baby would come out of her sister's navel.[32] As usual with Clara, there was a degree of inconsistency in her approach. At one moment she wanted to keep her youngest daughter innocent, even objecting to her displaying her legs in public when she was acting in amateur dramatics, and making her wear stockings while swimming.[33] At another moment, she was concerned that Agatha was too naïve, so she encouraged her to read gritty novels by the French realist novelists, which would expose her to the harsh realities of life.[34] Inevitably, Auntie-Grannie joined in too, providing a far from sentimental education for her inexperienced granddaughter. In *Unfinished Portrait*, the grandmother offers 'dark hints' about the difficulties of married life. She was surprisingly candid about the dangers of contracting a sexually transmitted disease from a husband or marrying a man who then had an affair with one of the servants.[35]

This ambivalence about sex education was typical of Clara's generation; many mothers only enlightened their daughters when they were about to get married, or even left them to be initiated on their wedding night. Unlike Virginia and Sylvia, Agatha did not rebel against her mother's sexual codes; she accepted the double standard for men and women. Even decades later, in a period of greater sexual freedom, she championed the concept of purity for young girls. In her autobiography, she explained, 'I do not think we felt in the least repressed because of it. Romantic friendships, tinged certainly with sex or the possibility of sex, satisfied us completely.'[36]

21

Literary Ambitions

As photographs of a radiant Agatha having fun with her friends show, she enjoyed her social life to the full, but there was another private side of her which needed expression. Her inner self could only be released through the arts. Agatha had a great love of music and dreamed of becoming a concert pianist or an opera singer, but her fear of performing and the limitations of her voice meant she eventually ruled these options out. Writing was another way for her to express herself and as both her mother and sister wrote short stories, it was natural for her to follow in their footsteps. Clara was the person who first encouraged Agatha to become a writer. Reflecting on her power over her daughter, Agatha's grandson Mathew Prichard says, 'When Clara told her to write a book, what did she do? She wrote a book.'[1]

In Agatha's first attempts at storytelling the voice sounds more like her mother's than her own; the unworldly themes are a far cry from her later crime fiction. Max Mallowan described his wife's more fanciful stories as 'a natural product of Agatha's peculiar imagination'.[2] Her unorthodox way of perceiving the world was inherited from Clara. In *Unfinished Portrait*, the mother is described as having something of the mystic about her as she had 'a vision, a perception of unseen things'.[3] While Clara was alive, the 'peculiar imagination' that mother and daughter shared was given free rein in Agatha's writing, while later it made only occasional appearances.

The sole surviving story by Clara is 'Mrs Jordan's Ghost', a morality tale and ghost story narrated by the unhappy spirit of a dead woman. Shortly before her death, a man comes into Mrs Jordan's music shop and plays a piano she is selling. His 'soft sweet' music awakens her soul and as she listens a rhyme about a restless spirit, condemned to wander the earth because of a crime committed in the past, comes into her head. The man agrees to buy the piano and leaves, but the rhyme continues repeating for Mrs Jordan, making her feel that she will go mad because it reminds her of past transgressions.

During the night Mrs Jordan becomes ill and dies, but her soul remains trapped because of her guilty past. When the man takes the piano to his home, her spirit goes with him and hovers over his family. Whenever he plays the haunting music, 'an unknown power' touches her soul and her ghost appears. Gradually, the music transforms her and, observing the family's kindness to each other, Mrs Jordan repents of her sins. Finding redemption, her spirit is freed, and she joins 'a choir of voices, rich with melody and love'.[4]

The sentimental tone and subject matter of her story was very Victorian and, other than a skill at creating suspense, it demonstrates minimal literary merit. However, it does illustrate Clara's influence on her daughter's writing as similar themes appear in her early fiction. Agatha later described her juvenile works as 'stories of unrelieved gloom in which most of the characters died'.[5]

According to Agatha, her writing began as a pastime but developed into a passion. When she was about 17 years old and recovering from influenza, Clara suggested that she should try writing a story to entertain herself. At first Agatha was unsure, but her mother convinced her saying, 'Of course you can, darling. You just begin <u>now</u>.'[6] Clara then brought her an exercise book used for laundry lists and Agatha started writing. She thoroughly enjoyed it and her 6,000-word story, 'The House of Beauty', just flowed.

Influenced by Edgar Allan Poe and M.R. James, in 'The House of Beauty' Agatha wrote about the boundaries between the real and imaginary world. The story expressed many of Clara and Agatha's shared preoccupations. Reflecting their mutual love of Ashfield, it features an enchanting white house on a hill, which appears to the hero, John Segrave, in a dream. At first it is an image of perfect beauty, but his dreams take on a terrifying quality (reminiscent of Agatha's nightmares about the gunman) when he senses a malevolent 'Thing' lurking within. Segrave's feelings for the house become linked to his attraction to Allegra Innes Carr, a fragile young woman, who is psychic and has such a sensitive soul that her 'perfect comprehension left her defenceless'.[7]

When they first meet, John and Allegra experience an immediate rapport. Echoing Clara's idea in 'Mrs Jordan's Ghost' that the spiritual side of a person is released through music, Allegra reveals her inner self by playing the piano brilliantly. Allegra's genius is 'akin to madness', however, and her performances become disturbing when she plays discordant notes as though she is possessed.[8] The curse of hereditary insanity stalks the story, suggesting the mental illness in Clara's family concerned both mother and daughter.[9]

Although the plot occasionally verges on gothic melodrama, 'The House of Beauty' is a gripping tale which showed Agatha's potential as a writer. Like Clara, she knew how to build suspense and intrigue her readers, but she already demonstrated a literary ability which eluded her mother.[10] When Clara read it, she instantly recognised Agatha was a natural storyteller. Perhaps sensing that her daughter could succeed where she had failed, Clara gave her Madge's old typewriter and encouraged her to write more.

Growing in confidence, Agatha followed in Madge's footsteps and was soon sending off short stories to magazines under the pseudonyms Mac Miller, Nathaniel Miller and Sydney West. At first, she did not have much success, but, undeterred, she continued to polish her craft. Some of the early stories later appeared in magazines and in a collection of twelve short stories published as *The Hound of Death* in 1933. Written between her teenage years and her late thirties, their tone varies but the majority are about mental or psychic disturbance.

In many of them we still hear Clara's voice, but others begin to sound more like the mature Agatha. 'The Lamp' has so many echoes of 'Mrs Jordan's Ghost' it could have been written by the same hand. In the story, Mrs Lancaster buys a house which is haunted by a little boy. She does not believe in ghosts, but her father and young son see the spirit of the dead child. Like Mrs Jordan, the boy's ghost is trapped on earth and lonely, but once he connects with the living child, he finally finds peace. Even the style of Agatha's and Clara's stories is similar; a rhyme is repeated, and the ending is equally sentimental.[11]

Although other stories in *The Hound of Death* are less overtly like Clara's, their exploration of the supernatural is part of her literary legacy. Mother and daughter's shared interest in psychic phenomena was far from unique, but the way they tried to reconcile it with their faith was more unusual.

Orthodox Christianity taught that you should not dabble in the occult. But since both Clara and Agatha knew from personal experience that some people had 'the gift', the question was 'how to use it?'

In the late Victorian and Edwardian era there was a growing interest in psychic phenomena, which became even more common after the carnage of the First World War as grieving families desperately tried to communicate with their lost loved ones. In 1882, the Society for Psychical Research had been set up to understand psychic or paranormal events and abilities. Their areas of study included hypnotism, dissociations, thought-transference, mediumship, apparitions and haunted houses.

Agatha's early short stories deal with these phenomena and show a detailed knowledge of the latest thinking. Her approach to the super-natural is carefully nuanced and, like Clara in 'Mrs Jordan's Ghost', any sensationalism is tempered by a strong moral message. Agatha was sympa-thetic to characters who try to discover the laws of the universe to increase knowledge, but critical of those who experiment for their own egotistical ends. In her stories, there are people who genuinely have psychic powers, but there are also plenty of charlatans who fake supernatural phenomena or exploit it for financial gain.[12] In 'The Last Séance', the medium, Madame Simone, is genuinely able to communicate with the spirit world, but she is increasingly reluctant to use her gift. Her fiancé persuades her to do so one final time, with dire consequences for them both.[13] The message is clear: there are forces we do not yet completely understand, and they must be handled with care.

'The Last Séance' also examines another primitive elemental force which can be dangerous: the maternal instinct. Madame Simone's nemesis is Madame Exe, a bereaved mother who wants to contact her dead child. The medium says that she is afraid of the word 'mother', explaining, 'A mother's love for her child is like nothing else in the world. It knows no law, no pity, it does all things and crushes down remorselessly all that stands in its path.'[14] This idea that obsessive maternal love can be destruc-tive was to recur in Agatha's later novels. Virginia Woolf felt the same, writing in her novel *The Waves* about 'the bestial and beautiful passion of maternity'.[15] In a letter to her sister Vanessa, she described maternal pas-sion as 'immeasurable and unscrupulous'. Claiming Vanessa would 'fry us to cinders' for her daughter, she added, 'You are a mere tool in the hands of passion. [...] I don't like profound instincts – not in human relationships.'[16]

In her later fiction, Agatha continued writing about primal passions but in a less overt way. As she grew older, her mother's voice faded to just an occasional whisper; her mature authorial voice was more down-to-earth and less moralistic than Clara's. Her most successful plots were firmly rooted in the material rather than spiritual world and supernatural occurrences usually had a rational explanation.

Enjoying writing short stories, Agatha began to write her first novel, *Snow Upon the Desert*, which drew on her recent trip to Egypt. Acting as her sounding board, Clara suggested that she should get advice from their family friend Eden Phillpotts. The experienced author complimented her on her realistic dialogue but advised her to cut out the moralising tone.[17] Although he recognised her potential, in their circles it was more acceptable for a young woman to be an amateur lady writer than a serious professional author. Mr Phillpotts advised, 'Art is second to life and if you are living just now (we only live by fits and starts) then put art out of your mind absolutely.'[18] Agatha could never completely forget her writing, but her focus was about to turn elsewhere as one of those rare moments of intense living finally arrived.

22

Growing Apart

In October 1912, Agatha went to a dance at Ugbrooke House, Chudleigh given by Lord and Lady Clifford. That evening was to change the course of her life. Archie Christie, a debonair young man with curly blond hair, had come down from the garrison at Exeter for the party. He danced very well and had an easy charm and confidence. The chemistry between Agatha and Archie was so intoxicating, he decided that first night she was the woman he wanted to marry. A few days later, Archie appeared on his motorbike at Ashfield. Only Clara was there when he arrived but on Agatha's return, using the code they had devised for these occasions, Clara found out that her daughter wanted him to stay for supper. The evening went well, and Archie was soon a regular visitor.[1]

Immediately, Clara sensed that Archie Christie was different from Agatha's other suitors. Trying to keep control over her daughter's life, she stipulated that they could go to a concert together but not have tea in a hotel; however, suddenly such inconsistencies made her rules seem arbitrary.[2] Agatha was falling in love and experiencing emotions she had never felt before. It was a case of opposites attracting. Archie and Agatha had very different personalities but that made him even more exciting. Compared to her other mild-mannered boyfriends there was a hint of danger; he was a brave young man who was not afraid of anything. A second lieutenant in the Royal Field Artillery, he was about to join the newly formed Royal Flying Corps. His single-minded determination to marry her made her previous boyfriends' affections seem lukewarm.

When Agatha and Archie got engaged it was 'a terrible shock' for Clara.[3] He represented a threat to her relationship with her daughter as the pull of sexual attraction competed with Agatha's filial devotion. He was the one man who could take her daughter away from her physically and emotionally. A good judge of character, it seems Clara had doubts whether a man as handsome as Archie would stay faithful. Aware of Agatha's vulnerability, she was afraid he would hurt her sensitive daughter. Another anxiety was that Archie had only his subaltern's pay and a small allowance. When Clara quizzed the young man about his prospects it did little to endear her to her future son-in-law.[4]

Once Agatha had made up her mind, Clara had no choice but to accept the situation. A similar dynamic plays out in *Unfinished Portrait*, where the mother does not trust her daughter's fiancé, but she loves her child too much to cause her pain.[5] Agatha and Archie had a prolonged and often stressful engagement during which they would break off their relationship but then get back together. At one point, Agatha seriously considered giving up her hopes of happiness to stay with her mother because Clara was losing her sight due to cataracts. Archie convinced her such self-sacrifice would be a mistake.

When the First World War began, the intensity of their feelings was heightened by fears Archie would be killed in action. Agatha told her mother she wanted to marry him as soon as possible and, as usual, Clara was able to imagine what she was going through. Mrs Miller admitted that she would have felt the same.[6] No date was fixed for a wedding, but the idea was in Agatha's mind. During Archie's Christmas leave the couple decided to get married in a quickly arranged service in Bristol on Christmas Eve 1914. Although Clara realised it was likely, they did it without telling her beforehand. It was one of the few secrets Agatha ever kept from her mother and the night before she could not stop thinking about what Clara and Madge would say.[7] It was not the type of wedding Clara had dreamt of for her daughter. Dressed in her winter coat and a purple velvet hat, Agatha married Archie in a low-key ceremony attended by just the vicar and a witness.

It was the closest Agatha ever came to rebelling against her mother and it symbolised the competing hold her new husband had over her. Only once she was safely married did she dare telephone Clara to tell her the news. Madge was furious with her for not telling them first and Agatha immediately felt guilty. The newlyweds travelled to Torquay to spend

Christmas Day at Ashfield, and once Clara saw how ecstatic her daughter was, she forgave her.[8]

Thanks to the war, Agatha's life changed very little once she was married. Archie returned to fight, and she continued to live with her mother and grandmother at Ashfield. Trained as a Voluntary Aid Detachment, she worked long hours nursing, then after two years she became an assistant in the dispensary. By taking on a medical role, Agatha was once again fulfilling one of the dreams Clara had been unable to pursue. Although Agatha claimed never to have wanted to be a career girl, circumstances had turned her into a young working woman. The situation only changed when near the end of the war Archie was posted to the Air Ministry in London. Finally, Agatha's married life really began when she left her Torquay home and moved into a small flat in London with her husband. Auntie-Grannie wept when she left, but Clara put on a brave face and wished her well in her new life.[9]

Living away from her mother meant Agatha had to grow up and take on the adult responsibilities of being first a wife and then a mother. She did not find it easy as she was lonely and missed her friends and family. It was hard for Clara too and in *Unfinished Portrait* when the daughter visited her mother, she found her looking wilted; she soon revived once they were reunited.[10] When she became pregnant, Agatha needed Clara more than ever. Returning to Ashfield for the birth, once again her mother took control of her life. The night before the baby was born, Clara was in her element, calmly and efficiently sorting out everything with the nurse. Archie and Agatha were more nervous as they worried that she might die in childbirth, but having her mother with her calmed her and the effect was the same as when she was a child. In *Unfinished Portrait*, during the daughter's labour the mother stays with her holding her hand. The daughter 'instinctively' felt better 'at the sight of that sweet smiling face [...] As in nursery days she felt 'everything would be all right now that Mummy was here'.[11]

On 5 August 1919, Agatha gave birth to a baby girl whom they named Rosalind Margaret Clarissa, reflecting both Agatha's devotion to Shakespeare and her mother and grandmother.[12] Clara's delight at the birth of her granddaughter is captured in a poem she wrote to welcome Rosalind into the world. Her style had hardly changed since she wrote her sentimental verses to Fred half a century earlier. She wrote:

Forth from the Misty Way, jewel of night,
In Luminous zone, is my Rosalind's flight

Describing this rite of passage as 'a miracle', she felt an immediate connection with her granddaughter, writing:

Angels are guarding, and guiding her straight
Heaven has meant her for my divine fate.[13]

Agatha found it easier being a daughter than a mother. She did not immediately feel the instinctive attachment to her child that Clara had felt for her. In *Unfinished Portrait*, the daughter experiences a sense of unreality as though she was 'playing the part of the Young Mother. But she did not feel at all like either a wife or a mother, instead, she felt like a little girl come home after an exciting but tiring party.'[14] In her novels, Agatha explored how different women reacted to motherhood. She divided mothers into two camps: those who put their children first and the others who were more concerned about their husbands. Both by nature and nurture, she was in the latter group.

Trusting Clara more than anyone else, Agatha left her baby with her while she returned to London to be with Archie and sort out a new flat and childcare. Shortly after Rosalind's birth, Margaret Miller died aged 92 and with her death went part of the income which allowed Clara to keep her house. Even though she was now establishing her own home, Agatha's heart belonged to Ashfield, and she still could not bear the thought of it being sold.

Agatha returned as often as possible to Torquay and occasionally gave parties for her friends in her old home. At a fancy-dress 'Poodle Party' all the guests dressed as dogs. While Agatha donned an astrakhan headdress and wore Archie's dinner jacket, a concession was made for Clara, who was allowed to come as a butterfly; it was a far more fitting reflection of her inner self.[15]

23

Agatha Finds Her Niche

Ironically, the young woman who had seen her vocation as marriage was soon to discover that it was easier to be successful in her professional than her private life. Since being a child, Agatha had experimented with different genres. Influenced by her mother, she had already written poetry, short stories and her first novel. She really found her niche, though, when she began to write detective stories. Once again, the instigation had come from within her family, but this time it was her sister Madge, not her mother, who spurred her on.

The two sisters discussed a detective story they had just read which they considered particularly good. Agatha said that she would like to try writing one. Her sister replied that they were very difficult, and she bet Agatha would not be able to do it. Galvanised by her sister's challenge, Agatha was determined to prove her wrong. She did not do it right away, but 'the seed had been sown'.[1]

The idea came to fruition during the First World War when Agatha was working as a pharmacist. As she learned about different medicines which could be used to poison a victim and came across Belgian refugees, she began writing her first Hercule Poirot book. Clara was very enthusiastic about the idea and, like a literary midwife, supported her through the whole process.[2] When Agatha became tangled in the complicated plot, her mother suggested that she should take a holiday and write without any distraction. Agatha took her advice and after a fortnight in a hotel on Dartmoor, only interrupting her writing for walks on the moors, she finished the book.[3] When her first novel, *The Mysterious Affair at Styles*, was finally published in America in 1920 and England in 1921 she acknowledged her mother's influence by dedicating it to her.

The story shows how much Clara's childhood haunted Agatha's imagination. The murder victim Emily Inglethorp's relationship with her stepsons John and Lawrence and her orphaned protégée Cynthia is reminiscent of Clara's feelings for her aunt Margaret. Although Mrs Inglethorp was outwardly kind and generous, she always wanted something in return and never allowed people to forget what she had done for them. Her husband's description of her as a self-sacrificing, noble character sounds like Clara's teenage poem to her aunt; it is platitudinous rather than heartfelt. Mrs Inglethorp, like Mrs Miller, was respected rather than genuinely loved.[4] She was to be the first of a long line of worthy but unlovable matriarchs in Agatha's novels.

At first, Agatha claimed writing a detective story was just an isolated experiment, done to prove her sister wrong and she had no intention of writing more books. She emphasised that she was an amateur rather than a professional and that she treated it as fun.[5] Perhaps part of the reason Agatha played down the importance of her writing was not to alienate her husband. She had been brought up by her mother and grandmother to make men feel superior. Agatha's attitude seems to have been similar to Julia Stephen's; she knew women were intellectually equal and emotionally as strong as men, but she paid lip service to male superiority. Virginia Woolf was well aware of this male need, but she openly challenged it. Even though Sylvia Plath was born decades later than Agatha, she had also absorbed this attitude; it was only towards the end of her life that she openly rebelled against it.

Agatha believed that if a woman used her feminine wiles skilfully she could lead a fulfilling life without alienating her husband.[6] Her attitude makes it sound like a game – where women manipulated the men into doing what they wanted without them realising it. In a passage in her autobiography which could equally have been describing Julia Stephen's modus vivendi, she wrote:

> You've got to hand it to Victorian women, they got their menfolk where they wanted them. They established their frailty, delicacy, sensibility – their constant need of being protected and cherished. Did they lead miserable, servile lives, downtrodden and oppressed? Such is not my recollection of them.[7]

By her own standards, Agatha cleverly played it just right and, rather than feeling threatened by his wife's burgeoning career, Archie supported it. He suggested that she should continue writing to supplement their income. With her husband's consent, she began to approach her writing in a more professional way than she had previously.[8] When she wrote her next story, a newspaper paid £500 to serialise it. Neither Agatha, Archie nor Madge could believe it, but of course Clara could; her faith in her daughter was unshakeable.[9] She was soon earning enough money to buy a larger family home in Sunningdale, Berkshire and the Christies took a flat in Scotswood, a Victorian country house. She was also able to buy her first car and, wanting to share her good fortune with her mother, she drove her Morris Cowley down to Ashfield to take Clara for drives in the countryside.[10]

It seems Agatha was more comfortable being a writer than a mother. Her bond with Rosalind was very different from her rapport with Clara. In *Unfinished Portrait*, the grandmother gets on very well with her granddaughter, but her daughter always comes first. Miriam tells Celia, '"She's not you, my precious." […] Her heart was all Celia's.'[11] However, a letter from Clara to Agatha suggests her bond with her granddaughter was stronger than this quotation suggests. In one of her last letters, Clara sent, 'My love to Rosalind. She knows and understands her Grandma and her Grandma loves and understands her.'[12] This understanding was what had always really mattered in their family relationships. There is no doubt that Agatha loved her daughter deeply and relished watching her develop, but they did not have that unique understanding she had with Clara. Sharing her father's sense of humour, Rosalind was like Archie. Even as a small child it was clear that, unlike her mother and grandmother, she had a practical rather than an imaginative nature.

As a mother, daughter and wife, Agatha was now balancing many competing claims on her. When Rosalind was a toddler, Agatha was faced with a dilemma. Bored with his city job, Archie became the financial adviser on The Empire Tour which was to drum up interest in the Dominions for the Empire Exhibition, due to be held in London in 1924. He wanted his wife to travel with him around the world. Taught by the Miller matriarchy that a wife should put her husband first, even before her children, if she wanted to keep him, Agatha agreed to go with him.[13]

We get an insight into what her thinking might have been in her novel *Ordeal by Innocence*, which explored different models of motherhood.

Comparing a 'normal' mother to a female cat, the local doctor explains, 'She has her kittens, she's passionately protective of them, she'll scratch anyone who goes near them. And then in a week or so, she starts resuming her own life.' She will still protect her offspring if they are in danger but 'as they grow up she cares less and less about them and her thoughts go more and more to the attractive Toms in the neighbourhood. That's what you might call the normal pattern of the female life.'[14] It seems Agatha shared his opinion as she voices a similar sentiment in her autobiography.

Ordeal by Innocence is a cautionary tale for wives. Rachel Argyle's 'maternal obsession' meant her life became so dominated by her children that she shut her husband out.[15] Feeling that he did not count anymore, at first he withdrew, then he had an affair with his secretary. In the novel, any blame for his infidelity is placed squarely on her not him because she was by nature a mother, not a wife.[16]

The same could never be said of Agatha and she was going to take no such risks with her husband. Agatha was excited at the prospect of travelling the world, but she was concerned about leaving her 2-year-old daughter and her aging mother. Clara was adamant that Agatha should go. She told her, 'A wife ought to be with her husband – and if she isn't then he feels he has a right to forget her.'[17] Reassured, in January 1922 Agatha set off with Archie leaving Rosalind in the care of her mother and sister. Visiting South Africa, Australia, New Zealand, Canada and the United States, the Christies were away for almost a year.

As always, Agatha wanted Clara to share her experiences. Like Sylvia Plath in her letters home, Agatha wrote in detail describing a wider world than her mother had experienced. To help Clara picture the landscapes, she compared them to familiar places in Devon. She joked, 'No matter where Millers go, they always say it is just like Torquay!'[18] Written to entertain her mother, her letters exude enthusiasm. As she described characters, recreated their dialogues, and recounted amusing anecdotes, they read like instalments in one of her novels.

Agatha made the most of every moment, socialising on board ship, surfing in Honolulu and exploring every aspect of the local culture. At times, though, she was homesick; she told Clara that she thought about her '<u>so</u> much' and wished she was with her to share the experiences.[19] When she saw a baby on board ship it made her miss her daughter. Another difficult day was Rosalind's third birthday in August. She told her mother, 'I think of my little Poppet such a lot and get more and more homesick for her.'[20] As they were separated for so long, she worried her daughter would forget her. She wrote to her:

> I expect you love Uncle Jim [Madge's husband] and Aunt Punkie [Madge] very much now, but if anyone asks you 'who do you love' you must say 'Mummy.' I think about you such a lot my own baby, (I) shall come back by and by to my little Rosalind.[21]

When her parents finally returned, Rosalind treated them as strangers, deferring instead to her aunt Madge.[22] The little girl was to remain close to her aunt for the rest of her life.

While Agatha was away, she heard Madge's play, *The Claimant*, was to be performed in London's West End. She wrote to her mother half-joking, 'I shall be furious if she arrives "on film" before I do.'[23] Reflecting their very different personalities, while Madge's literary success was spectacular but short-lived, Agatha's was to be steady and sustained. While her daughters were making a success of their lives, the one perennial concern for Clara was her son, Monty. He had served in the army but afterwards he never settled into a permanent career. Farming in Kenya, he enjoyed a louche lifestyle, spending too much money, drinking excessively and womanising. During the war he was wounded in the arm and when it later became infected, it seemed that he might die. He decided to return to England to live out his final days. Protective of her mother, Agatha was particularly concerned when he moved in with Clara. Mother and son had never got on well, but Clara hoped that they could now develop a loving relationship. Agatha was sceptical and her qualms were proved right.

Monty moved into Ashfield accompanied by his black servant, Shebani. Trying to control the pain from his wound, Monty had become addicted to drugs. According to Agatha, looking after her drug-addicted son almost killed Clara.[24] He treated her staff badly and was no more considerate towards his mother, complaining that he could not stand her fussing over him. Only Shebani made the situation remotely tolerable because he chastised Monty for the way he treated Clara. After a year, Shebani returned to Africa, leaving Monty to terrorise the household. As visitors arrived at Ashfield, he used to shoot his revolver out of his bedroom window. Eventually, the police were called but Monty talked his way out of the situation. At this point, Madge and Agatha stepped in to protect their mother. They paid for a bungalow on Dartmoor for their brother and left him in the charge of a housekeeper who was able to manage Monty in a way his mother had never been able to.[25]

Now in her early seventies, Clara was increasingly frail. While Agatha was away on the Empire Tour, she worried about whether her mother was looking after herself. She wrote to Monty asking him to monitor Clara and make sure she changed her clothes after gardening because she often got herself sopping wet hosing the garden.[26] When Agatha returned, she noticed a deterioration in her mother. Clara was more awkward with people and Agatha's staff found her difficult to get on with because she always thought she knew best.[27] Getting things out of proportion, she seemed devastated by a situation but would then forget about it shortly afterwards.[28]

Agatha still enjoyed spending time with Clara as often as possible. A poignant photograph of three generations in the garden at Ashfield captures their relationship; Agatha is in the centre with one arm around her robust-looking little girl, Rosalind, but looking very closely at the picture you can see that her other hand is tightly clasping Clara's as if she cannot bear to let her mother go. In *Unfinished Portrait*, she described a daughter watching her aging mother slip away from her. Every time she saw her looking more fragile 'her heart had a sudden squeezed feeling'.[29] She wrote, 'The love between them was stronger than ever.' Although the mother looked 'a tiny old woman – grey – faded', she came alive again after a few days with her daughter and she would say, 'I've got my girl back.' Agatha was boosted by these visits too, because she experienced the unconditional love she only received from her mother. In her fictionalised version of this time, she wrote that she enjoyed resuming their old roles and feeling:

> that happy tide of reassurance sweeping over her – the feeling of being loved – of being <u>adequate.</u> For her mother, she was perfect. [...] Her mother didn't want her to be different [...] She could just be herself.[30]

Wanting to make the most of the time they had left together, Agatha knew just what would give Clara pleasure. Knowing how much her mother had always loved clothes, for one of her last birthdays she sent her a carefully chosen coat. Clara was delighted, but she admitted how unwell she felt. She wrote, 'The coat is lovely, just right and will be <u>most</u> useful this summer. I did not expect to live to wear it, but I think I shall now!!!' [31] Mother and daughter were too honest with each other to be able to deny what was happening. Clara's health was failing and Ashfield was becoming too much for her. She lived there with a companion, but she told Agatha that she felt too weak to bother about getting a gardener. For a change of scene, Clara came to stay in an adjacent flat in Sunningdale, where she enjoyed happy days playing with Rosalind. When the Christies moved into Styles, a large mock-Tudor house with a pleasant garden in the area, Clara readily offered advice to her daughter about how to run her household. [32] When Aurelia Plath behaved in a similar way with Sylvia, her daughter blamed her for interfering, but Agatha uncritically accepted her mother's interventions. Whether Archie found it so easy having his mother-in-law around is open to question, but Clara did not stay for long. Instead, she took some rooms in a friend's house in London and occasionally returned home. When Agatha and Archie went on holiday to the Pyrenees, she looked after Rosalind at Ashfield. [33] While in Torquay, Clara became ill with bronchitis. Realising it was serious, first Agatha then Madge rushed to be with her. Madge decided that Clara could be better cared for at her home, so she was moved to Abney Hall. At first, she seemed to improve but it was only a brief remission.

The 'psychic osmosis' between mother and daughter lasted until the end. On 5 April 1926, as Agatha was travelling on a train to Manchester to see Clara, she suddenly sensed that something had happened to her. She wrote, 'I felt a <u>coldness</u>, as though I was invaded all over, from head to feet, with some deadly chill and I thought: "Mother is dead."'[34] Agatha wrote about Clara's death in both her autobiography and *Unfinished Portrait*. As the daughter looked at the dead body of 'her little gallant mother [...] lying there so still and strange with flowers and whiteness and a cold, peaceful face',[35] she tried to be as positive as possible.

Unlike Julia's posthumous relationship with Virginia, Clara did not haunt her daughter. Their relationship was resolved, not riddled with the issues which plagued both Virginia's and Sylvia's feelings towards their mothers. Rather than trying to call Clara back, Agatha set her free. Drawing on her Christian faith, she realised that her mother's vibrant personality had moved on and it was 'only the shell that remains'.[36] She knew that Clara had found the last few years trying and had increasingly felt her worn-out body was a 'prison' from which she longed to be released. However, although she could rationalise it, nothing could take away the acute pain Agatha experienced at losing the person she had always been able to rely on most in this world. In the novel, the daughter realises she no longer has her mother's 'steadfast love and protection'. A feeling of panic sweeps over her as she knows 'the bottom had fallen out of her world' and she thinks, 'I'm alone now.'[37]

The Model: Julia Jackson photographed by Julia Margaret Cameron. (The Picture Art Collection / Alamy Stock Photo)

Pre-Raphaelite Muse: Julia painted by Edward Burne-Jones. (The Picture Art Collection / Alamy Stock Photo)

The Great Beauty: Julia photographed by Henry Herschel Hay Cameron. (Historic Images / Alamy Stock Photo)

The Perfect Partner: Herbert Duckworth circa 1867. (Smith College Special Collections)

Inconsolable: Julia grieving with her baby son Gerald. (Heritage Images / Alamy Stock Photo)

Julia's second husband, Sir Leslie Stephen. (Smith College Special Collections)

A Rare Moment of Intimacy: Julia with Virginia on her lap. (Smith College Special Collections)

The Holiday Home: Talland House, St Ives. (Historic Images / Alamy Stock Photo)

Inseparable: Stella and Julia. (Smith College Special Collections)

In Harmony: Virginia with her parents reading. (Smith College Special Collections)

An Unconventional Marriage: Virginia with her husband Leonard.
(Smith College Special Collections)

The romantic miniature of Clara on her wedding day. (Christie Archive Trust)

Home: Ashfield, Torquay. (Christie Archive Trust)

A Much-Loved Child: Agatha with her father. (Christie Archive Trust)

Agatha and her mother. (Christie Archive Trust)

Mistress of the House: Clara at Ashfield. (Christie Archive Trust)

A Matriarchy: Agatha with her cousin and Auntie-Grannie. (Christie Archive Trust)

Her First Marriage: Agatha with Archie. (Christie Archive Trust)

A Wise Woman: Clara remains a powerful influence. (Christie Archive Trust)

Motherhood: Agatha holding baby Rosalind. (Christie Archive Trust)

Hard to Let Go: Agatha holds Clara's hand, with Rosalind beside her. (Christie Archive Trust)

Second Chance: Agatha with Max.
(Christie Archive Trust)

A Close Bond: Agatha with her grandson,
Mathew. (Christie Archive Trust)

Determined Young Woman: Aurelia Schober 1930. (ARCHIVIO GBB / Alamy Stock oto)

The Soulmate: Karl von Terzaghi. (ARCHIVIO GBB / Alamy Stock Photo)

The Husband: Otto Plath. (ARCHIVIO GBB / Alamy Stock Photo)

Aurelia, Otto and Sylvia having a picnic. (ARCHIVIO GBB / Alamy Stock Photo)

A Devoted Mother: Aurelia cuddles Sylvia. (ARCHIVIO GBB / Alamy Stock Photo)

The Little Nurse: Sylvia puts on a brave face during her father's illness. (ARCHIVIO GBB / Alamy Stock Photo)

Recovering: Sylvia with her mother and brother Warren in 1950.
(ARCHIVIO GBB / Alamy Stock Photo)

The Start of a New Era: Sylvia leaving home. (ARCHIVIO GBB / Alamy Stock Photo)

A Grand Passion: Sylvia and Ted Hughes. (ARCHIVIO GBB / Alamy Stock Photo)

Last Visit: Aurelia, Sylvia and her two children in 1962. (Everett Collection / Alamy Stock Photo)

24

Missing

The period after Clara's death is one of the most closely examined episodes in Agatha's life as it culminated in her going missing and being found, under an assumed name, in Harrogate. In her autobiography, Agatha wrote that this time was 'one I hate recalling. As so often in life, when one thing goes wrong, everything goes wrong.'[1] Her disappearance has often been treated by Christie observers as a great mystery, but was it really so inexplicable?

Much emphasis has been placed on Agatha's reaction to her husband Archie's infidelity; less notice has been taken of the fact that she went missing shortly after her beloved mother had died. The combination of losing the two people who were essential to her security and sense of self within months of each other would have been devastating for anyone. If Clara is given the rightful place in her daughter's life, what happened seems hardly surprising. For most people, the death of a parent is disorienting; for women who were as sensitive as Virginia and Agatha and who were so psychically linked to their mothers, it seems inevitable this loss would profoundly affect their mental health.

Agatha's grandson, Mathew Prichard, thinks her mother's death even more than her separation from her husband explains what happened. He says, 'Let's assume that she didn't get divorced from Archie and her marriage was in a fairly normal state; I still think my grandmother would have been very, very upset and possibly even disturbed when her mother died.'[2] Agatha herself also primarily attributed her breakdown to losing Clara. In a letter written to a close friend more than three decades later, she explained:

Too many troubles all at once (my mother to whom I was devoted had died after a rather harrowing illness for one thing) breaks anybody down – and then something happens – earache, toothache, gastritis, lapses of memory, sleep walking and even buckets of tears – just because one can't start the car! How merciful that everything passes.[3]

In the days immediately after Clara's death, Agatha needed Archie, but he was in Spain and did not attend the funeral. On his return, he suggested that they should go abroad because she needed some 'fun' to distract her. It was the last thing she wanted – instead she needed to grieve. Later, she was to regret her decision, believing she should have done what her husband wanted, but to an observer his attitude sounds insensitive.[4]

Instead of going abroad, Agatha went to Torquay with Rosalind to sort out Ashfield. Returning to her childhood home without Clara to greet her was a harrowing experience. Like Talland House for Virginia, Ashfield had always been synonymous with her mother and as Clara had deteriorated, it had become more dilapidated. Unable to cope with the upkeep of a large house, she had lived in only two rooms. It was soul-destroying to find Ashfield crammed full of her mother's belongings but Clara not there. Although it was incredibly painful, Agatha forced herself to sift through drawers of old letters and photos, and trunks full of old clothes.

At first, Agatha repressed her grief and tried to carry on as normal, but her intense emotions could not be suppressed for long. For the first time in her life, she felt terribly afraid. Her mind was confused, and when she tried to write a cheque, she could not remember her name to sign it. She wrote, 'I felt exactly like Alice in Wonderland touching the tree.'[5] Her reaction reveals how closely her identity was intertwined with Clara's; without her mother she was no longer sure of exactly who she was.

After Clara's death, Agatha hoped her husband would fill the void. In *Unfinished Portrait*, the wife awaits her husband's visit with 'passionate intensity' thinking that without him she would want to die.[6] Sadly, Archie failed to rise to the occasion because he could not cope with people if they were ill or unhappy.[7] When he finally arrived, she sensed something was wrong; the chemistry between them had vanished and he seemed like a stranger. During the visit, Archie told her that he had fallen in love with another woman and wanted a divorce. This revelation was like a bomb-shell; Agatha had not seen it coming. Although Clara had always warned her that she would have to work hard to keep an attractive man like Archie, Agatha had blithely believed that he would be faithful. His infidelity could not have come at a worse moment as she no longer had her mother to support and advise her. Like Virginia after her mother died, Agatha suffered the double disillusionment of being let down by the man in her life when she most needed his support.

Characteristically, Agatha blamed herself for her husband's infidelity. Indoctrinated by the Miller matriarchy, she repeated their mantra that she should never have left a handsome man like him alone. Unlike Virginia, who fought back against the destructive men in her life, Agatha turned her anger inwards, failing to acknowledge fully that Archie was the one at fault, the one who had broken his marriage vows and betrayed her.

Overwhelmed with her double loss, Agatha's physical and mental health deteriorated. The slightest problem could make her burst into tears. She did not want to eat, and she began to suffer from insomnia. She would dream about the past and then wake up terrified, not sure exactly what was the matter. She had never needed her mother more. In *Unfinished Portrait*, the distraught daughter pleads, 'Oh Mother, Mother, come back to me, Mother.'[8] Her anguished cries echo Virginia's pleas to her mother, voiced through Lily Briscoe in *To the Lighthouse*. In moments of crisis, both women had a visceral need for the solace only a mother could provide.

Agatha hoped that leaving Ashfield and returning home to Sunningdale would mark a return to normal life. Hating the thought of divorce, she wanted to make it up with Archie. She had believed he was the love of her life and that they would always be together. In the 1920s there was a social stigma attached to divorce and it also went against Agatha's religious principles. Nor did she want her daughter to grow up without both her parents. The change of scene did not improve the situation and there was no permanent reconciliation.

Agatha began to feel increasingly physically and mentally ill. In *Unfinished Portrait*, the heroine is afraid that she will go mad as her thoughts were confused and she forgot things. Occasionally, she suffered from suicidal thoughts. Like Virginia, it seems that Agatha's mental health problems were linked to the loss of her mother. In the novel, half-awake in the night, the bereaved daughter wandered around the house looking for her mother, believing that if she found her 'everything would be all right'. On one occasion, she started walking to the police station to ask for help in tracing her.[9]

Perhaps *Unfinished Portrait* provides the greatest insight into what Agatha was feeling during this crisis; although it is a fictionalised version, it has an emotional truth. In her autobiography, written many years later, she chose not to revisit the episode in detail.[10] In the novel, the heroine decides she needs to go away because she can no longer bear the pain. She had gone beyond the point where she cared about anything; even her child no longer mattered.[11] In real life, by December 1926 Agatha had become so isolated in her depression that she was unwilling or unable to reach out to her loved ones for help.

When Agatha went missing from her Sunningdale home there was massive publicity. The press speculated whether the famous author had died by suicide and appeals were made to find her. The story escalated and her motivation was questioned. Rather than accepting she had suffered a breakdown, some people suggested that she had staged her disappearance in a bid to frame her unfaithful husband for murder or done it as a publicity stunt to promote her latest book. Eventually, after eleven days, she was found staying under an assumed name in a hotel in Harrogate, suffering from a complete loss of memory. Archie collected her from the spa town and took her to Abney Hall to be reunited with her daughter and sister. Years later, Rosalind recalled how when she saw Agatha again, she seemed somehow absent – it was not like a mother embracing a daughter.[12] Her description is reminiscent of the photos of Julia with her children after Herbert Duckworth's death; she was also present but absent. Both women had been shattered by unbearable loss and had withdrawn into themselves.

After this frightening episode, Madge insisted that her sister should see a psychiatrist. Agatha reluctantly agreed to go for therapy in Harley Street. We get an insight into what she felt about these sessions in her Westmacott novel *Giant's Bread*. When Vernon Deyre has lost his memory, he goes to a doctor who seems able to see deep within him. Like Agatha, Vernon does not want to go over his traumatic experience again. The psychiatrist explains to him that he must face his issues otherwise his memory loss might recur. When Vernon does what his doctor says he finally finds peace.[13] It seems that in real life, using hypnosis, the psychiatrist helped Agatha to retrieve much of her memory of the traumatic episode, but there were still some blanks. Two decades later, she was still trying to reconstruct these disconcerting gaps. After the war, she visited the Regius Professor of Pastoral Theology at Oxford, who was a well-known psycho-analyst. Apparently, he told her that her experience had been extremely serious and although he could not help her replace the missing hours, he tried to help her overcome her self-reproach.[14]

Even with professional help, Agatha was never able to unravel exactly what had happened. There has been much speculation about what was going on in her mind; the disappearance and its causes have been explored so extensively elsewhere it is unnecessary to go over old ground here.[15] One biographer argues convincingly that it was an extreme reaction to prolonged physical and emotional stress and shock. She suggests her condition sounds like Transient Global Amnesia, an isolated episode in which the person affected becomes disorientated but remains alert, capable of general understanding and management of themselves. No new memories are made at the time which creates a blank, but afterwards those who have experienced it will remember who they are and recognise people in their circle.[16]

The destabilising experience was an episode neither Agatha nor her family wanted to dwell on. However, what she had gone through gave a greater depth to her writing. Her personal experience of mental health problems meant that she understood how extreme circumstances could dramatically affect even a normally well-balanced person and make them behave out of character.

Biographer Janet Morgan argues it would be wrong to imagine that Agatha ever seriously considered taking her own life. She claims that had she wanted to, her pharmaceutical knowledge would have made it easy.[17] Recent biographer Lucy Worsley believes Agatha had a suicidal thought about driving into the quarry at Newlands Corner in Surrey, but because her daughter was in the car, she immediately dismissed the idea. On Saturday, 4 December, she made 'a half-hearted attempt' to kill herself but it was not 'very determined' nor 'well-planned'.[18] Agatha's second husband, Max Mallowan, believed that his wife came close to suicide.[19] In *Unfinished Portrait*, Celia, the character based on Agatha, makes a first suicide attempt during a period of nervous collapse. Later in the novel, when she surveys the wreckage of her life, she is once again on the point of a suicide attempt. On both occasions, Celia's life is saved by strangers intervening.

Agatha's experience made her think deeply about whether suicide was ever justified. In her later work she argued eloquently against it. Although she understood how a person could be so desperate this action appeared the only way out, her strong religious faith made her oppose it. In her short story 'The Man from the Sea', published three years after her breakdown, two characters are on the point of suicide because they believe their lives are no longer worth living. A stranger, Mr Satterthwaite, intervenes, arguing that there may be a divine plan for them in the future. Just by being in the right place at the right time, they might do something life changing for another person.[20] A similar argument appears in her novel *Towards Zero*, written more than a decade later. Angus MacWhirter tries to take his own life after his wife leaves him, but he is also saved by a stranger. By the end of the novel, he understands that his survival is a miracle which benefits both himself and someone else.[21] His plea to another person thinking of suicide, 'Don't throw yourself over! Nothing's worth it. <u>Nothing</u>. Even if you are desperately unhappy', seems to have been Agatha's hard-won view.[22]

In later life, Agatha did not deny her breakdown, but nor did she want it to define her. In her autobiography, she wrote that when something traumatic happened a person should 'take one brief look, and say, 'Yes, this *is* part of my life; but it's done with. It is a strand in the tapestry of my existence. I must recognise it because it is *part* of me. But there is no need to dwell upon it.'[23] Agatha's attitude about how to deal with traumatic incidents in the past was strikingly different from Sylvia Plath's and Virginia Woolf's, partly reflecting their different personalities but also their different attitudes to psychiatrists and psychoanalysis. Agatha was interested in how the mind worked and kept up to date on the latest theories, animatedly discussing Freud, Jung, Moore and Wittgenstein.[24] However, her writing suggests ambivalence to the professional study of the mind. In her *Autobiography* she wrote about admiring detective stories written as morality tales before people had 'begun to wallow in psychology'.[25]

In her novels there are reputable psychiatrists but also charlatans. In *They Do It with Mirrors*, Dr Maverick fails to impress Miss Marple. She thinks he is abnormal himself and her down-to-earth approach to human nature could not have been more different from his view that everyone is a little mad.[26] In *Third Girl*, Dr Stillingfleet is a reputable psychiatrist. When the heroine, Norma Restarick, worries that she is going mad he joins Poirot in normalising the situation. Poirot tells her that psychiatrists and psychologists have grand names for mental health problems but often the condition is not serious and can be easily cured with proper treatment. These episodes occur if someone has too much mental strain caused by worry, studying too much for exams, or broken love affairs; they can also be triggered by a person dwelling too much on religion or their relationship with their parents.[27]

After her breakdown, Agatha made a full recovery. Her mental health problems were very different from Virginia's and Sylvia's. Her crisis was triggered by specific circumstances, the combination of her mother's death and Archie's adultery. Except for a brief period during the Second World War, once again in reaction to events, there is no evidence that she ever experienced depression again. This was partly due to her temperament but also because of the firm foundation laid by her good relationship with her mother. Agatha believed that nature was at least as important as nurture. She wrote, 'Naturally, a lot depends on temperament. You are a happy person, or you are of a melancholic disposition. I don't know that you can do anything about <u>that</u>. I think it is the way one is made.'[28] Agatha believed that a sanguine personality was the greatest gift and that she was fortunate to be blessed with that temperament. She wrote in her autobiography:

I have always thought life exciting, and I still do [...] I like living. I have sometimes been wildly despairing, acutely miserable, racked with sorrow, but through it all I still know quite certainly that just to <u>be</u> alive is a grand thing.[29]

25

Agatha's New Life

Rather than ending her life in 1926, Agatha began a new one. With Clara and Archie gone forever she had to re-establish the small circle she relied upon. Although she could never completely recreate the rapport she had with her mother, her most satisfying relationships in later life had echoes of that formative bond. First with her second husband and then with her grandson, she experienced a similar understanding. Like the other authors in this book, Agatha still needed mothering and the people who loved her stepped in to protect her.

Once her grief subsided, Agatha made the most of her changed circumstances. Released from the responsibilities of being a wife and daughter, she experienced a new freedom. She had to balance her desire to live her own life to the full with the needs of her daughter, however. The divorce from Archie complicated Agatha's relationship with Rosalind. Although she was the innocent party, Agatha feared her daughter blamed her. In her novel *Third Girl*, the title character's reaction to her parents' divorce seems to have reflected what Agatha believed Rosalind felt. Although her father went off with another woman, the daughter idolised him and was critical of her mother. She thought that her father loved her; it was just her mother he disliked.[1]

Unlike Clara's unconditional love, Agatha took nothing for granted with Rosalind. In her novel *Death Comes as the End*, the Egyptian woman Renisenb's thoughts as she looked at her young daughter Teti seem to have reflected Agatha's feelings. Renisenb realises that her child is not a replica of her but a totally separate individual. She thought:

She is Teti. She is alone, as I am alone, as we are all alone. If there is love between us we shall be friends all our life – but if there is not love she will grow up and we shall be strangers.[2]

Instead of repeating the past, Agatha developed her own model of motherhood. Rather than being too tied to each other, she wanted her daughter to feel free.[3] Some of her novels explore a child's desire for freedom. In *Five Little Pigs*, the governess, Miss Williams, disapproves of children receiving too much attention from their parents because if a child is watched over too closely, they try to escape and be unobserved. Instead, she advocates 'healthy neglect', where the mother is busy with her own life and the child realises their parent is fond of them but is not fussed over.[4] These comments suggest that perhaps, in retrospect, Agatha felt that being so close to Clara had restricted her. Loving someone so much and feeling responsible for them meant you never felt truly free. Although having a person who totally understood your feelings was reassuring it could invade your privacy.

In the years immediately after her divorce, Agatha enjoyed travelling the world. She was no longer the naïve girl who believed in romantic dreams. It was while on an archaeological dig in the Middle East she found love again with the archaeologist Max Mallowan. As Max was fourteen years younger than her, she had not thought of him as a potential suitor but gradually friendship turned into a companionable partnership. The couple married in September 1930, marking the end of a profoundly unhappy period for Agatha. Max filled part of the void left by Clara's death. Her grandson, Mathew Prichard, explains:

The fact her mother was no longer there may have had some bearing on her willingness to marry again because she probably realised that she could not go on living a life that no longer existed. She knew in her heart of hearts that she needed something to concentrate on and to help her live another life of her own.[5]

Like Julia Stephen in her second marriage, this time Agatha did not give herself completely. She loved her new husband deeply, but she always held something back. Max wrote that she had 'a quality of elusiveness'.[6]

The loss of her mother and Archie had nearly destroyed her so for self-protection she could not risk unleashing the same 'dangerous intensity of affection' again. Agatha found a new serenity which did not depend so much on other people. Friends thought psychoanalysis had changed her perspective, but she attributed it to reading J.W. Dunne's *An Experiment with Time*.[7] Rather than taking things so personally, she realised life could be unfair and she put herself in the hands of fate. She told Max that she was afraid of being too detached, but he replied that she should recognise the benefits of being able to take an impersonal view.[8]

Part of her second husband's appeal was that he made her feel like Clara did. They seemed to understand each other almost before they spoke.[9] In *Unfinished Portrait*, the character of Michael is based on Max. In the novel, Celia describes him as like a mother to her because he was so gentle.[10] In a letter to Agatha written in 1931, Max describes her as 'my lover and my first child'.[11] After more than a decade of marriage, Agatha still thanked Max for helping her to come to terms with the loss of her mother. She wrote, 'I remembered a day in Alep when you comforted me on the anniversary of my mother's death – speaking with such faith and such sincerity.'[12] Max recognised Agatha's vulnerability and made her feel safe again. Like Leonard Woolf with Virginia, he protected her but also gave her the freedom to be herself. She was able to have a fulfilling career as well as the security of marriage. In return, she supported his archaeological work and was lenient about his close friendships with other women.[13]

Like the other mothers in this book, Agatha was concerned about the effect remarriage would have on her daughter. Before marrying Max, she consulted Rosalind who approved. There was none of the emotional blackmail used by Sylvia Plath to prevent her mother remarrying. Instead, Rosalind was pragmatic; she thought her mother should marry again and she liked Max more than any of Agatha's other suitors.[14]

After their marriage, following Clara's advice, Agatha always put her husband first. Joining Max on his archaeological digs, she left Rosalind at boarding school under the supervision of her sister Madge. Occasionally, Rosalind wrote letters to her mother suggesting she resented being left and wondering when her mother would come to collect her. Many modern mothers would blanch at the idea of leaving their child for long absences abroad, but parenting in the 1930s was very different from our own era. Rosalind was at boarding school with many girls whose parents lived abroad. Agatha was certainly not the only mother to spend long periods travelling, nor was she unique in making her husband's needs a priority. Clementine Churchill did the same, enjoying months away from her children.[15]

Rosalind grew up to be a very independent young woman. Agatha had her own life to lead and so did Rosalind. From an early age, Agatha treated her daughter as an autonomous individual who could make her own choices. When deciding which school Rosalind should go to, she listened to her daughter rather than imposing her views. It was a very different dynamic from the one between Clara and Agatha. While her mother was alive, Agatha had nearly always relied on her opinion. Rosalind was critical, claiming, 'My grandmother was a dangerous woman. Strong and dangerous. My mother never thought she was wrong.'[16] Her negative comment suggests that she preferred to rely on her own judgement rather than deferring to her mother.

Unlike Clara, Agatha did not get involved in her daughter's love life. When Rosalind fell in love with Hubert Prichard, a major in the army, Agatha met him a few times and liked him. The couple decided to marry in June 1940, but Rosalind only informed her mother at the last minute. Not wanting to make a big 'fuss', she only told Agatha because she was under 21 and her future husband made her. When her mother said she would like to come to the wedding, Rosalind reluctantly agreed. Playing down any hurt, Agatha wrote that it made her laugh because it illustrated how 'oyster-like' her daughter was.[17] Perhaps, on this occasion, she understood Rosalind because she had only told Clara about her wedding to Archie after it had happened.

Three years later, when Rosalind was about to give birth, Agatha was anxious because she feared something might go wrong, though she did not tell her daughter how she felt. Agatha joined Rosalind, who was staying with her Aunt Madge, for the birth. She was overjoyed when her grandson Mathew was born on 21 September 1943.[18] Tragically, Rosalind's husband Hubert was killed in action in 1944 during the D-Day invasion of Normandy. As soon as she heard her son-in-law was missing, Agatha rushed to be with her daughter. She admired Rosalind's courage but could not tell what she was really feeling. Although she felt deeply for Rosalind, she did not know exactly how to help her. Unsure of what to say, she kept quiet, feeling that was what Rosalind would have wanted, though she was never sure this was what Rosalind required. She later wrote, 'The saddest thing in life and the hardest to live through is the knowledge that there is someone you love very much whom you cannot save from suffering.'[19] Lacking the understanding she had with Clara, Agatha always approached Rosalind tentatively, never daring to break down the emotional barriers between them.

Like Clara, Agatha did not take her relationships for granted. Instead, she worked at them, carefully thinking about the characters involved, and trying to give them what they needed. Mathew Prichard explains, 'If my mother and I were available, she made every effort to be in the right place at the right time and to spend time with us.' Agatha, whom Mathew called 'Nima', would visit them in their Welsh home or invite them to stay with her at Greenway, her Georgian house in Devon. Her grandson believes that she knew from her own experience 'the value of time spent in the family and the recuperative effects'.[20] Mathew adds, 'My mother was a very undemonstrative person. She wasn't the sort of fellow to throw her arms around her mother when she arrived, or anything like that, but it was quite obvious that she valued these visits.'[21]

Mother and daughter grew closer, but it was never as effortless as Agatha's relationship with Clara. Her bond with her grandson was more like that precious rapport, although this time she was in the maternal role. Grandmother and grandson just understood each other. Mathew says, 'To put it simply, some people get on and are really close to each other and some people just are not.'[22] He believes that he is more like his grandmother than his mother.[23] Agatha never spoke to him directly about Clara, but indirectly her influence was felt as he saw the great emphasis Agatha placed on family life. As home had always meant so much to her, she understood what her 8-year-old grandson was going through when he went to preparatory school in Berkshire. At weekends, she drove over from Wallingford and took him back to her home. 'It didn't just happen by accident', he recalls. 'She made Sunday lunch free so that I could have roast chicken with her. It sounds very ordinary, but it wasn't. It meant everything to me because I was very homesick.'[24] As he grew older, Mathew wanted his school and university friends to meet Agatha. She thrived in the company of young people. Rather than behaving like an elderly famous author, she was genuinely interested in Mathew's friends, asking them about their studies and making it feel just like a normal family lunch.

Repeating Clara's parenting, Agatha never pushed her grandson to achieve, but she encouraged him in the right direction. Mathew explains:

> Rather than giving me lectures or trying to teach me things, she found out what really interested me at school and then she tried, very gently, almost without me noticing, to show me what she thought was the best of this particular thing I happened to be interested in.[25]

They shared a great love of music and went on trips together to Salzburg and the Wagner Festival in Bayreuth. On one occasion, Mathew joined Agatha and Max with two of his university friends. The students camped while the Mallowans stayed in a hotel. Each day the young people picked Agatha and Max up in their car and had lunch together, followed by a game of bridge, before going to the theatre. Mathew remembers, 'They were tremendous times; I've never forgotten those couple of weeks.'[26]

During the 1950s, Mathew became aware of 'what a star' his grandmother was. Sharing a love of the theatre, he was particularly impressed when *The Mousetrap* opened in the West End.[27] He had a special interest in the play because when he was 9, Agatha set up a trust for him assigning to it copyrights of the novel *They Do It with Mirrors* and the play *Three Blind Mice* (better known as *The Mousetrap*), which became the longest running play in the history of British theatre.

The whole family were involved in Agatha's professional life. Rosalind was fiercely protective, carefully controlling how her mother's work was used.[28] Rosalind told her exactly what she thought and, to a degree, Agatha valued her opinion, but they did not always agree. Mathew believes that mixing the personal and professional affected his mother and grandmother's relationship. He explains, 'I think my mother suffered a bit from being the person who it was always down to, to criticise her mother if things weren't going right with her work. The rest of us didn't have to do that.'[29]

Except for the period after her mother's death and a brief hiatus during the Second World War when Max was working abroad, Agatha was fortunate to be surrounded throughout her life by people who loved and supported her. She recognised how important this stability was to her well-being. In April 1954, when Agatha and her family were playing Confessions, she described her idea of misery as 'the people I love to go away'.[30] In her later life that never happened again; by carefully nurturing her relationships, she found the lasting security she needed. As she confessed in the game, she had once again reached a point where her present state of mind was 'Deeply Happy'.[31]

26

Clara's Literary Legacy

Clara's lasting influence on her daughter was felt in Agatha's literature as well as her life. As one of the most successful authors of all time, Christie was known as a brilliant storyteller, a talent she had inherited from Clara. As if she was still writing for her intellectually impatient mother, she never allowed purple prose to slow down a pacey plot. Taking her at face value, many critics failed to recognise the profound person who lay beneath the popular veneer, but she did not want them to know the real her. She gave the public what they wanted while maintaining her carefully guarded privacy.

In her *Autobiography*, Agatha claimed that at first she saw her occupation as being a married woman and writing as a sideline.[1] Gradually, as she became more famous, she saw it as her business to write, but like any job it left her with a longing to also do other things.[2] Even at the end of her life, when she was the bestselling author in the world – after the Bible and Shakespeare – she wrote, 'I do not quite feel as though I am an author. I still have the over-lag of feeling that I am pretending to be an author.'[3]

Perhaps her self-effacing approach was a legacy from the Miller matriarchy, which had instilled in her that a woman should never put her career before her husband and family.[4] In theory, Agatha was not a feminist, but in practice the story was different. In her *Autobiography* and interviews, her attitude to women's rights remained essentially the same as when she was a young woman in the Edwardian era. Even in later life, when women's roles had dramatically changed and she had enjoyed an extremely successful career, she was sceptical about whether sex equality had made women happier. In 1962, she told a journalist that she believed women had been 'foolish' to give up their privileged position, forfeiting 'the joys of leisure and creative thought, and perfecting of home conditions'.[5] These 'joys' had made up Clara's life, and her daughter believed it was fulfilling and had not made her mother a lesser person.

Rather than talk about sex equality, Agatha's life demonstrated it was possible for a woman to be as successful as any man. As Mathew Prichard explains:

> She was one of the first women who genuinely created a career for themselves. She was certainly no feminist, but she wrote as a living, and she was completely unashamed about it. It was what she wanted to do; it never even entered her mind to do anything else or that it would make any difference whether she was a woman or a man. She just did it naturally.[6]

A similar sex equality is evident in her female characters, who are a diverse range of women. Some conform to traditional roles, but others have careers and unconventional relationships.[7] Many of her heroines do not accept the patriarchal line, and are more ambitious and hard-headed than the male characters.[8] Perhaps influenced by her benign father and dominant Auntie-Grannie, unlike in Virginia and Sylvia's work, in Agatha's novels it is often the women not the men who are domestic tyrants. Rather than defining people by their gender, Agatha believed that people should be treated as individuals. In her novel *Appointment With Death*, when the nursery governess Miss Pierce says it is 'nice' that women are now able to do things, Sarah, a successful doctor, disagrees. She replies that it is 'nice' when any human being can do something worthwhile, irrespective of their gender. She disapproved of differentiation between the sexes, explaining that some girls were businesslike while some men were 'muddle-headed'. She concludes, 'There are just different types of brains. Sex only matters where sex is directly concerned.'[9]

Unlike the other authors in this book, Agatha remained an observer of women's lives rather than a crusader for their rights. She had strong views, but her writing was essentially to entertain, not proselytise. Faith not feminism was most important to her, and she was cynical about political ideology of all kinds.[10] Perhaps as a subtle challenge to Virginia Woolf's feminist theories, Agatha claimed she never needed a room of her own to write. She explained that she could do it anywhere; all she required was a steady table and a typewriter.[11] Historian Gillian Gill explains, Agatha did not need a room, because she was one of those rare women who owned whole houses, bought with her own money earned from her writing, not gained from inheritance or marriage.[12]

Unlike Virginia and Sylvia, she never complained that juggling domestic responsibilities detracted from her ability to work. Agatha claimed that she snatched time to write when she was not involved in other enjoyable activities. She willingly abandoned her work for a family picnic, a walk in the garden or lunch with friends. However, beneath her down-to-earth veneer, there were more similarities with Plath and Woolf than any of them would have admitted.

Writing was more important to Agatha than her descriptions of her working life suggested. Her friend A.L. Rowse thought that it was essential to her well-being. He observed that Agatha lived a double life; there was the outer person who had a full and normal social life, but there was also the inner life of the imagination.[13] One side of her life supported the other; she needed the stability of her home and family to be able to write, and her books financed her lifestyle. Her writing was also beneficial for her mental health. As it was for Virginia and Sylvia, Agatha's writing was a form of catharsis; it helped her to work out her true feelings in an environment which she could control.

Her husband, Max Mallowan, believed that she expressed who she really was in the pages of her books. He wrote that although she surrounded herself with 'an inbuilt armour off which any questionnaire was liable to glance like a spent arrow', she had been 'more generous than most writers in self-revelation' in her literature.[14] For a reader hoping to understand the real Agatha and her relationships, there are some clues in her detective fiction, but the real revelations come in the six Westmacott novels.[15] Written under a pseudonym, her identity as the author was only revealed in *The Sunday Times* in 1949. When asked why she used a pseudonym for those books, she explained, 'I like keeping them to myself [...] so that I can write exactly what I like. You can write a bit of your own life into them in a way, if nobody knows it's you.'[16]

Agatha's family knew how important these novels were to her. Max Mallowan believed that in them she found her 'true release'.[17] Mathew Prichard agrees, describing the Westmacott novels as 'to a greater or lesser extent autobiographical'.[18] They allowed his grandmother to explore in more detail human psychology which particularly interested her. Her daughter Rosalind described them as 'bitter-sweet stories about love'. She wrote that in them Agatha explored family relationships and 'love in some of its most powerful and destructive forms'.[19] During her lifetime Rosalind never wanted the Mary Westmacott novels to appear under the name Agatha Christie.[20] Perhaps they were just too personal for her to want them to be openly identified as by her mother.

In her Westmacott novels, Agatha was writing very much as Clara's daughter, expressing the 'inner sensitivity', 'dangerous intensity of affection' and 'exceptional imagination' that mother and daughter shared.[21] They are the successors of the early short stories she wrote under Clara's influence. The first Westmacott novel, *Giant's Bread*, published in 1930, is dedicated 'To the Memory of my Best and Truest Friend My Mother'. In the book, Agatha explores themes which interested both mother and daughter. Through the hero, Vernon Deyre, who is a composer, she develops further their ideas about the power of music to possess the soul.

Four years later, Agatha published *Unfinished Portrait*, giving us the greatest insight into her childhood and her relationship with Clara.[22] It is her equivalent of Virginia's novel *To the Lighthouse*, as in *Unfinished Portrait* Agatha worked through her feelings for her mother and recreated the woman who had dominated her early life. However, the task was easier for Agatha than for Virginia because as she always understood her mother it was natural for her to imagine herself into Clara's mind. For both writers, exploring their bond with their mothers through fiction was cathartic; while Virginia exorcised her mother's ghost, Agatha recaptured the woman she adored. While one is a type of ghost story, the other is a love letter.

Unlike Virginia, Agatha wrote as a mother as well as a daughter and having personal experience of two different models of motherhood influenced her writing. Like Sylvia writing about her feelings about being a mother after the birth of her children, Agatha's Westmacott novels are about her relationship with Rosalind as well as Clara. In *Unfinished Portrait*, the heroine explains why she was careful not to interfere in her daughter's life. She asks, 'How can you judge for someone else? You might ruin their lives when you thought you were helping them.'[23]

In several of the Westmacott novels, Agatha questioned what made a good mother. In *Absent in the Spring*, Joan Scudamore discovers that her self-image is completely different from the way her husband and children see her.[24] Writing it allowed Agatha to explore unsettling questions which she sometimes asked herself: 'Who am I? What am I like really? What do all the people I love think of me? Do they think of me as I think they do?'[25] Perhaps she had only been certain of the answers with Clara.

Like Virginia and Sylvia, Agatha returned to the mother–daughter relationship in different formats throughout her career. In a later Westmacott novel, *A Daughter's a Daughter*, she examined how this close bond can turn toxic.[26] The Westmacott novels show that the balance between a supportive and destructive love is fragile. A possessive relationship can be claustrophobic and sacrificial love can destroy rather than redeem. Although the characters involved do not intend to do each other harm – they are not bad people and often want to do the right thing – due to the combination of characters, it goes wrong. They also illustrate that there is not just one model of motherhood which works; it depends on the personalities involved. A repeated theme is that it can be dangerous to interfere too much in another person's life. That person knows best what is right for them and should be left to make choices for themself. The quest in life should not be for happiness, but to experience life to the full, even if that involves unhappiness, because that is the only way to grow up and become the person you are meant to be.

These novels suggest that over the decades Agatha periodically reassessed her relationship with Clara, first by recreating it and then by comparing it with alternatives. Using a pseudonym and fiction was a safe place to explore complicated emotions that it might have seemed disloyal to express openly. Like Virginia and Sylvia's fictionalised portrayals of their family relationships, there is a 'fusion' of different people in the characters and some manipulation of real events, but read carefully with those caveats, they reveal Agatha's growing understanding of complicated family dynamics.

Decades after losing her mother, Agatha finally wrote a non-fiction account of her relationship with Clara in her autobiography. She began when she was 59 and completed it over the next fifteen years. Having thought long and hard about the mother–daughter bond, it seems her final assessment of her feelings for Clara had come full circle, as there is very little difference between her novel *Unfinished Portrait*, written shortly after losing her mother, and her memoir written at the end of her life.[27] Both books show that Agatha believed the positives of her bond with Clara far outweighed any negatives. The section in her autobiography about her mother's death is entitled 'The Land of Lost Content', and this line from A.E. Housman's poem in *A Shropshire Lad* perfectly captures her nostalgia. The remembrance of times past was comforting but it was also tinged with sadness because she knew they would not come again.

In 1974, when Agatha had a heart attack and was confined to bed, she reread her Westmacott novels. She told her agent that she thought *Unfinished Portrait* was one of the best.[28] As she approached the end of her life, she looked back on her time with her mother with gratitude. Like Virginia shortly before her death by suicide during the Second World War, revisiting her childhood provided Agatha with a place of sanctuary, but unlike Woolf's reminiscing there were few negative emotions. Like her heroine in *Unfinished Portrait*, she went back 'deliberately to a childish world, finding there a refuge from the world's cruelty'.[29]

Agatha never stopped missing Clara, but in contrast to the other authors in this book, her relationship with her mother was resolved. Perhaps, as she grew older, she realised that it was not as perfect as she had once thought. Her novels suggest that it had limited her freedom. To some extent it had placed a burden on her as after her father's death she felt responsible for Clara. Her dependence on her mother had also prevented her from fully growing up until Clara died. Overall, though, she knew that by any standards they had enjoyed a good relationship.

Her positive experience of unconditional devotion from her mother made her a person who believed in love and, even after the disillusioning episode with Archie, that fundamental faith remained. When the right person came along, first her husband Max then her grandson Mathew, she experienced that understanding and sense of belonging she had felt with Clara again. Her later loves were different, mother love is unique, but strong.

When Agatha was dying, her husband and grandson were by her side. Knowing how much Mathew meant to her, Max asked him to stay with them at her Wallingford home as she slipped away. Once she had died, Mathew was about to go home but Max said to him, 'I would just like you to go in and have a look at her and make sure she's all right. I think Nima would like you to stay a bit longer.' Mathew recalls:

I wandered in every hour or two to sort of check up on her and, would you believe it? I felt a sort of almost uncanny sense that when I was in there she was in some form or other still alive. I can't explain it, but it did feel like that, and it felt entirely natural.[30]

Mathew's experience was reminiscent of Agatha's sixth sense of knowing when Clara died. It reflected the indestructible connection between one generation and another, undestroyed even by death.

Part Three

Aurelia and Sylvia

The Outsider

Sylvia Plath had two totally different relationships with her mother, Aurelia, playing out simultaneously. Reflecting the duality of her personality, there was a bond between mother and daughter as intense and loving as Agatha's with Clara, but running alongside that version, in Sylvia's mind there was an equally powerful relationship which was full of hatred and resentment. Emphasising the 'psychic osmosis' she had with Sylvia, Aurelia clung to her belief in the strength of the first version until she was made brutally aware of the extent of the second after her daughter's death.

Similar to the other mothers in this book, Aurelia was an outsider. During her childhood, her Germanic ethnicity caused problems. Instead of being seen as attractively cosmopolitan like Julia, she was treated as an enemy alien. Her mother's experience of being the 'other' was to influence Sylvia's poetry; Aurelia believed that it aroused her interest in minority groups.[1] Writing about victims of the powerful was to inspire some of Plath's most unforgettable poems and short stories.

Aurelia's experience was typical of many daughters of immigrants. Her father, Franz Schober, was a hard-working man who spoke four languages. He was born in Bad Aussee, near Salzburg, Austria. His mother, who came from a wealthy family, died when he was 10 years old. After her death, Franz's father squandered his late wife's fortune on a Viennese showgirl, leaving scant money to support his large family. At the age of 14, Franz had to leave home and earn a living. By the age of 20 he had travelled across Europe, working briefly in Italy and France before moving to England. He was highly intelligent and wanted to study medicine, but his opportunities were limited.[2] After working for two years as a servant in Kent, he sailed to America to begin a new life.

Arriving in Boston on 1 June 1902, he joined a Viennese friend, Josef Grunwald, running a boarding house. Two years later, Josef's teenage sisters joined him. At just 16, it was a life-changing step for Aurelia Grunwald and she soon started a relationship with her brother's friend, Franz.[3] In July 1905, the young couple married and the following year, on 26 April, their first child Aurelia Frances was born.[4] Hardly more than a child herself, when her daughter was born, Mrs Schober relied on her close-knit family network for support. The family rented accommodation in the Boston suburb of Jamaica Plain.

When Aurelia was 5, her younger sister Dorothy was born and eight years later Frank Junior completed the family. As with the Millers and Stephens, the division of labour in the Schober household followed the traditional rules of separate spheres for men and women. Aurelia's mother ran the home while her husband worked as head waiter in a smart hotel in Boston. Having to serve people all day at work, Franz was determined to be master of his own home.[5] Aurelia was brought up in a Catholic household with rigid rules about right and wrong.

Living in a predominantly Italian and Irish area, the Schobers stood out from their neighbours.[6] As first-generation immigrants, they negotiated a fine line between assimilating into American society and maintaining their own culture. Trying not to advertise their German roots, Franz anglicised his name to Frank and the Grunwalds changed their name to Greenwood. As the First World War began, it would take more than a change of name to make the Schobers fit in. As a small child, Aurelia did not play with other children in the neighbourhood. When she started school, she entered a hostile environment. It did not help that her parents spoke German at home and she could not speak English. On her first day, she felt completely isolated. Standing in the corner of the playground, listening to the other children shouting at her but not understanding what they were saying, she picked up on two words: 'Shut up!' When she repeated those words to her father, she received her first and only spanking. Once Aurelia explained that she did not know what the words meant, Frank apologised.

The bullying did not end there, as a gang of children used to call Aurelia 'spy-face'. When her fellow pupils pushed her off the school bus steps, the driver did nothing to intervene. These episodes were bruising experiences for a sensitive young girl, ones she would remember for the rest of her life; she would pass on this sense of injustice to her children.[7] Like Agatha who felt the pain of her mother's childhood as acutely as if she had experienced it herself, Sylvia Plath empathised with her mother's suffering. Getting inside her mother's mind, she later wrote short stories, 'The Shadow' and 'Superman and Paula Brown's New Snowsuit', about a child's experience of being ostracised by her peers.[8]

Realising they needed to do even more to assimilate, Frank became an American citizen, and the family began to speak English rather than German at home. Aurelia was brought up to conform and climb her way up within the existing system. The family always voted Republican and supported President Theodore Roosevelt. The Schobers wanted Aurelia to have opportunities which had been denied them. They saved up for her to have ballet lessons. Like her daughter, Aurelia showed a desire to be the centre of attention. Years later, she recalled appearing as a firefly in her ballet school's performance. On the dimly lit stage, dancing in her winged costume with little blinking flashlights in her hands, she felt 'exalted'. Watching her parents' proud faces in the front row of the audience, although Aurelia was only in the chorus, she fantasised about being the prima ballerina.[9]

Aurelia's progress at school became a family project. Although they could hardly afford it, her parents bought her all the books she needed and then worked through them with her. As she grew older, reading fiction provided escapism for Aurelia and through novels she entered a fairer world.[10]

Frank had always been industrious and by the time Aurelia was 12 his hard work paid off. The family bought a three-bedroomed house at 892 Shirley Street, Point Shirley in Winthrop, Massachusetts. In the neat rows of houses, aspiring working and middle-class families lived respectable suburban lives. The Schobers' new house was close to the beach and boasted sea views.[11] Although it was not grand, like Talland House for Virginia and Ashfield for Agatha, this 'sea-bitten house' was to have a profound influence on Aurelia and later her daughter.[12] The sound and smell of the ocean entered their souls and became an essential element for both women's mental well-being.

Aurelia described her home life as 'peaceful' and 'loving', but there were tensions beneath the surface. She grew up in a patriarchal household where Mr Schober made the important decisions. Like in Virginia's and Agatha's families, although the pretence was maintained that the father was in charge, as time went on the family was really run by a matriarchy. The women were emotionally stronger than the men and, in a crisis, they took over. During the mid-1920s Frank lost the family's money through foolish investments. The situation was made worse as his career prospects were ruined by first Prohibition and then the Great Depression, which ended the era of grand hotels. Afterwards, Frank had to rely on seasonal work in hospitality.[13] He blamed himself rather than events beyond his control. Like Agatha's father's reaction to his family's financial crisis, Frank's spirit was broken. His failure to be a good provider changed the balance in his marriage and he handed over management of the family finances to his competent wife.[14]

With the work ethic inherited from her parents and the need to earn her own money instilled in her, Aurelia was determined to succeed. From the age of 14 she took part-time jobs to help pay for her tuition fees. She was not willing to spend the rest of her life in a job which did not stimulate her intellectually. Developing her self-worth by achieving, she was determined to better herself, but she soon came up against barriers. As the daughter of a waiter, it was uncertain she could go to college and if she did, she would be the first in her family to do so.[15] Instead of going to university, her father wanted her to have a vocational education and become a good businesswoman.[16] As Mr Schober was paying, he decided she should go to a secretarial college. In 1924, she enrolled at Boston University's College of Practical Arts and Letters, an all-female college which educated young women in secretarial skills and the arts.

During her college years, Aurelia made the most of every opportunity. Taller than her classmates, she was a high-profile student who literally stood out from the crowd. Juggling academic studies with a hectic social life, she was judged by her peers to be among the busiest and most studious in the class. Loving words, Aurelia was known as the 'class dictionary'. She became vice president of the Writers' Club and edited the junior yearbook. As editor-in-chief, she used the same carrot and stick techniques she would later apply as a mother; her student staff claimed they would never forget those 'would-be scoldings and those cherished words of approval and praise'. Aurelia also had a theatrical streak and, as president of the German Club, she took leading roles in student amateur dramatics. Playing the male star of the show, she was described as 'sensational'.[17]

As she worked her way through the American and British literary canon, she lived vicariously through the characters. The poetry of Emily Dickinson became her 'bible'. Like Clara and Agatha, Aurelia and her mother read the books together and discussed them. Mrs Schober also had a love of learning which had been thwarted; as she said to her daughter, 'More than one person can get a college education on one tuition.' Decades later, Aurelia was to apply the same principle to Sylvia's university experience, using it to broaden her own horizons even further.[18]

As with the other mothers in this book, Aurelia also had literary aspirations. When she was 17, a banal poem entitled 'Forbidden Fruit' was published in her high school yearbook; a few years later another poem, 'A Child's Wish', appeared in a college publication. Although she showed no poetic gift, her theme of a visit to the beach and hunting for mermaids would later appeal to her daughter; the lure of the sea became part of their shared mythology.[19]

Aurelia's passion for learning meant that she wanted to continue her education and become a teacher not a secretary. Studying for two years on the teaching track of the bachelor's degree programme, she graduated with a Bachelor of Secretarial Sciences. After graduating she took up a teaching post at Melrose High School in Massachusetts.[20] However, she was determined to rectify her vocational rather than academic degree and after a year, she returned to college at Boston University Graduate School to study for a master's degree in English and German which would enable her to teach languages and literature.[21] Once again, she relished the intellectual challenge and particularly enjoyed studying philosophy.

Unlike more privileged girls, Aurelia had to fight every step of the way to fulfil her potential. She had the talent, the dedication and the ambition, but as a young woman without a private income she could only get so far. She was the living embodiment of Virginia Woolf's argument in *A Room of One's Own*, which was written at the time Aurelia was going through college. Like Woolf's imaginary heroine, Shakespeare's sister, Sylvia Plath's mother was limited by her gender and her class from realising all her dreams. Aurelia's experiences were to shape her attitude to Sylvia's life; like Clara with Agatha, she was determined that her daughter would have the opportunities she had missed out on. She vowed that her children would never have to work in a menial job which did not fulfil them.[22]

28

The Genius Soulmate

Like the other women in this book, Aurelia was a romantic who shared their 'dangerous intensity of affection'. As a teenager reading novels, she also imagined herself as a heroine who would have her life transformed by marrying the right man.[1] Unlike Julia, she was not a great beauty, but she was attractive in a fresh-faced, athletic way. Her power over men would come from her intellect and indomitable will. Prefiguring her daughter decades later, only an exceptional man could measure up to her exacting standards.

In 1926, Aurelia began working in a summer job for Karl von Terzaghi, a professor at the Massachusetts Institute of Technology (MIT). Twenty-three years older than her, Karl was a charismatic figure. Born in Prague, he was a pioneer in the science of soil mechanics and a skilled civil engineer. A flamboyant character, his first marriage failed. According to his biographer, he was very attractive to the opposite sex because he loved women with his body and soul.[2] His sex drive competed with his work ethic, and he confessed in his diary that he was 'hunting for the great adventure'.[3]

Arriving in America in 1925 he soon became one of Boston's most eligible men. A skilled conversationalist in three languages, Karl was a Renaissance man who was as eloquent speaking about the arts as he was about science. Never a man to underestimate his own talents, one observer described him as a 'very egocentric person', who was 'a restless, fearless adventurer, a charming humourless cosmopolitan – and sometimes a bragging showman with immense craving for recognition'.[4]

When Aurelia was employed to type up Karl's manuscript, their relationship soon changed from professional to personal. As she worked into the evening, Karl asked her to join him for dinner. Afterwards, he wrote in his diary that he thoroughly enjoyed the company of 'the warm-hearted, clever girl'.[5] Although he was in his forties and balding, Aurelia was soon fascinated by her boss. As she listened to him talk about his cosmopolitan life, she believed that she was in the presence of 'a true genius in both the arts and the sciences'.[6] Looking for a mentor, Aurelia avidly devoured the reading lists he gave her on poetry, philosophy, Greek drama and Russian literature. The experience of having her intellectual horizons extended affected her for the rest of her life. It made her realise how narrow her world had been and that self-education could be an exciting lifelong adventure.[7]

There was a hint of risk-taking about their relationship which must have added to his appeal. He offered excitement rather than security, writing that the 'very moment you overcome fear and desire you leave the domain governed by the law and you become free'.[8] Over the next two years, the couple enjoyed an intense relationship. The dynamic of the experienced professor and his naïve protégée appealed to them both. Perhaps having 'a daddy issue' similar to her daughter's,[9] Aurelia was overwhelmed by receiving attention from this sophisticated man. In return, Karl was flattered by the hero worship of this attractive student. Like Sylvia decades later in her relationship with Ted Hughes, there was a strong element of self-dramatisation in their affair. He called her 'Lilly', the nickname for an idealised German-speaking girl, and she treated him as the genius he believed himself to be.[10]

The couple were very compatible and liked doing the same things. They enjoyed hiking, camping and dancing together but most important to Aurelia they shared intellectual pleasures. They went to art galleries, museums and concerts, and enjoyed watching plays, operas and the latest films. Giving her a tantalising glimpse of a stimulating future, they socialised with his academic friends. After a Sunday afternoon trip to a museum, Karl wrote in his diary about feeling 'warm and happy to be in the company of a girl who obviously likes me'. Aurelia confessed to him that she sometimes had feelings of loneliness which became 'insupportable'. She feared the chances of finding the right partner were exceedingly small. Karl was moved by her honesty, but he had some reservations about the 'sweet child'. He disliked her handwriting and complained that there was 'something stiff and sober in it, which I can't quite digest'.[11]

By October 1926, the relationship was serious enough for Aurelia to introduce Karl to her parents. He recalled the evening in his diary. Infantilising Aurelia, he wrote about how his 'dear little girl with shining brown eyes', showed him 'her treasures, the beach, and the walls and the sea she loves'. Although he was nearly the same age as Mr and Mrs Schober, they welcomed him into their family. He reciprocated by idealising 'the light and beauty of the home', and their neighbourhood as 'a little world in itself'. He described Aurelia's mother as 'a plump little lady with irregular features, brutish forehead, but loveable and kind and good-natured', while her father came across as 'serious, official, simple but sincere'.

The evening went well and ended romantically. As Karl walked back to the station with Aurelia and her father by the ocean in the moonlight, he revealed his feelings with a kiss. Seeing Aurelia with her family had made a good impression on him. He wrote:

> The picture of the girl was with me: her innocence, her happiness at her wealth in her modest surroundings, the blessings of an education paid for by the self-restraint of conscientious parents, a bud, on the point of becoming a flower.[12]

On New Year's Eve he felt optimistic; for the first time since arriving in America there was 'some warmth and sunshine, opportunities for love'.[13] After walking in the hills with Aurelia, he forgot about the pressures of work and felt 'gloriously happy'. He found her combination of 'perfect innocence, affection and sensitivity' irresistible, and, in her company, he felt childlike, free and enthusiastic. At this point he described their friendship as platonic, but it was not to stay that way for much longer.

In May, they spent a weekend camping with his university colleagues. As they swam together in the lake, he enjoyed seeing her in a bathing suit noting that she looked 'well-built and very pretty'. Later, as they exchanged passionate kisses on the beach at Winthrop, 'the cheeks of the dear girl were glowing, her eyes sparkled, and she could hardly master her tenderness'. She told him how proud she was of him and explained:

> Sometimes you are for me the mature experienced man, sometimes I have the feeling of perfect comradeship, enjoying with you on equal

terms, and sometimes, if you are tired you are like a younger brother, and I have motherly feelings as if you were a boy.[14]

Increasingly, Karl behaved as a prospective husband. Although he was the same age as many of her teachers, he partnered Aurelia at her junior prom. He met her friends and was pleased to discover they were homely, sincere girls. At 4 a.m., they drove back to her home to share the post-prom breakfast prepared by Mrs Schober and he then slept in Aurelia's bedroom.[15]

Their relationship was becoming increasingly intense. During an afternoon spent in the Blue Hills, they went into the woods and 'played like children, enjoying each other, our lips, the heat of our cheeks, the fire in our eyes, listening, feeling, giving and feeling'. After a thunderstorm drove them out of the woods, as they walked home the tension between them mounted. Aurelia told Karl that a friend had written a character sketch describing her 'self-sufficiency, conceit, intolerance and sensitivity'. Karl replied that these were just the personality traits which he saw in her and which put a barrier between them. He told her, 'You will never make a man friend unless you get rid of your self-sufficiency!' He defined self-sufficiency as:

> The opposite of unlimited capacity for love. The opposite of true art and of true research. To be shut off from views towards what can be accomplished, inside and outside ourselves [...] To see our own circle rigidly surrounded by a fence, the inside of the fence superior to what is outside. No desperate dash towards an ideal goal, since no such goal can be perceived.[16]

His comments foreshadowed criticisms Sylvia would make of her mother's limitations. Evidently Karl's remarks hurt Aurelia, and when they kissed goodbye, she almost wept. Perhaps trying to prove she was far from self-sufficient, when they next spent a weekend together, it seems that they made love for the first time. Karl wrote:

> Lilly's (Aurelia's) tenderness and love broke out during these two days, like a beautiful flower. She repented so sincerely for whatever might have hurt me, and displayed her affection so touchingly, that I could not help surrendering whatever reserves were left. [...] It was as if my whole

being was purified and enlivened by her presence, and I began to wonder how I could exist during the last year without the sweet companion enjoying with me and sharing whatever inspires me. Love again, after years of confinement.[17]

In the summer, Aurelia took a holiday office job at Camp Maqua, Poland, Maine. With log cabins around a large lake, it was a romantic setting. When Karl visited, they went boating on the lake or swimming, then every evening there was singing and storytelling around the campfire. The passionate nature of their relationship was recorded in Karl's diary. He wrote that seeing Aurelia again made him feel five years younger. Lying together on the lakeside, in their own intimate world, Karl relished 'the passionate kisses of the girl, curled up on the blanket and pressing her body against mine, trembling with overflowing tenderness'.

The following day, as Aurelia swam in the lake, he admired 'the subtle strength and gracefulness of the slender body of my girl'. After watching the sunset, they spent the evening on the lake shore experiencing again 'the delight of perfect and unrestricted communion with my girl'. When he had to return to Boston at the end of the week, the memory of 'a week in fairyland' went with him.[18] After their idyllic time together, he believed that perhaps his eternal search for fusion with a woman was over.[19]

It seemed their relationship was the real thing for them both. Half a century later, Aurelia still recalled the thrill and excitement of becoming the most important person in another's life.[20] Sounding remarkably like Sylvia when she wrote about falling in love with Ted Hughes, Aurelia remembered her relationship with Karl in rapturous terms, writing to her granddaughter Frieda:

For the first time, I felt transfigured, beautiful: all was possible. Indeed [...] for a time, it was almost impossible for me to concentrate on anything else – that beloved face appeared between me and anything I was trying to read or study. I felt I spilled joy from every pore; the whole world and everything in it were beautiful. We shared it all then – for a little over two years – the music, the arts, books, our ideas on every possible subject, the earth, the sky, the sea; our hopes and dreams for ourselves and each other.[21]

Aurelia's passion for Karl shows a different perspective from her traditional image. In Sylvia's writing, her mother comes across as a conventional, sexless, rather dried-out, middle-aged woman. In Karl's diaries and in her letters about their relationship, a very different picture emerges. She appears as a passionate, sexy young woman who understood sexual attraction and could write about it with a verve worthy of her daughter.

Although Karl fell in love with Aurelia, the depth of his feelings proved ephemeral. She saw him as the perfect man to father her brilliant children.[22] However, while for her he was *the* one, for him she was just one among many; the fantasy they created together was not part of his long-term reality. Karl's biographer minimises their relationship, not even naming Aurelia, and lists a young woman matching her description as just one of his conquests during this time.[23]

By the end of the summer, Aurelia was becoming increasingly dependent on Karl. One evening on their way home, she suddenly turned to him and begged him not to overwork. She told him that without him her life had no meaning.[24] On another occasion, when it was time to say goodbye, she could hardly control her feelings; she pleaded that she was willing to make any sacrifice for him. Karl wrote in his diary that he felt torn by conflicting feelings. He wondered, 'What should I do with my love for this child?'[25]

In October, when Aurelia broke her ankle and was admitted to hospital Karl sat solicitously by her bedside. Part of him found her 'irresistible in her efforts to express her love and tenderness and show that she considers her life inseparably bound to mine'. But the other part of him wanted to pull away. He wrote in his diary, 'I am still striving. Could I dare to tie this young and loving and sincere child to my existence? Would she never regret? What with those periods when I am absorbed in my work, and she, lonesome, waiting?'[26]

Although he was beginning to have doubts, Karl did not end their relationship. He spent Christmas Eve with Aurelia and her family, describing it as 'a delightful, old-fashioned' celebration. When the couple talked about her friends who were about to get married, it seems Aurelia was hoping for a commitment from him, but Karl was not prepared to make one.[27] One evening, as he left her, he turned around and saw her through the window leaning against the wall crying her eyes out.[28]

The turning point came in April 1928. He wrote in his diary that he had thought seriously about marriage, but decided against it because 'one marries the family'.[29] It seems that as he got to know the Schobers better, he began to dislike Aurelia's parents.[30]

It seems likely that Aurelia's willingness to surrender herself to him sexually also played a part in his decision. Her innocence had been a large part of her initial attraction. Inserted into his diary at the page where he wrote about not marrying her is a letter addressed to 'Darling'. We cannot be sure to whom it was written but it sets out his attitude to female sexuality.[31] He wrote, 'You certainly must admit that I am far from being a puritan. Yet, at the outset of our acquaintance I was inwardly shocked more than once by your attitude towards matters of sex.' He explained that 'a high type of female' would never 'yield to a superficial impulse of desire', because soul and body were inseparable. For such an original man he sounded surprisingly conventional as he added that men were 'instinctively repelled' by thoughts that their chosen female 'associated with physical love pure and simple, far more desire'.[32]

It seems the double standard, which allowed men to have sex with as many women as they wished but penalised women if they did not 'save' themselves for marriage, played a part in the breakdown of their relationship. If Aurelia lost her virginity to Karl, it is likely that she did it in the hope that he would marry her. The fact he had decided against it was a catastrophic blow that could affect her future marriage prospects.

Karl did not immediately tell Aurelia about his decision, but she sensed their relationship had changed. In the summer, he spent several months away working in Central America. She agonised over the separation and feared that he did not need her anymore. On his return to Boston, Karl began to plan his next career move; he intended to take up a professorship in Vienna and had no intention of taking Aurelia with him. In November, when they went for a hike together, weeping while she kissed him, she asked, 'What will become of me if you leave?'[33] In a suitably dramatic finale to their affair, after seeing a performance of *Carmen*, they had the talk Aurelia had dreaded. Karl finally ended their relationship, writing, 'It was like a farewell and symbolic. Lilly (Aurelia) does not want to be an "episode" and I can offer no more. The dear little girl. She takes life so seriously.'[34]

For a woman of Aurelia's emotional intensity, the break-up was devastating. The future she had always dreamt of was within her grasp and at the last moment was snatched away. She suffered additional humiliation shortly afterwards. Just a fortnight after his relationship with Aurelia ended, Karl started dating Ruth Doggett. A doctoral student in geology at Harvard, Ruth was more Karl's professional equal.[35] A year after this new relationship began she achieved the goal that had eluded her predecessor. After taking up his professorship in Vienna, Karl proposed to Ruth, and they married a few months later in the summer of 1930. Karl's explanation of why he now felt able to marry makes an observer wonder if Aurelia was too dependent on him. He claimed Ruth was 'the only type I could live with. A girl honestly and strenuously striving to build a world of her own.'[36] Their marriage emphasises what Aurelia missed out on. Ruth lived the life her rival had fantasised about with Karl. She became 'more than a wife' to him, sharing in all aspects of his work, enjoying frequent trips abroad and pursuing her own academic research.[37]

Aurelia's rejection by Karl is the key to understanding much of what unfolds later. Losing her first love was one of the major tragedies in her life, on a par with Julia losing Herbert, Clara's loss of Fred or Agatha's divorce from Archie, but because, unlike them, she was not married to her lover, its emotional importance was overlooked by friends and family at the time and her daughter's biographers since. Karl was to her what Ted Hughes was to Sylvia: her genius, demi-god and soulmate. Neither woman could lose such a great love with equanimity; the intensity of their passion made it dangerous. Like everything with Aurelia, its effects simmered beneath the surface rather than exploded in the open. She soldiered on but how she reacted to this betrayal was to have long-term consequences, not just for herself but for her daughter. The depth of her hurt did not make her in the best place to become the wife of another man. Decades later she admitted that the pain remained until Sylvia was born.[38] It is telling that it was becoming a mother, rather than her marriage, which helped her recover from Karl. It was to be her daughter, not her husband, who became the next focus of her intense devotion.

29

Second Best

In Aurelia's life the realist always competed with the romantic. She was heartbroken by Karl's rejection, but she was a pragmatist and, rather than retreat into a corner, she picked herself up and tried again. As Agatha's attitude to marriage emphasised, Aurelia lived in an era when a woman's destiny was still often in the hands of her husband. If Aurelia wanted to move up in the world, she had to find another exceptional man to fill the gap left by Karl.

For a while, she thought that she had found what she was looking for in a middle-aged biology professor, Otto Plath. Finishing her Boston University Master's Degree in English and German, Aurelia was working on a bilingual thesis about the Swiss physician, alchemist and philosopher Paracelsus as a literary and historical figure.[1] To help her research, the head of the German department advised her to take the course in Middle High German run by Otto Plath.[2] When she met Professor Plath, she asked him if she could join his course, but he replied that he could only run it with a minimum of ten students. Never one to be deterred, Aurelia rallied her fellow students and made sure fifteen registered.[3]

Superficially, Otto shared many similarities with Karl; two decades older than Aurelia, he was also a pioneer in his field, the study of bumblebees. A handsome man, she described him as 'a very fine-looking gentleman [...] with extraordinarily vivid blue eyes and a fair ruddy complexion'.[4] However, unlike her previous love, Otto was a shy, donnish figure. Disappointed in his first marriage, he had retreated into a bachelor existence. A disillusioned romantic, it seems that when Aurelia focused her attention on him, he believed that he had finally found his match.

Aurelia realised he was attracted to her when he asked her to recite during lessons. Flustered, he could not meet her eyes and looked down at his shoes. Abiding by the rules that professors were forbidden to socialise with students, he did not ask her out until she had finished her final examination.[5] On the last day of the semester, when Aurelia came to say goodbye, she found Otto alone in the German office. Playing with his pen and still avoiding looking directly at her, he asked Aurelia if she would like to join him for a weekend with some faculty friends. Although the invitation was a surprise, she agreed to go because after Karl's treatment she was ready for some fun.[6]

During the weekend their relationship changed. Otto told her that her thesis had impressed him, and he wanted to get to know her better. He then surprised Aurelia by confiding about his unsuccessful first marriage. Even at this early stage, he evidently envisaged marrying her, because he explained that if he started a serious relationship with a young woman, he would get a divorce.[7]

Although the weekend had gone well, Aurelia had learned not to put her life on hold while waiting for a marriage proposal. She continued with her planned career path. Her academic potential is plain to see in the thesis she wrote on Paracelsus. Academic theses are often notoriously dull, but not this one; it is beautifully written and vividly captures the spirit of the man and his age. Her sophisticated scholarship shows that she was able to communicate complex ideas in lucid language. Interweaving German and English, her precise use of words highlights her bilingual ability.

Her dissertation gives us an insight into what interested her. An alchemist who was thought to have magical powers, Paracelsus was portrayed by contemporaries as a 'saint or as in league with the devil'.[8] While reading about him, Aurelia explored attitudes to the occult.[9] Like Clara and Agatha, she realised the potential dangers of dabbling with forces beyond her control and distinguished between the positive and negative use of supernatural powers.[10] Later, Sylvia also became fascinated by the occult, but she did not handle it with the same care as her mother.

In her introduction, Aurelia explained that she chose to write about Paracelsus because he was 'a searcher for truth'.[11] Challenging conventional doctrines, he explored the ideas of pagan and Eastern religions. Her attraction to him suggests that, like Clara and Julia, Aurelia was also a seeker after truth who questioned orthodox religion. Although she had been brought up a Catholic, she became a Unitarian, a branch of Christianity which believes that Jesus was inspired by God in his moral teachings, but he was not a deity or God incarnate.

In her thesis, Aurelia's passion for scholarship shines through, making it seem even more unfair that she lived in an era when someone of her gender and class could not fulfil her youthful promise. Once again, reading like a case study for Virginia Woolf's feminist theories, instead of becoming a high-flying academic or writer she had to rein in her ambition. During the summer, she took a temporary job as the manager of the business office of two camps for underprivileged children in New York. On returning home, she became a German and English teacher at Brookline High School, one of the state's best public schools.

Aurelia had a gift for teaching. Once, a school inspector came to watch one of her lessons and was amazed by her creativity. Teaching *Ivanhoe* she memorised the highly charged scene between the hero and heroine and then acted out the parts. Her class loved it and reacted with excitement to the novel. After watching her performance, the inspector came up to her, 'shaking his head in wonderment', and saying, 'Sheer genius; sheer genius.'[12] Once again, like her ballet performance, Aurelia enjoyed performing and showed a desire to be centre stage. Talented though she was, however, her career opportunities were limited. She accepted her best chance of living the life she desired was to marry a brilliant academic rather than become one herself, and this was due to lack of opportunity rather than ability.

When Aurelia returned in the autumn, her relationship with Otto intensified. As they hiked together, Otto introduced her to ornithology and entomology. In return, she shared her love of drama and literature with him, going to the theatre to see the plays of Ibsen and Shaw. Her dreams of a collaborative academic life now had a new hero. Otto and Aurelia discussed working together on joint projects, even planning groundbreaking research on 'The Evolution of Parental Care in the Animal Kingdom'.[13]

In some ways, Aurelia had more in common with Otto than Karl. They both came from aspirational immigrant backgrounds. Born in 1885, Otto had grown up in Grabow, Posen Province in the Polish Corridor territory of Germany. His father, Theodore, was a master blacksmith who travelled abroad selling equipment, leaving his wife, Ernestine, to bring up their six children.[14] As a child with a sweet tooth who loved honey, Otto became fascinated by bumblebees and developed a passion for entomology.

Growing up in one of the poorest regions of Germany, Otto believed he could have a better life in America. His grandparents had already emigrated to Wisconsin and aged 15 he joined them. Recognising his intellectual potential, his grandfather agreed to send him to Northwestern College, Wisconsin, with the condition that he would train to be a Lutheran minister. Once at the Lutheran Seminary, he suffered a crisis of faith because as an admirer of Darwin, he was shocked to find his theory of evolution was banned there. Otto's experience had echoes of Leslie Stephen's renunciation of religion at Cambridge. After six months of soul-searching, Otto realised the ministry was not for him. Rather than supporting his decision, his grandparents gave him an ultimatum: if he broke his promise and did not become a minister, he would no longer be part of the family. Even when his parents moved to America the family bond was never fully re-established.[15]

Determined to continue with his education, Otto enrolled at the University of Washington where he completed a Master of Arts degree in German. After completing his degree, he became first a research assistant then a teaching fellow in Berkeley's German Department. In 1912 he married 23-year-old Lydia Clara Bartz. The marriage was a disaster due to a combination of sexual incompatibility and financial problems and Lydia soon returned to her family.[16] Both Otto and Aurelia came to their new relationship with deep emotional scars. Neither Otto's estrangement from his family nor his attitude to his first wife augured well for the future; it meant he was used to fending for himself and living a bachelor existence.

As well as his disastrous personal relationships, Otto had suffered in his professional life. Like the Schober family, he was made to feel that he was an outsider in his adopted country. During the First World War he was victimised because of his German background. In October 1918, he was investigated by the FBI for suspected 'pro-German' leanings. Otto was eventually cleared of any pro-German sympathies, but he lost his chance of an instructorship at Berkeley at least partly due to his enemy alien status. Understandably, his treatment made him bitter.[17]

After these experiences, Otto became a wary character who did not confide easily in people.[18] However, he rebuilt his life through sheer hard work. He spent four years studying biology at Harvard. In 1921, to guarantee his patriotism was never questioned again, he filed for naturalisation papers and later became an American citizen. By the time he met Aurelia, his life was back on track; having completed his doctorate he became an assistant professor of biology at Boston University.[19]

A photograph of him at this time shows an immaculately dressed tall, slim, good-looking man with a dimple in his chin, standing in front of a blackboard. Yet there is something slightly arrogant and threatening about his pose; with his hand in his pocket, the other firmly gripping a book, he looks a controlling man, tightly wound like a spring with repressed emotions. In contrast, a companion photograph of Aurelia in her first teaching job shows a wholesome young woman who, in her ankle socks and sensible shoes, still looks like a schoolgirl. An observer could foresee the power dynamic that might develop between this controlling older man and naïve young woman, except it would be more complicated than this because, beneath Aurelia's innocent image, she had an iron will which was as strong as her husband's.

If Aurelia noticed any warning signs, she chose to ignore them and when Otto proposed she readily accepted. On 4 January 1932, Otto obtained a divorce from his first wife in Ormsby County, Nevada and married his new bride the same day. It seems Aurelia's parents were relieved to see her finally settle down because Mrs Schober drove the couple to Nevada for their wedding.[20] All Aurelia later recorded of this pivotal moment in her life was the dryness and dust of the place – this aridity was to be replicated in her marriage.[21]

The Full-Time Homemaker

The life Aurelia desired with Otto was much like the one Julia achieved with Leslie Stephen. She dreamed of being the wife of a brilliant academic and mixing in intellectual circles, but, like Julia, she was to discover that living with a man who desperately wanted to be a genius, but fell short, could be a soul-destroying experience. According to Sylvia's fictionalised account in *The Bell Jar*, as soon as her parents left Reno on their honeymoon, things started to go wrong when Otto said to Aurelia that they could stop pretending and now be themselves.[1]

The couple set up home in the ground-floor apartment of an elegant Arts and Crafts style building in Jamaica Plain.[2] Like Virginia and Agatha, Sylvia grew up in a family based on the Victorian idea of separate spheres for men and women. Unlike Julia and Clara, Aurelia was from a different generation and, having fought so hard for her education, she resented this unfair division of labour. Before their marriage, Otto had promised her that he wanted a modern, equal partnership, but the reality was different. He expected his wife to be a full-time homemaker while he was the head of the house. Left with little choice, Aurelia yielded to his wish and gave up her teaching career.

Setting his demands in context, in the 1930s there was a stigma to having a working wife. Many states in America had laws prohibiting married women from working.[3] As Agatha Christie's underplaying of her professional life when she was first married shows, attitudes were much the same in England. Aurelia was living during a transitional period for women; although they were beginning to receive more educational opportunities, the careers open to them were still limited. It was to take decades for Virginia Woolf's visionary views – of opening the professions more widely to women – to become accepted. Sexism was exacerbated by the economic climate. In the aftermath of the Great Depression, jobs were hard to come by for men as well as women. In January 1932, Otto's salary was cut by 20 per cent. The couple ironically dubbed this their wedding gift from the university, but, in the difficult economic environment, they felt fortunate that Otto had even kept his teaching post.[4]

Giving up the vocation Aurelia had worked so hard to achieve was a bad start to married life as it undermined her separate identity. Making her situation even more claustrophobic, Otto was a control freak who insisted on handling all the finances and even micro-managed where their food was bought.[5] He expected his wife's life to revolve around him. Admittedly, Aurelia had always dreamt of a collaborative intellectual partnership, but it did not live up to her expectations. In the first year of their marriage, they worked together on Otto's book, *Bumblebees and Their Ways*. A hint of Aurelia's resentment seeps through when she later complained 'all had to be given up for THE BOOK'. Otto now took charge of her further education and directed it to support his career. Aurelia had not learnt Latin, which was used in entomology classification. Feeling it was a gap in her education, Otto taught her the language. She then undertook an intensive course at Northeastern University to make her better able to help him.[6]

When Otto's book finally appeared, he acknowledged Aurelia's contribution, writing in the preface about 'the service of my wife, Aurelia S. Plath, who aided me greatly in editing the manuscript and proofreading'.[7] In this brief mention, Aurelia was cast as a glorified secretary rather than a gifted academic and writer in her own right. A recent biographer of Plath, Andrew Wilson, speculates that she contributed more to the work than her husband admitted; the book was written with a literary flair unusual in scientific works.[8] His view seems plausible; the vivid descriptions and elegant style are reminiscent of Aurelia's thesis on Paracelsus. It is much better written than Otto's earlier papers.[9] Aurelia later described how they collaborated; her husband set out the sources to use, then she read them and wrote the entire first draft which Otto then rewrote before submitting it.[10]

Like Julia Stephen, at first Aurelia did everything to help her husband fulfil his goals, but this left no time for her own ambitions. Unlike Julia, she did not have her own fulfilling role in the outside world, nor was she treated with the same devotion Leslie Stephen lavished on his wife. The self-sacrifice demanded by Otto did not come naturally to Aurelia.[11]

Thwarted in her professional ambitions, Aurelia channelled her considerable energy into bringing up her children. She explained that she was 'totally imbued with the desire to be a good wife and mother'.[12] Aged 46, Otto was equally keen to start a family so both parents were delighted when, on 27 October 1932, their daughter Sylvia was born. The Plaths approached parenting as seriously as they treated their academic work. Making it sound like an exam she could revise for, while pregnant Aurelia read books and magazines on child-rearing and then discussed the conflicting theories with her husband. An emotionally detached method was popular at the time. Child-rearing guru Emmett Holt's bestselling book warned mothers against cuddling children, playing with them, or displaying much affection. Babies should only be kissed on the forehead or cheek and the less the better. Similarly, a survey of articles in women's magazines from 1910 to 1935 showed many contributors considered that too much love was the greatest threat to a child's welfare.[13]

However, Otto and Aurelia rejected these ideas and favoured a more progressive model promoted by Friedrich Fröbel and Maria Montessori. Rejecting his own mother's rigid parenting, Otto believed in the natural unfolding of an infant's development. Aurelia also favoured a more child-centred approach; she fed her baby on demand and later wrote, 'Both my babies were rocked, cuddled, sung to, recited to and picked up when they cried.'[14]

Although both Aurelia and Otto were affectionate parents, there was also a clinical side to their child-rearing. Like scientists observing a specimen, they treated it as an intellectual exercise as much as an instinctive experience. When Sylvia was 6 months old, Otto held her against a rope attached to a bamboo shade and was delighted that her feet grasped the rope in the same way as her hands; he saw this as proof of man's evolutionary process.[15]

Like a researcher collecting data, Aurelia recorded every stage of her daughter's development in a baby book entitled 'The Record of Sylvia Plath by her "Mummy"'. Every detail was lovingly written down, from Sylvia's weight and height to her banal baby-talk. Aurelia's data collection sounds obsessive, but her behaviour should be set in the context of her era. An equally ambitious Boston mother behaved similarly. The matriarch of the political Kennedy dynasty, Rose Kennedy, also recorded every detail of her children's development with an eye to the future. Mrs Kennedy created a cataloguing system in which she kept index cards listing illnesses, treatments and measurements for each of her nine children.[16] Both Rose and Aurelia were following childcare guru Emmett Holt's advice that children should be weighed at standardised intervals and the data collated on index cards.[17]

In her early years, Sylvia was the shared project which united Aurelia and Otto. As they celebrated her first birthday, Aurelia wrote, 'Her daddy and I agree that the whole world doesn't hold another 1-year-old as wonderful and so sweet – at least it doesn't for us!'[18] On another occasion, as they looked in on their sleeping children, Otto whispered to her, 'All parents think their children are wonderful. We know!'[19]

With a demanding baby to look after, Aurelia's world could no longer revolve around Otto. His demands for a household geared towards his academic life became increasingly hard to maintain. Although it went against her strong-willed temperament, Aurelia realised that if her children were to grow up in a peaceful home, she would have to become more submissive.[20]

Otto's career was going well. He became a highly respected entomologist who was seen as a great man in his scientific field. Promoted to be a full professor at Boston University, he became known as the 'Bee King'.[21] However, like Leslie Stephen, although Otto was brilliant, he was never as successful as he wished. When he was frustrated with himself, he took it out on his wife. Behaving as though he was still a bachelor, Otto failed to provide Aurelia with the emotional intimacy or stimulating social life she desired. The dining room became his office with the table treated as his desk and the sideboard stacked with reference books. Aurelia was not supposed to move them. She only dared to invite friends to dinner on the one evening a week that Otto gave a course at Harvard night school. To avoid displeasing him, she drew a plan of where each item went and made sure they were correctly replaced before his return.[22]

We only have a portrait of their marriage from Aurelia's perspective. Without Otto's testimony, it can only be a one-sided picture. We also know that until Sylvia was born, Aurelia was still badly hurt by Karl. It seems that Otto was not the only half of the partnership who was unable to give themself completely to the marriage. Her lack of total emotional commitment does not excuse his controlling behaviour, but it perhaps adds to our understanding of why both husband and wife withdrew from each other and became disillusioned.

Years later, Sylvia asked her mother why she did not leave Otto if she was so unhappy with him. At first Aurelia looked blankly at her, but then replied that as it was the Depression, she would not have been able to get a job to support herself.[23] Feeling isolated in her marriage but unable to escape, Aurelia turned to her parents for support. As with the other authors in this book, Sylvia grew up in a matriarchy. In her autobiographical essay 'Ocean 1212-W', Sylvia wrote about their importance in her early life. Her grandparents' home was a sanctuary away from the tensions of her parents' fraught relationship.[24]

Aurelia and her mother were exceptionally close, not just emotionally but also in age. In a photograph of the two women together with baby Sylvia, they look almost identical. During the summer before and the one after Sylvia's birth, Mr and Mrs Schober let out their house and came to live with the Plaths. While Aurelia and Otto worked on his projects, her parents cared for their little girl. Aurelia wrote, 'Dad and Mother added their humour, love and laughter to what would otherwise have been too academic an atmosphere.'[25]

With four adults doting on her, Sylvia grew used to being the centre of attention. In April 1935, her time as the sole focus ended when her brother, Warren, was born. While Aurelia was in hospital, Sylvia went to stay with her grandparents. Like Agatha's visit to her grandmother while her mother was in America, Sylvia missed Aurelia. Describing this episode in 'Ocean 1212-W', she wrote about feeling that her mother had deserted her. Her grandmother was no substitute; Mrs Schober was a forceful character with strict rules. According to Sylvia, her grandmother did not properly inform her about what was happening.[26] However, years later, Aurelia challenged Sylvia's version, claiming that she had thoroughly prepared her daughter for the birth. She explained:

> She helped me get the clothes, and we talked about the baby coming before he was born. [...] And every time, she'd say 'Not today!' Because she knew that I was going away to get the baby. But it wasn't one of those instances where she was kept in ignorance and that her grandmother told her in her Victorian way. It wasn't that at all.[27]

Despite not being strictly autobiographically accurate, Sylvia's essay gives us an insight into her feelings. She recalled her possessive reaction to Warren's birth; it was the first time she had a real rival for her mother's attention. It was the start of her separation from Aurelia and the feeling that the fusion between them was over.[28]

Daddy's Girl

After Warren's birth, life was very different for Sylvia. In 1936, the family moved to Johnson Avenue, Winthrop to be nearer Aurelia's parents. They replaced their small apartment with a larger seven-room house which had a study for Otto and a well-stocked playroom for the children.[1] As a toddler, Warren suffered from health problems and when he was ill Sylvia was sent to her grandparents. Letters written by Aurelia to her daughter at the time suggest she felt torn between the competing needs of her children and husband. Like Julia, trying to do the best for everyone else left scant energy to look after her own needs.

Like the other mothers in this book, Aurelia was her children's first teacher. Every outing was turned into an opportunity to learn something new. On their daily walks, she encouraged them to observe nature and have 'a painter's eye as well as a writer's eye'.[2] Virtually as soon as Sylvia was born, Aurelia introduced her to poetry because she believed that even babies responded to the cadence of verse. When Sylvia was just a toddler, her mother taught her the alphabet and while Aurelia nursed Warren, the little girl would sit on the floor trying to read the newspaper by picking out the capital letters.[3] By the age of 5, she was reading fluently. After Aurelia read her poems by Robert Louis Stevenson, A.A. Milne, and Dr Seuss, she encouraged Sylvia to imitate them by making up her own rhymes and limericks.[4]

Aurelia and Otto sent Sylvia to the Sunshine School, a progressive pre-school. Classmates remembered her as a highly intelligent, imaginative, happy child.[5] When Sylvia returned home, seeing Aurelia was preoccupied with Warren, she became jealous and turned to Otto for attention. Sylvia monopolised mealtimes with her precocious conversation.[6] In her short story, 'Among the Bumblebees', she described how the sight of her mother cuddling Warren, like a Madonna with her child, made her almost gag, but then she noticed her father gazing at her with unconcealed devotion, and she felt triumphant.[7] Increasingly, the family divided in two, with Aurelia defending her delicate son while Otto favoured his precocious little girl. Father and daughter developed a special bond and she became his 'pet'.[8] A family friend remembered Otto speaking to Sylvia as if she was his intellectual equal, 'the recipient, the chosen one'.[9]

For Sylvia there was an element of competition between mother and daughter for Otto's love. Like Virginia as a small child with Leslie Stephen, the little girl did everything she could to endear herself to her father. Knowing he valued achievement, Sylvia played the piano for him and improvised dances. Before going to bed, she recited the poems she had learned and showed him her drawings.[10] Her last Father's Day card to Otto proclaimed that her heart belonged to Daddy.[11]

Realising his daughter was exceptionally intelligent, Otto shared his love of learning with her. Showing Sylvia how to catch bumblebees, he taught her the Latin names of insects.[12] Soon she was exclaiming '*Bombus bimaculatus!*' when she saw a bee.[13] She enjoyed just sitting with him, watching him correct his students' papers. Observing him lecture, she got a thrill from the power he exerted over his audience.[14]

Aurelia saw the father–daughter relationship differently from Sylvia. According to her, as an older father Otto never played with Sylvia nor took responsibility for her routine care. Aurelia remembered, 'She never went out with Daddy, never went to the beach with Daddy except in the evenings she would play the piano.'[15] In contrast, in 'Among the Bumblebees', the father and daughter do go to the beach together where they swim and run along the shore.[16] Responding to her daughter's story, Aurelia claimed that it was her father, Frank, not Otto, on these excursions. She argued that it was an example of how her daughter fused different characters together in her fiction.[17] However, the purpose of Sylvia's portrayal was to capture her strong bond with Otto rather than be strictly factually accurate. Perhaps she was indulging in wishful thinking, and it was what she would have liked to have done with her father. Whatever the truth, this was just one among many occasions where mother and daughter perceived the same events or relationships in totally different ways.

Sylvia's time with her father was to be all too brief. After Warren's birth, Otto withdrew more into himself and began to worry about his health. He lost weight, had a persistent cough and sinusitis. He became more irritable and was easily exhausted. A friend had recently died from lung cancer, and he self-diagnosed himself as having the same disease. Aurelia found it 'heart-breaking to watch a once handsome, powerfully built man lose his vigour and deteriorate physically and emotionally'.[18]

Otto was not an easy patient and he did nothing to help himself. When Aurelia appealed to him to get medical advice, he angrily exploded at her. Years later, Sylvia recalled her mother speaking to her father in a gentle low voice and Otto shouting at her.[19] Like Julia and Clara solicitously nursing their husbands, it was an exhausting time for Aurelia and most nights her sleep was disturbed. Once again, she felt torn between the needs of her husband and children. As Otto deteriorated, she kept Sylvia and Warren separate from their ailing father as she was concerned their noise would disturb him and they would be frightened by the sight of him suffering. The children ate separately and only saw their father for brief periods before bed. Sylvia remembered her father lying in his study on the sofa while her mother brought him meals on a tray.[20]

Otto continued to work for as long as possible. Aurelia supported him, updating his lectures, replying to letters, and marking students' work.[21] In August 1940, Otto's decline escalated. After stubbing his little toe, he started to limp and developed black and red streaks running up to his ankle. When Otto finally saw a doctor, his condition was very serious as he had an advanced state of diabetes mellitus.[22] As with other authors in this book as they observed their parent's illness, Sylvia did not understand exactly what was happening; she only later processed her intense emotions by writing about them. In 'Among the Bumblebees', she recalled the doctor's fateful visit and the whispered conversations with her mother. The little girl blamed the doctor and her mother for her father's decline.[23]

Over the next few months, as Otto went in and out of hospital, the family experienced a rollercoaster of crises interspersed with brief respites. Allowing Aurelia to dedicate herself to her husband's care, Warren stayed with his grandparents, but Sylvia wanted to remain with her parents. Involving the little girl, Otto's nurse cut down a uniform to fit her and called her 'my assistant'.[24] As Otto was thirsty, his daughter rushed up and downstairs bringing him jugs of water and fruit.[25] A photograph of Sylvia shows a little girl dressed as a nurse, looking immaculate with her tightly braided pigtails and a fixed smile on her face, but her eyes are not smiling and they reveal her carefully concealed anxiety.

In Sylvia's short story, there is a poignant description of going into her father's sick room and watching him sleep. As she looked at his thin face and listened to his shallow breathing, she tried to speak to him, but he did not respond because he had withdrawn into himself. As she left the room, she felt lost and betrayed.[26]

On the nurse's day off, Otto suggested that Aurelia should take a break with Sylvia and go to the beach. Feeling uneasy, she only left him for a short time, and then dropped Sylvia off at a friend's house. On her return, finding Otto collapsed on the stairs, she dragged him to his bed and gave him an insulin injection. Overnight he deteriorated; drenched in sweat and shaking with uncontrollable chills, he caught hold of his wife's hands and asked why he had been so 'cussed'. Unable to control her tears, or her resentment, Aurelia thought it need not have happened.[27]

The next day, as Otto's foot and leg had turned gangrenous, doctors decided that his leg would have to be amputated. It seemed to go well and Aurelia began planning for their future life together. Preparing her children for their father coming home, Aurelia explained to them about the operation. She struggled to get her head around what was happening, but as usual, she treated it as though she was revising for an exam. She talked to doctors about how to look after a diabetic and make him feel that he was still a 'whole man' and acceptable to her. Unfortunately, Otto seemed depressed and avoided discussing the future.

On 5 November 1940, Aurelia visited her husband in hospital. His condition was serious, and he seemed very weak. In his last few hours, he told her he did not mind dying but he would have liked to see how their children grew up.[28] After she arrived home, the doctor told her Otto had died from an embolism in his lung. He was 55 years old. Characteristically, Aurelia's first thoughts turned to her children. She waited until the next morning to tell them what had happened. When she went into her daughter's bedroom, Aurelia found her reading. Sylvia had been praying every night for her father to get better, so when she heard the news, she angrily told her mother that she would never speak to God again. Aurelia said that she could stay at home that day, but from under her blanket Sylvia replied that she wanted to go to school.[29] From now on academic achievement and later writing became the way Sylvia tried to exert control over a chaotic world.

On 9 November, Otto was buried under a modest slab on Azalea Path in Winthrop's town cemetery. Eight-year-old Sylvia and 5-year-old Warren did not attend the funeral. Trying to protect her children, Aurelia also decided not to let them see Otto's body in the funeral parlour. She believed they would not have recognised their father as his corpse bore no resemblance to the man she knew.[30] While Virginia had been traumatised by having to kiss her mother's dead body, Sylvia resented not being allowed to see her dead father or say goodbye to him properly. In her novel *The Bell Jar*, the heroine complained that her mother had never bothered with mourning, and that she had never had the opportunity to cry.[31] She thought it was odd that the family never visited his grave and she was angered by the minimal memorial Aurelia had chosen for him. Complaining about her mother's failure to confront what had happened, Plath wrote that it meant her father's death had always seemed unreal to her.[32]

Virginia and Agatha also described a sense of unreality after losing their parents. The similarity in all three authors' reactions suggests that there was no ideal formula to handle bereavement; the enormity of their loss was just too great. However, the way their surviving parents dealt with their grief greatly affected their daughters and had long-term repercussions. While Leslie Stephen wallowed in self-pity and ignored Virginia's needs, Clara Miller was open with Agatha and mother and daughter drew closer. In contrast, Aurelia hid her grief from her children, fearing that seeing her break down would traumatise them further. Decades later, vindicating her actions, she explained:

> What I intended as an exercise in courage for the sake of my children was interpreted years later by my daughter as indifference [...] I vividly remembered a time when I was a little child, seeing my mother weep in my presence and feeling that my whole personal world was collapsing. <u>Mother</u>, the tower of strength my one refuge, crying! It was this recollection that compelled me to withhold my tears until I was alone in bed at night.[33]

Aurelia's panic at seeing her mother as a vulnerable person for the first time echoes Agatha's experience when she witnessed Clara's collapse after her husband died. By trying to soldier on and pretend everything was fine, perhaps Aurelia subliminally taught Sylvia to conceal her true feelings. Although her stoicism was brave and done with the best intentions, the consequences were counterproductive in her relationship with her daughter.

The real tragedy is Otto did not need to die as he had a manageable disease. His death seems to have been as much due to a psychological as a physical problem that prevented him from seeking the help which could have saved him. Biographer Heather Clark suggests he may have been suffering from depression.[34] In later life, Sylvia saw his death as a 'slow suicide', and blamed Aurelia for not doing more to prevent it.[35] There was a history of mental health problems in Otto's family. When he first met Aurelia, he described his mother, Ernestine, as a melancholy person.[36] After moving to America, her mental health deteriorated; she suffered from age-related dementia and died in an asylum. One of Ernestine's daughters and a granddaughter also suffered from mental health problems. After Sylvia's first suicide attempt in 1953, one of Otto's sisters told Aurelia about this family history.[37] Surprisingly, Aurelia never shared this information with Sylvia. However, her daughter must have had some inkling because she alluded to it in *The Bell Jar*, writing that her father came from 'some manic-depressive hamlet' in Prussia.[38]

The loss of her father in her childhood exacerbated any hereditary predisposition for mental health problems. A Scandinavian study which observed the effect of parental death on children over a forty-year period found that, irrespective of cause, it was associated with an increased long-term risk of suicide.[39] Of course, this does not totally explain Sylvia and Virginia's tragic ends; Agatha experienced a similar childhood loss and lived a long and happy life. Yet this research does emphasise that the trauma of their early bereavement should not be underestimated. As Virginia wrote in her diary three decades after her mother's death, 'People never get over the early impressions of death I think. I always feel pursued.'[40]

Otto's death cast a long shadow over his family. While Agatha believed her parents had a very happy marriage and Virginia recognised her parents' relationship was mixed but strong, Sylvia grew up aware of the flaws in Otto and Aurelia's partnership. However, her relationship with her father was different from her mother's experience; she had been his favourite and there were shades of his personality in her. Sylvia identified with Otto and his side of the family. In 'Among the Bumblebees', the daughter believes she is more like her paternal than her maternal family.[41]

Like Virginia, Sylvia's writing is haunted by her lost parent. She tried to recreate her father and understand her complex feelings towards him. Virginia believed her father's idealised image of her mother in the *Mausoleum Book* stopped her being able to remember the real woman. Sylvia also tried to distinguish what Otto was really like by disentangling him from her mother's version. Both Virginia and Sylvia had to put a distance between themselves and their surviving parent if they were to see their dead parent from their own perspective. Like the Bloomsbury author's fluctuating feelings towards her dead parents, Sylvia's attitude towards Otto was ambivalent. She loved him but she was aware of his flaws and felt he had abandoned her.[42] At different periods in her life, depending on what was happening to her, she saw him from alternative perspectives.

The Pact

Shortly after Otto's death, Sylvia returned from school and handed her mother a piece of paper which read, 'I PROMISE NEVER TO MARRY AGAIN'.[1] Her classmates had made her cry by taunting her that she would soon have a stepfather. Devastated by the thought of a stranger replacing her father, she immediately took action to prevent it happening.[2] Aurelia signed her daughter's contract and Sylvia kept it folded in the back of her diary, in order to hold her mother to her promise.

Later in life Sylvia regretted her emotional blackmail; she realised that it would have been healthier for the whole family if Aurelia had remarried. Instead of channelling her energies into her children, her intensity would have been diluted. Excluding a new partner from the equation also meant that Sylvia, like Agatha, felt a burden of responsibility for her widowed mother's well-being.[3] When Sylvia went to college and met a classmate whose widowed mother remarried, she felt guilty. Aurelia had to reassure her that her decision had nothing to do with the promise.[4]

Perhaps their pact suited both parent and child at the time as it gave Aurelia an excuse to opt out of a part of her life which had been unsuccessful. Left a young widow in her thirties, Aurelia chose to shut down her romantic life prematurely. It is as likely that she did not marry again because of her past experiences as much as her daughter's demands; her rejection by Karl and her disappointment with Otto left her disillusioned. Like her daughter, she was a perfectionist, and it seems that if she could not have perfection in a partnership, she wanted nothing at all. However, she attributed her decision to putting her children first. She explained that she decided:

I never should marry again unless, in the years to come, I would have the opportunity to marry a man I respected, loved, and trusted to be a good father to my children and <u>whom</u> the children wanted to have for their father.[5]

Any responsible mother considers her children when selecting a new partner – both Julia and Agatha did the same before remarrying – but Aurelia's attitude goes further. She was once again putting her needs second; the suggestion that Sylvia and Warren, rather than she, could veto her choice of husband suggests a reversal of the normal power structure between a parent and child. Ultimately, sticking to the rules imposed by a grieving 8-year-old girl backfired on both mother and daughter. There are echoes of the destructive relationship in Agatha's Westmacott novel *A Daughter's a Daughter*, where the widowed mother and her daughter interfere in each other's love lives. By doing so, they damage their close relationship and resent each other.[6]

No sacrifice by Aurelia could make up for the loss of Otto. Like the other authors' experiences of losing a parent, the death of Sylvia's father marked the end of her 'seaside childhood'.[7] There was no pretence that the Plaths' family life had ever been idyllic, but it became even more difficult after Otto's death. The situation was exacerbated by the Second World War. In Sylvia's short story 'The Shadow', the threat to the father is not death but that he will be sent away to a camp for enemy aliens because of his German birth.[8] The girl reacts in the same way as Sylvia responded when Otto died, crying out that God would not let it happen, but when her mother told her that God would allow it, the girl bitterly replied that she would no longer believe in Him.[9] The similarities between fact and fiction suggest that as the war coincided with Otto's death, the two seismic events became linked in her subconscious. The world no longer seemed a secure place where goodness and justice would triumph.[10]

It was not just world events which added to the instability. Like Agatha and Clara's situation after Fred died, there were serious financial repercussions from Otto's death. He left no pension, and most of his life insurance was eaten up paying for his medical and funeral expenses.[11] With the family's income much reduced, Mrs Plath had no choice but to go back to work. In one way, returning to her career suited Aurelia; she had enjoyed teaching and was good at it, but now it was due to necessity rather than choice. In her generation there was stigma attached as it was unusual for a mother to be the single wage-earner. It put an additional strain on her which was reflected in her health. During Otto's illness she had developed a duodenal ulcer; now she suffered from gastric haemorrhages which required hospitalisation.[12] Like Agatha after her father's death, Sylvia worried that she would also lose her mother.[13] Tempted to just let go, Aurelia held on to the image of her children's faces before telling herself that it was just one fight more for their sake.[14]

Instead of being able to pursue her more risky career ambitions, Aurelia took the safer option and returned to teaching. She later told an interviewer, 'I had hoped to become a writer once, but I didn't feel that I could expose my children to the uncertainty of a writer's success or failure.'[15] Like the other mothers in this book, her literary ambitions were channelled into making up bedtime stories for her children; a particular favourite was about a teddy bear called Mixie Blackshort.

Aurelia made the best of her situation but even working exceptionally hard, she found it difficult to earn enough money. Teaching posts were in short supply and Aurelia had to take whatever she could get. Teaching Spanish and German, she became a substitute teacher at Braintree High School. She left home at 5.30 a.m. each morning and then three evenings a week she gave private Spanish lessons. She later told an interviewer, 'I had a man's responsibilities, but I was making a single woman's salary.'[16] Even with her parents helping care for the children, working such long hours was unsustainable, so after two terms Aurelia began teaching nearer to home at the Junior High School in Winthrop. Combining a full teaching programme with handling the school's finances, the stress of her job once again triggered her gastro-intestinal problems.

In summer 1942, the dean of the Boston University College of Practical Arts and Letters asked her to develop a medical secretarial training programme. Although it meant leaving the security of her steady job, she relished being in a more academic environment.[17] Vowing to make the course fascinating, she included basic anatomy, a brief history of medicine and medical record keeping. She later told an interviewer, 'I especially enjoyed knowing that I was preparing young women for a useful career.'[18]

Shortly before Sylvia's tenth birthday, the extended family moved to Wellesley, Massachusetts, setting up home at 26 Elmwood Road. The choice of location was made with a calculated eye to Sylvia's future.

Wellesley was a more affluent area with excellent schools. Most importantly, the prestigious Wellesley College, the private women's liberal arts college, offered a town scholarship for exceptional students.[19]

With its white clapboard and shutters, their new home was attractive but small. Warren and Mr and Mrs Schober had bedrooms of their own, but Aurelia and Sylvia shared a twin-bedded room. Although their living conditions were cramped, Aurelia and her mother took pride in creating a welcoming home. They were both excellent cooks and a childhood friend of Sylvia's remembered a warm, close-knit unit.[20] Her mother and grandmother were the lynchpins of the family. Aurelia tried to combine being the main breadwinner with a more traditional female role. The subliminal message was that it was possible to be both a successful career woman and a homemaker. Sylvia realised juggling work and children was only possible with the support of her grandmother, however. While Aurelia was teaching, Mrs Schober was always there.

Later in life, Sylvia suggested that she disliked being brought up in a matriarchy and the relationship between her grandmother and her mother was not ideal. She told her psychiatrist that Aurelia always remained a child while her grandmother was alive, cooking for her and looking after the children while she worked.[21] Her criticism is reminiscent of Agatha's daughter Rosalind's comments about her mother's dependence on her grandmother.

Managing family finances, Aurelia was frugal. Any money left over was spent on her children rather than herself and while she made do with second-hand clothes, she took pride in dressing Sylvia in new outfits.[22] She made sure her children were brought up to be careful with money. Sylvia had to help with household chores and get holiday jobs to supplement her income. However, according to Aurelia, she minimised Sylvia's workload so that she could enjoy her school life to the full. Teasingly nicknamed the 'prima donna', the household was run around her needs because, as Aurelia later explained, 'Sylvia required the most consideration.'[23] Observing her schoolmates' wealthier lifestyles, Sylvia resented the burden her family's relative poverty placed on her.[24] She later complained that she had been brought up with the Puritan attitude that being lazy or spending money on luxuries was rather wicked.[25]

As the atmosphere at home could be claustrophobic, Sylvia escaped to her own imaginary world. In a note to Aurelia, she told her mother she would like to give her fairy wings, so that she could enter her secret world, but as that was impossible, she would try to be a good girl instead.[26] This comment suggests that escaping through her imagination provided Sylvia with some much-needed privacy. She pretended she wanted Aurelia to be able to share it with her, but part of her enjoyed having a separate sphere away from her mother.

The Teacher

Aurelia was not just a mother to Sylvia, she was also her teacher. Even once her daughter started school, Mrs Plath remained her greatest intellectual influence. It was not just the emphasis she put on education and her high expectations which shaped her. At a formative stage in Sylvia's life, Aurelia told her stories which would become part of her personal mythology. She also introduced her to some of the writers who would inspire her later work.

Aurelia instilled the Protestant work ethic in her children, teaching them that by working hard they could achieve whatever they wanted.[1] It was obvious that Sylvia had great potential; when she did an IQ test, she achieved a score which put her in the genius range.[2] Her natural ability was matched by her capacity for hard work. Sylvia was soon awarded top grades in school. When she received straight As on her report, Aurelia was delighted and praised her. Inadvertently, this started a vicious circle which made Sylvia believe that she had to achieve to win her mother's love.

Outside the classroom, Mrs Plath encouraged her daughter to fill each moment with activities. She proudly recorded that in one year Sylvia wrote reports on forty books, became a dedicated Girl Scout, and continued with her piano lessons. An all-rounder, she socialised with friends at summer camps and enjoyed sailing and swimming. Encouraging Sylvia to write about her experiences, Aurelia put a diary in her Christmas stocking. Sylvia then asked for an undated journal because she wanted to record the 'big moments' of her life in more detail.[3]

Aurelia took every opportunity to expand her daughter's cultural horizons. Gratifyingly, Sylvia responded with enthusiasm. After a trip to an art exhibition followed by listening to a classical concert, Sylvia wrote in her diary, 'Magnificent'.[4] It was a great responsibility being the mother of such an impressionable child. Aurelia fed in material but never knew how it would come out, transformed by her daughter's uncanny imagination. When Sylvia was 7, Aurelia took her to the circus. The little girl sat spellbound in the darkened ring, fascinated by the juggler tossing his flaming torches in the air. Eleven years later, this incident inspired Sylvia's first collection of poems, *Circus in Three Rings*.[5]

When Sylvia was 12, Aurelia took her to see Shakespeare's *The Tempest*. Unlike Clara and Agatha's trips to the theatre, instead of being just for fun there was a didactic purpose. Like an English teacher setting an assignment, Aurelia said she would buy good tickets if Sylvia read the play first and could tell her the story.[6] Her daughter passed her test with flying colours. The performance was magical and both mother and daughter felt transported into another world. Sylvia described it as the biggest day of her life.[7] It had a lasting effect; themes from the play would recur in her later work. Her final collection of poetry is named *Ariel* after the spirit who is bound to serve the magician Prospero.

Compared to Clara, Aurelia appears as a pushy mother hothousing her daughter. However, setting her behaviour in the context of American culture of the era, it seems less extreme. Once again there were similarities between Aurelia's and Rose Kennedy's parenting. For Mrs Kennedy too, every occasion was turned into an academic exercise. When she took her children on outings to places of historic interest she would rattle off improvised maths challenges and encourage questions and discussion.[8] One of the Kennedy daughters later described her as 'more a teacher or an inspirer' than an affectionate mother.[9] Later, Rose admitted, 'My ambition was to have my children, morally, physically and mentally as perfect as possible.'[10] Both Rose's and Aurelia's attitude was partly due to their perfectionist personalities, but it also reflected the fashion for achievement-oriented child-rearing. It was believed that the correct mothering could set a child on a lifelong path of personal and social significance. The Republican Motherhood, centred in New England, encouraged women to raise patriotic children who would enter public service.[11]

Later, Aurelia claimed that, unlike her parents, she had always been determined her children should have absolute freedom of choice in their education and careers.[12] Yet the education she gave her daughter steered her towards becoming a writer. From when Sylvia was a small child, Aurelia shared her love of words and favourite literature with her. For the rest of their lives, sharing texts would play an integral part in creating intimacy between mother and daughter.[13] Perhaps because of her failed relationship with Karl, love and loss was a recurring theme; later a similar fear of abandonment would feature frequently in her daughter's work.

Sylvia remembered for the rest of her life her mother reading from Matthew Arnold's *The Forsaken Merman*.[14] The Merman marries a mortal and lives a joyously unconventional life with her under the sea, but when she leaves him to return to land, they are separated for ever.[15] The combination of the tragic story and evocative language had a profound effect on Sylvia. Like Virginia's heightened experience after her mother's death, Sylvia had her first visceral reaction to words as Aurelia recited the poem.[16]

The idea of an underwater world peopled by mermaids and mermen became part of mother and daughter's mutual mythology. In one of the few surviving poems written by Aurelia before Sylvia was born, she described a child on a beach searching for caves where mermaids hid.[17] In 'Ocean 1212-W', Sylvia described them both as 'sea-girls'.[18] As a child she believed in mermaids rather than God and Father Christmas. Her first memories were of the sound of the sea and her mother taking her to the beach, where she crawled straight towards the incoming wave and was only saved by Aurelia grabbing her.[19]

Another myth passed from mother to daughter, which once again explored love and abandonment, was the legend of the Lorelei. Aurelia often played her children a nineteenth-century German song inspired by folklore about a beautiful maiden who threw herself into the river in despair over a lover who betrayed her. Transformed into a siren, she sat on a rock combing her golden hair, luring fishermen to destruction.[20] In later life, Sylvia identified with this bewitching figure, and she drew on the myth in her poem 'Lorelei'.[21]

Mother and daughter spent hours reading the classics together. They studied Donne, Browning and Tennyson but there were also more recent female poets including Edna St Vincent Millay, Emily Dickinson and Sara Teasdale.[22] Recalling their long discussions about literature, Aurelia remembered it as a precious bonding experience.[23] However, unlike Agatha and Clara who informally critiqued the books purely for pleasure, the Plaths approached it in a more structured way, making detailed notes in the margins.[24]

Sylvia's response to literature was intense. When they read Millay's 'Renascence' she was particularly moved by the poet's descriptions of suffering. With her ability to absorb other people's experiences, she fixated on the lines about a starving man.[25] Considering Sylvia's extreme sensitivity, parts of Aurelia's reading list seem ill advised. For Christmas 1949, she gave her daughter a copy of Friedrich Nietzsche's philosophical fiction *Thus Spake Zarathustra*.[26] Associated with Nazism and atheism, Nietzsche's subversive ideas challenged conventional concepts of morality and decency.

Some of Nietzsche's ideas would spread dangerous ripples through Sylvia's life. In his advice to writers, Nietzsche declared 'of all that writing, I love only that which is written with blood. Write with blood and you will discover that blood is spirit.'[27] This became a mantra for Sylvia and her most memorable writing would be in blood – both her mother's and her own. Even more pernicious, Nietzsche glorified death as the ultimate fulfilment. He explained, 'What has become perfect, everything ripe – wants to die.'[28] The Nietzschean influence is evident in Sylvia's later poetry; in 'Lady Lazarus' the speaker calls dying an art,[29] while in 'Edge', the dead woman is described as perfected in the Nietzschean sense of the word.[30]

Inadvertently, Aurelia had introduced her daughter to destructive ideas which would become a permanent part of her imaginative landscape. Perhaps, like Clara giving Agatha realist French novels to read, Aurelia felt it would be better for her daughter to explore challenging ideas with her there to discuss it rather than coming across these concepts on her own. Sylvia's vulnerability meant she absorbed them deep within her. Unintentionally, some of the dark philosophy Aurelia shared with her daughter started a ball rolling which could not be stopped.

The lasting image we have of Aurelia is of the ultimate 'tiger' mum. In later life, Sylvia was to be critical of her mother's emphasis on academic achievement. Biographers also blamed Mrs Plath for pushing her daughter too hard to succeed. But is this picture fair? Aurelia claimed that rather than pushing her daughter towards her own desired goal, Sylvia had always set her own targets. At first, they were modest; they only grew as her daughter's ability became apparent. When Sylvia began writing poetry, she hoped that one day her verses would appear in Hallmark greetings cards. Sylvia's ambitions increased as a teenager; when she went to college, she set herself the triple goal of doing well academically, socially and in her writing. Aurelia emphasised this goal was 'one of her own choosing'.[31] Sylvia's brother, Warren, supported Aurelia's view. He did not believe that their mother pushed his sister too much, telling a biographer, 'Sylvia didn't need any pushing.'[32]

The reality is perhaps more nuanced, as it seems Sylvia and Aurelia's perfectionist personalities played off each other. At first, Mrs Plath was very aware of her daughter's gifts, and they worked as a team to get excellent results. Later, though, Sylvia's need to achieve developed a momentum beyond Aurelia's control. A school friend of Sylvia's, Louise Gisey White, explained that Mrs Plath 'expected a great deal of her, but Sylvia was just as motivated by herself'.[33] Financial necessity also played its part because Aurelia had learnt that a woman of her class had to work very hard to fulfil her potential. Sylvia's high school English teacher, Wilbury Crockett, said, 'I think she was driven by the thought that Sylvia and Warren might not get all that they ought to have. Financial security was a very real factor.'[34]

Sylvia's closest childhood confidante, Betsy Powley, was upset that Aurelia was turned into a 'scapegoat'. She explained, 'Whatever Aurelia did was for Sylvia's benefit. She sacrificed her whole self for her children.'[35] The trouble was, as Agatha's Westmacott novels show, too great a sacrifice is not what a child wants; it can turn love into a burden, a mother into a martyr.

34

Too Close for Comfort

Just when the close bond between Aurelia and Sylvia began to change is difficult to pinpoint. Rather than happening overnight, their relationship gradually altered. Nor was any rupture between them ever complete because their symbiotic relationship meant that while part of Sylvia longed to break free from her mother's influence, the other part remained dependent on her.[1] Until Sylvia went to college, her emotional tussles with her mother read like many teenage clashes with a protective parent. Her rebellions were minor; it is only with the benefit of hindsight that they appear to be the harbinger of more profound problems.

As she was growing up, their devotion seemed mutual. Like Agatha and Clara, widowed mother and daughter were exceptionally close. Echoing Virginia's attempts to please Julia, Sylvia used to slip her latest poems and drawings under Aurelia's napkin to discover on her return from work. For special occasions, she created exquisite cards with loving verses and illustrations.[2] According to Aurelia, her daughter was uncritical of her throughout her high school years. Aged 15, Sylvia said that when she became a mother, she wanted to bring up her children just as Aurelia had her.[3] Aurelia wrote that this was the remark she most treasured.[4]

Yet their relationship was not quite as harmonious as this comment suggests. In 1947, Aurelia was offered a position as dean of women at Northeastern University. She would have found the role rewarding, but when Sylvia screamed at her, 'For your self-agrandizement [sic] you would make us complete orphans!' her mother turned down the opportunity. The same dynamic was playing out when Sylvia made Aurelia sign her ultimatum not to remarry; her daughter was using emotional blackmail and Mrs Plath allowed her to do so. Rather than respecting Aurelia's self-sacrifice, Sylvia resented it, complaining that she did not have 'the guts to make the break'.[5]

As Sylvia became a young woman, there were times of great companionship between mother and daughter as they enjoyed pleasurable activities together; Aurelia relished taking Sylvia clothes shopping and going out to restaurants or the cinema. Mrs Plath looked back with nostalgia, writing that these years were 'such fun. The sharing meant so much.'[6] Sylvia's version was less rose-tinted. On one occasion, she was furious with Aurelia for refusing to buy her an expensive dress. In her diary, Sylvia wrote angrily that she hated her mother for not getting her the outfit. Yet even in this private journal, she edited her emotions and immediately apologised for her outburst, claiming that writing about it had got her frustration out of her system.[7] Like most teenagers, Sylvia wanted her independence, and she resented it when her mother was overprotective. When Aurelia would not allow her to go to Boston on her own to see the film *Gone with the Wind*, she mocked her mother's anxieties in her diary.[8] These occasional clashes should not be blown out of proportion, however, as they were comparatively few and at this point, criticisms of her mother were rare.

As Sylvia entered her late teens, Mrs Plath recognised that the boundaries between them had to be renegotiated. She gave her daughter more space and when Warren left for college, Sylvia had her own bedroom. Sylvia wrote about how much she loved having her private domain. She happily sat at her desk writing and contemplating the future.[9] One of Sylvia's friends remembered Aurelia was always pleased when the girls were together enjoying themselves.[10] Mrs Plath realised that Sylvia would now confide in her friends rather than her, but Sylvia still felt her mother understood her best and she valued talking to Aurelia about her increasingly changeable moods.[11] Handling her volatile daughter carefully, Mrs Plath thought before speaking and tried not to refer to anything Sylvia told her confidentially in the past.[12]

Tall and slim, Sylvia had a similar build to Aurelia but was more attractive than her mother had ever been. Her generous smile lit up any room and she was the vivacious centre of attention at parties. A life-enhancing character, she was popular and dated many boys. Rather than being jealous, Aurelia enjoyed seeing her daughter enjoying herself. Like Clara with Agatha, she took a close interest in Sylvia's love life. Wanting her to look her best, she helped her get ready for an evening out by setting her hair.[13] When Sylvia returned from a dance, Aurelia listened to her coming upstairs and, depending on the pace of her footsteps, she could immediately tell how the evening had gone. If it had been a success Sylvia would rush in and tell her all about it. Mrs Plath wrote that on these occasions she relished Sylvia's enjoyment as if it had been her own.[14]

In contrast to the other mothers in this book, according to Aurelia, she was frank with her daughter about sex – by the time Sylvia started dating, she knew the full facts of life. Sylvia felt able to ask her mother questions about many aspects of sexuality.[15] But in interviews with her psychiatrist, Sylvia painted a different picture. She recalled Mrs Plath warning her about the double standard, telling her that any eligible man would want his wife to be a virgin when they married, no matter how promiscuous he had been.[16] Later, Aurelia explained that she advised her daughter not to have sex before marriage – not because she condoned such sexist rules but due to societal pressures.[17] It seems Aurelia did not tell Sylvia about her own heartbreaking experience with Karl. Sylvia thought her mother did not understand sexual desire and was just being prudish – little did she know that Aurelia had learnt the hard way about the double standard.

America was a conservative country in the 1950s. It treated its daughters very differently from its sons. There was a backlash against the war years when women had taken on male roles and shown their competence. Once the conflict was over, they were expected to return home and become housewives. It was difficult for young women growing up in this era to know how to behave; the glimpse of freedom they had been given had been taken away from them and they were now expected to choose between a career and motherhood.

For a young woman who was as brilliant as Sylvia, the situation was particularly challenging. She intended to be a writer, wife and a mother. She wanted to live an active not a passive life and she envied men being able to combine a career and family.[18] To be the best writer possible, she needed the same opportunities as men to experience life to the full. She was envious of male sexual freedom, and in her journal she fantasised about being a man visiting bars and brothels. Aware that women experienced lust too, she resented the idea that female sexuality should be treated differently from male sexual behaviour. She described being a woman in this sort of hypocritical society as her tragedy.[19] Echoing Virginia Woolf's feminist ideas, she feared that if she had to repress her own desires, as Aurelia had done, she would either go mad or become neurotic.[20]

Sylvia faced a dilemma: conform or rebel. When she was 19, she wrote in her journal that the only free act available to a woman was accepting or refusing the man who wanted to marry her. Although she resented this limited sphere of action, she feared that she was beginning to accept it.[21] As Sylvia analysed her attitude, she noted a confusing ambivalence. Although in theory, like Virginia Woolf, she resented a sexist society which expected women to live vicariously through their husbands, like Agatha, she enjoyed the sexual attraction between men and women. She admitted that under certain circumstances she wanted to get married.[22] Part of her was an iconoclast but another part was conventional, and this clash created tension within her.

Sylvia appeared to be the perfect all-American girl. Her friends and teachers thought she was an exceptionally happy person.[23] For much of the time this was accurate; rather than thinking of herself as a depressive, she thought of herself as passionate and brave.[24] Aurelia also emphasised her daughter's immense capacity for joy. Yet behind the radiant veneer there was a darker side, which was also real. The two sides of her personality – the exuberant, confident girl, and the unstable, insecure young woman – coexisted. At different times, one side would overpower the other.

As a teenager, she first expressed her experience of psychological pain in the poem, 'I Thought That I Could Not Be Hurt', written after her grandmother accidentally ruined a picture she had created. In this poem, she described the emptiness inside her; this idea of a void within was to become a recurring theme.[25] Her writing could be cathartic, but it also encouraged her to delve into her darker side. During her teens, Sylvia began to send her poems and short stories to magazines. After many submissions, in August 1950 her first story was published in *Seventeen* magazine. Aurelia was very involved in the process, acting like an amateur literary agent. Like Clara's involvement in Agatha's early work, Aurelia brainstormed ideas with Sylvia when she had writer's block and, using her mother's suggestions, the story flowed. On at least one occasion, Mrs Plath provided the title. Once it was finished, she mailed off her daughter's work to potential publications. These collaborative experiences were enjoyed by them both and Sylvia lovingly expressed her gratitude.[26]

By her late teens, Sylvia was developing her own voice and her mother did not approve. Aurelia wanted her daughter to write morally uplifting stories.[27] However, Sylvia's melancholy works sold better than her happier ones. She discovered that detailed self-analysis, which involved drawing on her darker emotions, produced her best literature. Her mother believed that this was 'the beginning of the appeal of the tragic muse'.[28] Perhaps Sylvia's choice of subject matter was also too close to home. Her mother's experience seems to have inspired many of her stories. Almost half of those written in high school were about working-class women who had ambition but were prevented by circumstances from fulfilling their potential. Usually, the outcome for these women was bleak; they lived lonely, limited lives which undermined their mental health.[29]

Although Sylvia drew on her mother's life, her favourite subject was really herself. She found exploring her emotions both cathartic and creative. When she was 17, she described her conflicting emotions – the self-confidence and the destructive perfectionism which existed side by side. She feared she would never be able to achieve the perfection she desired.[30] When Sylvia was feeling negative about herself, her mother's fulsome praise could no longer boost her confidence. If Mrs Plath complimented her, she would dismiss it as only because she was her mother.[31] At times, whatever Aurelia did or said seemed to be wrong. Mrs Plath claimed that she was not unduly concerned by the change in their relationship because she remembered her own critical attitude to her parents when she was at college.[32]

On both large and small matters, Aurelia had a clear idea of what she thought best for her daughter, but this did not always coincide with Sylvia's views. Mrs Plath had always wanted Sylvia to go to Wellesley College, but instead her daughter chose Smith College, the independent liberal arts college in Northampton, Massachusetts. A girl had to be exceptional to get into either Smith or Wellesley. No doubt the fact Smith was further away from home than Wellesley was part of the appeal, as Sylvia wanted to experience the wider world. However, her choice had financial implications; if she enrolled at Wellesley, she could have received a full scholarship. Aurelia could not afford to pay the tuition fees for Smith's course. If Sylvia was to study there, she needed to be awarded one of their highly competitive scholarships. Even if she gained one, Aurelia would still have to contribute to her costs from her limited salary.[33]

Although it made life more difficult for Mrs Plath, like Clara with Agatha, she tried to see the situation from her daughter's perspective. She consulted with friends and family; Sylvia's English teacher and the family's minister were convinced that going to Smith would be good for Sylvia.[34] Once she had weighed up the options, Aurelia did everything she could to support her daughter. In September 1949, she wrote to Smith getting details about their application process. It seems that Aurelia may have already had concerns about Sylvia's mental health because when the college's letter stated that they required psychological tests, she underlined it in red pencil and wrote 'Inquire'.[35]

The fact Sylvia would only be able to attend Smith if she got a scholarship increased the academic pressure. Aurelia grew concerned as she watched her daughter work for eight hours at a time, even sometimes forgetting to eat.[36] By the time she was applying to college, her pursuit of excellence was taking on a pathological quality. In her essay 'America! America!' she used the vocabulary of disease to describe her obsession with getting into college, comparing it to a frightening virus.[37]

As usual, when Sylvia set herself a goal, she achieved it. She gained a place at Smith and was awarded a scholarship for her freshman year. Aurelia contributed to her fees, but Sylvia also received generous financial aid from several other sources, including the Olive Higgins Prouty Fund. When Virginia Woolf wrote 'we think back through our mothers if we are women', she had been referring to women writers as much as biological parents. The author Olive Higgins Prouty was to become one of Sylvia's 'literary mothers'. Aurelia had laid the foundations for her daughter's literary career,[38] but now Sylvia needed supplementary mother figures to help her develop further.

Mrs Prouty gave Sylvia an insight into the literary world which Aurelia could never offer. Olive Prouty had suffered from mental health problems, but rather than preventing her from becoming a bestselling writer it had provided her with material. Using the money she earned, Mrs Prouty funded a scholarship at her alma mater, Smith, for 'most promising young writer'. When Sylvia was awarded this scholarship, she felt her benefactress was a kindred spirit.[39] At their first meeting, the two women had an immediate rapport. Mrs Prouty asked Sylvia if she had ever written about her family. Sylvia explained that she had not because she came from such an ordinary home. Her mentor said it might seem that to her, but it would not be for other people, and she should mine this material in her work.[40] Later, Sylvia was to take her advice, with consequences for both her literary and biological mothers.[41]

35

Smith Girl

In September 1950, Sylvia left home to go to Smith. It was the moment both mother and daughter had been working towards for years, but the reality was different from the dream. During her college years, Sylvia experienced a rollercoaster of emotions. Aurelia wrote that if her daughter's mood swings were charted on a graph, it would resemble 'the contours of the Alps'.[1] There were exceptional high points but also devastating low ones. Mrs Plath travelled on this vertiginous journey with Sylvia, sharing her daughter's experiences as if they were her own.

Whenever they were apart, Sylvia wrote frequent letters home. Rather than being exclusively for Aurelia, the majority were intended to be read aloud to family and friends. If Sylvia wanted to keep a letter confidential, she wrote asking her mother not to share it.[2] While in her journal she felt free to express negative emotions, in this correspondence she often provided a more positive spin. Did Sylvia tell Aurelia what she wanted to hear because her mother could not stand the truth? Or was she reshaping reality because of her own psychological needs? Was she fashioning an image for the wider audience of family and friends? Biographer Heather Clark suggests that rather than the divergence being caused by Aurelia only demanding good news, mother and daughter were 'co-conspirators' in attempting to protect each other from anxiety.[3] However, they were unable to hide their true feelings from each other for long. Even when they failed to confront challenging emotions, they seeped through – shaping their relationship.

When Sylvia first arrived at Smith, she felt homesick. She wrote to Aurelia saying that for all her talk of becoming self-sufficient, she suddenly realised how much she still needed her mother.[4] She found it hard to make female friends because her competitive nature did not endear her to the other young women.[5] Many of them were wealthy and well connected and Sylvia was very aware of the difference between her home life and their luxurious lifestyles. Few of their mothers had to work, and while they were able to travel abroad in the vacations, Sylvia had to take holiday jobs. She resented having to work so hard to have what they took for granted.[6]

Although she was an outsider, Sylvia was soon outstanding in both her academic and social life. Like Agatha's letters to Clara describing travelling the world, Sylvia wanted Aurelia to share her exciting new life. She wrote detailed descriptions of her academic work, the famous speakers she heard, and the glamorous parties she attended. Years later, Aurelia was still writing enthusiastically about her daughter's letter describing an elite coming-out party. She wrote, 'Had Cinderella written a description of her evening at the prince's ball, it couldn't have been more rapturous than that which Sylvia described. [...] Oh new worlds opened that night as they continued to do throughout her life.'[7]

Exposed to this wider world, Sylvia began to see her family as unsophisticated and provincial. When she returned home, Aurelia did everything to pamper her, cooking her favourite food and keeping the house quiet so Sylvia could sleep late.[8] Despite all Aurelia's efforts, Sylvia was often critical in her journal. She denigrated her mother's choice of décor and the way she looked. Aurelia was aware that her daughter was looking down on her. She recalled how 'in the eyes of my Smith girl' her hair was not properly styled, her second-hand suits were unfashionable and her white blouses 'did nothing for me'. Although Aurelia claimed she was amused by her daughter's reaction she could not help thinking, 'I dress this way the better to provide for you, my dear.'[9]

Sylvia's feelings for her home were never consistent. Just a few months after complaining about the shabbiness, she complimented Aurelia on what a great job she did and how she loved her home with all her heart. She wondered whether staying in her friends' mansions would change her view but reassured her mother that, on the contrary, she felt a great pleasure and peace when she came back.[10] Part of Sylvia realised she was often over-critical of her family, but she could not help seeing her home through her wealthy friends' eyes.[11] In a letter to her brother, she expressed relief that Aurelia was having the house redecorated as it would mean when she brought boyfriends home, she would no longer have to dim the lights to avoid them seeing the worn wallpaper.[12]

Most of Sylvia's friends had already heard a great deal about Aurelia. When they finally met her, their opinions varied. One of Sylvia's best friends, Marcia Brown Stern, described Mrs Plath as 'bitter and careworn', with 'no room for colour – in her tone of voice or her hairdo or her aprons or her living room or inside her head'. Another friend, Nancy Hunter Steiner, saw it differently, perceiving that she was 'sweet and well-meaning and very intimidated by Sylvia'. A male friend, J. Melvin Woody, was also more sympathetic. He felt Aurelia was 'harmless', she was 'an intelligent, alert woman, who was probably much better qualified to deal with a daughter like that than most women'. Another male friend of Sylvia's, John K. Rosenthal, went even further, observing that Aurelia was a 'very attractive' woman and 'almost statuesque'.[13]

Sylvia's feelings for Aurelia were increasingly ambivalent. Similar to Virginia's posthumous feelings for Julia, her relationship with her mother was closely connected to issues about her identity. Fearing the boundaries between them were too blurred, she needed to distance herself from Aurelia. She could not always tell where her mother ended and she began. At times, she was afraid that her mother's personality was taking her over. Sometimes, when she was talking, she sounded just like Aurelia, and even her facial expressions reflected her.[14] Sylvia realised that being so close to her mother could be unhealthy for them both. She believed Mrs Plath was unable to be sufficiently detached from her and this made her feel her daughter's suffering more deeply than she did herself. Knowing how much her mother worried, Sylvia wanted to protect her from her mood swings.[15] Aurelia also recognised the risk in their exceptional closeness. She claimed there was 'a sort of psychic osmosis' between them and, although it could be 'very wonderful and comforting', it could also be 'an unwelcome invasion of privacy'.[16] Clara and Agatha had also experienced an almost telepathic understanding, but for them it remained positive. For Virginia Woolf, drawing too close to her dead mother became dangerous for her mental health.

Fearing that she was too dependent on her mother, Sylvia was determined to become more self-reliant and establish her own identity.[17] However, when she tried to pull away, she would suddenly be drawn back in. On one occasion, she described sitting in the car with her grandmother and mother and feeling intense love for them; there were no barriers between them. They stabilised her and after being with them she was able to return to her work feeling whole again.[18]

At other times, she wrote that the people who loved her were her enemies. She complained about her mother's pathetic desire for her to be happy.[19] According to Sylvia, Mrs Plath saw this as her purpose in life, but that put a pressure on her. It meant Sylvia always had to pretend to be all right in front of her.[20] It seems she came to the same conclusion as Agatha Christie in her Westmacott novels: that caring too much about your loved one being happy could be destructive because only that person could know what fulfilled them.

All three mothers in this book believed that the right marriage would be the key to their daughter's happiness. Similar to Clara with Agatha, Aurelia had ideas about the sort of man she wanted her daughter to marry. Both mothers wanted their daughters' husbands to be financially secure, kind men, who could provide stability; their daughters had other ideas. Although Sylvia tried dating eligible young men, those she was most attracted to were nonconformists; they could match her sexual and intellectual needs but might shock her mother.[21]

One of Sylvia's most serious relationships was with Dick Norton. The high-flying son of family friends, Dick matched her mother's criteria, but his closeness to 'Aunt Aurelia' did not endear him to her daughter.[22] Sylvia feared her boyfriend might admire her mother more than her. She wrote to Aurelia saying that Dick thought that daughters became like their mothers. Half-joking, she told Aurelia to stop being so competent and 'wonderful' because she was not sure she could measure up to her standards.[23] Similar to Virginia Woolf contrasting her mother's self-sacrificing femininity with her own, Sylvia compared herself to Mrs Plath. In her journal, she confessed that she lacked her mother's selfless love for other people and wondered if she should abandon her selfishness to serve others.[24] Many daughters, when they are establishing their identity, measure themselves against their mothers, but for Sylvia, it was an ongoing issue. At this stage, it made her self-critical, but later her criticism would turn on Aurelia.

As it became clear that Sylvia did not want to marry Dick, she worried about extricating herself from the relationship. Rather than finishing with him, she let it drag on. It turned into a difficult situation for Aurelia too, as Dick came to her for advice. Her attempts to soften the blow backfired – leaving him feeling that both mother and daughter had been condescending.[25]

The combination of pressures in her private life and academic demands took their toll on Sylvia. She became exhausted physically and mentally. In autumn 1952, she began to suffer from depression and experienced suicidal thoughts as once again she felt a 'nothingness' within. As she lost her sense of identity, she instinctively wanted her mother.[26] Needing to escape from responsibility, she wrote in her journal about returning to the womb.[27] Yet although her instinct was to run back to Aurelia, she did not wish to be dependent on her.[28] No longer able to appear positive, she told Mrs Plath exactly how she was feeling.[29] Deeply worried, Aurelia immediately phoned her daughter and calmed her down.[30] After returning home for Thanksgiving, Sylvia gradually began to regain her equilibrium.

Despite the mental health challenges, Sylvia's academic and literary career flourished. She published poems and stories in national magazines and won prestigious fiction and poetry prizes.[31] At this point, Sylvia's literary career remained a joint project; Aurelia often typed her daughter's submissions. Joking about her mother's help, Sylvia told her mother that when she was rich and famous, she would hire her as her private secretary and child carer and pay her a vast salary.[32]

Aurelia's support was far more than purely secretarial; her own literary skills made her, in a similar way to Clara with Agatha, a valued sounding board. Sylvia's letters to Aurelia are full of details about what she is writing. She particularly valued her mother's advice about writing for women's magazines.[33] When Sylvia won a prize, she enjoyed sharing her success with her mother, because Aurelia totally understood what this recognition meant to her.[34] In a reversal of roles, Sylvia encouraged Aurelia to launch her own literary career and even offered to edit her mother's work.[35] She suggested that Mrs Plath should write articles in women's magazines about her teaching jobs.[36]

This desire to create a more equal relationship, where Sylvia behaved as an adult who supported Aurelia, is evident at this time. She suggested that instead of working so hard, her mother should pamper herself. Aurelia should feel free to share any of her problems with her.[37] Sylvia told her brother that she was worried about their mother because she was suffering with her ulcer again. She suggested that they should take the financial pressure off her by trying to earn enough money to support themselves. She hoped that summer Aurelia would get some rest and relaxation and they would have a holiday together. However, in a telling comment, she added:

> You know, as I do, and it is a frightening thing, that mother would actually kill herself for us if we calmly accepted all she wanted to do for us. She is an abnormally altruistic person and I have realised lately that we have to fight against her selflessness as we would fight against a deadly disease.[38]

Aurelia's self-sacrifice and the need to repay her was to become a recurrent theme. Sylvia told her brother, 'After extracting her life blood and care for twenty years, we should start bringing in big dividends of joy for her.'[39] In 1953, Sylvia presented Aurelia with one of the biggest dividends so far but cashing it in was to have catastrophic consequences which neither mother nor daughter could have foreseen.

36

Crisis Point

In summer 1953, Sylvia was chosen to be a guest editor of *Mademoiselle* magazine. It was an incredible opportunity and promised to provide a brilliant launch for her career. Sylvia was thrilled by the prospect as the guest editorship introduced her to the cosmopolitan world she craved. Interviewing celebrities, attending fashion shows and receiving free tickets to the ballet, it seemed her ideal job.

Her novel *The Bell Jar* fictionalises events that summer. Esther Greenwood, the character based on Sylvia, takes up the guest editorship believing the world is full of possibilities, but gradually, she becomes disillusioned. She realises that so far, her life had been geared up to achieving academic goals, getting one prize or scholarship after another, but this was not how the real world worked. Plunged into sophisticated New York society, she felt out of her depth. Dressed immaculately in hats, gloves and wasp-waisted dresses, the guest editors epitomised feminine gentility. Yet, although Sylvia could play the role to perfection, something was missing. Writing for *Mademoiselle*, she felt pigeon-holed into the equivalent of women's work rather than more intellectual journalism.

At the end of her guest editorship, Sylvia returned to Wellesley disenchanted and exhausted. The atmosphere at home was already tense because Mrs Schober had been seriously ill. As Aurelia wrote, 'with us Grammy is the centre of our world'.[1] Closely intertwined as they were, anything which affected one member of the matriarchy had repercussions for the others. Worried about her mother, Aurelia's ulcer flared up again and her doctors ordered her to rest, but the stresses on her were about to escalate.

Aurelia knew something was wrong as soon as she picked up her tired, unsmiling daughter from the station.[2] Mrs Plath dreaded telling her that she had not been accepted on a prestigious Harvard summer school writing course. She knew that Sylvia would view it as a rejection of her as a writer.[3] On delivering the news, Aurelia watched as a look of shock and despair crossed her daughter's face.[4] Sylvia considered applying for a different course but wondered if the cost was worth it. She also realised that since both her mother and grandmother had health problems, she was needed at home. At first, she was full of good intentions, as she planned to combine academic research with spending quality time with her mother.[5] However, suddenly finding herself with nothing to do after so much stimulation, she experienced an emotional crash.[6] Everything overwhelmed her, and she once again began to lose her sense of identity. She was terrified about not living up to everyone's expectations. She tried to write but found her mind went blank; she thought she had permanently lost her literary gift and believed that if she was not a successful writer no one would be interested in her. She felt unworthy of the faith and money her mother and patrons had put into her.[7]

Inevitably, in a crisis the whole matriarchy became involved. Grammy reassured Aurelia that Sylvia just needed to rest and relax. Gradually, Sylvia began to confide in her mother.[8] Needing a purpose for the summer, Sylvia decided to learn shorthand. Aurelia agreed to teach her, but after a few lessons her daughter could not cope with even this task. Mrs Plath later regretted they had tried because it just added to Sylvia's sense of failure.[9]

As her mood deteriorated, Sylvia found it increasingly difficult to concentrate and the only book she read thoroughly was a collection of essays on Freud and abnormal psychology.[10] As she sank deeper into her depression, once again she wrote about wanting to return to the womb.[11] She was aware, though, that her mother could no longer make everything all right. During her mental health crisis, Sylvia had visions of murdering her mother. She later told her psychiatrist that she imagined strangling Aurelia because she was unable to protect her from the world.[12] In her autobiographical short story, 'Tongues of Stone', written two years later, the heroine has matricidal thoughts because she could not face her mother gradually declining and dying and not being there to support her. The heroine gets into bed with her mother, but it no longer makes her feel safe.[13] In *The Bell Jar*, Sylvia returned to this theme. Sharing the bedroom with her mother, Esther was irritated by Mrs Greenwood's snoring and fantasised about silencing her.[14] Like Virginia's feminist idea about killing the angel in the house, Sylvia's matricidal fantasy was as much about destroying the conventional model of femininity Aurelia represented as the real person.[15]

Demonstrating how her own identity was inextricable from her mother's, when Mrs Plath questioned her about scars on her legs from cutting herself, Sylvia caught hold of her hand and suggested that they should die together. Shocked, Aurelia hugged her and reassured her that she was ill and exhausted but had so much to live for.[16] After Sylvia's outburst, Mrs Plath took her to see their doctor, who recommended psychiatric counselling. Unfortunately, Sylvia did not get on with the male psychiatrist. When he prescribed a course of electroconvulsive therapy (ECT) Aurelia felt very alone and inadequate. Not knowing what else to do, she allowed the treatment to go ahead.[17]

A supportive neighbour drove mother and daughter to the hospital for the sessions. Her friend sat with Aurelia, holding her hand, while they waited for Sylvia to reappear. In the early 1950s, electroshock treatment was not well understood or regulated. Administered with no anaesthetic, Sylvia suffered from violent muscle spasms and felt as though she had been electrocuted. She emerged like a different person, lacking any of her old *joie de vivre*.

The Bell Jar suggests that Sylvia was aware of Aurelia's anguish. After she visited the psychiatrist, Esther could see her mother had been crying. She noted the strain Mrs Greenwood experienced while waiting for her daughter to emerge from treatment. But her mother had not experienced severe mental health problems herself, therefore she could not understand what her daughter was going through. After the first electroshock treatment, when Esther said she did not want to go again, her mother misunderstood and thought her daughter had just decided to be all right – as if deep-seated mental health problems could be solved by an act of will.[18] Of course, this was a fictional account, but it reflected what Sylvia believed her mother thought.

After the electroshock treatment, Sylvia was prescribed sleeping tablets which Aurelia locked away in a safe to give to her every night. When Sylvia saw a different psychiatrist, Dr Tillotson, he suggested her problems might be linked to sex. Aurelia disapproved of this line of questioning and insisted on attending sessions with her daughter. She believed Sylvia's issues were more to do with academic pressures than sexuality.[19] This could be seen as Aurelia failing to respect her daughter's privacy and preventing her talking to her psychiatrist confidentially. Aurelia's instincts on Dr Tillotson were right; unbeknown to her, he had been dismissed from a previous post for sexual misconduct with a young woman.[20]

It soon became clear that Sylvia was not getting better. As the start of a new college year approached, she became increasingly agitated. Financial pressures exacerbated the situation because Sylvia knew her treatment was costing Aurelia money she could ill afford. She feared being permanently incarcerated in a mental institution. Not wanting to be a burden on her family, she decided it would be better for everyone if she died by suicide.

In her depressed state, Sylvia identified with Virginia Woolf. Since being a teenager, the Bloomsbury author had been one of her 'literary mothers'. She first felt a rapport with her in high school when she read *Mrs Dalloway*.[21] At Smith, Sylvia increasingly identified with Virginia's life and work.[22] Whenever she needed inspiration or solace, she would turn to her predecessor, writing that she would like to be more like Virginia.[23] *To the Lighthouse* influenced her work; a discerning boyfriend detected similarities between Sylvia's short story 'Sunday at the Mintons' and Woolf's novel.[24] As she reached crisis point, she felt Virginia's suicide was repeating in her life. However, unlike her role model she could not drown herself.[25] During a trip to the beach, she began to swim far out to sea, but she was unable to go through with it because the life force within her was too strong.[26]

Sylvia chose an alternative way of ending it all. On 24 August 1953, when her mother was invited to see a documentary on Queen Elizabeth II's coronation, Sylvia said she would stay at home with her grandparents. According to Aurelia, her daughter was looking radiant that day, but she felt uneasy because she was aware that the cheerfulness was put on rather than real.[27] Once her mother had gone, Sylvia left a note for her on the dining-room table saying that she was going for a long walk. She took the sleeping tablets from the safe and went down into the crawl space beneath the house and started taking the tablets one by one.

Reflecting the 'psychic osmosis' which existed between mother and daughter, Mrs Plath had a similar telepathic experience to Agatha's when she instinctively knew her mother had died. As Aurelia was watching the film, she suddenly found herself 'filled with terror such as I had never experienced in my life. Cold perspiration poured down me; my heart pounded.'[28] When she got home, she found Sylvia's note. She immediately contacted the police, and friends and neighbours started searching the area. As Aurelia wrote, 'the nightmare of nightmares had begun'.[29]

In a bid to find her daughter, Mrs Plath did everything she could to publicise her daughter's disappearance. Like the reaction when Agatha went missing, Sylvia's story received extensive press coverage. Newspapers across the country ran front page stories on the 'beautiful Smith girl missing at Wellesley'. Aurelia talked to journalists and provided family photographs. She told *The Globe*, 'She (Sylvia) recently felt she was unworthy of the confidence held for her by the people she knew.' She added, 'For some time she has been able to write neither fiction, nor her more recent love, poetry.'

Aurelia's interview went into great detail about Sylvia's state of mind. In her traumatised state, this usually reserved woman spoke very candidly to journalists. Her intention was to increase the chances of her daughter being found. Although she had little choice, this could be seen as one of the first examples of how both mother and daughter would invade their own privacy. Inadvertently, it turned Sylvia's life into public property; from now on her mental health would be permanently linked in public perception with her writing.

As time passed, the whole family became more distraught. When Sylvia's former employer Mrs Cantor visited, Aurelia clung to her and asked her to pray with her. In the last hours before Sylvia was found, Aurelia seemed to be withdrawing from the world.[30] After three days, Sylvia's brother heard moaning coming from the crawl space. Investigating, he found his sister returning to consciousness. She survived because she had vomited up the pills. As she came around, she cut her face banging her head on the rocks in the cellar. An ambulance was called and she was taken to hospital. When Aurelia saw her daughter looking so vulnerable, she told her how thankful they were that she was alive and how much they loved her. Sylvia replied that her suicide attempt had been her 'last act of love'.[31] In *The Bell Jar*, Sylvia provides a fictionalised version of this encounter. The mother put on a smile, but she looked ill and seemed as if she was about to cry. Although her manner was loving, Esther detected she was reproachful. She just wanted her mother to go away.[32]

Sylvia was sent to the psychiatric ward at Massachusetts General Hospital. After a fortnight she was regressing. Not knowing what to do, Aurelia sought advice from her Unitarian minister, who recommended Sylvia should see Dr Erich Lindemann, a prominent psychiatrist. Aurelia was willing to do anything to make Sylvia better, but she was concerned about the cost and worried that a mental hospital might not be the right place for her sensitive daughter.

Fortunately, Sylvia's 'literary mother', Mrs Prouty, stepped in. It was a great relief for Aurelia to have the support of someone who understood mental health problems. Drawing on her own experience of having a breakdown, Olive Prouty was very sympathetic. When Aurelia was out of her depth, Mrs Prouty took charge. Aurelia told her that she had always been proud of being independent, but this crisis was too complex for her to handle alone. She would humbly accept any help available.[33]

Sensitive to Mrs Plath's feelings, Mrs Prouty acted as her ally not a rival for her daughter's affection. She impressed on Aurelia that she was Sylvia's mother, and it was up to her to decide what was right for her, but she was there to support her.[34] The two women worked closely together to get the best care. Writing with compassion, Mrs Prouty explained to Aurelia that when she had her nervous breakdown she needed to get away from her home and too much involvement from those she loved. Like Sylvia, she felt that she had become a burden to them. She recognised the ordeal Aurelia was going through and tried to reassure her that Sylvia would recover.[35]

Mrs Prouty paid for Sylvia to go to McLean Hospital in Belmont, Massachusetts. One of the best mental hospitals in the country, it created the atmosphere of a country club for its wealthy patients.[36] Most importantly, Sylvia had a new psychiatrist whom she liked. Only nine years older than Sylvia, Dr Ruth Beuscher had also been a precocious child. Patient and psychiatrist immediately got on well and considered themselves to be kindred spirits.[37] After talking to Sylvia, she diagnosed delayed adolescent turmoil.[38] She suggested that her patient was a perfectionist who, if she fell short of perfection, experienced feelings of worthlessness. She thought her depression was linked to her inability to reconcile her literary ambitions with marriage.

In *The Bell Jar*, Esther hated having visitors, particularly her mother. Mrs Greenwood believed the doctors felt she was at fault because they kept asking her questions. In response, she repeatedly asked her daughter to tell her what she had done wrong. On Esther's twenty-first birthday, Mrs Greenwood brought her favourite yellow roses, but her daughter just told her to keep them for her funeral and dumped them in a waste-paper basket.[39] This episode was closely based on real life. Recalling what happened later, Aurelia explained that she knew whatever she did would be taken the wrong way. If she did not mark Sylvia's birthday, her daughter would criticise her for ignoring the occasion, so she did what she felt was right and hoped her daughter would understand.[40]

In the novel, Esther believes that her mother is secretly embarrassed by the social stigma of having a daughter in a psychiatric hospital. However, she had decided to forgive her daughter. She put on her 'sweet martyr's smile' and told Esther that they would carry on where they left off, as if it had been a bad dream. This comment just confirmed her lack of understanding, because for her daughter it was the world that was a bad dream.[41] Years later, Aurelia refuted Sylvia's interpretation. She explained that she always saw her daughter's mental health problems as an illness which was 'to be fought through and conquered and I loved and treasured her'. It was the friend, who drove her to visit Sylvia each week, who made the comment about it being a bad dream, not Aurelia.[42]

Looking back on this terrible time, Mrs Plath claimed that her daughter blamed her for putting on a brave face. Sylvia complained that her mother could not relate to her suffering. In the past they had shared every experience; now she felt left on her own.[43] In fact, Aurelia was also living through her own worst nightmare. While Sylvia was in hospital, Aurelia's parents visited their son to get away from the stressful atmosphere. Rather than be on her own, Aurelia stayed with supportive friends.[44] To cope with the situation, Mrs Plath had weekly sessions with a psychologist. During one visit, Aurelia asked her doctor where she had been at fault and what she should change in herself to help Sylvia. The psychologist replied:

> You have been through a most harrowing experience, and you are doing magnificently! Follow your own instincts; they are sound. In Sylvia's present depression, no matter what you do or say just now, it will be wrong. Let her talk, but don't take issue with her present misconceptions.[45]

Aurelia also conferred with Dr Lindemann every week. He warned her against continuing to identify with her daughter. She must believe in his prognosis that Sylvia would recover completely. If Mrs Plath wished to help her, she must have a calm centre.[46] This took an incredible act of will and Aurelia meditated before seeing Sylvia to keep her emotions under control. Her stoicism was misinterpreted by her daughter, however. Mrs Plath believed that Sylvia later wrote her poem 'The Disquieting Muses', which was very critical of her, as an act of retaliation against her for appearing so optimistic.[47] When Aurelia asked Sylvia why she had written it, she replied, 'Oh that! Well, whenever you visited me in hospital, you were always so calm and confident that I would soon recover, I felt you had no conception of the psychological Hell I was going through.'[48]

In later years, Aurelia blamed Dr Beuscher for turning her daughter against her. In their sessions, Sylvia explored her emotions about her family and the past. Both Aurelia and Mrs Prouty were wary about Sylvia embarking on this sort of treatment. Aurelia was also frustrated that the psychiatrist refused to reveal details of what she discussed.[49] In *The Bell Jar*, Esther Greenwood easily admitted to her psychiatrist that she hated her mother, but in real life it was different. Dr Beuscher later told an interviewer that Sylvia had spent at least the first month in hospital saying that she loved her mother. Her psychiatrist said that she had 'to work hate admission out of Sylvia'.[50]

Dr Beuscher cannot be held solely responsible for planting the idea that Sylvia's problems were linked to her relationship with her mother. Her approach reflected the attitudes of society at the time. Blaming mothers for their children's emotional problems was mainstream in the early 1950s. Drawing on Freudian theories, many psychiatrists searched for the origins of their patients' neuroses in their childhood.[51] Attacking mothers became fashionable in popular culture as prominent psychiatrists published articles in women's magazines asking, 'Are American Moms a Menace?' According to one of Sylvia's friends, before her breakdown, she had been drawn to these ideas. Sylvia had read and discussed with her Philip Wylie's *Generation of Vipers*, which coined the term 'Momism' and blamed overbearing mothers for creating a generation of emasculated men.[52]

Aurelia was as aware as her daughter about the latest ideas. She later claimed that, during a visit, Sylvia had said that she had to prove to her doctors she understood the cause of her breakdown. Wanting to help her out, Aurelia replied carelessly, 'Well, use the old mother–daughter-conflict theme if it will help.' According to Mrs Plath, Sylvia then looked at her intently for a moment before saying, 'I hope you will never regret saying that, mother.' Aurelia added, 'Regret my unconsidered offer? Indeed, I have.'[53]

Wherever the idea originally came from, Dr Beuscher believed Sylvia had issues with female roles, her sense of identity and sex, and these problems were all linked to the negative mother figure. She believed that because Otto was an older father, there had been a type of sibling rivalry between Sylvia and Aurelia for his attention. She told Sylvia that she had encouraged her mother and other powerful women to dominate her.[54]

Both Mrs Plath and Mrs Prouty became increasingly suspicious of Dr Beuscher. The psychiatrist was developing a quasi-maternal relationship with her patient. During one session, Sylvia told her psychiatrist that she had become like a mother to her but without the disadvantages.[55] The therapy did not seem to be working as Sylvia was withdrawn and talking about suicide. Mrs Prouty and Aurelia were so dissatisfied that they considered moving her to another hospital. Dr Beuscher decided that the only way to break through was by administering more ECT sessions. To everyone's surprise and relief, after the electroshock therapy, Sylvia showed dramatic signs of recovery. Dr Beuscher believed this was partly because Sylvia convinced herself that she was better so that she did not have to undergo any further ECT.[56]

Recovering, Sylvia gave Aurelia her first hug since she had been ill and told her that she wanted to return to Smith.[57] Aurelia wrote, 'To see her eyes light up again and a genuine smile accompany her first embrace of me was cause for deep thanks-giving!'[58] Gradually, Sylvia pieced her life back together, but underneath her vulnerability remained.[59] Aurelia was also traumatised by what had happened. She wrote to Mrs Prouty, 'Periodically, I still have to battle with myself to combat the wave of terror I feel in connection with this continuing experience.' Aurelia had to summon up all her strength and focus on her work and responsibilities at home to channel her thoughts in a constructive direction.[60]

Sylvia's suicide attempt was the first time most of her friends realised she had serious mental health problems. Her breakdown alienated her further from the small town she had grown up in. In this era, mental health was treated as a taboo subject. One of Plath's neighbours said the stigma attached to her suicide was so strong it affected the whole neighbourhood. There was a sense of shame associated with what she had done.[61] She needed to escape from this narrow-minded world to build a new life.

By February 1954, Sylvia had recovered sufficiently to return to Smith to complete her senior year. To prevent her daughter having the additional pressure of a scholarship, Aurelia cashed in an insurance policy to finance it.[62] On the surface, Sylvia seemed to be back to her buoyant, happy self and was soon winning prizes and dating; Aurelia did not bounce back so rapidly. The toll her daughter's suicide attempt had taken on her was plain to see. In a photograph of Aurelia, Warren and Sylvia, Mrs Plath appears haunted. Painfully thin with her mouth set in a grim line, it looks as though she has physically absorbed her daughter's suffering.

Both mother and daughter tried to make sense of what had happened. Sylvia's choice of thesis suggests that she wanted to understand herself better. She wrote about the double in Dostoevsky's fiction. Her research helped her to address the two very different sides of her personality. The idea of the double also appealed to Aurelia. She believed that her daughter was never the same after her breakdown and it was the turning point in their relationship. She had been warned by Dr Lindemann that patients' personalities were sometimes totally altered by electroshock treatment, and she believed that after the therapy Sylvia began a double life.[63] There was still the good girl who did what was expected of her, but there was also a more rebellious person who was determined to break free. Sylvia's rebellion had echoes of Virginia's rejection of Julia's Victorian values which she replaced with her unconventional Bloomsbury lifestyle.

Reflecting this new stage, Sylvia bleached her hair blonder and adopted a more adventurous persona. She felt liberated to experiment sexually and abandon the middle-class morality her mother had instilled in her.[64] Thinking Aurelia would disapprove, she did not always tell her about her sexual encounters.[65] In her journal, Sylvia imagined her mother's thoughts: this was not her daughter; she was not her 'nice girl' anymore.[66]

Mrs Plath tried to be patient and understanding; she kept saying to herself, 'This is only a stage; it will pass.'[67] Sylvia also later tried to normalise this phase as just a delayed adolescent rebellion. She compared her relationship with Aurelia to the American colonies' desire to become independent from Mother England. She needed to get this rebellion out of her system and then she could return to a loving but less dependent relationship with her mother.[68]

Sylvia's boyfriend at this time, Richard Sassoon, assessed her conflicting emotions towards her mother, writing that she was simultaneously very

rebellious towards her but also very attached.[69] Their relationship fluctuated; one minute she would confide in her mother, the next withdraw. She
explained that she needed space.[70] Sylvia believed that developing a secure
sense of self was essential for her stability. She wrote to her brother that
being certain of your identity was the most important thing in life. To
reach that state involved no longer telling another person all your problems and seeking their advice or validation.[71]

It was difficult for Aurelia to accept this more distant relationship. She
later regretfully recalled that her daughter never called her 'mummy' again
after her breakdown, from then on it was always 'Mother'. Aurelia was hurt
because she had seen 'mummy' as a sign of affection, but Sylvia believed
it showed dependence.[72] Mrs Plath complained that her daughter seemed
to focus on the negative experiences in her childhood and forgot about
many of the positives. She viewed acts of love and kindness sceptically and
attributed cynical motives to them.[73]

It was not just the past that was causing conflict between mother and
daughter. They also clashed about what Sylvia should do next. Aurelia
wanted her daughter to earn some money, while Sylvia wanted an adventure. She told her mother that their ideas of success were very different and
that rather than being restricted by a set of career-oriented objectives, she
intended to experience as much as possible.[74] Asserting herself as an adult
not a child, Sylvia suggested that Aurelia should live her own life to the
full too, rather than postpone her personal fulfilment to some later date.
Recognising that they were similar and that they were both self-critical
and worried too much, Sylvia encouraged her mother to relax more for
the sake of her health.[75]

37

A Transatlantic Relationship

In June 1955, Sylvia graduated from Smith. It was a triumphant moment for both mother and daughter, marking the culmination of years of hard work. However, it had come at great cost to Aurelia; her duodenal ulcer had flared up again under the pressure of the past few years.[1] While she was in hospital for a gastrectomy, which removed a large part of her stomach, Sylvia phoned with news which she knew would give her mother a boost: she had been awarded a Fulbright Grant to study English at Cambridge University.[2] Aurelia was delighted, but it would take Sylvia even further away from her.

Mrs Plath had only recently been released from hospital on Sylvia's graduation day. Determined to be at the ceremony, she lay flat on a mattress as a friend drove her in her car. Aurelia described the sensation of floating as she joined her daughter. Her pride was mingled with relief; she was there to celebrate her daughter's recovery as much as her academic achievement. She wrote that she was just so happy to see Sylvia 'alive, well, and joyous'.[3]

Graduation marked the end of an era for Sylvia. Telling her brother that she would suffocate if she remained in America, she now felt strong enough to try her wings and fly far away.[4] Inevitably, the traumatic experience she had been through transformed her attitude. She believed that she had been reborn as a living Lady Lazarus.[5] Her ordeal reforged her into a woman who was better equipped to deal with the world.[6]

In autumn 1955, she crossed the Atlantic to take up her Fulbright Scholarship at Newnham College, Cambridge. Intending to 'find' herself, she aimed to meet the right man and establish her career before she came home.[7] Mother and daughter relied on letters to keep in touch. Knowing

Aurelia would relish every detail, once again Sylvia shared news about her academic work, glamorous social life, and love affairs. Later, Mrs Plath recalled her daughter's 'sparkling accounts' of cycling to lectures in the rain with her student's gown streaming out behind her, seeing the Queen and Prince Philip visit her college and going to a reception for the Russian leader at Claridge's.[8]

With an ocean between them, mother and daughter got on exceptionally well. Sylvia believed that this was because in their letters they created their desired image of themselves in relation to each other; Sylvia could be the glamorous golden girl, Aurelia the saintly mother. When they escaped from the emotional currents created when they were physically together, they were able to express interest and genuine love.[9]

Sylvia's journal entries were also positive about her mother. At a distance, she could see Mrs Plath from a more objective perspective, and she admired her hard work and resilience.[10] Living in different countries enabled both women to get on with their own lives. Promoted in her career, Aurelia was a highly respected member of staff who got on well with both her colleagues and pupils. She took pride in her work and believed it was providing a useful service to the community. But, as usual, she had to juggle her full-time job with family responsibilities. Her mother had been diagnosed with terminal cancer. Like Julia's and Clara's dutiful attitude towards the older generation, Aurelia was determined to care for her mother. Aware of what they were going through, Sylvia appreciated all her mother and grandmother had done for her.[11] She wished that she could be with them to support them.[12] She described Aurelia building a new life for herself while looking after Grammy as very courageous. Trying to give her mother something to look forward to, Sylvia wanted her to come to England and share her new world with her.[13] The visit would not just be for Aurelia's benefit; as the months passed, Sylvia was desperate to see her.[14]

Overall, Sylvia's two years at Cambridge were an exciting and fulfilling time. As well as her academic studies, she was writing poetry and short stories. Apparently, her fellow students thought of her as a second Virginia Woolf. However, her views were not always as feminist as her Bloomsbury predecessor. Expressing similar sentiments to Agatha Christie at the start of her writing career, Sylvia claimed that she did not want to be an academic or a career woman. She loved homemaking and thought that being a good wife and mother would enrich her life and writing.[15]

The desire to fulfil both sides of her complex personality once again began to cause problems. By February 1956, her relationship with Richard Sassoon was not going well. As she began to suffer moments of self-doubt, she felt homesick and missed her mother.[16] Concerned about her mental health, she saw the university psychiatrist and confided in Aurelia, who listened to her problems and provided reassurance.[17] She told her mother that she could not bear to return to America unmarried,[18] but reassured her that she was not about to marry just any man. She knew that most men would only accept part of her; she wanted someone who could encompass all her complexity.[19]

Shortly after setting out what she was looking for, she found it. In February 1956, she met the charismatic poet Ted Hughes. Intoxicated with the intensity of their passion, she wrote ecstatic letters to Aurelia overflowing with superlatives about finding her perfect match. Her poetry was flowing, and she had never felt more alive. She believed that she had finally established a firm sense of identity. The idyllic life she imagined with Ted had much in common with the fantasy world Aurelia had dreamed of with Karl.[20]

While Sylvia was falling deeply in love, the crisis at home was coming to a climax. On Aurelia's fiftieth birthday, Mrs Schober went into a coma and died three days later.[21] Fearing she might lose her mother as well, Sylvia worried about the toll her grandmother's death would take on Aurelia.[22] Her love affair with Ted Hughes filled her with joy, however, and she believed that she had never had more love to give.[23] Sylvia wanted Aurelia to draw on her new-found strength. Recognising that Mrs Plath had had many crosses to bear over the years, she told her that she wanted to take some of the burdens off her and walk beside her.[24]

The dynamics of the matriarchy were transformed with Grammy's death. Ted was replacing Aurelia as the most important person in Sylvia's life. No longer driven by the need for her mother's approval, like Agatha secretly marrying Archie, Sylvia decided she wanted to marry Ted before her mother had met him. Neither Archie Christie nor Ted Hughes fitted the model of the safe young men Clara and Aurelia wanted for their daughters. Knowing the influence their mothers had on them, perhaps neither daughter wanted to be talked out of her decision. Sylvia wrote to Aurelia asking her not to judge Ted on whether he could provide security.[25] Knowing what reception any advice would receive, Aurelia did nothing to dissuade her determined daughter.[26] When faced with a fait accompli, like Clara, Aurelia gracefully accepted the situation.

Sylvia told her mother that she would probably marry Ted the following year. To Aurelia's surprise, though, the couple decided to get married while she was in England. In the three days after she arrived, Aurelia rushed around London with her daughter organising the wedding. Rather than buy a new dress, Sylvia borrowed a pink knitted suit from her mother for the occasion. On 16 June 1956, Mrs Plath was the sole family witness at the service in the church of St George the Martyr in Bloomsbury.[27] Dazed by the pace of events, Aurelia was sick the night before and was still feeling unwell during the candlelit ceremony.[28]

Afterwards, Mrs Plath travelled with the couple to Paris on the first part of their honeymoon. To Sylvia's surprise, her mother was relaxed abroad.[29] While the newlyweds lingered in Paris before moving on to Spain, Aurelia continued with her tour of Europe. Mrs Plath got on well with her new son-in-law. She genuinely liked him and reassured Mrs Prouty that he was gentle and understanding.[30] She later wrote that as she got to know Ted, she 'loved the man and considered him an ideal mate for my creative daughter'.[31] Rather than being possessive, it seems Aurelia was relieved that there was now someone to share the responsibility of dealing with her volatile child.[32]

When the couple returned to England, Sylvia continued her studies at Cambridge. Fulfilling the homemaker image her mother and grandmother had cultivated, she filled her letters home with descriptions of the wonderful meals she was cooking.[33] Yet, at times, she found it hard juggling her work and housekeeping.[34] At this stage, Ted was more successful in his literary career than her. Repeating Aurelia's role in Otto's work, Sylvia typed Ted's poems and sent them to magazines. When Ted's collection of poetry *The Hawk in the Rain* won a prestigious prize, Sylvia told her mother that she was happier than if it was her own book.[35] She claimed that it would make it much easier when her work was accepted. Aurelia later noted that since being a child, Sylvia had always pandered to men's sense of superiority. Even at school, she claimed to be pleased if a boy beat her in a test.[36] This pandering to the male ego was just the sort of female behaviour Virginia Woolf warned against in her feminist writing.

Sylvia recognised the conflict within herself. Although part of her was happy making the perfect home for her outstanding husband, she feared domesticity would stifle her creativity. Once again, she turned to Virginia as a role model. Picking up Woolf's diary, she read that her predecessor overcame her depression after receiving a rejection by cleaning her kitchen. Sylvia wrote in her journal, 'Bless her, I feel my life linked to her somehow. I love her.'[37] She recommended that her mother should also read Virginia's diary.[38]

Aurelia preferred to see her daughter and son-in-law as the Victorian poetic duo, Elizabeth and Robert Browning.[39] Gradually, Ted and Sylvia developed a more equal literary partnership. Sylvia's poetic voice changed; instead of the gentility which gained her mother's approval, she unleashed a more authentic tone. Biographer Heather Clark argues that Aurelia represented 'the submissive self' which got in the way of 'the deeper, subversive poet self'. Ted encouraged her to move away from her carefully crafted, safe verse. Together they explored an alternative moral structure which valued 'self-expression rather than self-sacrifice'.[40]

Reunited

In June 1957, Sylvia and Ted moved to America. Having achieved her aim of finding a husband and establishing her career, Sylvia was eager to return home. While living in England, her relationship with Aurelia had been good. Both mother and daughter seemed secure and successful in their separate lives. Aurelia had been promoted to be an associate professor at Boston University. Sylvia was proud of her and wrote saying how much Ted also admired her.[1]

For her mother's fifty-first birthday, Sylvia sent an illustrated card with stylised sketches of Aurelia rushing around the world, sitting by the Eiffel Tower and climbing mountains. She praised her incredible mother who seemed to get younger each year. Knowing Aurelia had spent years caring for others, Sylvia now encouraged her to make the most of her life. She looked forward to having fun with her when they arrived in America.[2] Aurelia was equally excited about her daughter's return. To mark the occasion, she organised a belated wedding reception in a marquee in her backyard. Seventy guests were invited and as Sylvia introduced 'my Ted' to old friends, she could not have looked happier.[3]

Unfortunately, once mother and daughter were in the same country, their relationship deteriorated. It soon became clear that they did not want the same things from life. As a wedding present, Mrs Plath arranged for Sylvia and Ted to have a 'honeymoon' at Eastham on Cape Cod. Aurelia planned every detail to make it as romantic as possible. Knowing how much her daughter loved Nauset Beach, she rented a shingled cottage hidden away in the pines, with no phone, no car, only bicycles. Expecting Ted and Sylvia would want to write, Aurelia even left a new typewriter and some books for them.[4] It was Aurelia's dream, but not Sylvia's and she soon contacted her mother with a long list of items she needed to make this rustic retreat less basic.[5]

The difference between mother and daughter's professional aspirations also soon became clear. When Sylvia was offered a well-paid one-year renewable position teaching Freshmen English at Smith her mother was delighted.[6] Mrs Plath said she would have leapt at the chance. When Ted was also offered a teaching post at the University of Massachusetts, Aurelia considered it a miracle that they had both got college teaching jobs so close together.[7] For Mrs Plath, becoming an academic at a top college was the pinnacle of her ambitions, but her daughter's and son-in-law's vocations lay elsewhere.

Tensions between mother and daughter increased as the year progressed. Sylvia believed Aurelia was interfering in her life and envious of her opportunities.[8] Although she was good at teaching, Sylvia was not enjoying it. Working long hours, she was pursued by the old desire to be perfect.[9] Faced with anything less, she was tempted to run away from the situation. Sylvia wrote to her brother that she did not feel the sacrifice her job required was worth it. Unlike their mother, she was a writer, not a teacher.[10]

Financial pressures exacerbated the tensions between mother and daughter. Wanting Ted and Sylvia to have steady jobs with predictable incomes, Aurelia encouraged them to take on more teaching rather than dedicate themselves to their writing.[11] Sylvia complained that her mother's fears of financial disaster made her want them to put security above their poetic vocation.[12] The clash between them escalated partly because Aurelia was vocalising some of Sylvia's own concerns. Brought up by her mother to be frugal, she was also secretly worried about having enough money.[13] It was out of character for her not to have a structured career path. An undermining voice within her, amplified by her mother, questioned whether their poetry was good enough for them to succeed.[14]

Observing mother and daughter together, Ted became aware of the similarities between them. He became concerned that beneath Sylvia's Bohemian exterior lurked a more bourgeois character.[15] Many years later, in his collection of poems entitled *Birthday Letters*, he wrote about feeling that to please his wife and mother-in-law, he was being pushed to be more ambitious than he naturally was.[16]

Dissatisfied with her real mother, Sylvia once again turned to her literary one. Immersing herself in Virginia's writing, Sylvia felt that Woolf's vision could inspire her to write great literature.[17] She wrote that her predecessor's novels made hers possible and, in her most confident moments, she believed that she could do even better.[18] Inspiration was also coming from the occult as Ted and Sylvia used a Ouija board. These sessions provided ideas for Sylvia's poems and the title for her first collection of poetry, *The Colossus*.[19]

During this period, Sylvia wrote 'The Disquieting Muses', the first of her poems to specifically explore her relationship with her mother.[20] Her image of the pushy parent she created inflicted a lasting wound on Aurelia.[21] The mother in the poem does many of the things Mrs Plath did in Sylvia's childhood, making up bedtime stories, baking gingerbread and teaching rhymes to say when it thunders. However, less benignly, the mother pushes her child to achieve even in spheres for which she has little talent. Although she is not good at ballet or playing the piano, her mother ignores the reality. The poem suggests that the daughter's life was dominated by the quest for achievement.

Aurelia wanted to distance herself from the mother in the poem. She later claimed that her daughter had merged incidents from both their lives to create a 'fusion and violation of actual circumstances'.[22] She deconstructed the poem, explaining that it was her, rather than Sylvia, who had ballet lessons. She told Sylvia about her dancing and her daughter then appropriated her experience and treated it as her own.[23] Aurelia also challenged the idea that she made her daughter learn the piano. Apparently, when they lived in Winthrop, Sylvia had thoroughly enjoyed piano lessons with a friend of Aurelia's. When they moved to Wellesley, Sylvia wanted to go to the New England Conservatory of Music. Aurelia took on extra teaching sessions to pay for it and her daughter was offered a half scholarship. Although Sylvia was only an average student, she did well enough to play the viola in the school orchestra and made good progress playing Mozart, Beethoven and Brahms, as well as some 'boogie-woogie'.[24]

Whether the facts of the poem were accurate or not, it gives us an insight not only into Sylvia's feelings about her childhood but also her current attitude towards her mother. It reflected how Sylvia felt torn between being the good girl who did everything to please her mother and being a person who is committed to the disquieting forces represented by the muses.[25] It was not just the muses that were pulling Sylvia in a different direction from Aurelia; Ted represented the different life she could lead. Torn between her mother and husband, Sylvia chose Ted and following her literary vocation.

After teaching for a year, Sylvia left Smith to dedicate herself to writing full-time. When she told her mother, according to Aurelia, she remarked, 'The first year of teaching a lecture course is the very hardest – you are beginning from scratch. A second year would be much easier and give you a better recommendation if you ever wanted to return to teaching again.' Mrs Plath did not want to interfere, but she believed Sylvia should consider these facts. She was very careful not to say too much because she knew it was their right to run their lives as they thought best. She did not pressure her daughter to continue teaching because she was concerned about Sylvia's mental health. She explained, 'I thought that perhaps the frustration Sylvia implied might lead to another breakdown – something I wanted to avoid at all costs.' Sylvia was not behaving as Aurelia would have done in the same situation, but she had no choice but to accept her daughter's decision.[26]

The old pattern of Sylvia resenting her mother but still being dependent on her reasserted itself. She continued to expect her mother to provide practical help whenever she needed it.[27] Aurelia later wrote about how when Sylvia and Ted came to stay they expected her to attend to mundane tasks like getting their clothes washed, while they enjoyed literary discussions which she would have liked to have taken part in. She felt very left out and that they were treating her more like a domestic help than an intellectual equal.[28]

Although Sylvia was clashing with her mother, some of the imaginative seeds Aurelia had sown in her childhood were coming to fruition. In her poem 'Lorelei', Sylvia drew on the mythology Aurelia had passed on to her as a child about the beautiful siren with the death wish. She was also inspired by her 'ocean childhood' which she described as 'probably the foundation of my consciousness'.[29]

Without a routine to ground her, at times Sylvia suffered from writer's block. She wanted to get to the root of what was holding her back. In December 1958, Sylvia resumed her therapy with her psychiatrist, Dr Ruth Beuscher. These sessions marked another turning point in her relationship with Aurelia. The key moment came when her psychiatrist gave her permission to hate her mother. According to Sylvia, being able to admit her feelings was transformative. It made her feel like a new person, one completely alive and in tune with herself. She was angry with her mother and all mother figures who had wanted her to be a person who did not reflect the woman she really was.

Sylvia believed that her repressed hatred towards Mrs Plath paralysed her writing. As she had once written stories to win Aurelia's approval and affection, now she sometimes stopped writing because she believed her mother would appropriate her work. Her fears about her writing being rejected were tied up with thoughts that her mother would also reject her if she was not successful.[30]

Like Virginia imagining her mother's thoughts and motivations in *To the Lighthouse*, Sylvia often cast Aurelia's behaviour in the most negative light. During her therapy, she tried to imagine herself into Aurelia's mind, but she admitted that she was only expressing what she felt her mother felt. When Aurelia read what her daughter had written years later, she pointed out that Sylvia made so much of what 'SHE THOUGHT MOTHER THOUGHT!'[31] (Aurelia's capitals)

Dr Beuscher suggested that their sessions should focus on Sylvia's 'Electra Complex', the psychoanalytic term used to describe a daughter's sense of competition with her mother for the affections of her father. This involved exploring the hatred Sylvia had projected on to her mother following her father's death and how this anger against Aurelia had recently become mixed up with Sylvia's belief that her mother was undermining her marriage by her complaints that Ted should have a proper job.[32] As she analysed her parents' marriage, Sylvia claimed that Aurelia hated Otto and she, in turn, hated her mother for not loving him. She believed that part of Aurelia was relieved when he died because the thought of caring for him after his leg was amputated disgusted her. Aurelia later counteracted this accusation in her introduction to *Letters Home*, writing that she did everything possible to look after her husband and prevent him from feeling emasculated. In her unresolved grief, however, it seems Sylvia blamed Aurelia for 'killing' him.[33] She saw her mother as an enemy who had taken away her paternal ally.[34]

Sylvia recognised that Aurelia wanted her children to have the life she had missed out on. She worked incredibly hard to achieve this goal. Sylvia was angry at the unfair society which made a single mother struggle to support her family, but she was also critical of the woman who sacrificed so much that she turned herself into a martyr. It was a sacrifice that Sylvia did not want. She felt her mother expected something in return and when her children did not behave as she wished, Aurelia blamed them for worrying her.[35]

Recognising that Aurelia had experienced bad luck in her life, Sylvia wondered if her mother partly blamed her for what had happened. She thought that perhaps Aurelia hated her daughter as much as she hated her.[36] Although it appeared to the outside world that Sylvia was loved, and Aurelia believed she loved her, she did not feel loved.[37] She was only aware of her mother's anxiety, anger, jealousy and hatred.[38]

Sylvia believed Aurelia saw her daughter as an extension of herself. She thought her mother was envious of her life and part of Aurelia wanted to be her. When Sylvia was happy, it made Mrs Plath aware of what her life could have been if she had made better decisions.[39] One of Sylvia's greatest fears was becoming like Aurelia.[40] She believed that her mother's attitude prevented happiness because she thought that the minute you dared to be content, fate would strike some devastating blow.[41] Sylvia did not want her own potential for happiness to be crushed by this pessimistic outlook.[42]

Just as Aurelia could not help relating to every situation like a teacher, Sylvia could never switch off from being a writer. She intended to draw on this voyage of self-discovery in her work.[43] During the spring of 1959, she used some of this new material in her poetry. After visiting her father's grave for the first time, she wrote in her journal that she had wanted to dig him up. In her novel *The Bell Jar*, the heroine cried uncontrollably, as she felt that she had been cheated out of grieving for him properly. The experience inspired her poem 'Electra on Azalea Path', which drew on the name of where Otto was buried but also played on Aurelia's name.

Like for Virginia, there were potential dangers for Sylvia in returning to her past. Digging so deep within herself was incredibly painful.[44] She grieved that she did not have the relationship with her mother that she wanted. She now believed that she would never be able to have it. As she distanced herself from Aurelia, Sylvia transferred her dependence on to Dr Beuscher. She could tell her psychiatrist anything, and, unlike Aurelia, this 'mother' would not reproach her or ever stop listening. Instead of telling her what to do, she would help her find out what lay deep within herself and how she could best use it.[45]

Trying to deepen her understanding, Sylvia also studied the works of Freud and Jung.[46] As she read Freud, she believed that her suicide attempt had been a transference of murderous impulse from her mother on to herself. She appropriated his vampire metaphor and used it to describe Aurelia.[47] She was also influenced by Jung's claim that mothers who surrounded their children with excessive anxious care created tension in their children.[48] His writing on parental expectations and self-sacrifice also struck a particular chord. He stated that the worst thing a parent could do was to try to do their best for their children and live only for them. It placed conditions on a child which could never be fulfilled.[49]

Returning from the psychiatrist's chair to her real-life relationship with her mother was confusing. Sylvia wondered how she should deal with her powerful emotions and treat her mother. She did not want to be a hypocrite, nor did she want to be cruel.[50] When Aurelia joined Sylvia and Ted for Christmas, they had an enjoyable time together. Sylvia realised that she did not just hate her mother, she pitied and loved her too. She recognised that Aurelia did not realise the detrimental effect she had on her daughter. She kept telling herself that Aurelia could only encroach on her life if she allowed her to do so. She needed to develop a strong sense of self which could not be undermined by anyone else.[51]

39

Rites of Passage

Both Ted and Sylvia realised that their future was not in America. With no intention of continuing teaching and now pregnant, Sylvia wanted to combine writing with motherhood.[1] When they moved back to England in December 1959, Aurelia realised her daughter was leaving home for good. As Sylvia sorted out what she would take with her and planned for the arrival of her new baby, Mrs Plath recognised that although her daughter still looked like a high school student, she was now an adult woman and about to become a mother herself.[2]

Back in London, Ted and Sylvia moved into a small flat at 3 Chalcot Square. It was to be the start of a fertile period in their private and professional life. On 1 April 1960, their daughter, Frieda Rebecca, was born. Unlike Clara and Agatha who shared this rite of passage, Aurelia was far away from her daughter. Used to hospital deliveries in America, she was concerned about Sylvia having a home birth. However, all went smoothly and as soon as the midwife left, Sylvia phoned her mother.[3] It was three in the morning and the call was disconnected before Aurelia could find out what was happening. Mrs Plath spent an agonising hour pacing the floor, praying that everything was going well. Finally, Sylvia phoned again to excitedly announce that she had given birth to a daughter.[4] She sent her mother a sketch she had made of her baby which Aurelia described as 'unforgettable'.[5]

Sylvia felt 'reborn' with Frieda, as if her real life only started then.[6] Married to an outstanding man, writing poetry and enjoying her first child, she told her mother that she had never been so happy and fulfilled.[7] Her writing was flourishing as her collection of poetry, *The Colossus and*

Other Poems, was published in 1960. Despite the ecstatic letters, Aurelia read between the lines and was concerned. In Sylvia's poems about her dead father, she was not sure if she wanted to escape from him or recreate him.[8] The critic A. Alvarez wrote about the sense of threat in the poems, 'as though she was continually menaced by something she could see only out of the corner of her eye'.[9] Aurelia later noted that the fear expressed in these verses was very different from the positive tone of her letters.[10] She wrote:

> The toll of the death bell frightened me, as did the obsessive return to the period of emotional confusion and the horror of that first shock treatment. I so longed for her to free herself from these memories. I thought it best not to recall them to her, but to listen to any references she might make. I wanted us to make the present as good and wholesome as possible and to look courageously toward our future.[11]

However, Aurelia had to be careful about voicing any criticism because Sylvia accused her mother of wanting her to just write trite verse.

It was a productive time for Ted too; he won prestigious poetry prizes which confirmed his growing reputation. Their partnership was progressive by the sexist standards of their era; mutually supportive, they critiqued each other's work.[12] Both Sylvia and Ted delighted in their baby daughter, taking turns looking after her while the other wrote. While Sylvia had the bedroom and sitting room to work in, Ted had the small hallway. But when friends invited Ted to work in the study at their apartment, Sylvia resented it. Like Virginia Woolf's idea that a woman needs a room of her own to write, Sylvia admitted that she craved a study where she could be away from the distraction of hearing her baby.[13] In the end, Sylvia got her room; she enjoyed the peace of writing in their friends' study in the morning.

Mrs Plath had her own worries; Boston University decided to close its secretarial teaching department. Afterwards, Aurelia had to work twice as hard to earn the same amount of money and had to take additional work teaching medical shorthand or German. Revealing Sylvia had not forgotten her mother's dream of becoming a writer, she again suggested that Aurelia should write short stories for women's magazines, which she would edit.[14]

Although Aurelia lived far away, she wanted to be involved in her daughter and granddaughter's lives. Sylvia felt ambivalent; part of her was envious of her friends whose mothers lived nearby and she missed not having Aurelia close enough to share this joyful new experience. However, she was also aware that what she missed was an idealised version of the mother–daughter relationship, rather than the real thing. Sylvia resented any interference from Aurelia. She did not want to bring up her daughter in the same way her mother had parented her. When Aurelia sent her an endocrinologist's report on hormones and growth, suggesting that Sylvia could give Frieda something to limit her height,[15] Sylvia replied that she had no intention of tampering with nature and that it was so American of her to think that trying to make a person reach an ideal height would make them happy. She would be proud of her daughter whatever height she grew to.[16]

Increasingly, Sylvia relied on herself and her husband rather than her mother. When she had a miscarriage and appendectomy, she only told Aurelia about the difficult six months once it was over.[17] Her feelings were not the only thing she was keeping secret from her mother. In 1961, Sylvia began writing her autobiographical novel, *The Bell Jar*. Eight years after her suicide attempt, Sylvia believed she had the emotional distance to explore what happened through fiction. Knowing her mother would not like it, she avoided mentioning the novel in her letters home. The novel included derogatory images of many people, including her benefactor Mrs Prouty, her boyfriend Dick Norton, and his mother Millicent. The most merciless portrait was reserved for Aurelia. Sylvia poured all her negative emotions about her into the character of Mrs Greenwood, Esther's mother.

The novel was deeply personal, but also political. It was an indictment of 1950s America which set Sylvia's experience in a wider context. Influenced by the anti-psychiatry movement of R.D. Laing, she explored the link between insanity and repression. She wondered whether a person was sick, or had society made them mentally ill?[18] Like the gradual evolution of Virginia Woolf's feminist ideas, many of the themes Sylvia wrote about had been formulating for years. Since being a teenager, she had explored her attitudes to women's roles in her journal. In *The Bell Jar*, Sylvia used fiction to expose the dilemmas for young women caused by the sexual double standard. Her anger that women had to stay pure while men were able to live a double life is a major theme in the book. It also critiques the idea that once a woman is married, she should become just the launch pad for her husband's success, rather than pursuing her own career.

Wanting to finish the first draft by the end of May, Sylvia worked seven mornings a week, but it was still not completed before her mother's visit to England. As she relived memories of that traumatic period, it was not the best time for her mother to be coming.[19] In mid-June 1961, Aurelia arrived, looking forward to seeing her daughter, and her granddaughter for the first time. Sylvia was also excited about showing her new life to her mother and planned to make the trip as enjoyable as possible.[20] The reality of their reunion did not live up to their hopes. As Ted and Sylvia's flat was so small, Mrs Plath stayed in their friends' apartment. According to her host, one night Aurelia returned in tears, saying, 'Everything I do is wrong, I can't seem to do anything right.' She added, 'I just don't know how Ted stands it.'[21]

Although there were tensions, having her mother available to help with childcare was useful. Aurelia looked after Frieda while Ted and Sylvia went to stay with friends in France. When they returned, the whole family visited Ted's parents in Yorkshire.[22] Aurelia relished the drama of the landscape and liked Mr and Mrs Hughes, but she was critical of British standards of cleanliness and the ugliness of northern cities.[23]

During Aurelia's visit, Ted and Sylvia looked for a house in the country. Before Aurelia returned to America, they decided to buy Court Green, an ancient thatched house in Devon.[24] With its generous grounds, planted with apple trees, adjoining the churchyard, it was romantic but run-down. Sylvia was relieved that there was no opportunity for her mother to cast her critical eye over their new house because she did not want Aurelia pointing out its flaws. As money was tight, Aurelia and Ted's mother, Edith, agreed to lend the couple money so that they could buy the house. Aurelia offered to cover the full mortgage but, wanting to be as independent as possible, Ted refused.[25]

When Ted and Sylvia moved into their Devon home it needed a great deal of work. Sylvia was in her element creating a beautiful home and garden, painting the children's furniture with hearts and planting flowers. Rather than the image of the Laurentian literary bohemian she had previously cultivated, Sylvia now seemed to be conforming to a more traditional female role. Rather than rejecting her upbringing, she seemed to be trying to recreate it, even modelling herself on an idealised version of her mother. She looked for a second-hand piano so that she could play and sing to Frieda as Aurelia had to her.[26] Although she described herself as a 'pagan-Unitarian', she attended the parish church. She wrote to her mother that at difficult moments she found it useful to recite the prayer 'God is my help in every need', which Aurelia had taught her as a child.[27] Looking forward to their first Christmas at Court Green, Sylvia wanted to keep their family customs alive.[28] Not able to be with them, Aurelia sent a huge box of presents.[29]

In January 1962, Ted and Sylvia's second child, Nicholas, was born at Court Green. Sylvia relished having children and told Aurelia that it was the happiest experience of her life.[30] Once again, part of her felt homesick and missed her mother. Limited in what she could do to help, Aurelia showered her daughter with generous gifts. She sent Sylvia bras and pants and copious bottles of vitamins but also a top-of-the-range Bendix washing machine.[31] Although Sylvia raved about the appliance in letters to Aurelia, she complained to her friends about her mother, mocking her vulgar taste.[32]

In the Devon village, Sylvia was leading a double life. Few villagers knew she was a poet; they only saw the young wife and mother. However, while dealing with the mundane details of domesticity, in private Sylvia was reaching her full potential as a writer. Her first novel, *The Bell Jar*, had been accepted by Heinemann. When she submitted the manuscript, she discussed with her publisher whether she could be sued for libel. Dismissing the idea that her mother might sue, she claimed that she was not defaming Aurelia because she portrayed her as a dutiful, hard-working woman whose unpleasant daughter was ungrateful.[33] Tellingly, she published the novel under the pseudonym Victoria Lucas.

Her poetry was also entering a new phase and there was a fresh energy and freedom in her writing. It was exhilarating but also dangerous because she was drawing on the darker side of her nature. She began to write poems in the distinctive Ariel voice.[34] As she released the submerged force which had always been part of her inner self, her poetry came with a new urgency and power.[35]

Some of Sylvia's later work echoes Virginia Woolf. Perhaps influenced by the Bloomsbury writer's essay 'On Being Ill', she wrote about women's bodily experiences in a new way. Her poems 'Tulips' and 'Fever 103°' can be read as responding to Virginia's call for 'a new hierarchy of the passions;

love must be deposed in favour of a temperature of 104'.[36] Although she was never a mother herself, Woolf was interested in the intimate bodily functions involved in childbearing and the power of the maternal instinct.[37] Through the character of Susan in *The Waves* she explored its overwhelming potential. After reading this novel, Sylvia vowed to do even better than her role model; she believed that after having children she would be able to speak even deeper from her inner self.[38] In 1962, Sylvia went that step further by drawing on her own experience of being a mother in her verse play 'Three Women'. Set in a maternity ward, it explored three different versions of motherhood. First voice is the fulfilled mother with her son; second voice deals with the trauma of miscarriage; while the third voice gives birth to a daughter, who is given up for adoption. The descriptions of giving birth are visceral and bloody, but the poem goes beyond the personal to become universal. Sylvia was breaking new ground by examining how motherhood and creativity could be reconciled. One biographer describes it as 'probably the first great poem of childbirth in the language'.[39] According to Ted Hughes, after 'Three Women' there was a turning point in Sylvia's life and work as suddenly the ghost of her father reappeared.[40] The return of this spectre gave her some of her most unforgettable poetry, but it also pushed her to the edge.

40

The Final Visit

Everything Sylvia had always wanted seemed to be coming to fruition, but beneath the surface there were problems. Although Sylvia adored her children, she longed to have time on her own with her husband. Juggling childcare with her writing was also stressful.[1] Sylvia's moods were volatile and there were occasional outbursts. According to friends of Ted, she was possessive and could freeze people out if they demanded too much of his attention. By the summer of 1962, there was a genuine focus for her jealousy. When Ted and Sylvia moved to Devon, the Canadian poet David Wevill and his wife Assia took their London flat. The two couples became friends and in May the Wevills visited Court Green. Sensing an attraction between her husband and Assia, Sylvia became jealous.

At the end of June, Aurelia came to stay with her daughter. Sylvia wanted everything to appear perfect for her mother's first visit to Court Green. To welcome Aurelia she put an enamelled heart in a garland of flowers on her bedroom door and a silk scarf as a gift on her pillow.[2] The first week of the visit went well. Mrs Plath wrote to her son that it was one of the happiest times she had experienced in many years.[3] Aurelia was relieved that Frieda recognised her and Nicholas came willingly into her arms.[4] She enjoyed spending time with her daughter and grandchildren just pottering around the garden.

According to Aurelia, one evening Sylvia excitedly told her she was writing a trilogy. Although she did not refer to it by name, this was the first time Sylvia mentioned *The Bell Jar* to her mother. She explained that it was the view of life seen through the eyes of depression. The manuscript she had on her lap was the sequel, which was life seen through the eyes of health. It began when she came to England and ended with the birth of Frieda. Ted was the hero, and it was dedicated to him; she intended to give it to him as a surprise for his birthday. Sylvia then read extracts from this draft copy until she was interrupted by Nicholas crying and had to go upstairs to comfort him.[5] As she talked about the trilogy, Sylvia said to Aurelia, 'I feel I have been living a series of novels, really, and this is, so far, the most exciting part.'[6]

On a shopping trip to Exeter, Sylvia continued in a similar positive vein, telling her mother that she had everything she had ever wanted in her life. Aurelia, however, sensed that there was something wrong.[7] The tensions exploded into the open when Assia phoned Ted through a male colleague at her office. When Sylvia intercepted the phone call, she suspected a ruse and confronted Ted. According to Aurelia's account, Sylvia's face turned pale as she called her husband downstairs. From that moment, the atmosphere at Court Green changed. Sylvia went upstairs and, once the call was over, Ted followed her into their bedroom.[8] Sylvia later told a friend that she confronted Ted, but he denied everything. She then ranted and screamed at him.[9]

While Ted and Sylvia were in the bedroom, Mrs Plath looked after the children. According to Aurelia, when Nicholas began to cry because his feeding time was overdue, she walked the floor with him for over an hour, hoping that Sylvia would emerge to take him. Aurelia's back began to ache, but she just kept walking up and down with her grandson sobbing in her arms. Finally, she knocked on the door and asked Sylvia to take Nicholas. Ted and Sylvia were in bed, so Aurelia put the baby down, and left him with his parents.

Next day, Aurelia once again looked after her grandchildren while Ted and Sylvia talked. At first, she did not know what the problem was, and she wondered if it was work related. Later that afternoon, Ted left for London, saying to Aurelia he did not know when he would see her again. Once Ted had gone, Sylvia explained to her mother that the phone call had been from the woman Ted had been having an affair with.

According to Aurelia, on 10 July, in a scene worthy of 'a gothic horror story', Sylvia burned the sequel to *The Bell Jar* in a bonfire in the courtyard. Aurelia stood helplessly by with her grandson in her arms, trying to stop Frieda from joining her mother. When she later asked her daughter why she had done it, Sylvia said that the manuscript symbolised a time of joy in her life which now proved to be false, and the hero of the story was dead to her.[10]

The existence of a second novel, which may have been based on drafts of *Falcon Yard*, the novel Sylvia began in Cambridge, is open to question. The biographer Anne Stevenson disputed Aurelia's account. Stevenson's biography puts the timing of the bonfire before Assia's phone call. She claimed that Sylvia burnt Ted's papers, not her own. In Sylvia's poem 'Burning the Letters', she described seeing Assia's name on a fragment of paper among the embers. Stevenson also argued that there was no documentary evidence that the second novel ever existed.[11] In 2000, Plath's publishers also claimed that Sylvia did not write another novel besides *The Bell Jar* and reference to a sequel (entitled *Falcon Yard*) was inaccurate.[12] The truth about a second novel remains one of the contentious issues in Plath scholarship.

When Ted returned from London, Aurelia realised her daughter and son-in-law needed time to themselves and took a room in the local midwife Winifred Davies's house. She came every day to Court Green to spend time with her grandchildren, but she was careful not to outstay her welcome. A photograph taken of mother and daughter with the two children captures the tense atmosphere; both women look grim with fixed half-smiles on their faces and dark bags under their eyes. When Aurelia left Devon to return to America on 4 August, Sylvia, Ted and the two children saw her off at the station; only baby Nicholas was smiling. It was to be the last time she saw her daughter.[13]

Aurelia paid a heavy price for observing the events which unfolded at Court Green that summer. Both Aurelia and Sylvia were proud women who found it mortifying to be rejected by the men they loved. When Karl had ended their relationship, Aurelia had concealed her true feelings from everyone; her daughter could not do the same because her mother was with her. Aurelia believed that Sylvia later wrote her poem 'Medusa' to lash out at her because she was present at that fateful time.

When Sylvia wrote to Dr Beuscher, she explained that her mother witnessing her humiliation made it worse. She admitted Aurelia had been helpful looking after the children and did not pry, but she claimed her mother was the last person she wished to talk to about what was happening.[14] Once again, Sylvia imagined what her mother was thinking. She told her psychiatrist that she thought her mother hated her for depriving her of her vicarious dream. However, another part of Aurelia was glad about what was happening, because it confirmed her low opinion of men.[15]

In late summer, Sylvia proposed a legal separation from her husband, yet in September they travelled to Galway together to find a cottage for Sylvia to live in for the winter. After spending time together, Ted told his sister Olwyn that he thought his wife had changed and was becoming much more like her mother, whom he detested.[16] One of Sylvia's greatest fears was turning into Aurelia. As she found herself alone with two young children, the parallels became increasingly uncomfortable. Rather than her real mother, Sylvia turned to her replacement mother figure for advice. Dr Beuscher warned her not to repeat the same pattern as Mrs Plath and let a man turn her into a martyr. Sylvia replied that she was not her mother nor did she have masochistic tendencies. She had no intention of sacrificing herself to her children nor living through them and did not want her daughter to hate her as she had hated Aurelia.[17]

Her psychiatrist wielded a great deal of influence over her. According to Sylvia's latest biographer, it was Dr Beuscher who convinced Sylvia to divorce her husband.[18] She also advised her to settle child custody and finances as soon as possible. Mrs Prouty and Aurelia also advised Sylvia to take effective financial measures against Ted and dissolve the marriage.[19] Following their advice, she ordered Ted to leave. Aurelia hoped her daughter and grandchildren would return to America. She told Sylvia the family were willing to set her up in an apartment.[20] When Dr Beuscher heard Aurelia's offer, she gave Sylvia clear instructions not to return to the United States.[21] Sylvia told her mother that she wanted to make her life in England because if she started running away from things now, she would never stop. She intended to continue with her literary career and establish a fulfilling life in London. Tellingly, although she said how much she needed someone from home to be with her, she did not want her mother. She told Aurelia that she would like to see her Aunt Dot (Aurelia's sister) or her brother, but not her. She admitted that after the scenes Aurelia had witnessed, she could not face seeing her again until she had a successful new life.[22]

Explaining her reasons to Warren, Sylvia complained that Aurelia identified too much with her and it was not helpful.[23] Returning to the metaphor she had used years before, she told him that she must not go back to the womb.[24] She was determined to be self-reliant.[25] As usual when she was unhappy, Sylvia turned her anger on her mother both in conversations with friends and in her writing.

Left alone with the children at Court Green, Sylvia experienced an incredible surge of poetic energy. Like Virginia Woolf shortly before her suicide, Sylvia returned to thoughts of her childhood. It was as if she had to re-examine what had hurt her in the past before she could move on.[26] While the ghosts of Julia and Leslie haunted Woolf, Otto's spectre once again loomed over Sylvia. In these poems she lashed out at her father, mother and husband. In one of her most famous poems, 'Daddy', she portrayed Otto as a Nazi, while she identified with the Jews sent to concentration camps. Comparing domestic tyranny to fascist dictatorship was reminiscent of Virginia's ideas in *Three Guineas*. Exhilarated by what she had written, Sylvia wrote to her mother, 'It's over. My life can begin.'[27]

However, it was not over, and she attacked Aurelia in her poem 'Medusa'. The title played on Aurelia's name as 'Medusa' in Greek mythology was the gorgon who turned everyone who looked at her to stone. It was also the name of a species of jellyfish, *Aurelia medusae*. Her mother had once joked with Sylvia about this.[28] Now she used the idea to portray a love-destroying mother figure, who smothered her daughter. The final line was the most hurtful, 'There is nothing between us.'

After writing it, Sylvia wrote to her mother without mentioning the contents of the poem. She just told Aurelia that she was a genius of a writer and that she was writing the best poems of her life which would make her famous. She warned her mother not to suggest that she should write more cheerful works because when people were suffering it helped to know someone else went through dreadful experiences too.[29] And, if her poems upset her mother, that was her problem – she had always shied away from confronting difficult issues.[30]

When Ted read these *Ariel* poems, he recognised their brilliance but was shocked at the tone and wondered how Aurelia could survive such an attack.[31] Years later he was to write about how 'appalled' he was by the 'malice' of these new poems in his 'Trial' sequence. According to his poem, he was not just concerned about the effect these verses would have on Aurelia, he also feared the long-term repercussions for his wife. He wondered how she would go on living in a world in which she had 'condemned your parents, publicly / Into such everlasting furnaces?'[32]

Unaware of what her daughter had written, when Sylvia told Aurelia that she was feeling ill and needed a good nanny, Mrs Plath immediately tried to help. She contacted the midwife Winifred Davies asking her to keep an eye on Sylvia and find her a live-in nanny, whom she would pay for.[33] When Sylvia found out, she wrote an angry letter telling Aurelia not to bother Winifred. She did not want her money, which she should be saving for her retirement.[34]

Sylvia wrote to Dr Beuscher saying she despised Aurelia for her lack of courage and for making herself into a martyr.[35] In conversations with a friend, she described her as a 'demon mother' and complained that she was controlling and had pushed her beyond endurance to win prizes.[36] She told another friend that she had always needed to impress her mother with her successes. The end of her marriage seemed like a failure.[37]

Thousands of miles away, Aurelia felt helpless, unsure what to do to help her daughter. Making her feel even more cut off, Sylvia wrote to her less frequently. Once again, Mrs Prouty stood beside Aurelia as her ally. She was clear-sighted about Sylvia, recognising that her overwhelming grief at losing Ted was making her behave in ways beyond her control. Unlike Aurelia, she stood back and was the cool, calm voice of reason.[38] Nor was she afraid to tell Sylvia what she thought. When her protégée said she was intending to dedicate her next novel to her, Mrs Prouty reminded her of the debt she owed Aurelia. She told Sylvia that her mother loved her so much she would willingly die for her and it hurt her if Sylvia did not write to her regularly.[39] This willingness to sacrifice herself was part of the problem. Sylvia wrote an angry letter to her mother attacking her for saying that she could not live unless her daughter was reasonably happy; one person should never be so dependent on another. She asked her mother why she identified with her so much. Rather than making her want to confide it pushed her away.[40]

In December 1962, Sylvia and the children moved to London where she rented a flat in Fitzroy Road.[41] Aurelia was desperately worried about her daughter.[42] Uncertain how to handle her, she made practical suggestions trying to micromanage Sylvia's move from across the Atlantic.[43] Concerned she might be short of money, she sent her a cheque book. Once again, Sylvia reacted angrily, rejecting her mother's support.[44]

Trying to put a positive spin on the situation, on 6 December Sylvia phoned home and spoke to her mother in reassuring tones about her intention to build a fulfilling new life. Aurelia told her how much she admired her courage.[45] Sylvia tried to remain strong and positive, but increasingly she could no longer put on a brave face. During one of the coldest winters on record, she suffered from flu and the children had coughs and colds. Ted visited regularly and babysat when Sylvia needed a break, but she was not coping well on her own.[46] In her final weeks, she wrote more outstanding poems; however, this phenomenal literary output went hand in hand with acute emotional turmoil.

During Sylvia's final weeks, a conjunction of unfortunate circumstances came together. The coldest weather for years with frozen pipes, electricity cuts and the lack of a telephone made daily life even more difficult. The publication of *The Bell Jar* in January also pushed her nearer the edge.[47] Although Aurelia claimed Sylvia had mentioned writing a novel during her summer visit, it seems that her daughter first told her she was going to have a 'secret' novel published in a letter home in October 1962.[48] Ted said that Sylvia became paranoid about the novel, worrying that it would not be successful, but also that it would hurt her friends and family in America.[49] She admitted to Ted that Esther's anger towards her self-sacrificing and generous mother was a symptom of her madness.[50] Dreading the effect it might have, Sylvia told her mother not to tell anyone about it.[51]

Conscious her mental health was deteriorating, in late January Sylvia went to see her doctor. When she told him the history of her attempted suicide, he put her on a course of anti-depressants. Inadvertently, he prescribed tablets which her doctors in America knew she reacted badly to. As the medication was branded under a different name, she was unaware of its detrimental effects on her, and rather than helping, her condition worsened.

Aware of how serious the situation was, Sylvia confided in her mother again.[52] In her final letter to Aurelia on 4 February, she said she had not been in touch because she was lonely and felt awful. Once again, Aurelia had suggested she should return to America or at least send Frieda over to give her a break. Sylvia, though, had no intention of being separated from her daughter. To reassure her mother, she promised she was going to see a female psychiatrist.[53] Sylvia also wrote to Dr Beuscher saying that she feared losing her mind. She felt panic as she was faced with her mother's example of fear and self-sacrifice on one side and her beautiful children on the other. Her lack of a firm identity remained a problem, and she felt unable to be herself and love herself. She knew no one else could save her, but she recognised that she needed help.[54]

In her final days, circumstances conspired against her. Her London doctor tried unsuccessfully to find a suitable hospital to take her. Meanwhile, he was trying to get her an appointment with a female psychiatrist. She had fired her au pair and was waiting for a replacement.[55] On 11 February 1963, after leaving out bread and milk for her children and taping up their bedroom door, she turned on the gas oven and killed herself. Mrs Plath heard on 12 February when Ted sent a cablegram to her sister which told her that Sylvia had died yesterday but did not explain what had happened.[56]

Aurelia was too grief-stricken to leave her home, but her son and his wife flew over to Britain for the funeral in Yorkshire. At first, she assumed that Sylvia had died from pneumonia until Warren wrote to tell her that his sister had died from carbon monoxide poisoning from the gas stove.[57] Aurelia tried to make sense of why her brilliant daughter took her own life. On 4 March 1963, she wrote a letter to *The Observer* thanking Sylvia's friends and neighbours for their help. She ended it, 'Those who systematically and deliberately destroyed her know who they are.' She never sent the letter.[58] At first, in private, she blamed her daughter's death on Ted but later her attitude changed, and she shifted the blame on to Dr Beuscher.[59] She was also angry with her daughter, but gradually she stopped playing the blame game. She believed that some dark subconscious force engulfed Sylvia as she explored her past through her poetry. She ascribed her daughter's suicide to 'some darker day than usual'.[60]

According to a friend, in later life Aurelia had three or four explanations about why it happened, ranging from it being triggered by a chemical imbalance caused by the medication, to Sylvia being unable to face the consequences of publishing *The Bell Jar* or the failure of the au pair to arrive. Which explanation she favoured varied according to her mood on that day.[61] We also get an insight into Aurelia's thoughts from an article she kept, which she noted was particularly perceptive. In it, Erica Jong explained that at the end of her life Sylvia was exposed to stresses which would have crushed even the strongest person. She was seriously ill and lonely but determined not to show her desperate need for help to her family and friends. Jong concluded, 'Surely Sylvia Plath was the author of her own despair in that she was constantly drawn toward impossible challenges, but SHE WAS ALSO IMMENSELY BRAVE.'[62] The capitals are Aurelia's.

41

Aurelia Answers Back

No words can express the complex layers of pain felt by the loved ones of someone who dies by suicide. For Aurelia, her daughter's death was made even worse by the literary legacy she left behind. Sylvia's last works caught her at one specific moment in her life and in the act of revenge. If she had lived longer, her relationships and what she wrote about them may have changed, but, like an insect trapped in amber, the images she created remained fixed in the public imagination for evermore.

Aurelia did not read the *Ariel* poems, *The Bell Jar*, or her daughter's journals until after her death. Reading them, her concept of the loving relationship she thought they had was shattered. A very different picture emerged from the one in Sylvia's letters home. It must have been a totally disorienting experience for her as, like Joan Scudamore in Agatha Christie's *Absent in the Spring*, Aurelia realised that the way other people saw her did not match her self-image. She had to work out what had been real or unreal in her past and find a way of living with it. Not only did Aurelia suffer private pain she also experienced public humiliation when her daughter's works were published posthumously.

However, unlike the other mothers in this book, she could tell her side of their story. She reasserted control over the narrative and answered her daughter back. Although, like the daughters writing about their mothers in this book, she cannot be treated as a completely reliable narrator; what she said sheds light not only on her relationship with Sylvia but also on what it is like for a mother to have her private life put in the public domain by her daughter's writing. From now on there would be an ambiguity in

Aurelia's attitude to her daughter. She experienced a range of emotions including sadness, anger and bitterness, but there also remained an indestructible love and pride.

For the rest of her life, Aurelia would try to make sense of how there could be two different versions of their relationship. Even after years of analysing what happened she could not understand it. She wrote to a friend:

> It is so strange as I go back in memory – there was NEVER [Aurelia's capitals] contention between us. I loved her from the moment I knew I was to have a baby and was absolutely devoted to her all her life and beyond. But I do not want to be obsessed by the past now. [1]

Aurelia's claim that there was 'never' contention is a demonstrable exaggeration. Although Sylvia's negative emotions towards her mother were most starkly expressed privately, she had never entirely withheld her feelings of resentment from Mrs Plath.[2] As Plath scholars observe, the mother of someone who had lost their life to suicide might well say or claim things contrary to facts or do things to lessen their immense emotional pain.[3] Some of Aurelia's comments should be read like some of Sylvia's autobiographical writing as not necessarily strictly factually accurate but valuable because they give us an insight into how she tried to come to terms with what had happened.

Like Virginia Woolf trying to piece together exactly who her mother was, Aurelia had to reassess the daughter she thought she knew so well. Approaching it in a professional way, she gathered the evidence from her daughter's letters and literary works and compared them to her own memories. As Virginia found with her mother, no matter how hard Aurelia tried, Sylvia remained elusive.

When Aurelia first read her daughter's *Ariel* poems, she detected a pattern in Sylvia's work which had been hiding in plain sight since Otto's death. Aurelia later explained:

> I think it was an inbred fear that what she'd loved would leave her sometime and I think it haunted her all her life without making it known in words. I never was aware of it until I gathered poems together and found this pattern running straight through.[4]

After Karl's rejection, Aurelia also had this fear; perhaps she passed this legacy on to her daughter.

After *Ariel* was published in the US in 1966, Aurelia felt overwhelmed. Her life became a 'torment' as she had to deal with endless correspondence about 'Daddy'. Strangers phoned asking whether Otto had really been a Nazi.[5] She also suffered the humiliation of critics psychoanalysing her relationship with Sylvia. She could not understand the venom of her daughter's poems.[6]

Reading *The Bell Jar* was equally painful. She was shocked by its 'raging adolescent voice',[7] and believed it should 'never have seen the light of day'.[8] Aurelia concluded that Sylvia had got carried away with the dramatic effect of the story and did not fully realise what havoc she would cause for the characters who were so 'falsely cartooned'. After Ted told Aurelia that the novel's publication frightened Sylvia, Aurelia commented 'as it should have – she hurt people who had been thoroughly good, generous, and loving in regard to her. She sensed, I believe, that the book cost her the loss of her best friends.'[9] Aurelia thought that it played a part in Sylvia's death because she could not face the people she had hurt. The hardest person to face of all would have been her mother.

As Sylvia had not obtained a divorce from Ted Hughes, nor made a will, he inherited the copyright on her writing. He understood that for Aurelia's sake *The Bell Jar* should not be published in America. But there were rumours that he might lose control of the right to withhold it. A provision in the copyright law of the US meant that a work by a dead US citizen published outside the country did not have protection at home for longer than seven years. Any unscrupulous publisher could get hold of a copy of the English edition and print it. To prevent this happening, Ted wrote to his former mother-in-law, and his sister Olwyn, who was literary agent of the Plath estate, also discussed it with her. As it had been agreed that money from the publication of Sylvia's work would be used to benefit Frieda and Nicholas, Olwyn suggested that it would be better to publish an authorised version with editorial control and make some money for the children, than see an unauthorised version brought out and receive no money. Aurelia opposed the idea, but eventually she left the decision to Ted.[10]

To soften the blow, it was agreed Mrs Plath would receive $10,000 on publication. Extracts from a letter from Aurelia were included in an essay appended to the novel. In it, she claimed Sylvia had looked at people through the distorting lens of a bell jar. The strain her daughter was under when she wrote the novel, having recently had a miscarriage, appendicitis and given birth, meant that it gave the impression of showing 'the basest ingratitude'. It was for this reason that Sylvia had said to her brother that it must never be published in the US.[11]

In 1971, when *The Bell Jar* was published in America, it went straight into the bestseller list. The publication was humiliating for Aurelia as friends and family read her daughter's version of their relationship. Until the novel appeared, Sylvia's first suicide attempt had not been widely known about in America.[12] Aurelia later admitted to an interviewer that at times being known as Sylvia Plath's mother had been very difficult, particularly at this moment.[13]

After the novel was released, Aurelia was inundated with enquiries about their life together. Wanting to show a different side of her daughter's story, she decided to publish Sylvia's letters to her. Rather than a vindication, she described it as her 'last commitment to Sylvia's memory'.[14] She wanted to shape her daughter's posthumous reputation and create a more rounded picture. She explained that Sylvia's work had been presented in such a way that she was known only for the literature written during 'the two blackest periods of her life'. Describing the letters as 'an unpremeditated autobiography', she wanted to present a picture of the daughter she knew.[15]

The process of editing *Letters Home* was time-consuming and emotionally demanding. There were nearly 700 letters to go through and there were also copyright issues. While Mrs Plath had the physical possession of the letters, she had to get permission from Ted Hughes to publish them. He allowed it but reserved the right to final approval of the manuscript.

To accompany the letters, Mrs Plath wrote an introduction and commentary. Aurelia was later criticised for deliberately leaving out some pertinent material from the letters she selected.[16] Plath biographer Jacqueline Rose portrays Aurelia's attempts to control the narrative as a desire to 'assert the exclusive, inviolable intimacy of the mother–daughter relationship', even though by publishing them she undermined that intimacy.[17] The publication of the complete and unabridged letters shows that only 383 of the 856 letters written by Plath to her mother and family were published in *Letters Home*, and some of those were only excerpted.[18] Portions of some letters in which Sylvia had expressed anger or complained of illness had been removed.[19]

It seems that Mrs Plath, Ted and the book's editor were collectively responsible for what appeared.[20] Aurelia said that she only removed repetition and trivial domestic detail. She claimed that when she sent her draft to Ted, he suggested final cuts. Some were in the interest of economy, others for privacy.[21] Ted disagreed with some of Aurelia's interpretations; for instance, when his mother-in-law wrote about Sylvia 'renouncing the subservient female role', he commented that his wife was never subservient.[22]

Aurelia also claimed that her editor removed material, partly because there was a fear of libel lawsuits.[23] Mrs Plath was not always happy with the decisions. In her draft, she wrote a detailed account of her harrowing experiences after Sylvia's first suicide attempt. She wrote on the manuscript that her editor had crossed out some of her story.[24] She told a friend, 'The next book I write will be free of all censorship.'[25] Plath scholar Catherine Rankovic believes that some of Aurelia's unpublished passages were false, or 'idealized scenes', in which the dialogue was strangely stiff. Her experienced editor recognised them as face-saving fictions and deleted them.[26]

When *Letters Home* was published in 1975 it was a major achievement for Aurelia. It showed her writing ability and skill at editing. She wrote proudly to a friend that she was now classified as a writer.[27] It is tragic that it took her daughter's death for Mrs Plath to finally realise her long-term dream. Once *Letters Home* was published, Aurelia gave talks and interviews. One of the most prestigious events was the 'For the Authors' Series Talk' for Wellesley College Club in March 1976. As her speech and detailed notes show, she carefully constructed her argument, listing the key points to get across; she then repeated these in slightly different formats for the rest of her life. Piecing together her comments in talks, interviews and letters to friends we see how Aurelia tried to reclaim her daughter's life and work.

Rather than dwelling on the tragedy, Aurelia described Sylvia's life as 'an adventure story lived by an "electric" personality; as well as the unfolding of a sensitive, impressionable young girl into a determined, disciplined creative artist'.[28] She emphasised Sylvia's immense capacity for happiness and detested descriptions of her daughter as a 'mad poetess'. On a scrap of paper kept with the Wellesley notes, she wrote: 'Terms – "mad – madmen". Never so, the terms not used in connection to Robert Lowell and Anne

Sexton!' (other contemporary confessional poets). She underlined that Sylvia was 'never' the screaming figure portrayed in the film of *The Bell Jar*.[29] Her sensitivity on this issue is clear in a copy she kept of Sylvia's notes for her 1949 diary. In a predominantly positive passage, 17-year-old Sylvia wrote that she wanted to be both all-knowing and a little insane. Although it was only a light-hearted mention of madness, Aurelia crossed it out.[30]

An alternative image of her daughter's life was just part of Aurelia's project; she also wanted people to read her work differently. Sylvia's name had become synonymous with confessional literature.[31] Aurelia did not want Sylvia's writing to be read as autobiographically accurate. She emphasised that her daughter fused parts of her own life with Aurelia's, combined elements from different characters and manipulated events to achieve her artistic ends. Mrs Plath described it as a 'violation of actual circumstances', and nowhere was this 'violation' more evident than in *The Bell Jar*.[32] For a woman as precise in her language as Aurelia, the term 'violation' is telling; it suggests her daughter's portrayal of her affected her like a physical assault.

The idea that artists distort actual experience in their art is hardly shocking. Using the imagination to transform literal truth into emotional truth is part of the writer's craft. As Agatha's second husband, Max Mallowan, wrote, her novel *Unfinished Portrait* was 'a blend of real people and events with imagination. Only the initiated can know how much actual history is contained therein.'[33] Similarly, Virginia's *To the Lighthouse* was based on her imaginative impression of her family life. As one of 'the initiated', Aurelia was keen to draw clear lines between fact and fiction.

Mrs Plath explained that everyone Sylvia met potentially provided material for characters. Unfortunately, the images she created were often unflattering. In her youth, Sylvia admired the 'cruelly satirical' poems of Dorothy Parker and copied her style. Later, she developed this denigrating tone 'with more lethal impact'.[34] It could be cathartic for Sylvia because if she was angry with someone, she would write down her resentment and then be done with it.[35] However, as Aurelia complained, 'The sad thing is that the innocent "target" had to face this form of release in published form' and it became 'permanent as an epitaph on a tombstone'.[36]

A writer caricaturing her relatives was not unique to Sylvia; Virginia Woolf behaved similarly with her sister. Vanessa Bell complained to her husband:

Virginia since her youth has made it her business to create a character for me according to her own wishes and has now succeeded in imposing it upon the world that these preposterous stories are supposed to be certainly true because so characteristic.[37]

Knowing the risk, Vanessa only shared her innermost feelings with Virginia with reservations because she was never sure in what form they might be passed on to other people. Her daughter Angelica Garnett explained that it hurt because, 'Virginia's tongue, with unerring intelligence struck at her most vulnerable parts.'[38] The image her sister created was so brilliant but ruthless that there were moments when Vanessa hardly knew what she was really like. Vanessa found herself in 'a position of hopeless resistance because Virginia's need to destroy – albeit by an act of creation – was stronger than her own means of self-protection'.[39]

In an act of resistance, rather than accepting this was the nature of her daughter's creativity, Aurelia tried to deconstruct Sylvia's writing, as though by doing so she could take the hurt away. Like an English teacher, she analysed her daughter's works, explaining that 'because many times I knew the real-life character or event, I was much more aware of the manipulation than other people could be'.[40] Particularly galling for her was Sylvia's portrayal of Otto in her poem 'Daddy'. Mrs Plath explained that her husband never had any affiliation to the Nazi party and was a great advocate of the 'reverence for life'.[41] Reflecting her frustration with her daughter's obsession with her father, Aurelia wrote that Sylvia 'luxuriated in the interest aroused as she amplified her relationship with her father'.[42]

According to Mrs Plath, Sylvia's portrayal of their mother and daughter relationship had also been distorted beyond recognition. She challenged the image of herself as the over-ambitious mother in 'The Disquieting Muses', by taking it apart, line by line.[43] She also counteracted the portrayal of her as the love-destroying mother in the poem 'Medusa' by telling her side of the story. She suggested it was an act of revenge by Sylvia because she had witnessed the breakdown of her marriage. Similarly, she challenged her portrayal in *The Bell Jar* by sharing her version of what happened in 1953. In an interview for *The Listener*, when asked about the similarity between herself and Mrs Greenwood, she claimed there was 'very little'.[44]

Despite Mrs Plath's attempts to reshape the narrative, she did not have the final word. There was a backlash against her for putting private letters in the public domain. Author Janet Malcolm wrote:

'Mother, *how could you?*' would be any daughter's anguished response to an act of treachery like the publication of these letters: [...] It is one thing when some 'publishing scoundrel' somehow gets hold of a cache of your most private and unpremeditated letters after your death and prints them, and another when your own mother hands you over to posterity in your stained bathrobe and unwashed face; it is quite beyond endurance, in fact.[45]

Rather than protecting Sylvia's literary legacy, Malcolm argued that Aurelia had inadvertently damaged it. Although she did not blame a grieving mother for reacting in this way, she thought it could be seen as an act of 'unconscious aggression'. She explained:

It seems simply never to have occurred to Mrs Plath that the persona of *Ariel* and *The Bell Jar* was the persona by which Plath wished to be represented and remembered – [...] and that the face she showed her mother was not the face she wished to show the reading public.[46]

Sylvia's self-presentation in *Letters Home* is no less authentic than the way she portrays herself in her journals and poems; for Plath there were many selves and her writing reflects this.[47] An unintended consequence of the publication of *Letters Home* opened the door to more biographical studies. It encouraged Plath scholars to turn their scrutiny on the mother–daughter relationship.

In 1982, Ted Hughes allowed the publication of an abridged version of Sylvia's journals. They provided a different image from the one Aurelia had promoted. She described the terrible shock of reading them as she was once again forced to face that her daughter kept one part of her 'double' experience completely private from her.[48]

As a series of biographies were written about Sylvia, Aurelia was often disappointed by the results and it reopened old wounds. Perhaps the one person who could understand what it was like for her was her former son-in-law. As the people who had known Sylvia best and who bore the brunt of posthumous assessments of her life and work, a strange and often strained solidarity developed between Ted and Aurelia. In a similar position, they felt a degree of sympathy for each other. As Ted wrote to Al Alvarez, the critic and friend of Sylvia:

> Whatever Sylvia may be for your readers and for you, for her mother and me and her children, she is something different, she is an atmosphere we breathe. This is something apart from remembrance, it is a world imposed on us by the public consciousness of her and of our inevitable relationship to her. [...] For your readers it's five interesting minutes, but for us it is permanent dynamite.[49]

When Sylvia's feminism was debated and feminists attacked Ted Hughes, Aurelia tried to keep out of the controversy, although occasionally she got caught in the crossfire. When one biographer wrote critically about Ted, his former mother-in-law refused to endorse it. She commented, 'The sample chapters describe Sylvia as the abused woman and Ted the monster. Well, you can imagine my horror.' She explained that she did not want her name connected with anything related to Sylvia and Ted, adding, 'I WANT PEACE. [Aurelia's capitals] Ted is the father of my grandchildren – and at present we are in infrequent but pleasant communication. I don't want the errors of the past dug up, distorted, reported.'[50]

When her former son-in-law was made Poet Laureate in 1984, it was an emotional time for her. She told a friend how after Sylvia and Ted's wedding was over, her daughter whispered in her ear, 'I have just married the future Poet Laureate of England, Mother!' Aurelia added, 'How she would have rejoiced in this.'[51] During this decade, Sylvia's literary legacy brought Aurelia and Ted together again when psychiatrist Jane Anderson brought a libel action against Ted Hughes and the film company which made the film of *The Bell Jar*. She asserted that a character in the novel and the film was a 'portrait' of her and it had caused her substantial emotional anguish.[52] Ted's argument during the case had much in common with Aurelia's analysis. He argued that Plath was a symbolic artist who had been persistently misread as a confessional one.[53]

While in America, Ted visited Aurelia. He found her shrunken and hunched with age but as full of spirit as ever.[54] He wanted her to support him, but she did not wish to get too involved. Aurelia wrote to a friend, 'More than half the characters in that book – myself foremost – could make the same accusation [as Jane Anderson] [...] Strange that he should ask a favour of me after what I have endured through the journals and poems all these years.'[55] Eventually, the case was settled, but the widespread publicity upset Aurelia so much her gastric ulcer flared up.[56]

The court case made Ted Hughes reassess the legacy left by Sylvia. In February 1987, he wrote to a friend, setting out his analysis:

> Maybe I did help her (Aurelia) to keep up her self-delusion, and her sustained effort to delude the public too, about Sylvia's diabolical side. When she published Letters Home, she re-invented Sylvia as the ideal & angelic daughter – and consecrated her death as a martyrdom. This was all of a piece with her colossal effort to apologise for her daughter, & to persuade herself that the novel & the poems were screams extorted on the rack, & that all Sylvia's difficulties had been implanted in her somehow, by somebody else – mainly (in Aurelia's own mind) by her analyst Dr Beutscher [*sic*], who first gave Sylvia – after her attempted suicide – the resurrection mantra 'I hate my mother.' This image – sugar idol – of Sylvia became a divine icon, as you know. But of course it's a lie. And I colluded in the creation & propagation of it. What Aurelia saw – recognised – in the novel & poems as the voice of Sylvia's diabolical streak, she managed to represent as the voice of her suffering & martyrdom. And protecting Aurelia, I colluded – and promoted the cult which interpreted my continued silence in the blazing martyr-light shed by Sylvia's consecrated image. In which light I could only appear as a demon, the villain, the cause of all Sylvia's pains.[57]

Olwyn Hughes took a similar line in a letter to the writer Janet Malcolm. She blamed Aurelia's attitude that 'one must only see Sylvia's best side', describing it as 'sentimentalizing hypocrisy'. She explained:

> It's my belief that if Mrs Plath had said, when Sylvia died, 'She suffered from mental illness, but was a marvellous person and I loved her' the myth would never have happened. Unfortunately, Mrs Plath was

ashamed of mental illness – it has never been made clear, for instance, just how very ill Sylvia was with her first breakdown.[58]

The uneasy truce between Ted and Aurelia was maintained but it was fragile. Aurelia resented Ted owning the copyright of her daughter's work. Although the money made from Sylvia's writing was used for her grandchildren, her own failure to benefit more continued to rankle. She had received some money on the publication of *The Bell Jar* in America. She was also paid a $5,000 cash advance by her publishers Harper and Row for *Letters Home* and received a percentage of its royalties. In 1977, she sold most of her letters and material on her daughter to Indiana University's Lilly Library.[59]

Both Ted and Aurelia claimed that they wanted the whole truth about Sylvia to be told, but they had different truths. Like the enigmatic Julia Stephen, neither the people who had loved her nor biographers could completely recapture Sylvia. After yet another researcher bombarded Aurelia with intrusive questions, she wrote:

> It seems impossible that a true, decent, well-written biography will ever emerge, and I wish Sylvia could slip into the oblivion she seemed to desire. I am just worn out with this – naturally I MUST know what is going on – there is no escape.[60]

She tried not to be affected by what was written but it was hard. She told a friend, 'Of course, I care but I cannot afford to let it tear me apart as it has in the past.'[61] Part of her wanted to move on and live like a 'free human being', but she responded because she believed so much that was printed about her daughter was false. She was still trying to 'put the record straight'.[62]

In 1983, Aurelia provided her final written statement in *Ariel Ascending*, a collection of essays on Sylvia. Mrs Plath explained that constantly revisiting her daughter's life took its toll on her. She wanted to enjoy her own life rather than delving back 'into the tragic transformation of my daughter, whose loss is a constant pain, one that no critic of her writing has ever seemed to sense fully'.[63] Poignantly, she finished by writing, 'All I can say is that it is now I miss Sylvia most. [...] However, even while her loss is constantly with me, I find some measure of solace in the thought that her genius, evident in both her poetry and prose will endure.'[64] She was right, but that genius had come at a high cost for both mother and daughter. As Aurelia wrote to another Plath scholar, 'She [Sylvia] has posthumous fame – at what price to her children, to those of us who loved her so dearly and whom she has trapped into her past. The love remains – and the hurt. There is no escape for us.'[65]

Aurelia's Afterlife

For the rest of her life, Aurelia remained caught in a claustrophobic cycle with her daughter; however, there was another side to her later years. Despite the image of a single-minded woman whose every thought revolved around Sylvia, Mrs Plath had always had a full life of her own. Since Sylvia was a baby, she had responded to her daughter's demands, but that had not always been through choice. She had wanted her autonomy as much as Sylvia had.[1] Mrs Plath explained that she had always tried to foster her daughter's independence, not so that Sylvia could be free of her, but so that she could free herself from Sylvia. She wanted to live '<u>my</u> life – not to be drawn into the complexities and crises of hers. I loved spending time with the children – but wanted freedom which Sylvia refused to grant.'[2]

Rebelling against her daughter's caricature of her, she refused to live up to the myth of the martyred mother. She was angry about how she had been portrayed both by Sylvia and biographers. Instead of acting like a victim, she was determined to make the most of her life. Despite being irreparably scarred, she tried to be positive and carry on. As she wrote to a friend, even in the depths of grief, 'Whatever the cost, the awareness, the leaping up of the heart must remain with us.'[3]

With more time available, Aurelia finally tried to pursue her literary ambitions. She started writing a novel about her mother's Austrian childhood but did not continue because she was too busy caring for her father.[4] Mr Schober was suffering from dementia, so she did not tell him about Sylvia's death. As she nursed him, she longed for him to comfort her, but he had become like a child. She told a friend that at least as he clung to her hand, she felt his love.[5]

After his death, she was on her own for the first time. Left alone in the empty house with her memories, she felt like the Ancient Mariner, surrounded by fulfilled people, while she had an invisible but weighty albatross around her neck. She lectured herself about counting her blessings, but she admitted that it took all her strength.[6]

Family remained at the centre of Aurelia's life. Immediately after Sylvia's death, Aurelia proposed that Nicholas and Frieda could be raised in the US by Warren and his wife Margaret. Understandably, Ted wanted to bring up his children himself. Desperate to remain a part of her grandchildren's lives, Aurelia visited them in her summer holidays. She wanted them to know their mother's family loved them and that they would always be ready to provide a home for them in America.[7]

In June 1963, the first visit after Sylvia's death was difficult. Beforehand, Ted wrote to his former mother-in-law urging her not to smother the children with her transferred love for Sylvia, nor to make 'a battleground' of their loyalties. He dreaded 'the effects of that tense, watchful anxiety for them and everything about them which, I think, helped to make Sylvia's life so much more difficult than it need have been'.[8] During her stay, Aurelia visited Sylvia's grave in Yorkshire and saw her grandchildren. Ted found it a strain particularly when she once again asked him to allow his children to be raised in America.[9]

Bound together by circumstance, Ted and Aurelia continued to meet during her regular visits to see Frieda and Nicholas in England. Back in America, Aurelia had a strong family network. She stayed with Warren and his wife Margaret and their two daughters, Jenny and Susan, in their New York home at Christmas and for Warren's birthday. In the summer, she joined them on Cape Cod. Although distance made it difficult, her son and daughter-in-law did everything they could to support her. Aurelia became very fond of Margaret, describing her as a selfless, thoughtful person.[10]

Aurelia relished travelling and new experiences. While in Europe, she traced her Austrian roots and met her relatives. As well as cultural holidays, she treated herself to more relaxing breaks in the Caribbean. Fit enough to swim regularly and walk miles, even in her seventies, she remained a 'sea-girl', who wrote enthusiastically about a stay in the 'flowery paradise' of Bermuda.[11] She wished she had been able to travel more in her youth. When her granddaughter Jenny was studying in Florence, she wrote, 'Oh to be young and have such opportunities!'[12]

The Protestant work ethic remained deeply entrenched. She continued to work, partly because she needed the money but also for the routine. When the programme in Secretarial Studies was discontinued, to supplement her income, Aurelia taught at Cape Cod Community College.[13] She was proud of her professional life, telling an interviewer that, 'The high point of my teaching career has been contributing to the lives of my students.'[14] As she said to a fellow teacher, 'Who knows who you are encouraging to reach "the unreachable star"?'[15] Aurelia's maternal streak meant she took a personal interest in her students and their well-being. She described 'the longing to know them well and help them grow'.[16] When one of her favourite students developed glandular fever, she invited her to move in with her while she recovered. The young woman ended up staying for two years and remained close friends with Aurelia.

We get a strong impression of Mrs Plath's personality from an interview with Linda Heller in 1976. The insight comes not only from what the journalist wrote but from Aurelia's acerbic comments written on the article, which reveal she had a sharp tongue like her daughter. Ms Heller described Aurelia as speaking 'with the easy elegance of a poet and seems to have stepped out of a different era, a gentler, more romantic time'. Aurelia wrote beside this '(Where's my crinoline?!)' When the interviewer described her house papered in pastel flowers and rooms filled with highly polished furniture and cut-glass bowls, Aurelia rejected the sentimentalised image, commenting that she had used lemon wax the day before for the first time in months and she only owned two pieces of cut-glass.[17] As her reaction shows, she remained a demanding critic who resented trite clichés.

Although Sylvia's portrayal of her mother suggested that she was a loner who had little time to socialise, the reality was different. Aurelia had an active social life and a wide circle of friends built up over many years. She often cooked meals for them, ate out in restaurants, or went to the cinema. Quantifying her popularity as meticulously as she measured everything else, she told a friend that for her birthday she received thirty-one letters and cards, while at Christmas the number swelled to more than a hundred.[18]

In her final years, two new friends made a great difference to her life. Professor Richard Larschan and Leonard Sanazaro met Aurelia because of their interest in Sylvia, but both developed genuine friendships with her.

They valued her for who she was rather than whose mother she happened to be. They also felt sympathy for what she had been through.

The poet and academic Leonard Sanazaro first met Aurelia in the 1980s. As a great admirer of Sylvia's work, Leonard was so nervous about meeting his heroine's mother that he could hardly speak. The highlight of his visit was when Aurelia recited to him from Sylvia's verse play about motherhood, 'Three Women'. It was one of Mrs Plath's favourite works and she regularly performed it for avid listeners. It gives an insight into Aurelia's feelings for her daughter and why Sylvia's life turned out as it did. Looking at her baby son, the mother prays for him to be ordinary, not exceptional because it is the exception which interests the devil and breaks his mother's heart. She wills him to love her as she loves him.[19] Apparently, Sylvia quoted those lines in one of her last letters to her mother.[20] After listening to Aurelia's recitation, Leonard wrote that he would never forget that memorable moment.[21]

As Leonard taught at the University of Nevada, they did not see each other often, but they wrote regularly. His letters were sympathetic, making Aurelia feel safe to confide her true feelings. After inviting Leonard for a meal at her house, Mrs Plath said to him most determinedly, 'Sylvia knows I loved her and she loved me.' Leonard agreed, writing:

> This is really all there has to be, and anyone with any degree of sensitivity knows that these two facts are true beyond any shadow of doubt. Certainly, anyone who has ever been a parent and a child understands the love and complexities of these relationships.[22]

Increasingly, Aurelia treated Leonard like a second son, taking an interest in his career and giving him advice about his poetry and academic appointments. In return, he sent her the latest books, flowers on Valentine's Day, and advice about how to handle enquiries about her daughter.[23]

Determined to promote Sylvia as one of the most important poets of her era, Leonard wrote scholarly articles about Plath and produced a radio biography. Promising Aurelia control over what appeared, he said that her comfort and ease were more important to him than any radio script.[24] He explained that his primary motivation was love of Sylvia's work and dismay at the way it had been misunderstood and twisted beyond the author's intention. He also resented the injustice of the way her family had been abused and made to suffer.[25]

As Leonard researched, he discussed what he found with Aurelia. Tentatively, he told her that he believed it was 'not outside of Sylvia's capacity to be unfair at times to you and Mr Hughes though I don't think that unfairness was a major tenor of her personality'.[26] He also repeated his reassurance that, 'There is no doubt in my mind that Sylvia loved you. I wish, wish there was some way for me to wash all the pain away, such a hopeless wish!'[27] In the programme, Leonard encouraged listeners to separate Sylvia's life from her art. Focusing on what she accomplished, he challenged the idea of presupposing she had a tragic life.[28] When Aurelia read the script, she thanked him for creating 'a true picture and a comforting one'.[29] When the programme was broadcast in autumn 1983, she was even more ecstatic, writing, 'Dear, dear Leonard, It is absolutely glorious! WHAT AN EVENING! I have never in my life heard poetry read so magnificently [...] I sat spellbound, immovable, and my spirit soared; my heart rejoiced.'[30]

The only threat to their friendship came when Leonard told Aurelia he would like to deposit their correspondence in the Lilly Library. She made it plain that this would ruin their relationship, explaining:

> I write to you as I would to my son – no attention to form – just a chat on paper. Your suggestion could not avoid making me self-conscious and writing would become Work – not just release. Nothing of my scribbling is to be released. Let me be free![31]

Mrs Plath's second important new friendship was with Richard Larschan, a professor of English. They met in 1982 when he was riding his bicycle past Aurelia's house. He knew that Sylvia had lived at 26 Elmwood Road, but he was not aware that her mother still lived there. It was only when he spoke to the elderly woman reading on the front stoop that he discovered she was Aurelia. As Richard lived just around the corner, he asked her to tea. They got on so well that she stayed chatting for several hours.[32]

In 1983, Aurelia decided it was time to sell 26 Elmwood Road and move to North Hill, an assisted living retirement village in Wellesley. She did not wish to become a burden to anyone and wanted to move while she was still healthy. Aurelia spent over a year preparing for the move, getting increasingly stressed about it. She found it a tremendous wrench leaving the home she had lived in since Sylvia was a child. She told Leonard that she had to fight back tears at the thought.[33] The house had been her sanctuary; it was crammed with memories as well as the many items she had hoarded. One summer day, she took a break from the onerous task of sorting through her belongings and went to the beach for some fresh air and by chance, she met Richard and his family. After Richard's wife volunteered him to help, he began thrice-weekly sessions with Aurelia sifting through the papers, books and memorabilia. Together they sorted through four desks, three filing cabinets and four bureaus, preparing the material to be donated to Smith College.[34] Aurelia had kept everything in meticulous order and the letters were already neatly organised and tied with ribbons.[35] It was an emotional task. Mrs Plath wrote that she had been 'living Sylvia's life through reading and reading in every given detail and underscored by the causes beneath the words – some which I alone can know'.[36]

Since Sylvia's childhood, Aurelia had carefully annotated material associated with her daughter either in Gregg shorthand or longhand. After Sylvia's suicide she reread and annotated her daughter's letters for future scholars.[37] Trying to influence the reader's interpretation of the material could be seen as another attempt to build her narrative and defend herself, but perhaps it also had a more private purpose, enabling her to have the arguments with her dead daughter which had not been resolved while Sylvia was alive.[38]

The stress of moving took its toll on Aurelia's health. Her tendency to worry was exacerbated and her weight dropped to 100lb. She admitted to Leonard, 'I lecture myself on the folly of worrying to the extent I do. [...] At 77 I still have much to learn, much to correct. I panic too easily, for one thing.' However, she added that she must try not to be defeated and instead just 'accept our fallible humanity and have the strength to begin afresh each new day'.[39]

Aurelia continued to be anxious about money. Worrying about whether she could afford to live at North Hill, she drove an old, battered car and rarely bought new clothes. With echoes of Virginia still dressing up in Julia's dresses decades after her mother's death, in 1980 Aurelia was still wearing some of Sylvia's clothes.[40] It was as if dressing up in their loved one's outfits kept them close.

When Aurelia moved to her retirement apartment in 1984, Richard helped her with the paperwork for the sale of her house. Working so closely together they had formed a 'familial bond'.[41] Living closer than her relatives, Richard, his wife and two young daughters became like a second family to Aurelia. She often came to their house for dinner and would sit in their garden in a deckchair enjoying the normality of their home and the chance to mix with younger people.[42] She took a great interest in Richard's daughters, discussing books with them and inviting them to swim at North Hill and go with her to 'Grandparents' Day'.[43]

Richard grew very fond of Aurelia. He believed that she had lived her life courageously and he admired her independence and determination never to be a burden to anyone. Admittedly, she had a sentimental streak which could be cloying but she also had a good sense of humour and would laugh uproariously. He found her to be 'intelligent, thoughtful, kind and unselfish'.[44] There was an old-fashioned courtesy in her manner. She believed in 'decorum and doing things properly'; she always wrote thank-you notes and gave thoughtful gifts to show how much she appreciated his support.[45]

During the last decade of her life, Richard became another quasi-surrogate son, helping with both her practical and emotional needs. Aurelia wrote that he was the person she felt able to 'let it all out' to, knowing he would understand.[46] Richard recalls, 'I wouldn't have to probe. She would release whatever negative feelings she had about how she was victimised by Sylvia's opinions of her. She said it wasn't fair, asking, "Why should I be defined by her projections?"'[47]

Like Leonard, Richard became involved in helping her to get her side of the story across. She could trust him to give her good advice. When she wrote her final written statement for *Ariel Ascending*, Richard helped her get the tone right. He explains, 'I advised Aurelia to delete several paragraphs of her expatiating at excessive length about Sylvia's "normal childhood" in an excessively sentimental way that came across to me as very defensive.'[48]

Aurelia treated her move to North Hill as the opening of a fresh chapter in her life. She wrote with the enthusiasm of a young girl about attending lectures, classical music concerts, visiting sites of historic interest and art galleries. She remained a lifelong learner, who was always open to new ideas. She became so interested in outer space that she wanted to look through a powerful telescope at the galaxy. When Ronald Reagan was president, she was appalled by his policies and campaigned for a nuclear freeze.[49]

Literature remained her great passion. In her seventies, she took a course in modern poetry, which now included her daughter's work alongside the literary greats.[50] When she joined a poetry reading group, she enjoyed being able to shine.[51] She particularly relished reciting Sylvia's lines from 'Three Women'. As she told Leonard, 'I do read this well! That is beloved by everyone who hears it; it is the Sylvia, the true Sylvia whom I want them to meet – to know.'[52] Part of Aurelia still craved being the centre of attention and performing. Richard Larschan recalls how she reacted when he represented her interests with the producers of the *Voices and Visions* documentary about Sylvia. Richard rehearsed Aurelia for the interview by recording her on audiotapes and videos. Sitting in a rocking chair, looking neat in a kilt and Fair Isle jumper, Aurelia let her innermost feelings out. A listener can hear the hurt and anger in her voice: at times she was emphatic at others tearful. Virtually spitting out the words, she called 'Medusa' 'that STINKING' poem. As she quoted from 'The Disquieting Muses' she recited, '"Mother, Mother" the way she said it broke my heart.' She asked why her daughter ever wrote 'anything so cruel'.[53]

When the time for the interview came in November 1986, it was agreed that it would take place at Richard's home. At first, she refused to appear on camera, saying she would only be interviewed on tape. However, when she arrived looking immaculate, dressed in a new red jacket and with her hair freshly coiffed, she asked Richard if she should appear on camera. It was obvious that she wanted to be cajoled, so suddenly the plan changed, and she was filmed.[54] It was a riveting performance and there were echoes of Sylvia in her New England tones. She came alive with an almost feverish energy as she recited her daughter's poems, but when questioned about Sylvia's breakdown and suicide the suffering she had been through was apparent, etched in the lines on her face and the anguished expression in her dark brown eyes. Richard has no doubt Aurelia wanted her voice to be heard. When he asked if he could use the material he had recorded after her death, she liked the idea.[55] As someone who knew Aurelia well and observed her reaction to her daughter, Richard says, 'Aurelia internalised Sylvia as much as her daughter internalised her. She appropriated Sylvia's poetry.'[56]

The attention she gained from being Sylvia's mother was not always positive. She found it hard to make friends at North Hill. She felt particularly uncomfortable when Mildred Norton, Dick's mother who had also been caricatured in *The Bell Jar*, moved into the retirement village.[57] She believed people still judged her because of what Sylvia had written. She wrote:

> When they meet me, they speak of her and look at me so coldly that I shrink inside and feel judged then and there as an uncaring mother. I never defend myself (I have no reason to), but I feel the distance and long for closeness and friendship.[58]

Like Virginia's experience after Julia's death, Aurelia could never escape the shadow Sylvia cast over her life. Nor did she want to, because, as for the Bloomsbury writer with her mother, separating completely would be like losing her again. Aurelia's life was never easy. Gradually, macular degeneration deprived her of her sight. For the last years of her life, she was even more cut off from the world as she suffered from Alzheimer's disease.[59]

Richard remained a stalwart friend, visiting her regularly. When she was in hospital with pneumonia in 1992, he suggested that she should practise meditation exercises to reduce her stress. He encouraged her to visualise a sunlit shore with billowing waves and gently bobbing sailing boats. With her eyes closed and breathing more easily, Aurelia seemed to be benefiting from Richard's soothing tones. He recalled, 'Thinking the scene incomplete, however, without joyful sounds of children at play, I started to introduce them into the setting. Aurelia's eyes immediately shot open as she declared with pronounced emphasis, "No children!"' As Richard says, 'From what I had learned over our years of friendship, who could really blame her?'[60]

Aurelia recovered from the pneumonia, but the next two years were lived in a twilight zone, where she had limited sight, hearing and memory. Richard continued to visit, but she was now medicated and although at times she could be cogent, she was often confused. Her once carefully styled hair was now crudely cropped to make it easier to look after.[61] On 11 March 1994, death finally released Aurelia from this limbo. After a memorial service attended by close family and friends, she was buried in the Woodlawn Cemetery, Wellesley. Tellingly, she had chosen to be buried close to her parents rather than next to her husband, Otto, in Winthrop.[62]

A few years before her death, as she knew her powers were waning, Aurelia left clear instructions about what she most desired. She wrote to Leonard:

> I have one deep-seated wish: that the truth of my relationship with my beloved Sylvia would be made public. [...] I do not wish to leave this planet believing that I did not cherish, love, serve (sacrifice <u>gladly</u> for her) my daughter from the time of her birth [...] and still work to correct the terrible misconceptions concerning our relationship.[63]

As this statement makes clear, she wanted to write her own epitaph rather than have the one set in stone for her by her daughter's work.

Acknowledgements

This book has come to fruition thanks to a group of like-minded people. My mother, Bridget, has been with me every step of the way from when we first saw Virginia Woolf's quotation about mothers at the Tate of St Ives. As always, her support and encouragement has been essential.

Secondly, I would like to thank Lady Antonia Fraser and the Society of Authors for giving me the Antonia Fraser Award. It has allowed me to research the book to the high standard I would wish. Meeting Lady Antonia, who has been a role model throughout my literary career, has been a highlight of this project.

My book builds on the scholarship of excellent biographies by previous writers. I have also drawn on the novels, poetry and autobiographical work of the three writers and the memoirs of their family and friends. Speaking to people who knew them has really brought these women alive and added a deeper dimension. I would particularly like to thank Agatha Christie's grandson, Mathew Prichard, for talking to me about his grandmother, and for the generous hospitality shown by him and his wife, Lucy. Discussing Aurelia Plath with Professor Richard Larschan, a great friend during her final years, was enlightening. Experts have also generously shared their unrivalled knowledge. Joe Keogh, archivist at the Christie Archive Trust, Tony Medawar of the International Agatha Christie Festival, and Catherine Rankovic, the leading scholar on Aurelia Plath, have acted as sounding boards for my ideas and pointed me in the right direction.

Reading unpublished sources in archives across the world has added important original material to my book. I would like to thank the following libraries who made this project possible during the pandemic.

For my research on Julia and Leslie Stephen and their circle, the Henry W. and Albert A. Berg Collection of English and American Literature, the New York Public Library, Astor, Lenox and Tilden Foundations. I would like to thank the New York Public Library for allowing me to quote from the collections of Sir Leslie Stephen, William Holman Hunt, Julia Margaret Cameron, and James Russell Lowell. Letters from the Julia Stephen Collection are courtesy of the Charles Deering McCormick Library of Special Collections and University Archives, Northwestern University Libraries. The Lushington Papers at Surrey History Centre and the letters between Julia Stephen and her sister Mary Fisher, at King's College, Cambridge, provided new insights into relationships with family and friends.

For my research on Agatha Christie and her mother Clara, my visit to the Christie Archive Trust allowed me an intimate insight into their family relationships. Mathew Prichard has kindly allowed me to publish material from the archive including Agatha's unpublished play *The Lie* and unpublished family photographs.

For my research into the Plath family, Smith College Special Collections provided me with Linda Heller's article 'Aurelia Plath: A Lasting Commitment', Aurelia Plath's draft introduction and commentary for *Letters Home* and her 'For the Authors' Series Talk at Wellesley College Club. Letters between Aurelia Plath and Leonard Sanazaro are used courtesy of Lilly Library, Indiana University, Bloomington, Indiana. The Terzaghi Library at NGI, Oslo have permitted me to quote from Karl Terzaghi's diaries.

When dealing with such major literary figures being able to draw on the authors' own writing is vital. I am grateful to the literary estates and publishers of Virginia Woolf, Agatha Christie, Sylvia Plath and Ted Hughes for allowing me to quote from their works. For Virginia Woolf's and Leslie Stephen's literature I would like to thank the Society of Authors as the Literary Representative of the Estate of Virginia Woolf and the Estate of Leslie Stephen. Sarah Baxter at the SoA provided me with excellent advice. For Agatha Christie, John Mallowan has let me use material from Max Mallowan's *Memoirs*. Agatha Christie's Trustees, Agatha Christie Ltd and HarperCollins Publishers Ltd have granted permission to quote from her autobiography and novels. For my section on Sylvia and Aurelia Plath, the Ted Hughes Literary Estate and Faber and Faber Ltd have allowed me to use quotations from 'Trial' archive material in MS 88993/1/1 The British Library PER 3 and the *Letters of Ted Hughes*. The Sylvia Plath Literary Estate and the publishers Faber and Faber Ltd have agreed to me quoting from 'Ocean 1212-W' in *Johnny Panic and the Bible of Dreams*, *The Bell Jar*, *The Journals of Sylvia Plath 1950–62*, *Letters Home* and 'Medusa', *Collected Poems by Sylvia Plath*. In the US, Penguin Random House have granted permission to use a quote from *The Journals of Sylvia Plath*. I would also like to thank the Aurelia Plath Estate and Faber and Faber Ltd and in the US HarperCollins Ltd for allowing me to quote from *Letters Home*. Jenny Plath has kindly let me use her grandmother's unpublished writing. Becky Taylor at Faber and Faber worked tirelessly on my behalf.

Every effort has been made to contact copyright holders, but if there are any omissions we are happy to rectify them in future editions.

Working with a team who are in tune has been crucial throughout writing this book. My literary agent, Heather Holden-Brown, has been a wise adviser. My publisher, Laura Perehinec, at The History Press and my publicist, Cynthia Hamilton, have once again been a pleasure to work with. I would also like to thank their teams; Elly James and Rob Dinsdale at HHB Agency and Katie Beard and Alex Boulton at The History Press. Finally, I am grateful to my family for sharing this project with me. Although my mother has been the main player others have also played an important part; my husband John as my companion on research trips, my son Christopher as technical support, and my sister, Becky, as a good listener.

Select Bibliography

Alexander, Paul, *Ariel Ascending: Writings about Sylvia Plath* (New York: Harper and Row, 1985).

Annan, Noel Gilroy, *Leslie Stephen: His Thought and Character in Relation to His Time* (Cambridge, Massachusetts: Harvard University Press, 1952).

Badia, Janet, "'I May Hate Her, But That's Not All". Mother–Daughter Intimacy in the Plath Archive' in Anita Helle, Amanda Golden and Maeve O'Brien (eds), *The Bloomsbury Handbook to Sylvia Plath* (London, New York, Oxford: Bloomsbury Academic, 2022).

Barnard, Robert, *A Talent to Deceive: An Appreciation of Agatha Christie* (London: Fontana/Collins, 1979).

Bate, Jonathan, *Ted Hughes: The Unauthorised Life* (London: HarperCollins, 2015).

Bechdel, Alison (ed.), *Love Letters: Virginia Woolf and Vita Sackville-West* (London: Vintage, 2021).

Bell, Quentin, *Bloomsbury* (London: Weidenfeld and Nicolson, 1968).

—. *Virginia Woolf: A Biography* (London: The Hogarth Press, 1972).

Brain, Tracy, 'Sylvia Plath's Letters and Journals' in Jo Gill (ed.), *The Cambridge Companion to Sylvia Plath* (Cambridge: Cambridge University Press, 2006).

Bundtzen, Lynda K., *Plath's Incarnations: Woman and the Creative Process* (Ann Arbor: The University of Michigan Press, 1983).

Cade, Jared, *Agatha Christie and the Eleven Missing Days: The Revised and Expanded 2011 Edition* (London: Peter Owen Publishers, 2022 Kindle).

Chan, Chris, 'Agatha Christie's Witches', 3 October 2019. *The Home of Agatha Christie Website*.

Christie, Agatha, *An Autobiography* (New York: Dodd, Mead and Co, 1977).

—. *Appointment with Death* (London: HarperCollins, 2016).

—. *Come, Tell Me How You Live: Memories From Archaeological Expeditions in the Mysterious Middle East* (London: HarperCollins, 2015).

—. *Death Comes as the End* (London: HarperCollins, 2017).

—. *Five Little Pigs* (London: HarperCollins, 2013).

—. *Love Detectives: The Compete Quin and Satterthwaite* (London: HarperCollins, 2004).

—. *Ordeal by Innocence* (London: HarperCollins, 2017).

—. *Postern of Fate* (London: HarperCollins, 1973).

—. *Star Over Bethlehem including The Road of Dreams and Poems* (London: HarperCollins, 1924, 1965, 1973 Ebook).

—. *The Harlequin Tea Set and Other Stories* (London: William Morrow, 2012).

—. *The Hound of Death* (London: HarperCollins, 2016).

—. *The Lie: A Play by Agatha Christie* (Radio 4: 29/08/20).

—. *The Mysterious Affair at Styles* (United Kingdom: Printed by Amazon, 2022).

—. *Third Girl* (London: HarperCollins, 2015).

—. *Towards Zero* (London: HarperCollins, 2017).

Clark, Heather, *Red Comet: The Short Life and Blazing Art of Sylvia Plath* (London: Jonathan Cape, 2020).

Curran, John, *Agatha Christie's Complete Secret Notebooks: Stories and Secrets of Murder in the Making* (London: HarperCollins, 2020).

Dell, Marion, *A Vision of Beauty: A Biography of Julia Prinsep Stephen*. Website: The Elusive Julia Prinsep Stephen. 04/12/21.

—. *Virginia Woolf's Influential Forebears: Julia Margaret Cameron, Anny Thackeray Ritchie and Julia Prinsep Stephen* (Basingstoke: Palgrave Macmillan, 2015).

Dunn, Jane, *Virginia Woolf and Vanessa Bell: A Very Close Conspiracy* (London: Virago, 2000).

Edel, Leon (ed.), *Henry James. Letters. Vol. 4* (Harvard: Harvard University Press, 1974).

Garnett, Angelica, *Deceived with Kindness: A Bloomsbury Childhood* (London: Pimlico, 1995).

Gill, Gillian, *Agatha Christie: The Woman and Her Mysteries* (London: Robson Books, 1990).

—. *Virginia Woolf and the Women Who Shaped her World* (Boston, New York: Houghton Mifflin Harcourt, 2019).

Gillespie, Diane. F. and Elizabeth Steele (eds), *Julia Duckworth Stephen: Stories for Children, Essays for Adults* (New York: Syracuse University Press, 1987).

Gordon, Lyndall, *Virginia Woolf: A Writer's Life* (New York, London: W.W. Norton and Company, 1984).

Green, Julius, *Agatha Christie: A Life in Theatre* (London: HarperCollins, 2018).

Kalfopoulou, Adrianne, 'Voice Rehearsals and Personas in Sylvia's Letters to Aurelia' in Dale Salwak (ed.), *Writers and Their Mothers* (Hampshire: Palgrave Macmillan, 2018).

Keating H.R.F. (ed.), *Agatha Christie: First Lady of Crime* (London: Weidenfeld and Nicolson, 2020).

Kukil, Karen V. (ed.), *The Journals of Sylvia Plath 1950–1962* (London: Faber and Faber, 2000).

Larschan, Richard J., 'Art and Artifice in Sylvia Plath's Self-Portrayals' in Koray Melikoglu (ed.), *Life Writing: Autobiography, Biography, and Travel Writing in Contemporary Literature* (Munich: Ibidem Press, 2007).

—. 'Sylvia's Mother Said – though it took some doing …' *Times Higher Education*. September 8–14, 2012. Timeshighereducation.co.uk.

—. *Sylvia Plath and the Myth of the Monstrous Mother; Sylvia Plath and the Myth of the Omnipresent/Absent Father.* Educational videos published and distributed by Academic Instructional Media, Elizabeth Wilda (ed.), University of Massachusetts Amherst, 2001.

Lee, Hermione, *Virginia Woolf* (London: Vintage Books, 1997).

Lochnan, Katharine and Carol Jacobi (eds), *Holman Hunt and the Pre-Raphaelite Vision* (Ontario: Art Gallery of Ontario, 2008).

Logevall, Frederik, *JFK: Volume One* (New York: Viking, Random House, 2020).

Lowe, Gill (ed.), *Hyde Park Gate News: The Stephen Family Newspaper* (London: Hesperus Press, 2005).

Maida, Patricia D. and Nicholas B. Spornick, *Murder She Wrote: A Study of Agatha Christie's Detective Fiction* (Ohio: Bowling Green State University Popular Press, 1982).

Maitland, Frederic William, *The Life and Letters of Leslie Stephen* (New York and London: Duckworth and Co, 1906).

Makinen, Merja, *Agatha Christie: Investigating Femininity* (Basingstoke: Palgrave Macmillan, 2006).

Malcolm, Janet, 'The Silent Woman'. *Annals of Biography*, August 23 and 30. 1993 Issue.

Mallowan, Max, *Mallowan's Memoirs: Agatha Christie and the Archaeologist* (London: HarperCollins, 2010).

Middlebrook, Diane, *Her Husband: Ted Hughes and Sylvia Plath: A Marriage* (London, New York: Penguin Books, 2003).

Morgan, Janet, *Agatha Christie: A Biography* (London: HarperCollins, 2017).

Nicholson, Virginia, *Singled Out: How Two Million Women Survived Without Men After the First World War* (London: Penguin Books, 2008).

Nietzsche, Friedrich, *Thus Spoke Zarathustra* (London: Penguin Books, 1969).

Osborne, Charles, *The Life and Crimes of Agatha Christie: A Biographical Companion to the Works of Agatha Christie* (London: HarperCollins, 1999).

Perry, Barbara A., *Rose Kennedy: The Life and Times of a Political Matriarch* (New York, London: W.W. Norton and Co, 2013).

Plath, Aurelia Schober (ed.), *Letters Home. By Sylvia Plath 1950–1963* (London: Faber and Faber, 1975).

—. *The Paracelsus of History and Literature* (Boston: Boston University, 1930).

Plath, Otto, *A Muscid Larva of the San Francisco Bay Region Which Sucks the Blood of Nestling Birds* (Berkeley, California: University of California Publications in Zoology, 1919).

Plath, Sylvia, Foreword by Frieda Hughes. *Ariel: The Restored Edition* (New York, London: Harper Perennial, 2004).

—. *Collected Poems* (London: Faber and Faber, 1981).

—. *Johnny Panic and The Bible of Dreams* (London: Faber and Faber, 1979).

—. *The Bell Jar* (London: Faber and Faber, 2005).

Ramsey, G.C. *Agatha Christie: Mistress of Mystery* (New York: Dodd Mead and Co, 1967).

Rankovic, Catherine, 'Medusa's Metadata: Aurelia Plath's Gregg Shorthand Annotations' in Anita Helle, Amanda Golden and Maeve O'Brien (eds), *Bloomsbury Handbook to Sylvia Plath* (London, New York, Oxford: Bloomsbury Academic, 2022).

—. *Studying Aurelia Plath*. Blogspots. https://aureliaplath.blogspot.com.html.

Reid, Christopher (ed.) *Letters of Ted Hughes* (London: Faber and Faber, 2007).

Robyns, Gwen, *The Mystery of Agatha Christie: An Intimate Biography of the First Lady of Crime* (London: Penguin Books, 1979).

Rose, Jacqueline, *The Haunting of Sylvia Plath* (London: Virago, 2014).

Rosenman, Ellen Bayuk, *The Invisible Presence: Virginia Woolf and the Mother–Daughter Relationship* (Baton Rouge and London: Louisiana State University Press, 1986).

Rothenstein, William, *Men and Memories: Recollections 1872–1938* (Columbia: University of Missouri Press, 1978).

Rowse, A.L., *Memories of Men and Women* (Newton Abbot: Group of Book Clubs, 1981).

Saunders, Peter, *The Mousetrap Man* (London: Collins, 1972).

Schulkind, Jeanne (ed.), *Virginia Woolf, Moments of Being: Autobiographical Writings* (London: Pimlico, 2002).

Sigmund, Elizabeth and Gail Crowther, *Sylvia Plath in Devon: A Year's Turning* (Croydon: Fonthill, 2014).

Steinberg, Peter K. and Karen V. Kukil (eds), *The Letters of Sylvia Plath. Vols 1 and 2* (London: Faber and Faber, 2018).

Stephen, Leslie, *Social Rights and Duties: Addresses to Ethical Societies. Vol. 2* (London, New York: Macmillan, 1896).

—. *Mausoleum Book* (Oxford: Clarendon Press, 1977).

Stevenson, Anne, *Bitter Fame: A Life of Sylvia Plath* (Boston: Houghton Mifflin Co., 1989).

Thompson, Laura, *Agatha Christie: An English Mystery* (London: Headline Review, 2008).

Troubridge, Laura, *Memories and Reflections* (London: William Heinemann, 1925).

Wade, Francesca, *Square Haunting: Five Women, Freedom and London Between the Wars* (London: Faber and Faber, 2021).

Watts, Mary S., *George Frederic Watts: The Annals of an Artist's Life* (London: Macmillan and Co, 1912).

Westmacott, Mary (Agatha Christie), *Absent in the Spring* (London: HarperCollins, 2017).

—. *A Daughter's a Daughter* (London: HarperCollins, 2017).

—. *Giant's Bread* (London: HarperCollins, 2017)

—. *The Burden* (London: HarperCollins, 2017).

—. *The Rose and the Yew Tree* (London: HarperCollins, 2017).

—. *Unfinished Portrait* (London: HarperCollins, 2017).

Wilson, Andrew, *Mad Girl's Love Song: Sylvia Plath and Life Before Ted* (London: Simon and Schuster, 2013).

Wilson, Frances, *Burning Man: The Ascent of D.H. Lawrence*. London: Bloomsbury Circus, 2021.

Woolf, Leonard, *Beginning Again: An Autobiography of the Years 1911 to 1918* (New York and London: Harvest Books, 1964).

—. *Downhill All the Way: An Autobiography of the Years 1919 to 1939* (New York and London: Harvest Books, 1967).

—. *Sowing: An Autobiography of the Years 1880 to 1904* (New York and London: Harvest Books, 1960).

—. *The Journey Not the Arrival Matters: An Autobiography of the Years 1939 to 1969* (New York and London: Harvest Books, 1969).

Woolf, Virginia, *A Room of One's Own* (London: Grafton Books, 1989).

—. *Jacob's Room* (Oxford: Oxford University Press, 2008).

—. *Mrs Dalloway* (London: Grafton Books, 1976).

—. *On Being Ill* (London and Amsterdam: HetMoet, 2021).

—. *Selected Diaries* (London: Vintage Books, 2008).

—. *Selected Letters* (London: Vintage Books, 2008).

—. *The Art of Biography: A Collection of Essays* (London: Read and Co, 2021).

—. *The Collected Essays of Virginia Woolf* (London: Read Books Ltd, 2012).

—. 'The New Dress' (Great Britain: Amazon, 2022).

—. *The Voyage Out* (London: Penguin Books, 1992).

—. *The Waves* (London: Penguin Classics, 2019).

—. *The Years* (London: Vintage, 2000).

—. *Three Guineas* (Oxford: Oxford University Press, 2015).

—. *To the Lighthouse* (Hertfordshire: Wordsworth Classics, 2002).

Woolf, Virginia, Julia Margaret Cameron and Roger Fry, *Julia Margaret Cameron* (Los Angeles: The J. Paul Getty Museum, 2016).

Worsley, Lucy, *Agatha Christie: A Very Elusive Woman* (London: Hodder and Stoughton, 2022).

Notes

Introduction

1   Virginia Woolf, *A Room of One's Own* (London: Grafton Books, 1989) p.72.
2   Ibid., p.79.
3   Laura Thompson, *Agatha Christie: An English Mystery* (London: Headline, 2008).
4   Interview with Catherine Rankovic.
5   Interview with Mathew Prichard, 23 March 2022.
6   Virginia Woolf argued that what held all great writing together 'is something that one calls integrity [...] What one means by integrity, in the case of the novelist, is the conviction that he gives one that this is truth.' Woolf, *A Room*, p.69.
7   Richard Larschan points out that Aurelia became ambivalent about Sylvia becoming a professional writer. Though she was obviously proud of Sylvia's accomplishments and did encourage her ambitions, she expressed concern that Sylvia would have to 'compete' (Aurelia's word) in the world of professionals. Email from Richard Larschan, 24 October 2022.

Part One: Julia and Virginia

Chapter 1: The Dutiful Daughter

1   For a full discussion of what was fact, what fiction, see Marion Dell, *A Vision of Beauty: A Biography of Julia Prinsep Stephen* (Website: The Elusive Julia Prinsep Stephen).
2   Virginia Woolf, *To the Lighthouse* (Hertfordshire: Wordsworth Classics, 2002) p.7.
3   Gillian Gill writes it is an established fact that he was not a page. Gillian Gill, *Virginia Woolf and the Women Who Shaped her World* (Boston, New York: Houghton Mifflin Harcourt, 2019) p.7. Marion Dell believes that it is possible

he was a page; however, it is unlikely he held a formal position at court as a child as his name does not appear in any list of pages.

4   Gill, *Virginia Woolf*, p.4.
5   Sir Hugh Orange, *Account by Sir Hugh Orange of the Chevalier de l'Etang and his descendants in the Pattle Family.* (*c.*1940. The Bodleian Library, Oxford).
6   Gill, *Virginia Woolf*, pp.14–15.
7   Quentin Bell, *Virginia Woolf: A Biography* (London: The Hogarth Press, 1972) p.14.
8   Marion Dell, *A Vision of Beauty*.
9   For a full analysis of what really happened, see Dell, *A Vision*.
10   Hermione Lee, *Virginia Woolf* (London: Vintage, 1997) pp.87–9.
11   See Dell, *A Vision*.
12   Laura Troubridge, *Memories and Reflections* (London: William Heinemann, 1925) pp.6, 20.
13   Letters to his daughter Adeline in the British Library illustrate his involvement. See Dell, *A Vision*.
14   Leslie Stephen, *Mausoleum Book* (Oxford: Clarendon Press, 1977) p.26.
15   Ibid., pp.26–7.
16   According to Marion Dell's research this judgement seems unfair as when he returned to England Dr Jackson continued to be a well-respected doctor. His extensive knowledge of Indian diseases, particularly tetanus, led to him publishing a book on the subject and being an expert witness in a court case. He became a Fellow of the Royal College of Physicians in 1859. Dell, *A Vision*.
17   Virginia Woolf, 'Sketch of the Past' in Jeanne Schulkind (ed.), *Moments of Being: Autobiographical Writings* (London: Pimlico, 2002) p.98.
18   Marion Dell, *Virginia Woolf's Influential Forebears: Julia Margaret Cameron, Anny Thackeray Ritchie and Julia Prinsep Stephen* (Basingstoke: Palgrave Macmillan, 2015) p.125.
19   Virginia Woolf, 'Sketch of the Past', *Moments of Being*, p.97.
20   Stephen, *Mausoleum Book*, p.29.
21   There are hundreds of letters from Mary Fisher to Julia at Kings College, Cambridge.
22   Stephen, *Mausoleum Book*, p.34.
23   Bell, *Virginia Woolf*, p.17.
24   Stephen, *Mausoleum Book*, p.34.

Chapter 2: The Muse

1   Dell, *A Vision*.
2   31 May 1894, 'Books Worth Reading by Lady Henry Somerset. Tennyson and His Friends Part II', *The Women's Signal*.
3   Woolf, 'Sketch of the Past', *Moments of Being*, p.98.
4   Ibid., pp.97–8.
5   Virginia Woolf, *To the Lighthouse*, p.132.

6 Stephen, *Mausoleum Book*, p.29.
7 William Holman Hunt, quoted in Getty Education website.
8 William Holman Hunt to Maria Pattle Jackson, 17 June 1865 (The Henry W. and Albert A. Berg Collection of English and American Literature, The New York Public Library, Astor, Lenox and Tilden Foundations).
9 Stephen, *Mausoleum Book*, p.28.
10 'Julia Margaret Cameron', The National Portrait Gallery website.
11 Anny Thackeray, quoted in Virginia Woolf, Julia Margaret Cameron and Roger Fry, *Julia Margaret Cameron* (Los Angeles: The J. Paul Getty Museum, 2016) plate 38.
12 'Julia Margaret Cameron Photographs', V and A Collections website.
13 9 January 1869, 'Mrs Cameron's Photographs', *London Evening Standard*.
14 Stephen, *Mausoleum Book*, p.33.
15 Woolf, *To the Lighthouse*, p.132.
16 Virginia Woolf, *Jacob's Room* (Oxford: Oxford University Press, 2008) p.196.

Chapter 3: The Perfect Match

1 Woolf, 'Sketch of the Past', *Moments of Being*, p.99.
2 Stephen, *Mausoleum Book*, p.35.
3 Jane Lushington to Vernon Lushington, 28 March 1867 (Lushington Papers, 7854/3/6/3/4a)
4 Woolf, 'Sketch of the Past', *Moments of Being*, p.100.
5 Stephen, *Mausoleum Book*, p.37.
6 Woolf, 'Sketch of the Past', *Moments of Being*, p.100.
7 As tutor to the Prince of Wales, Herbert Fisher often spent two or three months at Sandringham without his wife. Stephen, *Mausoleum Book*, p.39.
8 Vernon Lushington to Jane Lushington, 19 August 1868 (Lushington Papers, 7854/3/5/7).
9 Stephen, *Mausoleum Book*, p.38.
10 Woolf, 'Sketch of the Past', *Moments of Being*, p.100.
11 Virginia Woolf, 'Reminiscences', *Moments of Being*, p.4.
12 'Sudden Death of Mr Herbert Duckworth', *Frome Times*, 28 September 1870.
13 Woolf, 'Sketch of the Past', *Moments of Being*, p.100.
14 Virginia Woolf, 'Reminiscences', *Moments of Being*, p.5.
15 Maria Jackson to Vernon Lushington, 28 January 1873 (Lushington Papers, 7854/3/10/93a-b).
16 Lee, *Virginia Woolf*, p.93.
17 Julia Margaret Cameron to Maria Jackson, 6 February 1878 (The correspondence of Julia Margaret Cameron and Julia Prinsep Stephen. The Henry W. and Albert A. Berg Collection of English and American Literature, The New York Public Library, Astor, Lenox and Tilden Foundations).
18 Woolf, 'Sketch of the Past', *Moments of Being*, p.99.
19 Stephen, *Mausoleum Book*, p.40.

20 Ibid.
21 Jane Lushington to Vernon Lushington, 6 September 1871 (Lushington Papers, 7854/3/6/7/21a).
22 Stephen, *Mausoleum Book*, p.41.
23 Woolf, 'Reminiscences', *Moments of Being*, p.5.

Chapter 4: A Meeting of Minds

1   Stephen, *Mausoleum Book*, p.22.
2   Noel Gilroy Annan, *Leslie Stephen: His Thought and Character in Relation to his Time* (Cambridge, Massachusetts: Harvard University Press, 1952) pp.1–2.
3   Stephen, *Mausoleum Book*, p.17.
4   Ibid., p.9
5   Ibid., p.31.
6   Lee, *Virginia Woolf*, p.71.
7   Ibid.
8   Ibid., p.101.
9   Stephen, *Mausoleum Book*, p.42.
10 Ibid., p.46.
11 Virginia Woolf, 'Reminiscences', *Moments of Being*, p.5.
12 Stephen, *Mausoleum Book*, p.47.
13 Ibid.
14 Ibid., p.48–9.
15 Ibid., p.65.
16 Julia Margaret Cameron to Maria Jackson, 6 February 1878 (The correspondence of Julia Margaret Cameron and Julia Prinsep Stephen. The Henry W. and Albert A. Berg Collection of English and American Literature, The New York Public Library, Astor, Lenox and Tilden Foundations).
17 Julia Margaret Cameron to Julia Stephen, 5 February 1878 (The correspondence of Julia Margaret Cameron and Julia Prinsep Stephen. The Henry W. and Albert A. Berg Collection of English and American Literature, The New York Public Library, Astor, Lenox and Tilden Foundations).
18 Leslie Stephen, quoted in Frederic William Maitland, *The Life and Letters of Leslie Stephen* (New York and London: Duckworth and Co, 1906) pp.314–15.
19 Leslie Stephen to Julia Stephen, 31 March 1877 (The Sir Leslie Stephen Collection. The Henry W. and Albert A. Berg Collection of English and American Literature, The New York Public Library, Astor, Lenox and Tilden Foundations).
20 Stephen, *Mausoleum Book*, p.51.
21 Ibid., p.50.
22 Leslie Stephen to Julia Stephen, autumn 1877 (The Sir Leslie Stephen Collection. The Henry W. and Albert A. Berg Collection of English and

American Literature, The New York Public Library, Astor, Lenox and Tilden Foundations).

23 Ibid.

24 Stephen, *Mausoleum Book*, p.52.

25 Leslie Stephen to Julia Stephen, 28 December 1877 (The Sir Leslie Stephen Collection. The Henry W. and Albert A. Berg Collection of English and American Literature, The New York Public Library, Astor, Lenox and Tilden Foundations).

26 Stephen, *Mausoleum Book*, p.57.

27 Leslie Stephen to Julia Stephen, 15 January 1878 (The Sir Leslie Stephen Collection. The Henry W. and Albert A. Berg Collection of English and American Literature, The New York Public Library, Astor, Lenox and Tilden Foundations).

28 Julia Duckworth to Jane Margaret Vaughan Williams, 14 January 1878 (Lushington Papers, 6536/253/2).

29 Julia Margaret Cameron to Leslie Stephen, 5 February 1878 (The Sir Leslie Stephen Collection. The Henry W. and Albert A. Berg Collection of English and American Literature, The New York Public Library, Astor, Lenox and Tilden Foundations).

30 Woolf, 'Sketch of the Past', *Moments of Being*, p.101.

31 Woolf, *Jacob's Room*, p.73.

32 Elizabeth Robins to VW, 4 May 1928, quoted in Jane Dunn, *Virginia Woolf and Vanessa Bell: A Very Close Conspiracy* (London: Virago, 2000) p.32.

33 Leslie Stephen to Julia Stephen, 11 August 1877 (The Sir Leslie Stephen Collection. The Henry W. and Albert A. Berg Collection of English and American Literature, The New York Public Library, Astor, Lenox and Tilden Foundations).

34 Stephen, *Mausoleum Book*, p.53.

35 Julia Margaret Cameron to Julia Prinsep Stephen, 5 February 1878 (The correspondence of Julia Margaret Cameron and Julia Prinsep Stephen. The Henry W. and Albert A. Berg Collection of English and American Literature, The New York Public Library, Astor, Lenox and Tilden Foundations).

36 Quoted in Alan Bell's introduction to Stephen, *Mausoleum Book*, p.xxi.

37 Henry James to Alice James, 17 February 1878, quoted in Lee, *Virginia Woolf*, p.94.

38 Annan, *Leslie Stephen*, p.100.

39 Stephen, *Mausoleum Book*, p.25.

40 Ibid., p.90.

41 Leslie Stephen to Julia Stephen, 20 April 1881 (The Sir Leslie Stephen Collection. The Henry W. and Albert A. Berg Collection of English and American Literature, The New York Public Library, Astor, Lenox and Tilden Foundations).

42 Woolf, 'Reminiscences', *Moments of Being*, p.6.

Chapter 5: The Absent Mother

1 This was Julia's aunt Virginia Somers' home. She had married Lord Eastnor, who owned a fairy-tale castle with a drawing room designed by Pugin, a deer park, lake and arboretum.

2 Stephen, *Mausoleum Book*, p.65.

3 Leslie Stephen to Julia Stephen, 1877 (The Sir Leslie Stephen Collection. The Henry W. and Albert A. Berg Collection of English and American Literature, The New York Public Library, Astor, Lenox and Tilden Foundations).

4 Stephen, *Mausoleum Book*, p.65.

5 Ibid., p.83.

6 Ibid., p.59.

7 Leslie Stephen to Julia Stephen, 5 April 1977 (The Sir Leslie Stephen Collection. The Henry W. and Albert A. Berg Collection of English and American Literature, The New York Public Library, Astor, Lenox and Tilden Foundations).

8 Leslie Stephen to Julia Stephen, 19 October 1881 (The Sir Leslie Stephen Collection. The Henry W. and Albert A. Berg Collection of English and American Literature, The New York Public Library, Astor, Lenox and Tilden Foundations).

9 Lee, *Virginia Woolf*, p.104.

10 Woolf, 'Reminiscences', *Moments of Being*, p.2.

11 Virginia Woolf, 'Old Bloomsbury', *Moments of Being*, p.44.

12 Lee, *Virginia Woolf*, p.101.

13 Woolf, 'Old Bloomsbury', *Moments of Being*, p.44.

14 Leslie Stephen to Julia Stephen, 29 April 1881 (The Sir Leslie Stephen Collection. The Henry W. and Albert A. Berg Collection of English and American Literature, The New York Public Library, Astor, Lenox and Tilden Foundations).

15 For a full discussion of Laura's plight see Gillian Gill. She wonders whether the Duckworth brothers sexually abused their stepsister as well as Virginia. Gill, *Virginia Woolf*, p.117.

16 Jane Lushington to Vernon Lushington, 1 August 1893 (Lushington Papers, 7854/3/6/20/29a-c).

17 Lee, *Virginia Woolf*, p.102.

18 Jane Lushington to Vernon Lushington, 1 August 1993 (Lushington Papers, 7854/3/6/20/29a-c).

19 Laura eventually died in an asylum in York in 1945. Bell, *Virginia Woolf*, p.22.

20 Leslie Stephen to Julia Stephen, 1 August 1893 (The Sir Leslie Stephen Collection. The Henry W. and Albert A. Berg Collection of English and American Literature, The New York Public Library, Astor, Lenox and Tilden Foundations).

21 Lee, *Virginia Woolf*, pp.103–4.

22 Woolf, 'Sketch of the Past', *Moments of Being*, p.106.

23 Woolf, 'Reminiscences', *Moments of Being*, p.15.

24 Ibid., p.14.

25 Ibid., p.15.

26 Ibid.

27 See below, letters written by Julia to Stella when Jem Stephen was obsessed with the younger woman.

28 Woolf, 'Sketch of the Past', *Moments of Being*, p.78.

29 Stephen, *Mausoleum Book*, p.32.

30 Woolf, 'Sketch of the Past', *Moments of Being*, p.93.

31 Woolf, *Jacob's Room*, p.10.

32 Lee, *Virginia Woolf*, p.119.

33 Woolf, 'Sketch of the Past', *Moments of Being*, p.94.

34 Ibid.

35 Ellen Bayuk Rosenman, *The Invisible Presence: Virginia Woolf and the Mother–Daughter Relationship* (Baton Rouge and London: Louisiana State University Press, 1986) p.10.

36 Woolf, 'Reminiscences', *Moments of Being*, pp.7–11.

37 Dr Maudsley published an influential article on this subject in 1874. Lyndall Gordon, *Virginia Woolf: A Writer's Life* (New York and London: W.W. Norton, 1984) p.55.

38 Leslie Stephen to Julia Stephen, 18 July 1877 (The Sir Leslie Stephen Collection. The Henry W. and Albert A. Berg Collection of English and American Literature, The New York Public Library, Astor, Lenox and Tilden Foundations).

39 Leslie Stephen to Julia Stephen, 19 July 1877 (The Sir Leslie Stephen Collection. The Henry W. and Albert A. Berg Collection of English and American Literature, The New York Public Library, Astor, Lenox and Tilden Foundations).

40 See Gordon, *Virginia Woolf*, p.74.

41 Virginia Woolf to Vita Sackville-West. Alison Bechdel, *Love Letters: Virginia Woolf and Vita Sackville-West* (London: Vintage, 2021) p.180.

42 Anna Snaith (ed.), 'Notes' in Woolf, *Three Guineas*, p.xvii.

43 Dell, *Virginia Woolf's Influential Forebears*, p.120.

44 For a full discussion of the stories see Diane F. Gillespie and Elizabeth Steele (eds), *Julia Duckworth Stephen: Stories for Children, Essays for Adults* (New York: Syracuse University Press, 1987).

45 Lee, *Virginia Woolf*, p.108.

46 Ibid., p.82.

47 Gill Lowe (ed.), *Hyde Park Gate News: The Stephen Family Newspaper* (London: Hesperus Press, 2005) p.viii.

48 Bell, *Virginia Woolf*, p.29.

49 Lee, *Virginia Woolf*, p.109.

50 Woolf, 'Sketch of the Past', *Moments of Being*, p.93.

51 Ibid., p.95.

52 Bell, *Virginia Woolf*, p.29.

53 Woolf, 'Sketch of the Past', *Moments of Being*, p.105.

54 Dell, *Virginia Woolf's Influential Forebears*, p.121.

55 Woolf, 'Sketch of the Past', *Moments of Being*, p.105.

56 Ibid., p.101.

57 Lee, *Virginia Woolf*, p. 56.

58 Leslie Stephen to Julia Stephen, 25 January 1891 (The Sir Leslie Stephen Collection. The Henry W. and Albert A. Berg Collection of English and American Literature, The New York Public Library, Astor, Lenox and Tilden Foundations).

59 Leslie Stephen to Julia Stephen, 17 April 1887 (The Sir Leslie Stephen Collection. The Henry W. and Albert A. Berg Collection of English and American Literature, The New York Public Library, Astor, Lenox and Tilden Foundations).

60 Leslie Stephen to Julia Stephen, 13 April 1884 (The Sir Leslie Stephen Collection. The Henry W. and Albert A. Berg Collection of English and American Literature, The New York Public Library, Astor, Lenox and Tilden Foundations).

61 Leslie Stephen to Julia Stephen, 3 August 1893 (The Sir Leslie Stephen Collection. The Henry W. and Albert A. Berg Collection of English and American Literature, The New York Public Library, Astor, Lenox and Tilden Foundations).

62 Leslie Stephen to Julia Stephen, July 1893 (The Sir Leslie Stephen Collection. The Henry W. and Albert A. Berg Collection of English and American Literature, The New York Public Library, Astor, Lenox and Tilden Foundations).

63 14 March 1892. Lowe, *Hyde Park Gate News*, p.42.

64 Leslie Stephen to Julia Stephen, 26 January 1894 (The Sir Leslie Stephen Collection. The Henry W. and Albert A. Berg Collection of English and American Literature, The New York Public Library, Astor, Lenox and Tilden Foundations).

65 For a full discussion of Julia's love for Adrian see the *Mausoleum Book*.

66 Woolf, '22 Hyde Park Gate', *Moments of Being*, p.32.

67 James Russell Lowell to Julia Stephen, 16 December 1889. (James Russell Lowell Collection, The Henry W. and Albert A. Berg Collection of English and American Literature, The New York Public Library, Astor, Lenox and Tilden Foundations).

68 21 March 1892. Lowe, *Hyde Park Gate News*, p.45.

69 George Meredith to Julia Stephen, 12 August 1884, quoted in Gillespie and Steele, *Julia Duckworth Stephen*, p.15.

70 For a full discussion of Gerald's sexual abuse and its effect on Virginia, see Lee, *Virginia Woolf*, p.126–7.

71 Virginia Woolf, quoted in Gordon, *Virginia Woolf*, p.9.

72 Woolf, 'Sketch of the Past', *Moments of Being*, pp.82–3.

Chapter 6: The Hostess

1 Woolf, 'Sketch of the Past', *Moments of Being*, p.94.
2 For a detailed description of Hyde Park Gate, see Woolf, '22 Hyde Park Gate' and 'Old Bloomsbury', *Moments of Being*, pp.31, 43–4.
3 Woolf, 'Old Bloomsbury', *Moments of Being*, p.44.
4 Woolf, 'Sketch of the Past', *Moments of Being*, p.119.
5 Stephen, *Mausoleum Book*, p.58.
6 Jane Lushington to Vernon Lushington, 1 August 1883 (Lushington Papers, 7854/3/6/20/29a-c).
7 James Russell Lowell to Julia Stephen, 2 August 1882 (The Henry W. and Albert A. Berg Collection of English and American Literature, The New York Public Library, Astor, Lenox and Tilden Foundations).
8 James Russell Lowell to Julia Stephen, 16 December 1888 (The Henry W. and Albert A. Berg Collection of English and American Literature, The New York Public Library, Astor, Lenox and Tilden Foundations).
9 James Russell Lowell to Julia Stephen, 11 January 1888 (The Henry W. and Albert A. Berg Collection of English and American Literature, The New York Public Library, Astor, Lenox and Tilden Foundations).
10 James Russell Lowell, quoted in Lee, *Virginia Woolf*, p.83.
11 James Russell Lowell to Julia Stephen, 8 October 1887 (The Henry W. and Albert A. Berg Collection of English and American Literature, The New York Public Library, Astor, Lenox and Tilden Foundations).
12 James Russell Lowell to Julia Stephen, 17 April 1888 (The Henry W. and Albert A. Berg Collection of English and American Literature, The New York Public Library, Astor, Lenox and Tilden Foundations).
13 James Russell Lowell to Julia Stephen, 10 May 1891 (The Henry W. and Albert A. Berg Collection of English and American Literature, The New York Public Library, Astor, Lenox and Tilden Foundations).
14 James Russell Lowell to Julia Stephen, 22 February 1884 (The Henry W. and Albert A. Berg Collection of English and American Literature, The New York Public Library, Astor, Lenox and Tilden Foundations).
15 James Russell Lowell to Julia Stephen, 9 November 1885 (The Henry W. and Albert A. Berg Collection of English and American Literature, The New York Public Library, Astor, Lenox and Tilden Foundations).
16 James Russell Lowell to Julia Stephen, 2 September 1890 (The Henry W. and Albert A. Berg Collection of English and American Literature, The New York Public Library, Astor, Lenox and Tilden Foundations).
17 James Russell Lowell to Julia Stephen, 22 February 1884 (The Henry W. and Albert A. Berg Collection of English and American Literature, The New York Public Library, Astor, Lenox and Tilden Foundations).
18 James Russell Lowell to Julia Stephen, 9 November 1885 (The Henry W. and Albert A. Berg Collection of English and American Literature, The New York Public Library, Astor, Lenox and Tilden Foundations).

19 When Dodgson died his obituary in the *London Daily Graphic* noted that 'like many bachelors, he was very popular with children and very fond of them'. Dodgson's nephew, Stuart Collingwood, published a biography that devoted two chapters to Dodgson's many 'child friends', including references to his hugging and kissing girls. Jenny Woolf, 'Lewis Carroll's Shifting Reputation,' *Smithsonian Magazine*, April 2010.

20 James Russell Lowell to Julia Stephen, 31 July 1889 (The Henry W. and Albert A. Berg Collection of English and American Literature, The New York Public Library, Astor, Lenox and Tilden Foundations).

21 James Russell Lowell to Julia Stephen, 23 August 1888 (The Henry W. and Albert A. Berg Collection of English and American Literature, The New York Public Library, Astor, Lenox and Tilden Foundations).

22 James Russell Lowell to Julia Stephen, 12 August 1888 (The Henry W. and Albert A. Berg Collection of English and American Literature, The New York Public Library, Astor, Lenox and Tilden Foundations).

23 Stephen, *Mausoleum Book*, p.80.

24 Woolf, 'Sketch of the Past', *Moments of Being*, p.118.

25 Ibid., p.122.

26 Leslie Stephen to Julia Stephen, 20 April 1881 (The Sir Leslie Stephen Collection. The Henry W. and Albert A. Berg Collection of English and American Literature, The New York Public Library, Astor, Lenox and Tilden Foundations).

27 Stephen, *Mausoleum Book*, p.62.

28 Susan Lushington to Vernon Lushington, 4 January 1890 (Lushington Papers, 7854/3/9/23a–c).

29 Woolf, 'Sketch of the Past', *Moments of Being*, pp.154–5.

30 Ibid., p.151.

31 Virginia Woolf, '22 Hyde Park Gate', *Moments of Being*, pp.31–2.

32 Ibid., p.32.

33 Stephen, *Mausoleum Book*, p.89.

34 Woolf, 'Sketch of the Past', *Moments of Being*, p.79.

35 Leslie Stephen letter, 1884, quoted in Lee, *Virginia Woolf*, p.29.

36 Virginia Woolf, quoted in Gillespie and Steele, *Julia Duckworth Stephen*, p.23.

37 Margaret Lushington to Susan Lushington, no date (Lushington Papers, 7854/3/5/1a).

38 Lee, *Virginia Woolf*, p.27.

39 Woolf, 'Reminiscences', *Moments of Being*, p.7.

40 Lee, *Virginia Woolf*, p.31.

41 Margaret Lushington to Susan Lushington, 19 September 1893 (Lushington Papers, 7854/4/5/5).

42 Woolf, 'Sketch of the Past', *Moments of Being*, p.93.

43 Woolf, *To the Lighthouse*, p.12.

44 19 December 1938, Virginia Woolf, *Selected Diaries* (London: Vintage Books, 2008) p.445.
45 Gordon, *Virginia Woolf*, p.15.
46 Woolf, 'Sketch of the Past', *Moments of Being*, p.79.
47 James Russell Lowell to Julia Stephen, 11 August 1887 (The Henry W. and Albert A. Berg Collection of English and American Literature, The New York Public Library, Astor, Lenox and Tilden Foundations).
48 Bell, *Virginia Woolf*, p.34.
49 See Margaret Lushington's letters to Susan Lushington (Lushington Papers).
50 Woolf, *To the Lighthouse*, p.5.
51 Stephen, *Mausoleum Book*, p.78.
52 Margaret Lushington to Susan Lushington, September 1893 (Lushington Papers, 7854/4/5/6).
53 Kitty was the model for Minta Doyle in *To the Lighthouse*.
54 Stephen, *Mausoleum Book*, p.77.
55 Woolf, 'Reminiscences', *Moments of Being*, p.15.
56 Ibid.
57 Woolf, 'Sketch of the Past', *Moments of Being*, p.110.
58 Woolf, 'Reminiscences', *Moments of Being*, p.19.
59 Woolf, *To the Lighthouse*, p.36.
60 Margaret Massingbred to Susan Lushington, 1895 (Lushington Papers, 7854/4/5/23a-b).
61 Stephen, *Mausoleum Book*, p.75.
62 Woolf, *To the Lighthouse*, p.5.

Chapter 7: The Angel Outside the House

1 Gillespie and Steele, *Julia Duckworth Stephen*, p.212.
2 Leslie Stephen to Mrs Jackson, Tuesday, no date (The Sir Leslie Stephen Collection. The Henry W. and Albert A. Berg Collection of English and American Literature, The New York Public Library, Astor, Lenox and Tilden Foundations).
3 Troubridge, *Memories and Reflections*, p.43.
4 Leslie Stephen to Julia Stephen, 8 February 1878 (The Sir Leslie Stephen Collection. The Henry W. and Albert A. Berg Collection of English and American Literature, The New York Public Library, Astor, Lenox and Tilden Foundations).
5 Stephen, *Mausoleum Book*, p.67.
6 Leslie Stephen to Julia Stephen, 18 April 1881 (The Sir Leslie Stephen Collection. The Henry W. and Albert A. Berg Collection of English and American Literature, The New York Public Library, Astor, Lenox and Tilden Foundations).

7   Virginia Woolf, 'Julia Margaret Cameron', 1926 *Julia Margaret Cameron* (Los Angeles: The J. Paul Getty Museum, 2016) p.32.

8   Maria Jackson to Stella Duckworth, 21 September, no year (Julia Stephen Collection. Courtesy Charles Deering McCormick Library of Special Collections and University Archives, Northwestern University Libraries MS 177).

9   Maria Jackson to Stella Duckworth, 25 August, no year (Julia Stephen Collection. Courtesy Charles Deering McCormick Library of Special Collections and University Archives, Northwestern University Libraries, MS 177).

10 Leslie Stephen to Maria Jackson, 9 January 1879 (The Sir Leslie Stephen Collection. The Henry W. and Albert A. Berg Collection of English and American Literature, The New York Public Library, Astor, Lenox and Tilden Foundations).

11 Maria Jackson to Stella Duckworth, 25 August, no year (Julia Stephen Collection. Courtesy Charles Deering McCormick Library of Special Collections and University Archives, Northwestern University Libraries, MS 177).

12 Stephen, *Mausoleum Book*, p.74.

13 Leslie Stephen to Julia Stephen, April 1887 (The Sir Leslie Stephen Collection. The Henry W. and Albert A. Berg Collection of English and American Literature, The New York Public Library, Astor, Lenox and Tilden Foundations).

14 Rothenstein, *Men and Memories: Recollections 1872–1938* (Columbia: University of Missouri Press, 1978) p.60.

15 Gill, *Virginia Woolf*, p.47.

16 Stephen, *Mausoleum Book*, p.75.

17 Lee, *Virginia Woolf*, pp.64–5.

18 Bell, *Virginia Woolf*, p.36.

19 Stephen, *Mausoleum Book*, p.78.

20 Woolf, 'Sketch of the Past', *Moments of Being*, p.108.

21 Julia Stephen to Stella Duckworth, no date (Julia Stephen Collection. Courtesy Charles Deering McCormick Library of Special Collections and University Archives, Northwestern University Libraries, MS 177).

22 Julia Stephen to Stella Duckworth, no date (Julia Stephen Collection. Courtesy Charles Deering McCormick Library of Special Collections and University Archives, Northwestern University Libraries, MS 177).

23 Lee, *Virginia Woolf*, p.65.

24 Stephen, *Mausoleum Book*, p.78.

25 Ibid., p.82.

26 Stephen, 'Cat's Meat' in Gillespie and Steele, *Julia Duckworth Stephen*, pp.166–87.

27 Woolf, 'Reminiscences', *Moments of Being*, p.9.

28 Ibid., p.7.

29 Ibid.

30 Stephen, *Mausoleum Book*, p.63.

31 Woolf, 'Sketch of the Past', *Moments of Being*, p.93.

32   Ibid., p.95.

33   Woolf, *To the Lighthouse*, p.4.

34   'Review', 27 January 1883, *Graphic*.

35   Jessie Raine Review, 14 June 1883, *Truth*.

36   Stephen, 'Notes from Sick Rooms' in Gillespie and Steele, *Julia Duckworth Stephen*, p.217.

37   Stephen, 'The Servant Question' in Gillespie and Steele, *Julia Duckworth Stephen*, p.248.

38   Gillespie and Steele, *Julia Duckworth Stephen*, p.206.

39   Woolf, 'Sketch of the Past', *Moments of Being*, pp.124–5.

40   'Mrs Leslie Stephen Pleads for Beer', *Western Morning News*, 17 October 1879.

41   Woolf, *To the Lighthouse*, p.7.

42   'The Appeal Against Female Suffrage', *The Queen*, 8 June 1889.

43   George Meredith to Julia Stephen, 1889, quoted in Gillespie and Steele, *Julia Duckworth Stephen*, p.15.

44   Stephen, 'Agnostic Women' in Gillespie and Steele, *Julia Duckworth Stephen*, pp.246–7.

45   Leslie Stephen, 'Forgotten Benefactors', *Social Rights and Duties: Addresses to Ethical Societies. Vol. 2.* (London, New York: Macmillan, 1896) p.250.

46   Woolf, *To the Lighthouse*, pp.30, 61.

47   Stephen, 'Forgotten Benefactors', p.258.

48   William Wordsworth, 'Lines Composed a Few Miles above Tintern Abbey'.

49   Stephen, 'Agnostic Women' in Gillespie and Steele, *Julia Duckworth Stephen*, p.243.

50   Ibid., p.242.

51   Stephen, *Mausoleum Book*, p.84.

52   Woolf, *To the Lighthouse*, p.57.

Chapter 8: The Martyr

1   Stephen, *Mausoleum Book*, p.33.

2   Woolf, *To the Lighthouse*, p.21.

3   Woolf, 'Sketch of the Past', *Moments of Being*, p.94.

4   Woolf, *To the Lighthouse*, p.21.

5   Stephen, *Mausoleum Book*, p.93.

6   Woolf, *To the Lighthouse*, p.147.

7   Woolf, 'Sketch of the Past', *Moments of Being*, p.149.

8   Ibid., p.117.

9   Woolf, *To the Lighthouse*, p.145.

10   Woolf, 'Sketch of the Past', *Moments of Being*, p.137.

11   Leslie Stephen to Julia Stephen, 20 April 1881 (The Sir Leslie Stephen Collection. The Henry W. and Albert A. Berg Collection of English and American Literature, The New York Public Library, Astor, Lenox and Tilden Foundations).

12 Leslie Stephen to Julia Stephen, 6 October 1886 (The Sir Leslie Stephen Collection. The Henry W. and Albert A. Berg Collection of English and American Literature, The New York Public Library, Astor, Lenox and Tilden Foundations).

13 Leslie Stephen to Julia Stephen, 4 October 1887 (The Sir Leslie Stephen Collection. The Henry W. and Albert A. Berg Collection of English and American Literature, The New York Public Library, Astor, Lenox and Tilden Foundations).

14 Stephen, *Mausoleum Book*, pp.87–8.

15 Vernon Lushington to Kitty Lushington, 8 September 1890 (Lushington Papers, 7854/5/1/80a-b).

16 Kitty Lushington to Vernon Lushington, 10 April 1890 (Lushington Papers, 7854/3/7/33a-b).

17 Smith Elder to Julia Stephen, 3 May 1889 (The Sir Leslie Stephen Collection. The Henry W. and Albert A. Berg Collection of English and American Literature, The New York Public Library, Astor, Lenox and Tilden Foundations).

18 James Russell Lowell to Julia Stephen. 4 December 1889. (The Henry W. and Albert A. Berg Collection of English and American Literature, The New York Public Library, Astor, Lenox and Tilden Foundations).

19 Stephen, *Mausoleum Book*, p.89.

20 Ibid., p.60.

21 Woolf, *To the Lighthouse*, p.46.

22 Matthew Arnold, 'Dover Beach'.

23 Woolf, 'Reminiscences', *Moments of Being*, p.9.

24 Woolf, *To the Lighthouse*, p.113.

25 Stephen, *Mausoleum Book*, p.90.

26 Leslie Stephen to Julia Stephen, 2 January 1895 (The Sir Leslie Stephen Collection. The Henry W. and Albert A. Berg Collection of English and American Literature, The New York Public Library, Astor, Lenox and Tilden Foundations).

27 Susan Lushington to Vernon Lushington, 14 March 1895 (Lushington Papers, 7854/3/9/85a-b).

28 Henry James to Theodora Sedgwick, 30 March 1895, quoted in Gillespie and Steele, *Julia Duckworth Stephen*, p.23.

29 11 March 1895. Lowe, *Hyde Park Gate News*, p.189.

30 Woolf, 'Reminiscences', *Moments of Being*, p.11.

31 The condition could possibly be traced back to 1879 when she had nursed a severe case of the fever a few months after she herself had a difficult childbirth. Gordon, *Virginia Woolf*, p.21.

32 Leslie Stephen to Julia Stephen, no date (The Sir Leslie Stephen Collection. The Henry W. and Albert A. Berg Collection of English and American Literature, The New York Public Library, Astor, Lenox and Tilden Foundations).

33 Woolf, 'Reminiscences', *Moments of Being*, pp.15–16.

34 Stephen, *Mausoleum Book*, p.96.

35 Woolf, 'Sketch of the Past', *Moments of Being*, p.95.
36 Ibid., p.102.
37 Virginia Woolf, 12 September 1934, Diary, quoted in Lee, *Virginia Woolf*, p.131.
38 Woolf, 'Sketch of the Past', *Moments of Being*, pp.102–3.
39 Ibid., pp.102–3.
40 Woolf, 'Reminiscences', *Moments of Being*, p.11.
41 Margaret Massingbred (Lushington) to Vernon Lushington, 9 May 1895 (Lushington Papers, 7854/3/8/113a-b).

Chapter 9: The Family Falls Apart

1 Woolf, 'Reminiscences', *Moments of Being*, p.4.
2 Woolf, *To the Lighthouse*, p.111.
3 Woolf, 'Reminiscences', *Moments of Being*, p.13.
4 Woolf, *To the Lighthouse*, p.114.
5 Stephen, 'Forgotten Benefactors', p.253.
6 Woolf, 'Reminiscences', *Moments of Being*, p.18.
7 Stephen, *Mausoleum Book*, p.13.
8 Woolf, 'Sketch of the Past', *Moments of Being*, p.103.
9 Woolf, 'Reminiscences', *Moments of Being*, p.17.
10 Lee, *Virginia Woolf*, p.177.
11 Ibid., p.134.
12 Ibid., p,135.
13 Leonard Woolf, *Beginning Again: An Autobiography of the Years 1911 to 1918* (New York and London: Harvest Books, 1964) pp.75–6.
14 For a full discussion of Virginia's mental health, see Lee, *Virginia Woolf*, p.175.
15 18 December 1937, Woolf, *Selected Diaries*, p.422.
16 Woolf, 'Reminiscences', *Moments of Being*, p.18.
17 Lilly (no surname) to Stella Duckworth, 18 August 1895 (Julia Stephen Collection. Courtesy Charles Deering McCormick Library of Special Collections and University Archives, Northwestern University Libraries, MS 177).
18 Woolf, 'Sketch of the Past', *Moments of Being*, p.104.
19 Stephen, *Mausoleum Book*, p.104.
20 Ibid., p.102.
21 Lee, *Virginia Woolf*, p.136.
22 Ibid., p.138.
23 Lee, *Virginia Woolf*, p.139.
24 Gordon, *Virginia Woolf*, p.47.
25 Kitty Maxse (Lushington) to Susan Lushington (Lushington Papers, 7854/4/22/4/4c).
26 Lee, *Virginia Woolf*, p.136.
27 Woolf, 'Reminiscences', *Moments of Being*, p.27.
28 Gordon, *Virginia Woolf*, p.21.

29 Leonard Woolf, *Sowing: An Autobiography of the Years 1880 to 1904* (New York and London: Harvest Books, 1960) p.182.

30 Virginia Woolf to Vita Sackville-West, 13 May 1927. Bechdel, *Love Letters*, p.110.

31 Woolf, 'Sketch of the Past', *Moments of Being*, p.148.

Chapter 10: An Abuse of Trust

1 Gordon, *Virginia Woolf*, p.38.

2 Woolf, 'Sketch of the Past', *Moments of Being*, p.130.

3 Woolf, 'Old Bloomsbury', *Moments of Being*, p.45.

4 Kitty Maxse (Lushington) to Susan Lushington, no date (Lushington Papers, 7854/4/22/4/46).

5 Woolf, 'Reminiscences', *Moments of Being*, p.27.

6 Woolf, 'Sketch of the Past', *Moments of Being*, p.146.

7 Quoted in Lee, *Virginia Woolf*, p.149.

8 Woolf, '22 Hyde Park Gate', *Moments of Being*, p.34.

9 Woolf, 'Sketch of the Past', *Moments of Being*, p.157.

10 Woolf, '22 Hyde Park Gate', *Moments of Being*, p.42.

11 Woolf, 'Old Bloomsbury', *Moments of Being*, p.44.

12 Woolf, 'Reminiscences', *Moments of Being*, p.29.

13 Lee, *Virginia Woolf*, p.157.

14 Quoted in Lee, *Virginia Woolf*, p.158.

15 For a full discussion see Lee, *Virginia Woolf*, p.159.

16 Woolf, 'Old Bloomsbury', *Moments of Being*, p.124.

17 Ibid., p.45.

Chapter 11: The Rebellion

1 Woolf, 'Old Bloomsbury', *Moments of Being*, p.47.

2 'Old Bloomsbury Manuscript', Monks House Papers, Sussex, A16, quoted in Lee, *Virginia Woolf*, p.208.

3 Gordon, *Virginia Woolf*, p.116.

4 Quentin Bell, *Bloomsbury* (London: Weidenfeld and Nicolson, 1968) pp.42–3.

5 Vita Sackville-West, quoted in Bell, *Virginia Woolf*, p.6.

6 Woolf, 'Old Bloomsbury', *Moments of Being*, p.56.

7 Ibid., pp.52–3.

8 Ibid., p.60.

9 Lee, *Virginia Woolf*, p.235.

10 Woolf, 'Reminiscences', *Moments of Being*, p.8.

11 Ibid.

12 *Virginia Woolf*, 'I am Christina Rossetti', *The Art of Biography: A Collection of Essays* (London: Read and Co, 2021) p.15.

13 For a full discussion of Virginia Woolf's approach to biography, see Gordon, *Virginia Woolf*, pp.vi, 6.

14 Lee, 'Introduction', *Moments of Being*, p.xv.

15 Quoted in Lee, *Virginia Woolf*, p.307.

16 Woolf, *To the Lighthouse*, p.113.

17 Ibid., p.130.

18 Woolf, 'Old Bloomsbury', *Moments of Being*, p.57.

19 Leonard Woolf, *Sowing*, pp.185–6.

20 Virginia Woolf, *Selected Letters* (London: Vintage Books, 2008) p.74.

21 Virginia Woolf to Ethel Sands, 9 February 1927 in Woolf, *Selected Letters*, p.215.

22 5 September 1926 in Woolf, *Selected Diaries*, p.219.

23 15 September 1926 in Woolf, *Selected Letters*, p.220.

24 20 December 1927 in Woolf, *Selected Letters*, p.238.

25 Virginia Woolf, *The Voyage Out* (London: Penguin Books, 1992) p.77.

26 Ibid., p.234.

27 Rosenman, *The Invisible Presence*, p.25.

28 Woolf, 'Old Bloomsbury', *Moments of Being*, p.141.

29 Bell, *Virginia Woolf*, pp.24–5.

30 Lee, *Virginia Woolf*, p.180.

31 18 December 1937 in Woolf, *Selected Diaries*, p.422.

32 Jane Dunn, *Virginia Woolf and Vanessa Bell: A Very Close Conspiracy* (London: Virago, 2000) p.4.

33 Vanessa Bell to Virginia Woolf, quoted in Dunn, *Virginia Woolf and Vanessa Bell*, p.91.

34 Rosenman, *The Invisible Presence*, pp.10–11.

35 Quoted in Lee, *Virginia Woolf*, p.168.

36 Virginia Woolf to Madge Vaughan, July 1906, in Woolf, *Selected Letters*, pp.21, 27.

37 Virginia Woolf to Katharine Arnold-Forster, 9 October 1919, in Woolf, *Selected Letters*, p.114.

38 Gordon, *Virginia Woolf*, p.184.

39 21 December 1925, in Woolf, *Selected Diaries*, p.203.

40 Virginia Woolf to Vita Sackville-West, 19 November 1926 in Bechdel, *Love Letters*, p.76.

41 Virginia Woolf to Vita Sackville-West, 29 January 1929 in Bechdel, *Love Letters*, p.175.

42 Vita Sackville-West to Harold Nicolson, 27 September 1928 in Bechdel, *Love Letters*, p.160.

43 Vita Sackville-West to Harold Nicolson, 17 August 1926 in Bechdel, *Love Letters*, p.72.

44 Vita Sackville-West to Virginia Woolf, 16 February 1929 in Bechdel, *Love Letters*, p.179.

45 Quoted in Lee, *Virginia Woolf*, p.593.

Chapter 12: Haunting Virginia

1   Woolf, 'Reminiscences', *Moments of Being*, p.12.
2   Woolf, 'Sketch of the Past', *Moments of Being*, p.92.
3   Woolf, Draft of *To the Lighthouse*, p.187, quoted in Gordon, *Virginia Woolf*, p.37.
4   Virginia Woolf, 'The New Dress' (Great Britain: Printed by Amazon, 2022).
5   Quoted in Lee, *Virginia Woolf*, p.566.
6   Ibid.
7   Ibid., p.567.
8   Quoted in Lee, *Virginia Woolf*, p.568.
9   Virginia Woolf, *On Being Ill* (London and Amsterdam: HetMoet, 2021) p.29.
10 Lee, *Virginia Woolf*, p.623.
11 Gordon, *Virginia Woolf*, p.20.
12 Woolf, *To the Lighthouse*, p.147.
13 Gordon, *Virginia Woolf*, p.38.
14 Woolf, 'Sketch of the Past', *Moments of Being*, p.92.
15 For a full discussion of Virginia's writing of the novel, see Gordon, *Virginia Woolf*, pp.28–9.
16 17 October 1934, Woolf, *Selected Diaries*, p.360.
17 Dell, *Virginia Woolf's Influential Forebears*, p.176.
18 Lee, *Virginia Woolf*, p.477–8.
19 Vanessa Bell to Virginia Woolf, May 1927, quoted in Lee, *Virginia Woolf*, p.480.
20 Virginia Woolf to Vanessa Bell, May 1927, quoted in Gordon, *Virginia Woolf*, p.29.
21 Lee, *Virginia Woolf*, pp.480–1.
22 Vita Sackville-West to Virginia Woolf, 12 May 1927, in Bechdel, *Love Letters*, p.109.
23 Virginia Woolf to Vita Sackville-West, 13 May 1927, in Bechdel, *Love Letters*, p.110.
24 Lee, *Virginia Woolf*, p.481.
25 Woolf, *To the Lighthouse*, p.133.
26 Woolf, 'Sketch of the Past', *Moments of Being*, p.93.
27 Ibid., p.96.
28 Virginia Woolf, *The Waves* (London: Penguin Classics, 2019) pp.211, 222.
29 From *The Waves*, quoted in Lee, *Virginia Woolf*, p.726.
30 Virginia Woolf, *The Years* (London: The Hogarth Press, 1937)

Chapter 13: Killing the Angel

1   Lee, *Virginia Woolf*, p. 81.
2   Ibid., p.279.
3   Woolf, *A Room of One's Own*, p.46.
4   Ibid.
5   Ibid., p.35.

6   Ibid., pp.85, 103.
7   Virginia Woolf, 'Professions for Women', *The Collected Essays of Virginia Woolf* (London: Read Books Ltd, 2012) p.284.
8   Ibid., p.286–8.
9   Lee, *Virginia Woolf*, p.598.
10 Virginia Woolf, *Three Guineas* (Oxford University Press, 2015) p.99.
11 Stephen, 'Agnostic Women' in Gillespie and Steele, *Julia Duckworth Stephen*, p.246.
12 Woolf, *Three Guineas*, p.101.
13 Ibid., p.160.
14 Ibid., p.158.
15 Ibid., p.187.
16 Virginia was not the first to make this connection. Jane Harrison's 'Epilogue on the War: Peace and Patriotism' written during the First World War made a similar argument. Anna Snaith (ed.), 'Introduction' in Virginia Woolf, *Three Guineas*, p.xxx.
17 Ibid., p.206.
18 Woolf, 'Thoughts on Peace in an Air Raid', *The Collected Essays of Virginia Woolf*, p.292.
19 Lee, 'Introduction', *Moments of Being*, p.xii.
20 Woolf, 'Sketch of the Past', *Moments of Being*, p.116.
21 While Virginia said she began to write this memoir on 16 April 1939, she may have started it before. Dell, *Influential Forebears*, p.135.
22 Woolf, 'Sketch of the Past', *Moments of Being*, p.92.
23 22 December 1940 in Woolf, *Selected Diaries*, p.497.
24 Woolf, 'Sketch of the Past', *Moments of Being*, pp.132, 140.
25 Gordon, *Virginia Woolf*, p.276.
26 Woolf, *To the Lighthouse*, p.135.
27 The coroner emphasised the effect of world events on her sensitive nature but Leonard claimed that private rather than public matters had led to her suicide. She feared having another breakdown and that she would never write again.
28 Leonard Woolf, *The Journey Not the Arrival Matters: An Autobiography of the Years 1939 to 1969* (New York and London: Harvest Books, 1969) p.79.
29 Virginia Woolf to Vanessa Bell, March 1941, in Woolf, *Selected Letters*, p.442.

Part Two: Clara and Agatha

Chapter 14: The Poor Relation

1   Mary Westmacott (Agatha Christie), *Unfinished Portrait* (London: HarperCollins, 2017) pp.71–2.
2   'Find a Grave.' Online Website.
3   Agatha Christie, *An Autobiography* (New York: Dodd, Mead and Co, 1977) p.29.

4   Ibid., p.36.
5   Westmacott, *Unfinished Portrait*, p.71.
6   'Find a Grave.'
7   Christie, *An Autobiography*, p.29.
8   'Find a Grave.'
9   'Browning Takes Great Central Mining Company', *Taunton Courier and Western Advertiser*, 28 March 1860.
10 Lucy Worsley, *Agatha Christie: A Very Elusive Woman* (London: Hodder and Stoughton, 2022) p.10.
11 Christie, *An Autobiography*, p.5.
12 Ibid.
13 'Confessions Album'. The Christie Archive Trust.
14 Christie, *An Autobiography*, p.5.
15 Laura Thompson, *Agatha Christie: An English Mystery* (London: Headline, 2007) p.11.
16 Christie, *An Autobiography*, p.5.
17 Agatha Christie, 'Witch Hasel', Version 2. The Christie Archive Trust.
18 Thompson, *Agatha Christie*, p.12.
19 Agatha Christie, *Ordeal by Innocence* (London: HarperCollins, 2017) p.139.
20 Ibid., p.171.
21 Agatha Christie, 'Wireless', *The Hound of Death* (London: HarperCollins, 2016) p.103.
22 Christie, *An Autobiography*, p.6.
23 Janet Morgan, *Agatha Christie: A Biography* (London: HarperCollins, 2017) p.3.
24 Ibid., p.4.
25 Christie, *An Autobiography*, p.155.
26 Ibid.
27 Clara Miller, 'To M.M.' The Christie Archive Trust.
28 Christie, *An Autobiography*, p.85.
29 Agatha Christie Mallowan, *Come, Tell Me How You Live: Memories from Archaeological Expeditions in the Mysterious Middle East* (London: HarperCollins, 2015) p.6.
30 'Confessions Album'. The Christie Archive Trust.
31 Ibid.

Chapter 15: The Wonderful Hero

1   Clara Miller, 'To F.A.M.'. Switzerland, May 1878. The Christie Archive Trust.
2   Clara Miller, 'An Ideal'. The Christie Archive Trust.
3   For a full description of their romance see Agatha Christie, *An Autobiography*.
4   Christie, *An Autobiography*, p.35.
5   Morgan, *Agatha Christie*, p.5.
6   Embroidered pocketbook from Clara to Fred. Kept in The Christie Archive Trust.

7   'Confessions Album'. The Christie Archive Trust.

8   Miller, 'An Ideal'. The Christie Archive Trust.

9   Clara Miller, 'Violets'. The Christie Archive Trust.

10 Clara Miller, 'Two Loves Two Lives. To F.A.M.'. The Christie Archive Trust.

11 Clara Miller, 'To F.A.M.'. 31 October 1877. The Christie Archive Trust.

12 Ibid.

13 Clara Miller, 'A Love Song'. The Christie Archive Trust.

14 Miller. 'To F.A.M.'. Switzerland, May 1878. The Christie Archive Trust.

15 Morgan, *Agatha Christie*, pp.5–6.

16 Christie, *An Autobiography*, p.3.

17 'Confessions Album'. The Christie Archive Trust.

18 Christie, *An Autobiography*, p.4.

19 In 1909 Frederick Boehmer, aged 57, shot himself in a railway carriage. His body was discovered at Maidenhead railway station. 'Tragic Discovery at Maidenhead Railway Station: A Captain Found Shot', *The Maidenhead Advertiser*, 27 October 1909.

20 Worsley, *Agatha Christie*, p.11.

21 Westmacott, *Unfinished Portrait*, p.285.

22 Ibid., p.330.

23 Christie, *An Autobiography*, p.5.

24 Ibid., p.8.

25 Westmacott, *Unfinished Portrait*, p.90.

26 Christie, *An Autobiography*, p.8.

27 Max Mallowan, *Max Mallowan's Memoirs: Agatha and the Archaeologist* (London: HarperCollins, 2010) p.196.

Chapter 16: The Homemaker

1   Christie, *An Autobiography*, p.9.

2   Ibid., p.518.

3   Ibid., p.106.

4   Annie Caan (1897), quoted on Facebook page Torbay Undiscovered, Lost, Forgotten.

5   Find a Grave Website. Margaret Frary 'Madge' Miller Watts.

6   'Ashfield, Torquay', *The Morning Post*, 31 December 1889.

7   Christie, *An Autobiography*, p.7.

8   Ibid.

9   Worsley, *Agatha Christie*, p.6.

10 Morgan, *Agatha Christie*, p.10.

11 Worsley, *Agatha Christie*, p.4.

12 Ibid.

13 Mallowan, *Mallowan's Memoirs*, p.204.

14 Christie, *An Autobiography*, p.9.

15 Mallowan, *Mallowan's Memoirs*, p.204.

16 Christie, *An Autobiography*, p.39.

17 Gwen Robyns, *The Mystery of Agatha Christie: An Intimate Biography of the First Lady of Crime* (London: Penguin Books, 1979) p.36.

18 Christie, *An Autobiography*, p.98.

19 Agatha Christie, quoted in Robyns, *The Mystery of Agatha Christie*, p.61.

20 Decades later Adelaide admitted that she had been the long-term victim of her father's incestuous attentions. Fortunately for Agatha, Eden Phillpotts' interest in her was purely professional. He later acted as a literary mentor to the budding novelist. For a full discussion of Eden Phillpotts, see Julius Green, *A Life in Theatre* (London: HarperCollins, 2018) pp.39–41.

21 Patricia D. Maida and Nicholas B. Spornick, *Murder She Wrote: A Study of Agatha Christie's Detective Fiction* (Ohio: Bowling Green State University Popular Press, 1982) p.17.

22 Christie, *An Autobiography*, p.38.

23 Ibid.

24 Ibid., p.16.

25 Ibid.

26 Ibid., p.17.

27 Ibid., p.15.

28 Ibid., p.18.

29 Ibid., p.12.

30 D.H. Lawrence was one of the celebrities attracted to Theosophy. See Frances Wilson, *Burning Man: The Ascent of D.H. Lawrence* (London: Bloomsbury Circus, 2021) p.122.

31 'The Theosophical Society', *Western Morning News*, 7 August 1893.

32 Christie, *An Autobiography*, p.2.

33 Ibid.

34 Ibid., p.191.

35 Agatha Christie quoted in Morgan, *Agatha Christie*, p.194.

36 Ibid.

37 Rowse, *Memories of Men and Women*, p.80.

38 Agatha Christie, *Star Over Bethlehem including The Road of Dreams and Poems* (London: HarperCollins. Ebook).

39 Gillian Gill, *Agatha Christie: The Woman and Her Mysteries* (London: Robson Books, 1990) p.208.

Chapter 17: The Devoted Mother

1 Christie, *An Autobiography*, p.313.

2 Clara Miller to Agatha Miller, no date. The Christie Archive Trust.

3 Frederick Miller to Agatha Miller, 15 June 1894. The Christie Archive Trust.

4 Westmacott, *Unfinished Portrait*, p.88.

5 Christie, *An Autobiography*, p.14.

6   Ibid., p.70.

7   Westmacott, *Unfinished Portrait*, p.93.

8   Talk with Mathew Prichard. September 2021.

9   Christie, *An Autobiography*, p.50.

10   Ibid., p.12.

11   Mallowan, *Mallowan's Memoirs*, p.196.

12   Agatha Christie, quoted in G.C. Ramsey, *Agatha Christie: Mistress of Mystery* (New York: Dodd, Mead and Co, 1967) p.12.

13   Christie, *An Autobiography*, p.34.

14   Agatha Christie, *Postern of Fate* (London: HarperCollins, 1973) pp.5–7, 11–13.

15   Christie, *An Autobiography*, p.4.

16   Christie, *Postern of Fate*, p.13.

17   Ibid., p.84.

18   Christie, *Star Over Bethlehem*.

19   Agatha Christie, quoted in Ramsey, *Agatha Christie: Mistress of Mystery*, p.12.

20   Ibid., p.13.

21   Mallowan, *Max Mallowan's Memoirs*, p.196.

22   Christie, *An Autobiography*, p.33.

23   Ibid., p.105.

24   Ibid., p.34.

25   Ibid., p.117.

26   Julius Green, *Agatha Christie: A Life in Theatre* (London: HarperCollins, 2018) p.34.

27   After she became a well-known authoress, her early poetry was published in *The Road of Dreams*. This collection was published in 1924. Morgan, *Agatha Christie*, p.46.

28   Agatha Christie, *Death Comes as the End* (London: HarperCollins, 2017) pp.161, 235.

29   Green, *Agatha Christie*, p. 262.

30   Christie, *An Autobiography*, p.27.

31   Frederick Miller to Agatha Miller, 27 June 1897. The Christie Archive Trust.

32   Clara Miller to Agatha Miller, 17 November, no year. The Christie Archive Trust.

33   Christie, *An Autobiography*, p.31.

34   Robyns, *The Mystery of Agatha Christie*, p.252.

35   Green, *Agatha Christie*, p.2.

36   Westmacott, *Unfinished Portrait*, p.88.

Chapter 18: Nightmares

1   Christie, 'The Road of Dreams', *Star Over Bethlehem*.

2   Christie, *An Autobiography*, p.25.

3   Morgan, *Agatha Christie*, p.30.

4   Christie, *Ordeal by Innocence*, pp.211, 213.

5   Christie, *An Autobiography*, p.42.

6   Morgan, *Agatha Christie*, p.31.

7   For a more detailed discussion, see Christie, *An Autobiography*, p.57.

8   Ibid., p.92.

9   'Heart Attacks'. The Christie Archive Trust.
10 Frederick Miller to Clara Miller, 24 October 1901. The Christie Archive Trust.
11 Westmacott, *Unfinished Portrait*, p.101.
12 Christie, *An Autobiography*, p.93.
13 Frederick Miller to Clara Miller, 9 May 1901. The Christie Archive Trust.
14 Frederick Miller to Clara Miller, 24 October 1901. The Christie Archive Trust.
15 Agatha Christie to Frederick Miller, no date. The Christie Archive Trust.
16 Quoted in Christie, *An Autobiography*, p.101.
17 Westmacott, *Unfinished Portrait*, p.101.
18 Christie, *An Autobiography*, p.100.
19 Westmacott, *Unfinished Portrait*, p.101.
20 Christie, *An Autobiography*, p.101.
21 Westmacott, *Unfinished Portrait*, p.102.
22 Christie, *An Autobiography*, p.100.
23 Westmacott, *Unfinished Portrait*, p.104.
24 Two quotations clipped in Frederick Miller's Burial Service. The Christie Archive Trust.
25 Westmacott, *Unfinished Portrait*, p.105.
26 Christie, *An Autobiography*, p.101.
27 Westmacott, *Unfinished Portrait*, p.102.
28 Christie, *An Autobiography*, pp.102–103.
29 Ibid.
30 Westmacott, *Unfinished Portrait*, p.103.
31 Ibid. 106.

Chapter 19: The Widow

1   Christie, *An Autobiography*, p.107.
2   Ibid., p.105.
3   Ibid., p.109.
4   These figures were also to inspire her Mr Quin stories. Agatha Christie, 'Author's Foreword', *Love Detectives: The Complete Quin and Satterthwaite* (London: HarperCollins, 2004).
5   Charles Osborne, *The Life and Crimes of Agatha Christie: A Biographical Companion to the Works of Agatha Christie* (London: HarperCollins, 1999) p.38.
6   After she became a well-known authoress, her early poetry was published in *The Road of Dreams*. This collection was published in 1924. Morgan, *Agatha Christie*, p.46.
7   Agatha Christie, 'Down in the Wood', quoted in Morgan, *Agatha Christie*, p.75.
8   For a full discussion of Agatha's love of Shakespeare, see Green, *Agatha Christie: A Life in Theatre*.
9   Agatha Christie, quoted in Green, *Agatha Christie*, p.9.
10 Woolf, *On Being Ill*, p.38.
11 Christie, *An Autobiography*, pp.136–7.

12 Christie, *An Autobiography*, quoted in Green, *Agatha Christie*, p.2.
13 Agatha Miller's 'Confessions', 27 October 1903. The Christie Archive Trust.
14 Westmacott, *Unfinished Portrait*, p.91.
15 Christie, *An Autobiography*, p.106.
16 Ibid., p.138.
17 Westmacott, *Unfinished Portrait*, p.113.
18 Christie, *An Autobiography*, p.116.
19 Morgan, *Agatha Christie*, p.38.
20 Westmacott, *Unfinished Portrait*, p.128.
21 Robyns, *The Mystery of Agatha Christie*, p.46.
22 Dorothy Hamilton-Johnston quoted in Robyns, *The Mystery of Agatha Christie*, p.46.
23 Christie, *An Autobiography*, pp.141–3.
24 Agatha Christie, 'Heritage', *Star Over Bethlehem*.

Chapter 20: The Confidante

1 Westmacott, *Unfinished Portrait*, p.91.
2 Ibid., p.169.
3 Agatha Christie, *The Lie* (Performed on Radio 4). Copyright Christie Archive Trust.
4 Christie, *An Autobiography*, p.118.
5 Green, *Agatha Christie*, p.43.
6 Christie, *An Autobiography*, p.118.
7 Ibid., p.120.
8 Ibid., p.119.
9 Morgan, *Agatha Christie*, p.40.
10 Christie, *An Autobiography*, p.156.
11 Westmacott, *Unfinished Portrait*, p.139.
12 Ibid., p.143.
13 Ibid., p.169.
14 Christie, *An Autobiography*, p.157.
15 Ibid., pp.163–4.
16 Ibid., p.97.
17 Westmacott, *Unfinished Portrait*, p.162.
18 Ibid., p.155.
19 Worsley, *Agatha Christie*, p.42.
20 Christie, *An Autobiography*, pp.189–95.
21 Westmacott, *Unfinished Portrait*, p.157.
22 Christie, *An Autobiography*, p.232.
23 Ibid., p.234.
24 Ibid., p.36.
25 Ibid., p.232.
26 Agatha Christie, *The Lie* (Performed on Radio 4). Copyright Christie Archive Trust.

27 Christie, *An Autobiography*, pp.229–33.
28 Ibid., p.231.
29 Mallowan, *Mallowan's Memoirs*, p.206.
30 Christie, *An Autobiography*, pp.422–3.
31 Agatha Christie, quoted in Ramsey, *Agatha Christie: Mistress of Mystery*, p.57.
32 Christie, *An Autobiography*, p.115.
33 Ibid., p.113.
34 Westmacott, *Unfinished Portrait*, p.157.
35 Ibid., p.173.
36 Christie, *An Autobiography*, p.158.

Chapter 21: Literary Ambitions

1   Interview with Mathew Prichard, 23 March 2022.
2   Max Mallowan was talking about Agatha's Mr Quin stories. Mallowan, *Mallowan's Memoirs*, p.205.
3   Agatha Christie writing as Mary Westmacott in *Unfinished Portrait*, p.125.
4   Clara Miller, 'Mrs Jordan's Ghost'. The Christie Archive Trust.
5   Agatha Christie Quoted in Ramsey, *Agatha Christie*, p.13.
6   Gwen Petty's account to Gwen Robyns, quoted in Robyns, *The Mystery of Agatha Christie*, p.39.
7   Agatha Miller, 'The House of Beauty'. The Christie Archive Trust.
8   Ibid.
9   Worsley, *Agatha Christie*, p.11.
10 This story was drastically revised and published as 'The House of Dreams' in *Sovereign Magazine* in January 1936. Morgan, *Agatha Christie*, p. 49.
11 Christie, 'The Lamp', *The Hound of Death*.
12 See 'Wireless' and 'The Mystery of the Blue Jar', *The Hound of Death*.
13 Christie, 'The Hound of Death', *The Hound of Death*.
14 Christie, 'The Last Séance', *The Hound of Death*, p.232.
15 Woolf, *The Waves*, p.99.
16 Virginia Woolf to Vanessa Bell, 21 April 1927. Woolf, *Selected Letters*, p.222.
17 Osborne, *The Life and Crimes of Agatha Christie*, p.4.
18 Eden Phillpotts to Agatha Christie, quoted in Morgan, *Agatha Christie*, p.53.

Chapter 22: Growing Apart

1   Christie, *An Autobiography*, pp.200–201.
2   Ibid., p.201.
3   Ibid., p.203.
4   Ibid., p.203.
5   Westmacott, *Unfinished Portrait*, p.189.
6   Christie, *An Autobiography*, p.221.

7   Ibid., p.224.
8   Ibid., p.226.
9   Ibid., p.247.
10 Westmacott, *Unfinished Portrait*, p.212.
11 Ibid., p.231.
12 Christie, *An Autobiography*, p.254.
13 Clara Miller, 'The Birth of Rosalind', 5 August 1919. The Christie Archive Trust.
14 Westmacott, *Unfinished Portrait*, p.231.
15 Morgan, *Agatha Christie*, p.79.

Chapter 23: Agatha Finds Her Niche

1   Christie, *An Autobiography*, p.198.
2   Ibid., p.244.
3   Ibid., p.245.
4   Agatha Christie, *The Mysterious Affair at Styles* (United Kingdom: Printed by Amazon, 2022) p.34.
5   Christie, *An Autobiography*, p.263.
6   Ibid., p.122.
7   Ibid.
8   Ibid., p.266.
9   Ibid., p.305.
10 Ibid., p.321.
11 Westmacott, *Unfinished Portrait*, pp.259–60.
12 Clara Miller to Agatha Christie, no date. The Christie Archive Trust.
13 Christie, *An Autobiography*, p.274.
14 Christie, *Ordeal by Innocence*, p.83.
15 Ibid.
16 Ibid., p.101.
17 Morgan, *Agatha Christie*, pp.87–8.
18 Agatha Christie to Clara Miller, February 1922. The Christie Archive Trust.
19 Agatha Christie to Clara Miller, 6 February 1922. The Christie Archive Trust.
20 Agatha Christie to Clara Miller, 5 August 1922. The Christie Archive Trust.
21 Agatha Christie to Rosalind Christie, no date, Pretoria. The Christie Archive Trust.
22 Christie, *An Autobiography*, p.294.
23 Agatha Christie to Clara Miller, 9 May 1922. The Christie Archive Trust.
24 Christie, *An Autobiography*, p.314.
25 Ibid., p.315.
26 Agatha Christie to Monty Miller, 23 June 1922. The Christie Archive Trust.
27 Christie, *An Autobiography*, pp.327–8.
28 Ibid., p.417.
29 Westmacott, *Unfinished Portrait*, p.283.
30 Ibid., p.260.
31 Clara Miller to Agatha Christie, 28 February, no year. The Christie Archive Trust.

32   Ibid.
33   Morgan, *Agatha Christie*, p.126.
34   Christie, *An Autobiography*, p.334.
35   Westmacott, *Unfinished Portrait*, p.286.
36   Christie, *An Autobiography*, p.334.
37   Westmacott, *Unfinished Portrait*, pp.286–7.

Chapter 24: Missing

1   Christie, *An Autobiography*, p.333.
2   Interview with Mathew Prichard, 23 March 2022.
3   Agatha Christie to Christianna Brand in 1962. Letter recently sold at auction by Brand's estate. Copy provided by The Christie Archive Trust.
4   Christie, *An Autobiography*, p.334.
5   Ibid., p.336.
6   Westmacott, *Unfinished Portrait*, p.288.
7   Ibid., p.259.
8   Ibid., p.307.
9   Ibid., pp.307–313.
10   Christie, *An Autobiography*, p.340.
11   Westmacott, *Unfinished Portrait*, p.321.
12   Morgan, *Agatha Christie*, p.153.
13   Mary Westmacott (Agatha Christie), *Giant's Bread* (London: HarperCollins, 2017) p.398.
14   Morgan, *Agatha Christie*, pp.148–59.
15   For full descriptions and suggestions about what might have happened, see the biographies of Agatha Christie by Laura Thompson, Janet Morgan and Lucy Worsley.
16   Morgan, *Agatha Christie*, pp.viii-ix.
17   Ibid., p.134.
18   Worsley, *Agatha Christie*, pp.125–30.
19   Mallowan, *Mallowan's Memoirs*, p.201.
20   Agatha Christie, 'The Man from the Sea', *Love Detectives: The Complete Quin and Satterthwaite* (London: HarperCollins, 2004) p.109.
21   Agatha Christie, *Towards Zero* (London: HarperCollins, 2017).
22   Ibid., p.203.
23   Christie, *An Autobiography*, p.337.
24   Morgan, *Agatha Christie*, p.363.
25   Christie, *An Autobiography*, p.424.
26   Agatha Christie, *They Do It with Mirrors* (London: HarperCollins, 2016) pp.54–5.
27   Agatha Christie, *Third Girl* (London: HarperCollins, 2015) p.95.
28   Christie, *An Autobiography*, p.121.
29   Ibid., p.xiii.

Chapter 25: Agatha's New Life

1   Christie, *Third Girl*, p.142.
2   Christie, *Death Comes as the End*, p.196.
3   Christie, *An Autobiography*, p.319.
4   Agatha Christie, *Five Little Pigs* (London: HarperCollins, 2013) pp.134–5.
5   Interview with Mathew Prichard, 23 March 2022.
6   Mallowan, *Mallowan's Memoirs*, p.195.
7   Christie, *An Autobiography*, p.366.
8   Max Mallowan, quoted in Morgan, *Agatha Christie*, p.357.
9   Christie, *An Autobiography*, p.400.
10 Agatha Christie writing as Mary Westmacott, *Unfinished Portrait*, p.336.
11 Max Mallowan to Agatha Christie, 25 October 1931. The Christie Archive Trust. Quoted in Worsley, *Agatha Christie*, p.201.
12 Agatha Christie to Max Mallowan, 1944. The Christie Archive Trust.
13 For a full discussion of their marriage see Laura Thompson's and Lucy Worsley's biographies.
14 Christie, *An Autobiography*, p.402.
15 See Rachel Trethewey, *The Churchill Girls: The Story of Winston's Daughters* (Cheltenham: The History Press, 2021).
16 Quoted in Thompson, *Agatha Christie*, p.36.
17 Christie, *An Autobiography*, p.474.
18 Janet Morgan, *Agatha Christie*, p.243.
19 Christie, *An Autobiography*, p.487.
20 Interview with Mathew Prichard, 23 March 2022.
21 Ibid.
22 Ibid.
23 Talk with Mathew Prichard, September 2021.
24 Interview with Mathew Prichard, 23 March 2022.
25 Ibid.
26 Ibid.
27 'Foreword. Mathew Prichard'. Green, *Agatha Christie*, p.v.
28 For a full discussion of Rosalind's relationship with her mother see Thompson, *Agatha Christie*.
29 Interview with Mathew Prichard, 23 March 2022.
30 Agatha Christie, 'Confessions', 19 April 1954. The Christie Archive Trust.
31 Ibid.

Chapter 26: Clara's Literary Legacy

1   Christie, *An Autobiography*, p.418.
2   Ibid., p.456.
3   Ibid., p.504.

4 Gillian Gill puts Agatha's attitude to her writing in the context of Gilbert and Gubar's theories in *The Mad Woman in the Attic*, about the 'anxiety of authorship' experienced by female writers. See Gill, *Agatha Christie*, pp.209–10.

5 Quoted in Thompson, *Agatha Christie*, p.26.

6 Interview with Mathew Prichard, 23 March 2022.

7 Merja Makinen, *Agatha Christie: Investigating Femininity* (Basingstoke: Palgrave Macmillan, 2006) pp.1, 14.

8 Gill, *Agatha Christie*, p.7.

9 Agatha Christie, *Appointment With Death* (London: HarperCollins, 1938) p.84.

10 Gill, *Agatha Christie*, p.8.

11 Christie, *An Autobiography*, p.419.

12 Gill, *Agatha Christie*, p.10.

13 Rowse, *Memories of Men and Women*, p.89.

14 Mallowan, *Mallowan's Memories*, p.195.

15 Robert Barnard claims that her detective fiction reveals very little of Agatha's feelings or opinions and that this detachment is one of her great strengths as a puzzle-maker. Robert Barnard, *A Talent to Deceive: An Appreciation of Agatha Christie* (London: Fontana/Collins, 1979).

16 Julian Symons, 'Agatha Christie Talks to Julian Symons About the Gentle Art of Murder', *The Sunday Times*, 15 October 1961. Quoted in Cade, *Agatha Christie and the Eleven Missing Days*.

17 Mallowan, *Mallowan's Memories*, p. 209.

18 Interview with Mathew Prichard, 23 March 2022.

19 'The Mary Westmacotts', *The Home of Agatha Christie Website*.

20 Talk with Mathew and Lucy Prichard, September 2021.

21 These quotes came from people who would know. Max Mallowan describes her 'inner sensitivity' and 'exceptional imagination', while Agatha herself used the term 'dangerous intensity of affection'. Westmacott, *Unfinished Portrait* p.91.

22 Mallowan, *Mallowan's Memories*, p.195.

23 Westmacott, *Unfinished Portrait*, p.334.

24 Mary Westmacott (Agatha Christie), *Absent in the Spring* (London: HarperCollins, 2017).

25 Christie, *An Autobiography*, p.485.

26 Mary Westmacott (Agatha Christie), *A Daughter's a Daughter* (London: HarperCollins, 2017).

27 There are slight differences; for example, the ages of characters and the dates of events are slightly different. Celia only has one sibling, a brother called Cyril and the grandmother lives in Wimbledon not Ealing but many of the same anecdotes are repeated in both the autobiography and the novel.

28 Cade, *Agatha Christie and the Eleven Missing Days*.

29 Westmacott, *Unfinished Portrait*, p.15.

30 Interview with Mathew Prichard, 23 March 2022.

Part Three: Aurelia and Sylvia

Chapter 27: The Outsider

1   Aurelia Plath (ed.), *Sylvia Plath. Letters Home. Selected and edited by Aurelia Schober Plath* (London, Boston: Faber and Faber, 1976) p.4.

2   Karl Terzaghi's Diary, 26:1, 24 October 1926. Quoted in Catherine Rankovic, 'Otto was a Rebound', Studying Aurelia Plath, 20 July 2019 (https://aureliaplath.blogspot.com/2019/07/otto-plath-was-rebound.html. Retrieved 13 November 2021).

3   Heather Clark, *Red Comet: The Short Life and Blazing Art of Sylvia Plath* (London: Jonathan Cape, 2020) p.22.

4   For a detailed account of Sylvia's heritage see Andrew Wilson, *Mad Girl's Love Song: Sylvia Plath and Life Before Ted* (London: Simon and Schuster, 2013) p.22.

5   Conversation with Catherine Rankovic, 14 November 2021.

6   Catherine Rankovic has pointed out that their immediate neighbours were German or Austrian while Irish immigrant families lived a few blocks away. Catherine Rankovic, 'Aurelia Plath's Birthplace and the Myth of her Childhood', Studying Aurelia Plath, 16 February 2021 (https://aureliaplath.blogspot.com/2021/02/aurelia-plaths-real-childhood-home.html).

7   Aurelia Plath, *Letters Home*, p.4.

8   Clark, *Red Comet*, p.23.

9   Aurelia Plath, 'Letters Written in the Actuality of Spring' in Paul Alexander (ed.), *Ariel Ascending: Writings About Sylvia Plath* (New York: Harper and Row, 1985) p.215.

10   Aurelia Plath, *Letters Home*, p.5.

11   Clark, *Red Comet*, p.23.

12   Sylvia Plath, 'Ocean 1212-W', *Johnny Panic and the Bible of Dreams* (London: Faber and Faber, 1979) p.119.

13   Catherine Rankovic, 'The White Waiter: Sylvia Plath's Grandfather at Work', Studying Aurelia Plath, 2 March 2021 (https://aureliaplath.blogspot.com/2021/03/the-white-waiter-sylvia-plaths.html).

14   Aurelia Plath, *Letters Home*, p.3.

15   Email from Catherine Rankovic, 31 October 2022.

16   'Commentary for *Letters Home* by AP. Typescript (originals and carbons), (34) pages (some full pages, some on scraps of paper). Handwritten note by AP on first page. "Carbons from Preface and Commentaries. Some not submitted." Handwritten comments and deletions by AP, including indication of whether or not item was included in published version of *Letters Home*.' Sylvia Plath Collection (MRBC-MS -00045). Mortimer Rare Book Collection Repository Box 30 Folder 67. Smith College Special Collections.

17   For Aurelia's early achievements, see Rankovic, Studying Aurelia Plath. Website.

18   Aurelia Plath, *Letters Home*, p.5.

19 Catherine Rankovic, '"Forbidden Fruit": Aurelia Plath's Poems', Studying Aurelia Plath, 11 February 2021 (https://aureliaplath.blogspot.com/2021/02/forbidden-fruit-aurelia-plaths-poems.html).
20 Catherine Rankovic, 'Aurelia Moves Out of the House', Studying Aurelia Plath, 9 March 2021 (https://aureliaplath.blogspot.com/2021/03/aurelia-moves-out-of-the-house.html).
21 Information on Aurelia Plath's early life from Catherine Rankovic's Studying Aurelia Plath website.
22 Aurelia Plath, *Letters Home*, p.5.

Chapter 28: The Genius Soulmate

1   Aurelia Plath, *Letters Home*, p.5.
2   Richard E. Goodman, *Karl Terzaghi: The Engineer as Artist* (Virginia: Virginia ASCE Press, 1998) p.34.
3   Karl Terzaghi's Diary, 26:1, 31 October 1926 (The Terzaghi Library, NGI, Oslo) pp.125–6.
4   Reint de Boer, *The Engineer and The Scandal: A Piece of Science History* (Springer Science and Business Media, 12 December 2005).
5   Karl Terzaghi's Diary. 26:1. 24 August 1926 (The Terzaghi Library) p.6.
6   Aurelia Plath, *Letters Home*, p.6.
7   Ibid.
8   Karl Terzaghi's Lectures, quoted in Goodman, *Karl Terzaghi*, p.91.
9   Catherine Rankovic thinks Aurelia 'probably had a daddy issue' and saw Karl as her only chance to marry. Email 31 October 2022.
10 Catherine Rankovic, 'Aurelia Plath's First Love', Studying Aurelia Plath, 9 May 2019 (https://aureliaplath.blogspot.com/2019/05/aurelia-plaths-first-love.html).
11 Karl Terzaghi's Diary, 26:1, October 1926 (The Terzaghi Library) p.100.
12 Ibid., 24 October 1926 (The Terzaghi Library) pp.107–112.
13 Karl Terzaghi's Diary, 25:3, 31 December 1926 (The Terzaghi Library) p.147.
14 Karl Terzaghi's Diary, 27:1, 30 May 1927 (The Terzaghi Library) pp.15–18.
15 Ibid., 13 May 1927 (The Terzaghi Library) p.21.
16 Ibid., May/June 1927 (The Terzaghi Library) pp.37–40.
17 Ibid., 13 June 1927 (The Terzaghi Library) pp.45–6.
18 Ibid., 29 July 1927 to 1 August 1927 (The Terzaghi Library) pp.62–72.
19 Ibid., 6 August 1927 (The Terzaghi Library) p.100.
20 Letter from Aurelia Plath to Frieda Hughes, 21 April 1978, Cruickshank Archive. Quoted in Wilson, *Mad Girl's Love Song*, p.24.
21 Ibid.
22 Aurelia Plath, *Letters Home*, p.6.
23 Goodman, *Karl Terzaghi*, p.111.
24 Karl Terzaghi's Diary. 27:1, 6 August 1927 (The Terzaghi Library) p.100.
25 Ibid., 29 September 1927 (The Terzaghi Library) p.130.
26 Ibid., 2 October 1927 (The Terzaghi Library) pp.134–5.

27 Ibid., 4 December 1927 (The Terzaghi Library) p.167.

28 Karl Terzaghi's Diary. 27:2, 18 January 1928 (The Terzaghi Library) pp.6–7.

29 Ibid., 6 April 1928 (The Terzaghi Library) p.62.

30 Conversation with Catherine Rankovic, 14 November 2021.

31 Catherine Rankovic thinks this letter may have been for Ruth Doggett, Karl's future wife, as he wrote it while travelling on a steamer line.

32 Karl Terzaghi to 'Darling', 17 July, no year. Insert in Diary 27:3 (The Terzaghi Library).

33 Karl Terzaghi's Diary. 27:2, 6 November 1928 (The Terzaghi Library) p.103.

34 Ibid., 3 December 1928 (The Terzaghi Library) p.131.

35 Conversation with Catherine Rankovic, 14 November 2021.

36 Quoted in Goodman, *Karl Terzaghi*, p.111.

37 Ibid., p.121

38 Letter from Aurelia Plath to Frieda Hughes, 21 April 1978. Cruickshank Archive, quoted in Wilson, *Mad Girl's Love Song*, p.24.

Chapter 29: Second Best

1 Catherine Rankovic, 'Otto Plath was a Rebound', Studying Aurelia Plath, 20 July 2019 (https://aureliaplath.blogspot.com/2019/07/otto-plath-was-rebound.html).

2 Letter from Aurelia Plath to Frieda Hughes, 29 September 1973. Cruickshank Archive, quoted in Wilson, *Mad Girl's Love Song*, p.16.

3 Aurelia Plath, *Letters Home*, p.6.

4 Ibid.

5 Letter from Aurelia Plath to Frieda Hughes, 29 September 1973. Cruickshank Archive, quoted in Wilson, *Mad Girl's Love Song*, p.16.

6 Aurelia Plath, *Letters Home*, pp.6–7.

7 Ibid.

8 Aurelia Plath, *The Paracelsus of History and Literature* (Boston: Boston University, 1930) p.70.

9 Ibid., 'Introduction'.

10 Ibid., pp.20–1.

11 Ibid., 'Introduction'.

12 Aurelia Plath to Leonard Sanazaro, 2 December 1984 (Sanazaro MSS. Lilly Library, Indiana University, Bloomington, Indiana).

13 Aurelia Plath, *Letters Home*, p10.

14 Clark, *Red Comet*, p.7.

15 For a full discussion of Otto's early life see Plath, *Letters Home*, pp.8–10.

16 Letter from Aurelia Plath to Frieda Hughes, 24 March 1978. Cruickshank Archive, quoted in Wilson, *Mad Girl's Love Song*, p.19.

17 Clark, *Red Comet*, p.14.

18 Ibid., p.16.

19 Wilson, *Mad Girl's Love Song*, p.20.

20 Conversation with Catherine Rankovic, 14 November 2021.
21 Leonard Sanazaro to Aurelia Plath, 19 June 1983 (Sanazaro MSS. Lilly Library, Indiana University, Bloomington, Indiana).

Chapter 30: The Full-Time Homemaker

1 Sylvia Plath, *The Bell Jar* (London: Faber and Faber, 2005) pp.80–1.
2 Clark, *Red Comet*, p.30.
3 Ibid., p.26.
4 'Commentary for *Letters Home* by Aurelia Plath'. Smith College Special Collections.
5 Aurelia Plath, *Letters Home*, p.13.
6 'Commentary for *Letters Home* by Aurelia Plath'. Smith College Special Collections.
7 Wilson, *Mad Girl's Love Song*, p.21.
8 Andrew Wilson cites the opening of the first chapter of *Bumblebees and Their Ways*: 'If one takes a walk on a clear, sunny day in middle April, when the first willows are in bloom, one may often see young bumblebee queens eagerly sipping nectar from the catkins. It is a delightful thing to pause and watch these queens, clad in their costumes of rich velvet, their wings not yet torn by the long foraging flights which they will be obliged to take later.' Quoted in Wilson, *Mad Girl's Love Song*, pp.21–2.
9 O.E. Plath. *A Muscid Larva of the San Francisco Bay Region Which Sucks the Blood of Nestling Birds* (Berkeley, California: University of California Publications in Zoology, 1919).
10 Aurelia Plath, *Letters Home*, p.12.
11 Clark, *Red Comet*, p.26.
12 Aurelia Plath, *Letters Home*, p.10.
13 Fredrik Logevall, *JFK: Volume 1* (New York: Viking, Random House, 2020) p.48.
14 Aurelia Plath, *Letters Home*, p.10.
15 Ibid., p.12.
16 Logevall, *JFK*, p.46.
17 Ibid., p.48.
18 Aurelia Plath's Baby Book for Sylvia, quoted in Wilson, *Mad Girl's Love Song*, p.27.
19 Aurelia Plath, *Letters Home*, p.16.
20 Ibid., p.13.
21 Clark, *Red Comet*, p.18.
22 Aurelia Plath, *Letters Home*, p.12.
23 Sylvia Plath to Dr Ruth Beuscher, 22 September 1962. Quoted in Clark, *Red Comet*, p.752.
24 Sylvia Plath, 'Ocean 1212-W', *Johnny Panic and the Bible of Dreams*, pp.119–20.
25 Aurelia Plath, *Letters Home*, p.13.
26 Sylvia Plath, 'Ocean 1212-W', *Johnny Panic and the Bible of Dreams*, pp.119–20.

27 Aurelia Plath taped interview with Richard Larschan, 30 October 1986.
28 Sylvia Plath, 'Ocean 1212-W', *Johnny Panic and the Bible of Dreams*, pp.19–20.

Chapter 31: Daddy's Girl

1 Wilson, *Mad Girl's Love Song*, p.29.
2 Linda Heller, 'Aurelia Plath: A Lasting Commitment,' draft, 8p, Photocopy of typescript with corrections and comments by AP, 2/24/76. Sylvia Plath Collection (MRBC-MS-00045). Mortimer Rare Book Collection. Box 30 Series 11 and 12 Folder 54. Smith College Special Collections.
3 Aurelia Plath, *Letters Home*, p.16.
4 Ibid., p.19.
5 Clark, *Red Comet*, p.39.
6 Aurelia Plath, *Letters Home*, p.19.
7 Sylvia Plath, 'Among the Bumblebees', *Johnny Panic and the Bible of Dreams*, p.260.
8 Clark, *Red Comet*, p.35.
9 Harriet Rosenstein interview with Perry and Shirley Norton, 1971–4. Quoted in Clark, *Red Comet*, p.35.
10 Aurelia Plath, *Letters Home*, p.19.
11 Quoted in Clark, *Red Comet*, p.42.
12 Sylvia Plath, 'Among the Bumblebees', *Johnny Panic and the Bible of Dreams*, p.264.
13 Clark, *Red Comet*, p.35.
14 Sylvia Plath, 'Among the Bumblebees', *Johnny Panic and the Bible of Dreams*, p.261.
15 Video. *Poets of New England: Sylvia Plath and the Myth of the Monstrous Mother.*
16 Sylvia Plath, 'Among the Bumblebees', *Johnny Panic and the Bible of Dreams*, p.263.
17 Aurelia Plath, *Letters Home*, p.22.
18 Aurelia Plath, draft introduction to *Letters Home*. Smith College Special Collections.
19 Sylvia Plath, 'Among the Bumblebees', *Johnny Panic and the Bible of Dreams*, p.264.
20 Ibid.
21 Aurelia Plath, *Letters Home*, pp.16–18.
22 Ibid. 22.
23 Sylvia Plath, 'Among the Bumblebees', *Johnny Panic and the Bible of Dreams*, p.266.
24 Aurelia Plath, *Letters Home*, p.23.
25 Sylvia Plath, 'Among the Bumblebees', *Johnny Panic and the Bible of Dreams*, p.264.
26 Ibid., p.266.
27 Aurelia Plath, *Letters Home*, p.23.
28 Clark, *Red Comet*, p.46.
29 Aurelia Plath, *Letters Home*, pp.24–5.

30   Ibid., p.25.
31   Sylvia Plath, *The Bell Jar*, p.161.
32   Ibid., p.159.
33   Aurelia Plath, *Letters Home*, pp.27–8.
34   Clark, *Red Comet*, p.35.
35   Ibid., p.46.
36   Aurelia Plath, *Letters Home*, p.13.
37   Clark, *Red Comet*, p.8.
38   Sylvia Plath, *The Bell Jar*, p.30.
39   For a full discussion of this research see Clark, *Red Comet*, p.49.
40   15 April 1924. Virginia Woolf, *Selected Diaries*. (London: Vintage Books, 2008) p.181.
41   Sylvia Plath, 'Among the Bumblebees', *Johnny Panic and the Bible of Dreams*, p.259.
42   Clark, *Red Comet*, p.19.

Chapter 32: The Pact

1   Aurelia Plath, *Letters Home*, p.25.
2   Interview with Ruth Geissler, 12 February 2011. Quoted in Wilson, *Mad Girl's Love Song*, p.37.
3   Sylvia's friend Elizabeth Compton Sigmund made this suggestion in Elizabeth Sigmund and Gail Crowther, *Sylvia Plath: A Year's Turning* (Croydon: Fonthill, 2014) p.20.
4   Clark, *Red Comet*, p.47.
5   Aurelia Plath, *Letters Home*, p.25.
6   Mary Westmacott (Agatha Christie), *A Daughter's a Daughter* (London: HarperCollins, 2017).
7   Sylvia Plath, 'Ocean 1212-W', *Johnny Panic and the Bible of Dreams*, p.124.
8   This was a genuine threat for Germans living in America as a detention centre had been set up in East Boston to house German detainees. Clark, *Red Comet*, p.53.
9   Sylvia Plath, 'The Shadow', *Johnny Panic and the Bible of Dreams*, pp.335–8.
10   Ibid.
11   Aurelia Plath, *Letters Home*, p.29.
12   Ibid., p.28.
13   Sylvia Plath, 27 December 1958 in Kukil, *The Journals of Sylvia Plath 1950–1962* (London: Faber and Faber, 2000) p.446.
14   Clark, *Red Comet*, p.921.
15   Heller, 'Aurelia Plath: A Lasting Commitment'. Smith College Special Collections.
16   Ibid.
17   Aurelia Plath, *Letters Home*, p.28.
18   Heller, 'Aurelia Plath: A Lasting Commitment'. Smith College Special Collections.

19 Aurelia Plath, *Letters Home*, p.29.
20 Pat O'Neal quoted in Clark, *Red Comet*, p.68.
21 Sylvia Plath to Dr Beuscher, 28 September 1962. Quoted in Clark, *Red Comet*, p.67.
22 Wilson, *Mad Girl's Love Song*, p.39.
23 Aurelia Plath, 'Letters Written in the Actuality of Spring' in Alexander, *Ariel Ascending*, p.214.
24 Sylvia to Dr Beuscher, quoted in Clark, *Red Comet*, p.48.
25 7 May 1957. Aurelia Plath, *Letters Home*, p.310.
26 Wilson, *Mad Girl's Love Song*, p.43.

Chapter 33: The Teacher

1   Sylvia Plath, 'America! America!', *Johnny Panic and the Bible of Dreams*, p.35.
2   Clark, *Red Comet*, p.63.
3   Aurelia Plath, *Letters Home*, pp.29–30.
4   Clark, *Red Comet*, p.69.
5   Aurelia Plath, 'For the Authors' Series Talk at Wellesley College Club, 16 March 1976. Sylvia Plath Collection (MRBC-MS-00045). Mortimer Rare Book Collection. Box 30 Folder 58. Smith College Special Collections.
6   Aurelia Plath, *Letters Home*, p.31.
7   Wilson, *Mad Girl's Love Song*, p.55.
8   Logevall, *JFK*, p.48.
9   Quoted in Barbara A. Perry, *Rose Kennedy: The Life and Times of a Political Matriarch* (New York, London: W.W. Norton and Co, 2013) p.80.
10 Quoted in ibid., p.50.
11 Logevall, *JFK*, p.48.
12 'Commentary for *Letters Home* by Aurelia Plath'. Smith College Special Collections.
13 For a full discussion of the link between reading, writing and intimacy for them, see Janet Badia, '"I May Hate Her, But That's Not All": Mother–Daughter Intimacy in the Plath Archive' in Anita Helle, Amanda Golden and Maeve O'Brien (eds), *The Bloomsbury Handbook to Sylvia Plath* (London, New York, Oxford: Bloomsbury Academic, 2022) pp.219–33.
14 Sylvia Plath, 'Ocean 1212-W', *Johnny Panic and the Bible of Dreams*, p.118.
15 'The Forsaken Merman', *Encyclopaedia Britannica*. Website.
16 Sylvia Plath, 'Ocean 1212-W', *Johnny Panic and the Bible of Dreams*, p.118.
17 Catherine Rankovic, '"Forbidden Fruit": Aurelia Plath's Poems', Studying Aurelia Plath, 11 February 2021 (https://aureliaplath.blogspot.com/2021/02/forbidden-fruit-aurelia-plaths-poems.html).
18 Sylvia Plath, 'Ocean 1212-W', *Johnny Panic and the Bible of Dreams*, p.118.
19 Ibid., p.35.
20 'Lorelei. German Legend', *Encyclopaedia Britannica*. Website.
21 Sylvia Plath, 'Lorelei', *Collected Poems* (London: Faber and Faber, 1981) pp.94–5.

22 Aurelia Plath, *Letters Home*, p.19.
23 Ibid., p.31.
24 Clark, *Red Comet*, p.103.
25 Aurelia Plath, *Letters Home*, p.32.
26 For a full analysis of Nietzsche's influence on Sylvia see Wilson, *Mad Girl's Love Song*, pp.106–108.
27 Friedrich Nietzsche, *Thus Spoke Zarathustra* (London: Penguin Classics, 1969) p.67.
28 Ibid., p.331.
29 Sylvia Plath, 'Lady Lazarus', *Collected Poems*, pp.244–7.
30 Sylvia Plath, 'Edge', *Collected Poems*, pp.272–3.
31 Aurelia Plath, 'For the Authors' Series Talk at Wellesley College Club, 16 March 1976. Smith College Special Collections.
32 Warren Plath to Edward Butscher, 31 August 1975. Quoted in Clark, *Red Comet*, p.22.
33 Quoted in Wilson, *Mad Girl's Love Song*, p.54.
34 Wilbury Crockett's interview with Harriet Rosenstein. Quoted in Catherine Rankovic, 'Beyond "Medusa" and "Mrs Greenwood": From the Rosenstein Papers', Studying Aurelia Plath, 8 June 2021 (https://aureliaplath.blogspot.com/2021/06/beyond-medusa-and-mrs-greenwood-from.html).
35 Betsy Powley Wallingford quoted in Clark, *Red Comet*, p.21.

Chapter 34: Too Close for Comfort

1   Clark, *Red Comet*, p.91.
2   Aurelia Plath, *Letters Home*, p.29.
3   Ibid., p.37.
4   Clark, *Red Comet*, p.31.
5   Aurelia Plath draft introduction to *Letters Home*. Smith College Special Collections.
6   Aurelia Plath, *Letters Home*, p.38.
7   Quoted in Clark, *Red Comet*, p.93.
8   Ibid.
9   Notes from Sylvia Plath's diary 1949, in 'Commentary for *Letters Home* by Aurelia Plath'. Smith College Special Collections.
10 Clark, *Red Comet*, p.121.
11 Ibid., p.120.
12 Aurelia Plath, *Letters Home*, p.32.
13 Clark, *Red Comet*, p.76.
14 Aurelia Plath, *Letters Home*, p.38.
15 Dr Ruth Beuscher interview with Aurelia Plath, 15 September 1953. Quoted in Clark, *Red Comet*, p.96.
16 Sylvia Plath, Notes on interview with Ruth Beuscher, 12 December 1958 in Kukil, *The Journals*, p.432.

17 Dr Ruth Beuscher interview with Aurelia Plath, 15 September 1953. Quoted in Clark, *Red Comet*, p.96.
18 Sylvia Plath, (121) in Kukil, *The Journals*, p.98.
19 Sylvia Plath, (62) in Kukil, *The Journals*, p.77.
20 Sylvia Plath, 3 November 1952, in Kukil, *The Journals*, p.51.
21 Sylvia Plath, (62) in Kukil, *The Journals*, p.54.
22 Ibid.
23 Wilson, *Mad Girl's Love Song*, p.42.
24 Clark, *Red Comet*, p.xx.
25 Sylvia Plath, 'I thought I could not be hurt'. Quoted in Aurelia Plath, *Letters Home*, p.33.
26 Clark, *Red Comet*, p.88.
27 Ibid.
28 Aurelia Plath, *Letters Home*, p.36.
29 Clark, *Red Comet*, pp.122–3.
30 Sylvia Plath, 'Diary Supplement' titled 'Reflection of a 17-Year-Old', 13 November 1949. Aurelia Plath, *Letters Home*, p.40.
31 Ibid., p.32.
32 Ibid., p.37.
33 Wilson, *Mad Girl's Love Song*, p.102.
34 'Notes Toward the Introduction', 'Commentary for *Letters Home* by Aurelia Plath'. Smith College Special Collections.
35 Wilson, *Mad Girl's Love Song*, p.101.
36 Clark, *Red Comet*, p.125.
37 Sylvia Plath, 'America! America!', *Johnny Panic and the Bible of Dreams*, pp.35–6.
38 Conversation with Catherine Rankovic, 14 November 2021.
39 Wilson, *Mad Girl's Love Song*, p.133.
40 Ibid., p.138.
41 Sylvia based characters on both her mother and Mrs Prouty in *The Bell Jar*.

Chapter 35: Smith Girl

1 Aurelia Plath, 'For the Authors' Series Talk at Wellesley College Club, 16 March 1976. Smith College Special Collections.
2 Catherine Rankovic, email 31 October 2022.
3 Clark, *Red Comet*, p.152.
4 27 November 1950. Aurelia Plath, *Letters Home*, p.60.
5 Clark, *Red Comet*, p.139.
6 Kukil, *The Journals*, p.36.
7 Aurelia Plath, 'For the Authors' Series Talk at Wellesley College Club, 16 March 1976. Smith College Special Collections.
8 Clark, *Red Comet*, p.162.
9 Aurelia Plath, draft introduction to *Letters Home*. Smith College Special Collections.

10 11 August 1951. Aurelia Plath, *Letters Home*, pp.72–3.

11 Sylvia Plath, 29 March 1951 in Kukil, *The Journals*, p.53.

12 Sylvia Plath to Warren Plath, 12 May 1953. Aurelia Plath, *Letters Home*, p.112.

13 These comments come from notes and tapes of 1970s interviews with Sylvia Plath's friends in the Harriet Rosenstein Research Files at Emory University. Quoted in Catherine Rankovic, 'Beyond "Medusa" and "Mrs Greenwood": From the Rosenstein Papers', Studying Aurelia Plath, 8 June 2021 (https://aureliaplath.blogspot.com/2021/06/beyond-medusa-and-mrs-greenwood.html).

14 Sylvia Plath, 15 June 1951 in Kukil, *The Journals*, pp.64–5.

15 Wilson, *Mad Girl's Love Song*, pp.207–208.

16 Aurelia Plath, *Letters Home*, p.32.

17 Wilson, *Mad Girl's Love Song*, p.42.

18 Sylvia Plath, 29 March 1951 in Kukil, *The Journals*, p.70.

19 Sylvia Plath, (121) in Kukil, *The Journals*, p.98.

20 Wilson, *Mad Girl's Love Song*, p.141.

21 Anne Stevenson, *Bitter Fame: A Life of Sylvia Plath* (Boston: Houghton Mifflin Co, 1989) p.40.

22 Clark, *Red Comet*, pp.165–6. For a full discussion of Sylvia's relationships with men also see Wilson, *Mad Girl's Love Song*.

23 16 May 1951. Aurelia Plath, *Letters Home*, p.70.

24 Sylvia Plath, (121) in Kukil, *The Journals*, p.98.

25 Clark, *Red Comet*, p.230.

26 Sylvia Plath, 14 November 1952 in Kukil, *The Journals*, p.153.

27 Sylvia Plath, 3 November 1952 in Kukil, *The Journals*, p.149.

28 Ibid.

29 Clark, *Red Comet*, p.163.

30 Ibid., p.212.

31 'About the Author: Meet Sylvia Plath' in Sylvia Plath, *Ariel: The Restored Edition* (London, New York: Harper Perennial, 2004) p.2.

32 23 February 1953. Aurelia Plath, *Letters Home*, p.103.

33 For a full discussion of Aurelia's role see Janet Badia, '"I May Hate Her"' p.224.

34 11 June 1952. Aurelia Plath, *Letters Home*, pp.87–8.

35 7 February 1952. Aurelia Plath, *Letters Home*, p.83.

36 15 May 1953, Sylvia Plath to Warren Plath, 12 May 1953. Aurelia Plath, *Letters Home*, p.114.

37 5 November 1952. Aurelia Plath, *Letters Home*, p.95.

38 Sylvia Plath to Warren Plath, 12 May 1953. Aurelia Plath, *Letters Home*, p.112.

39 Sylvia Plath to Warren Plath, 12 May 1953. Aurelia Plath, *Letters Home*, p.113.

Chapter 36: Crisis Point

1 Aurelia Plath to Marcia Brown, summer 1953. Quoted in Wilson, *Mad Girl's Love Song*, p.260.

2 Aurelia Plath, *Letters Home*, p.123.

3   Biographer Andrew Wilson puts forward the theory that rather than Sylvia being rejected from the O'Connor course, Aurelia might have decided it would be better for the family if her daughter spent the summer at home. In her usually meticulously kept archives of material relating to Sylvia there is no rejection letter from Harvard and Aurelia told Sylvia's friend Marcia that her daughter had given up the idea of attending the summer school because of her problems at home. Wilson, *Mad Girl's Love Song*, p.261.

4   Aurelia Plath, *Letters Home*, p.123.

5   Clark, *Red Comet*, p.260.

6   'About the Author: Meet Sylvia Plath', in Sylvia Plath, *Ariel: The Restored Edition*, p.3.

7   29 November 1956. Aurelia Plath, *Letters Home*, p.133.

8   Ibid., pp.123–4.

9   Clark, *Red Comet*, p.261.

10 Ibid., p.265.

11 Sylvia Plath, Letter June–July 1953 in Kukil, *The Journals*, Appendix 5.

12 Sylvia Plath, Notes on interviews with Ruth Beuscher, 12 December 1958 in Kukil, *The Journals*, p.433.

13 Sylvia Plath, 'Tongues of Stone', *Johnny Panic and The Bible of Dreams*, p.271.

14 Sylvia Plath, *The Bell Jar*, p.118.

15 Sylvia Plath, 14 July 1953 in Kukil, *The Journals*, p.187.

16 Aurelia Plath, *Letters Home*, p.124.

17 Ibid.

18 Sylvia Plath, *The Bell Jar*, pp.130, 139–40.

19 Clark, *Red Comet*, p.273.

20 Wilson, *Mad Girl's Love Song*, p.265.

21 Sylvia Plath, 3 January 1957–11 March 1957 in Kukil, *The Journals*, p.269.

22 Clark, *Red Comet*, p.xxii.

23 Kukil, *The Journals*, p.44.

24 Wilson, *Mad Girl's Love Song*, pp.228–9.

25 Sylvia Plath, 3 January 1957–11 March 1957 in Kukil, *The Journals*, p.269.

26 Sylvia Plath to E., 28 December 1953. Aurelia Plath, *Letters Home*, pp.130–1.

27 Ibid., p125.

28 Ibid.

29 Ibid.

30 Clark, *Red Comet*, p.275.

31 Aurelia Plath, *Letters Home*, p.125.

32 Sylvia Plath, *The Bell Jar*, p.166.

33 Aurelia Plath to Olive Higgins Prouty, 29 August 1953. Quoted in Clark, *Red Comet*, p.278.

34 Olive Higgins Prouty to Aurelia Plath, 22 October 1953. Quoted in Clark, *Red Comet*, p.291.

35 Olive Higgins Prouty to Aurelia Plath, 2 September 1953. Aurelia Plath, *Letters Home*, p.127.

36 Wilson, *Mad Girl's Love Song*, p.277.

37 Clark, *Red Comet*, p.287.
38 Ibid., p.290.
39 Sylvia Plath, *The Bell Jar*, p.195.
40 Clark, *Red Comet*, p.292.
41 Sylvia Plath, *The Bell Jar*, p.227.
42 Clark, *Red Comet*, p.292.
43 Aurelia Plath to Judith Kroll, 1 December 1978. Quoted in Clark, *Red Comet*, p.292.
44 'Commentary for *Letters Home* by Aurelia Plath'. Smith College Special Collections.
45 Ibid.
46 Aurelia Plath, 'For the Authors' Series Talk at Wellesley College Club, 16 March 1976. Smith College Special Collections.
47 Aurelia Plath to Judith Kroll, 1 December 1978. Quoted in Clark, *Red Comet*, p.292.
48 Aurelia Plath, 'For the Authors' Series Talk at Wellesley College Club, 16 March 1976. Smith College Special Collections.
49 Andrew Wilson, *Mad Girl's Love Song*, p.282.
50 Interview Dr Ruth Beuscher with Harriet Rosenstein, 16 June 1970. Quoted in Catherine Rankovic, 'A Birthday Present for Aurelia', Studying Aurelia Plath, 26 April 2021 (https://aureliaplath.blogspot.com/2021/04/a-birthday-present-for-aurelia.html).
51 Clark, *Red Comet*, p.303.
52 Ibid., p.176.
53 'Commentary for *Letters Home* by Aurelia Plath'. Smith College Special Collections.
54 Clark, *Red Comet*, p.302.
55 Ibid., p.303.
56 Wilson, *Mad Girl's Love Song*, pp.283–7.
57 Aurelia Plath, *Letters Home*, p.129.
58 'Commentary for *Letters Home* by Aurelia Plath'. Smith College Special Collections.
59 Sylvia Plath to E., 28 December 1953. Aurelia Plath, *Letters Home*, p.131.
60 Aurelia Plath to Olive Higgins Prouty, 9 December 1953. Quoted in 'Commentary for *Letters Home* by Aurelia Plath'. Smith College Special Collections.
61 Sylvia Plath. Quoted in *Sylvia Plath – Inside the Bell Jar*. BBC Four. 10 October 2021.
62 Aurelia Plath, *Letters Home*, p.134.
63 Aurelia Plath, 'Letters Written in the Actuality of Spring' in Alexander, *Ariel Ascending*, p.216.
64 Clark, *Red Comet*, p.346.
65 For a full discussion of Sylvia's love life see Wilson, *Mad Girl's Love Song*.
66 Clark, *Red Comet*, pp.363–4.

67 Aurelia Plath, *Letters Home*, p.134.
68 Clark, *Red Comet*, pp.324, 336.
69 Richard Sassoon to Harriet Rosenstein, quoted in Clark, *Red Comet*, p.364.
70 30 August 1954. Aurelia Plath, *Letters Home*, p.140.
71 Sylvia Plath to Warren Plath, 28 July 1955. Aurelia Plath, *Letters Home*, p.178.
72 Aurelia Plath interview with Richard Larschan on tape.
73 Aurelia Plath, *Letters Home*, p.134.
74 Sylvia Plath to Aurelia Plath, 10 April 1955 excised from the letter dated 11 February in *Letters Home*. Quoted in Wilson, *Mad Girl's Love Song*, pp.339–40.
75 29 January 1955. Aurelia Plath, *Letters Home*, p.154.

Chapter 37: A Transatlantic Relationship

1 Aurelia Plath, *Letters Home*, p.138.
2 25 April 1955. Aurelia Plath, *Letters Home*, p.175.
3 'Commentary for *Letters Home* by Aurelia Plath'. Smith College Special Collections.
4 Clark, *Red Comet*, p.366.
5 Wilson, *Mad Girl's Love Song*, p.12.
6 6 February 1956. Aurelia Plath, *Letters Home*, p.215.
7 Sylvia Plath, 3 January 1957–11 March 1957 in Kukil, *The Journals*, p.270.
8 Aurelia Plath. 'For the Authors' Series Talk at Wellesley College Club, 16 March 1976. Smith College Special Collections.
9 Sylvia Plath, 27 December 1958 in Kukil, *The Journals*, p.449.
10 3 March 1956. Aurelia Plath, *Letters Home*, p.220.
11 20 January 1956. Aurelia Plath, *Letters Home*, p.209.
12 2 February 1956. Aurelia Plath, *Letters Home*, p.213.
13 Kukil, *The Journals*, p.203.
14 Clark, *Red Comet*, p.444.
15 Sylvia Plath to Olive Higgins Prouty, 13 December 1955. Aurelia Plath, *Letters Home*, p.201.
16 Stevenson, *Bitter Fame: A Life of Sylvia Plath* (Boston: Houghton Mifflin Co, 1989) p.71.
17 25 February 1956. Aurelia Plath, *Letters Home*, p.220.
18 29 January 1956. Aurelia Plath, *Letters Home*, pp.212–13.
19 25 January 1956. Aurelia Plath, *Letters Home*, p.211.
20 Kukil, *The Journals*, p.221.
21 Aurelia Plath, *Letters Home*, p.241.
22 Kukil, *The Journals*, p.236.
23 3 May 1956. Aurelia Plath, *Letters Home*, p.248.
24 23 April 1956. Aurelia Plath, *Letters Home*, p.240.
25 Clark, *Red Comet*, p.440.
26 Ibid., p.444.
27 Sylvia Plath to Warren Plath, 18 June 1956. Aurelia Plath, *Letters Home*, p.258.

28 Clark, *Red Comet*, p.447.

29 Ibid., p.449.

30 Ibid., p.462.

31 Aurelia Plath to Leonard Sanazaro, 8 September 1986 (Sanazaro MSS. Lilly Library, Indiana University, Bloomington, Indiana)

32 Clark, *Red Comet*, p.498.

33 Ibid., p.479.

34 24 February 1957. Aurelia Plath, *Letters Home*, p.297.

35 Ibid.

36 Ibid.

37 Sylvia Plath, 3 January 1957–11 March 1957 in Kukil, *The Journals*, p.269.

38 25 March 1957. Aurelia Plath, *Letters Home*, p.305.

39 Clark, *Red Comet*, p.480.

40 For a full discussion of Ted Hughes' influence on Sylvia see Clark *Red Comet*, pp.20–1.

Chapter 38: Reunited

1 28 April 1957. Aurelia Plath, *Letters Home*, p.309.

2 7 May 1957. Aurelia Plath, *Letters Home*, p.310.

3 Clark *Red Comet*, p.498.

4 Ibid., p.499.

5 Ibid.

6 Stevenson, *Bitter Fame*, p.105.

7 Aurelia Plath to Leonard Sanazaro, 8 September 1986 (Sanazaro MSS. Lilly Library, Indiana University, Bloomington, Indiana).

8 Clark, *Red Comet*, p.481.

9 Sylvia Plath journal entry, 1 October 1957, 'Letter to a Demon'. Quoted in Stevenson, *Bitter Fame*, p.115.

10 Sylvia Plath to Warren Plath, 5 November 1957. Aurelia Plath, *Letters Home*, p.329.

11 Sylvia Plath, Notes on interviews with Ruth Beuscher, 12 December 1958 in Kukil, *The Journals*, p.433.

12 Sylvia Plath, 11 May 1958 in Kukil, *The Journals*, p.381.

13 Richard Larschan, 'Art and Artifice in Sylvia Plath's Self-Portrayals' in Koray Melikoglu (ed.), *Life Writing: Autobiography, Biography and Travel Writing in Contemporary Literature. Proceedings of a Symposium Entitled 'The Theory and Practice of Life Writing: Auto/biography, Memoir and Travel Writing in Post-modern Literature.'* (Stuttgart: ibidem-Verlag, 2007).

14 Sylvia Plath, Notes on interviews with Ruth Beuscher, 12 December 1958 in Kukil, *The Journals*, p.436.

15 Clark, *Red Comet*, p.502.

16 Ibid., pp.474–5.

17 Sylvia Plath, 23 February 1958 in Kukil, *The Journals*, p.337.

18 Sylvia Plath, 20 July 1957 in Kukil, *The Journals*, p.337.
19 Stevenson, *Bitter Fame*, p.136.
20 Ibid., pp.124–6.
21 For a full discussion of the content of the poem and Aurelia's reaction to it, see earlier chapter.
22 Quoted in Wilson, *Mad Girl's Love Song*, p.53.
23 See earlier comments on 'Superman and Paula Brown's New Snowsuit'.
24 Aurelia Plath. 'Letters Written in the Actuality of Spring' in Alexander, *Ariel Ascending*, p.216.
25 *Voices and Visions: Sylvia Plath*. Documentary.
26 Aurelia Plath to Leonard Sanazaro, 8 September 1986 (Sanazaro MSS. Lilly Library, Indiana University, Bloomington, Indiana).
27 Clark, *Red Comet*, pp.505–506.
28 Aurelia Plath to Leonard Sanazaro, 20 January 1988 (Sanazaro MSS. Lilly Library, Indiana University, Bloomington, Indiana).
29 5 July 1958. Aurelia Plath, *Letters Home*, p.346.
30 Sylvia Plath, 27 December 1958 in Kukil, *The Journals*, p.448.
31 Aurelia Plath to Leonard Sanazaro, 8 September 1986 (Sanazaro MSS. Lilly Library, Indiana University, Bloomington, Indiana).
32 Jonathan Bate, *Ted Hughes: The Unauthorised Life* (London: William Collins, 2015) p.144.
33 Sylvia Plath, Notes on interviews with Ruth Beuscher, 12 December 1958 in *The Journals*, pp.429–31.
34 Ibid., p.433.
35 Ibid., pp.429–31.
36 Stevenson, *Bitter Fame*, p.146.
37 Sylvia Plath, 27 December 1958 in Kukil, *The Journals*, p.446.
38 Ibid., p.432.
39 Sylvia Plath, 27 December 1958 in Kukil, *The Journals*, p.449.
40 Sylvia Plath, 12 December 1958 in Kukil, *The Journals*, p.437.
41 Sylvia Plath, 16 December 1958 in Kukil, *The Journals*, p.441.
42 Sylvia Plath, 12 December 1958 in Kukil, *The Journals*, pp.432–3.
43 Sylvia Plath, 27 December 1958 in Kukil, *The Journals*, p.447.
44 Ibid., p.446.
45 Sylvia Plath, 12 December 1958 in Kukil, *The Journals*, p.435.
46 Clark, *Red Comet*, p.xxi.
47 Sylvia Plath, 27 December 1958 in Kukil, *The Journals*, p.447.
48 Clark, *Red Comet*, p.573.
49 For a full discussion on Carl Jung's influence on Sylvia see Wilson, *Mad Girl's Love Song*, p.39.
50 Sylvia Plath, Notes on interviews with Ruth Beuscher, 12 December 1958 in Kukil, *The Journals*, p.436.
51 Sylvia Plath, 26 December 1958 in Kukil, *The Journals*, p.445.

Chapter 39: Rites of Passage

1   Bate, *Ted Hughes*, p.144.
2   Aurelia Plath, *Letters Home*, p.356.
3   Clark, *Red Comet*, p.597.
4   Aurelia Plath, *Letters Home*, p.373.
5   Aurelia Plath, 'For the Authors' Series Talk at Wellesley College Club, 16 March 1976. Smith College Special Collections.
6   Stevenson, *Bitter Fame*, p.234.
7   Aurelia Plath, *Letters Home*, p.274.
8   *Voices and Visions: Sylvia Plath*. Documentary.
9   A. Alvarez, quoted in Stevenson, *Bitter Fame*, p.203.
10 Aurelia Plath, *Letters Home*, p.359.
11 Aurelia Plath, 'Letters Written in the Actuality of Spring' in Alexander, *Ariel Ascending*, p.217.
12 'A Discussion with Frieda Hughes' in Sylvia Plath, *Ariel: The Restored Edition*, p.8.
13 27 August 1960. Aurelia Plath, *Letters Home*, p.392.
14 Clark, *Red Comet*, pp.611–12.
15 Both Sylvia and Aurelia were tall; it seems Aurelia believed it would be more advantageous as a woman to be shorter. Clark, *Red Comet*, p.599.
16 Aurelia Plath, *Letters Home*, p.376.
17 Stevenson, *Bitter Fame*, p.212.
18 Clark, *Red Comet*, p.xxi.
19 The first draft was completed in August 1961. Stevenson, *Bitter Fame*, p.213.
20 Clark, *Red Comet*, p.656.
21 Dido Merwin, quoted in Stevenson, *Bitter Fame*, p.214.
22 Ibid., p.218.
23 Clark, *Red Comet*, p.659.
24 Aurelia Plath, *Letters Home*, p.359.
25 30 July 1961. Aurelia Plath, *Letters Home*, p.422.
26 Stevenson, *Bitter Fame*, p.235.
27 Clark, *Red Comet*, pp.669–70.
28 15 December 1961. Aurelia Plath, *Letters Home*, p.440.
29 Stevenson, *Bitter Fame*, p.230.
30 12 March 1962. Aurelia Plath, *Letters Home*, p.450.
31 7 February 1962. Aurelia Plath, *Letters Home*, p.446.
32 Clark, *Red Comet*, p.678.
33 Ibid., p.673.
34 Frieda Hughes 'Foreword' in Sylvia Plath, *Ariel: The Restored Edition*, p.xii.
35 Ibid., p.xiii.
36 Woolf, *On Being Ill*, p.29.
37 Kate Flint. 'Introduction' in Woolf, *The Waves*, p.xxxiii.

38 Diane Middlebrook, *Her Husband: Ted Hughes and Sylvia Plath – A Marriage* (London, New York: Penguin Books, 2003) p.193.
39 Stevenson, *Bitter Fame*, pp.232–4.
40 Ibid., p.236.

Chapter 40: The Final Visit

1   Clark, *Red Comet*, p.685.
2   Ibid., p.717.
3   Ibid.
4   Aurelia Plath. 'For the Authors' Series Talk at Wellesley College Club, 16 March 1976. Smith College Special Collections.
5   Ibid.
6   Ibid.
7   Aurelia Plath, *Letters Home*, p.458.
8   Aurelia Plath. 'For the Authors' Series Talk at Wellesley College Club, 16 March 1976. Smith College Special Collections.
9   Clark, *Red Comet*, p.722.
10 Aurelia Plath. 'For the Authors' Series Talk at Wellesley College Club, 16 March 1976. Smith College Special Collections.
11 For Anne Stevenson's full argument, see *Bitter Fame*, p.251.
12 30 October 2000. Plath's publisher to a deputy provost of the University of Massachusetts. 'Sylvia's Mother Said – though it took some doing …' Richard J. Larschan.
13 Aurelia Plath, *Letters Home*, p.458.
14 Clark, *Red Comet*, p.725.
15 Sylvia Plath to Dr Beuscher, 20 July 1962. Quoted in Clark, *Red Comet*, p.732.
16 Ted Hughes to Olwyn Hughes, September 1962. Quoted in Clark, *Red Comet*, p.752.
17 Clark, *Red Comet*, pp.50–2.
18 Ibid., p.289.
19 Stevenson, *Bitter Fame*, p.257.
20 Aurelia Plath, *Letters Home*, p.464.
21 Clark, *Red Comet*, p.762.
22 Aurelia Plath, *Letters Home*, p.465.
23 18 October 1962. Aurelia Plath, *Letters Home*, p.472.
24 16 October 1962. Aurelia Plath, *Letters Home*, p.469.
25 Sylvia Plath to Aunt Dotty, 14 December 1962. Aurelia Plath, *Letters Home*, p.487.
26 Frieda Hughes, 'Foreword' in Sylvia Plath, *Ariel: The Restored Edition*, p.xv.
27 Quoted in Stevenson, *Bitter Fame*, p.265.
28 Ibid., p.266.
29 21 October 1962. Aurelia Plath, *Letters Home*, p.473.
30 Sylvia Plath to Aurelia Plath, 25 October 1962. Quoted in Clark, *Red Comet*, pp.791, 795–6.

31 Clark, *Red Comet*, p.853.
32 Ted Hughes, 'Trial', sections 16, 13 and 14. The British Library PER 3 MS 88993/1/1. Quoted in Clark, *Red Comet*, p.853.
33 Aurelia Plath, *Letters Home*, p.470.
34 21 October 1962. Aurelia Plath, *Letters Home*, p.473.
35 Sylvia Plath to Dr Beuscher, 21 October 1962. Quoted in Clark, *Red Comet*, p.784.
36 Clark, *Red Comet*, p.780.
37 Ibid., p.845.
38 Olive Higgins Prouty to Aurelia Plath, 27 October 1962. Quoted in Clark, *Red Comet*, p.792.
39 Olive Higgins Prouty to Sylvia Plath, 27 November 1962. Quoted in Clark, *Red Comet*, p.823.
40 Aurelia Plath to Sylvia Plath, 29 November 1962. Quoted in Clark, *Red Comet*, p.824.
41 Frieda Hughes, 'Foreword' in Sylvia Plath, *Ariel: The Restored Edition*, p.xiii.
42 Clark, *Red Comet*, p.824.
43 Ibid., p.823.
44 Ibid.
45 Ibid.
46 Frieda Hughes 'Foreword' in Sylvia Plath, *Ariel: The Restored Edition*, p.xiv.
47 Clark, *Red Comet*, p.852.
48 Badia, '"I May Hate Her"', p.229.
49 Clark, *Red Comet*, p.703.
50 Ibid., p.304.
51 25 October 1962. Aurelia Plath, *Letters Home*, p.477.
52 Clark, *Red Comet*, p.841.
53 Sylvia Plath to Aurelia Plath, 4 February 1963. Quoted in Clark, *Red Comet*, p.866.
54 Sylvia Plath to Dr Ruth Beuscher, 4 February 1963. Quoted in Clark, *Red Comet*, p.869.
55 'About the Author: Meet Sylvia Plath' in Sylvia Plath, *Ariel: The Restored Edition*, p.4.
56 Aurelia Plath, *Letters Home*, p.500.
57 Clark, *Red Comet*, p.900.
58 Ibid., p.918.
59 Ibid., p.921.
60 Ibid., p.918.
61 Interview with Richard Larschan, 2 January 2022.
62 Erica Jong, 'Review of *Letters Home*', *The Los Angeles Times*. In Aurelia Plath's notes, 'For the Authors' Series Talk at Wellesley College Club, 16 March 1976. Smith College Special Collections.

Chapter 41: Aurelia Answers Back

1 Aurelia Plath to Leonard Sanazaro, 20 January 1986 (Sanazaro MSS. Lilly Library, Indiana University, Bloomington, Indiana).
2 Badia, '"I May Hate Her"', p.229.
3 Catherine Rankovic. Email, 31 October 2022.
4 Aurelia Plath interview. *Voices and Visions: Sylvia Plath*. Documentary.
5 Catherine Rankovic, 'Aurelia Plath's Live-in Students', Studying Aurelia Plath, 16 March 2021 (https://aureliaplath.blogspot.com/2021/03/aurelia-plaths-live-in-students.html).
6 Bate, *Ted Hughes*, p.254.
7 Aurelia Plath, 'For the Authors' Series Talk at Wellesley College Club, 16 March 1976. Smith College Special Collections.
8 Aurelia Plath to Miriam Baggett, 7 July 1966. Clark, *Red Comet*, p.921.
9 Aurelia Plath to Leonard Sanazaro, 20 January 1988 (Sanazaro MSS. Lilly Library, Indiana University, Bloomington, Indiana).
10 Bate, *Ted Hughes*, p.304.
11 Aurelia Plath in 'Sylvia Plath: A Biographical Note' by Lois Ames in *The Bell Jar* (New York: Harper and Row, 1971) pp.214–15. Quoted in Bate, *Ted Hughes*, p.304.
12 Bate, *Ted Hughes*, p.305.
13 Heller, 'Aurelia Plath: A Lasting Commitment'. Smith College Special Collections.
14 Ibid.
15 Aurelia Plath, 'For the Authors' Series Talk at Wellesley College Club, 16 March 1976. Smith College Special Collections.
16 Ibid.
17 Jacqueline Rose, *The Haunting of Sylvia Plath* (London: Virago, 2014) p.81.
18 Peter K. Steinberg and Karen V. Kukil (eds), *The Letters of Sylvia Plath* (London: Faber and Faber, 2018) 2 Vols.
19 Clark, *Red Comet*, p.934.
20 For a detailed discussion of what happened read Diane Middlebrook, *Her Husband*, pp.239–41.
21 For a full discussion of the editing see Rose, *The Haunting of Sylvia Plath*.
22 Bate, *Ted Hughes*, p.352.
23 Clark, *Red Comet*, p.935.
24 Aurelia's note. 'Commentary for *Letters Home* by Aurelia Plath'. Smith College Special Collections.
25 Aurelia Plath to Miriam Baggett, 13 November 1974. Quoted in Clark, *Red Comet*, p.935.
26 Catherine Rankovic. Email, 31 October 2022.
27 Aurelia Plath to Leonard Sanazaro, 9 February 1984 (Sanazaro MSS. Lilly Library, Indiana University, Bloomington, Indiana).

28 Aurelia Plath, 'For the Authors' Series Talk at Wellesley College Club, 16 March 1976. Smith College Special Collections.

29 Aurelia Plath notes, 'For the Authors' Series Talk at Wellesley College Club, 16 March 1976. Smith College Special Collections.

30 Notes from Sylvia Plath's diary, 1949. 'Commentary for *Letters Home* by Aurelia Plath'. Smith College Special Collections.

31 Bate, *Ted Hughes*, p.8.

32 Aurelia Plath, 'Letters Written in the Actuality of Spring' in Alexander, *Ariel Ascending*, p.216.

33 Mallowan, *Max Mallowan's Memoirs*, p.195.

34 Aurelia Plath, 'For the Authors' Series Talk at Wellesley College Club, 16 March 1976. Smith College Special Collections.

35 Ibid.

36 Ibid.

37 Vanessa Bell to Clive Bell, 25 June 1910. Quoted in Bell, *Virginia Woolf*, p.163.

38 Angelica Garnett, *Deceived with Kindness: A Bloomsbury Childhood* (London: Pimlico, 1995) pp.20–1.

39 Virginia Woolf to Duncan Grant 1917. Quoted in Garnett, *Deceived with Kindness*, p.23.

40 Aurelia Plath, 'Letters Written in the Actuality of Spring' in Alexander, *Ariel Ascending*, p.215.

41 Aurelia Plath to Helen Vendler, 5 January 1976 29–47. SPC Smith College. Quoted in Clark, *Red Comet*, p.15.

42 Aurelia Plath notes, 'For the Authors' Series Talk at Wellesley College Club, 16 March 1976. Smith College Special Collections.

43 See earlier chapter for Aurelia's comments on this poem.

44 Interview Aurelia Plath with Robert Robertson, 'About *The Bell Jar*', *The Listener* vol 95, pp.515–16. Quoted in 'Aurelia Speaks About "Mrs Greenwood"', Studying Aurelia Plath, 19 September 2016 (https://aureliaplath.blogspot.com/2016/00/aurelia-speaks-about-mrs-greenwood.html).

45 Janet Malcolm, 'The Silent Woman', *Annals of Biography*, 23 and 30 August 1993. Reproduced in *The New Yorker*.

46 Ibid.

47 Badia. '"I May Hate Her"', p.226.

48 Clark, *Red Comet*, p.935.

49 Ted Hughes to Al Alvarez, November 1971. Quoted in Clark, Red Comet, p.811.

50 Aurelia Plath to Leonard Sanazaro, 1 February 1985 (Sanazaro MSS. Lilly Library, Indiana University, Bloomington, Indiana).

51 Aurelia Plath to Leonard Sanazaro, 17 January 1985 (Sanazaro MSS. Lilly Library, Indiana University, Bloomington, Indiana).

52 Bate, *Ted Hughes*, p.7.

53 Ibid., p.11.

54 Ibid., p.433.
55 Aurelia Plath to Leonard Sanazaro, 26 March 1986 (Sanazaro MSS. Lilly Library, Indiana University, Bloomington, Indiana).
56 Aurelia Plath to Leonard Sanazaro, 23 February 1986 (Sanazaro MSS. Lilly Library, Indiana University, Bloomington, Indiana).
57 Ted Hughes to Lucas Myers, 14 February 1987. Christopher Reid (ed.), *Letters of Ted Hughes* (London: Faber and Faber, 2007) pp.536–7.
58 Olwyn Hughes, quoted in Janet Malcolm, 'The Silent Woman', *Annals of Biography*, 23 and 30 August 1993.
59 Catherine Rankovic, 'How Much Money Did Aurelia Make From Sylvia's Work', Studying Aurelia Plath, 30 March 2021 (https://aureliaplath.blogspot.com/2021/03/how-much-money-did-aurelia-plath-make.html).
60 Aurelia Plath to Leonard Sanazaro, 20 January 1986 (Sanazaro MSS. Lilly Library, Indiana University, Bloomington, Indiana).
61 Aurelia Plath to Leonard Sanazaro, 2 May 1985 (Sanazaro MSS. Lilly Library, Indiana University, Bloomington, Indiana).
62 Aurelia Plath to Leonard Sanazaro, 1 December 1982 (Sanazaro MSS. Lilly Library, Indiana University, Bloomington, Indiana).
63 Aurelia Plath, 'Letters Written in the Actuality of Spring' in Alexander, *Ariel Ascending*, p.214.
64 Ibid., p.217.
65 Aurelia Plath to Judith Kroll. Quoted in Stevenson, *Bitter Fame*, p.302.

Chapter 42: Aurelia's Afterlife

1   Interview with Richard Larschan, 2 January 2022.
2   Aurelia Plath's copy of Judith Kroll's *Chapters in a Mythology* (SPC, Smith), quoted in Clark, p.921.
3   Aurelia Plath to Miriam Baggett, 4 December 1966. Quoted in Clark, *Red Comet*, p.923.
4   Conversation with Catherine Rankovic, 14 November 2021.
5   Aurelia Plath to Miriam Baggett, 19 April 1966. Quoted in Clark, *Red Comet*, p.920.
6   Clark, *Red Comet*, p.920.
7   Ibid, p.921.
8   Ted Hughes to Aurelia Plath, 13 May 1963. Reid, *Letters of Ted Hughes*, pp.218–19.
9   Clark, *Red Comet*, p.909.
10 Aurelia Plath to Leonard Sanazaro, 28 December 1985 (Sanazaro MSS. Lilly Library, Indiana University, Bloomington, Indiana).
11 Aurelia Plath to Leonard Sanazaro, 9 June 1982 (Sanazaro MSS. Lilly Library, Indiana University, Bloomington, Indiana).

12 Aurelia Plath to Leonard Sanazaro, 3 March 1984 (Sanazaro MSS. Lilly Library, Indiana University, Bloomington, Indiana).

13 Catherine Rankovic, 'Move Over, Daddy: Professor Aurelia Plath's University Teaching Career', Studying Aurelia Plath, 21 July 2021 (https://aureliaplath. blogspot.com/2021/07/move-over-daddy-professor-aurelia.html).

14 Heller, 'Aurelia Plath: A Lasting Commitment'. Smith College Special Collections.

15 Aurelia Plath to Leonard Sanazaro, 2 February 1983 (Sanazaro MSS. Lilly Library, Indiana University, Bloomington, Indiana).

16 Aurelia Plath to Leonard Sanazaro, 2 February 1983 (Sanazaro MSS. Lilly Library, Indiana University, Bloomington, Indiana).

17 Comments from Aurelia Plath on Heller, 'Aurelia Plath: A Lasting Commitment'. Smith College Special Collections.

18 Aurelia Plath to Leonard Sanazaro, 28 December 1983 (Sanazaro MSS. Lilly Library, Indiana University, Bloomington, Indiana).

19 In Aurelia Plath's notes, 'For the Authors' Series Talk at Wellesley College Club, 16 March 1976. Smith College Special Collections.

20 Heller, 'Aurelia Plath: A Lasting Commitment'. Smith College Special Collections.

21 Aurelia Plath to Leonard Sanazaro, 20 January 1986 (Sanazaro MSS. Lilly Library, Indiana University, Bloomington, Indiana).

22 Ibid, 22 January 1983.

23 Ibid.

24 Ibid, 5 April 1983.

25 Ibid, 29 January 1983.

26 Ibid, 21 July 1983.

27 Ibid, 23 September 1983.

28 Ibid, 19 June 1983.

29 Aurelia Plath to Leonard Sanazaro, 28 July 1983 (Sanazaro MSS. Lilly Library, Indiana University, Bloomington, Indiana).

30 Ibid, 6 November 1983.

31 Ibid, 10 June 1983.

32 Notes from Richard Larschan, December 2021.

33 Aurelia Plath to Leonard Sanazaro, 20 April 1983 (Sanazaro MSS. Lilly Library, Indiana University, Bloomington, Indiana).

34 Ibid., 26 April 1983.

35 Richard Larschan email to Catherine Rankovic.

36 Aurelia Plath to Leonard Sanazaro, no date (Sanazaro MSS. Lilly Library, Indiana University, Bloomington, Indiana).

37 For a full discussion of the annotations see Catherine Rankovic, 'Medusa Metadata: Aurelia Plath's Gregg Shorthand Annotations' in Anita Helle, Amanda Golden and Maeve O' Brien (eds) *Bloomsbury Handbook to Sylvia Plath* (London, New York, Oxford: Bloomsbury Academic, 2022).

38 See Tracy Brain, 'Sylvia Plath's Letters and Journals' in Jo Gill (ed.), *The Cambridge Companion to Sylvia Plath* (Cambridge: Cambridge University Press, 2006).

39 Aurelia Plath to Leonard Sanazaro, 28 December 1983 (Sanazaro MSS. Lilly Library, Indiana University, Bloomington, Indiana).

40 Catherine Rankovic, 'How Much Money Did Aurelia Make From Sylvia's Work', Studying Aurelia Plath, 30 March 2021 (https://aureliaplath.blogspot.com/2021/03/how-much-money-did-aurelia-plath-make.html).

41 Richard Larschan notes, December 2021.

42 Interview with Richard Larschan, 2 January 2022.

43 Richard Larschan notes, December 2021.

44 Richard Larschan notes, December 2021.

45 Richard Larschan interview, 2 January 2022.

46 Aurelia Plath to Leonard Sanazaro, 11 October 1986 (Sanazaro MSS. Lilly Library, Indiana University, Bloomington, Indiana).

47 Richard Larschan interview, 2 January 2022.

48 Richard Larschan email, 31 December 2021.

49 Aurelia Plath to Leonard Sanazaro, 2 February 1983 (Sanazaro MSS. Lilly Library, Indiana University, Bloomington, Indiana).

50 Ibid., 8 October 1983.

51 Ibid., 22 December 1986.

52 Ibid.

53 Richard Larschan's interview with Aurelia Plath for *Sylvia Plath and the Myth of the Monstrous Mother* for a multi-media project called 'Poets of New England'. Shown to the author by Richard Larschan, 2 January 2022.

54 Richard Larschan notes, December 2021.

55 Richard Larschan later used some of this material in *Sylvia Plath and the Myth of the Monstrous Mother* and *Sylvia Plath and the Myth of the Omnipresent/Absent Father* for a multi-media project called 'Poets of New England', Richard Larschan Notes, December 2021.

56 Richard Larschan interview, 2 January 2022.

57 Clark, *Red Comet*, p.922.

58 Aurelia Plath to Leonard Sanazaro, 20 November 1986 (Sanazaro MSS. Lilly Library, Indiana University, Bloomington, Indiana).

59 Conversation with Catherine Rankovic, 14 November 2021.

60 Richard Larschan, 'Sylvia's Mother Said – though it took some doing'.

61 Richard Larschan notes, December 2021.

62 Email from Richard Larschan, February 2022.

63 Aurelia Plath to Leonard Sanazaro, 8 September 1986 (Sanazaro MSS. Lilly Library, Indiana University, Bloomington, Indiana).

Index